STREET-LEVEL GOVERNING

Stanford Studies in Middle Eastern
and Islamic Societies *and* Cultures

STREET-LEVEL GOVERNING

Negotiating the State in Urban Turkey

Elise Massicard

STANFORD UNIVERSITY PRESS

Stanford, California

STANFORD UNIVERSITY PRESS

Stanford, California

A version of this work was originally published in French in 2019 under the title *Gouverner par la proximité: une sociologie politique des maires de quartier en Turquie* [Governing by Proximity: A Political Sociology of Neighborhood Headmen in Turkey] © 2019, Éditions Karthala, Paris.

Printed in the United States of America on acid-free, archival-quality paper

Cataloging-in-Publication Data available from the Library of Congress

Library of Congress Control Number: 2022931637

ISBN 9781503628410 (cloth)
ISBN 9781503631854 (paper)
ISBN 9781503631861 (digital)

Cover photo: Istanbul wall displaying a muhtar election poster. Jean-François Perouse.

Cover design: Rob Ehle
Typeset by Newgen North America in Brill 10.5/14.4

To Gabriel and Ariane

Contents

Abbreviations

AKP. Adalet ve Kalkınma Partisi (Justice and Development Party), conservative party originating in the Islamist movement

AP. Adalet Partisi (Justice Party), conservative (1961–81)

BDP. Barış ve Demokrasi Partisi (Peace and Democracy Party), left-wing, pro-Kurdish (2008–14)

CHP. Cumhuriyet Halk Partisi (Republican People's Party), Kemalist

HDP. Halkların Demokratik Partisi (People's Democratic Party), left-wing and pro-minority

İMDP. İstanbul Mahalle Dernekleri Platformu (Platform for Istanbul Neighborhood Associations)

MERNİS. Merkezi Nüfus İdare Sistemi, central population administration system

MHP. Milliyetçi Hareket Partisi (Nationalist Movement Party)

MİT. Milli İstihbarat Teşkilatı (National Intelligence Agency)

NGO. Nongovernmental organization

RP. Refah Partisi (Prosperity Party) Islamist (1983–98)

SCF. Serbest Cumhuriyet Fırkası (Free Republican Party), liberal (1930)

SHP. Sosyaldemokrat Halk Partisi (Social Democratic People's Party), left-wing (2002–10)

SOYBİS. Sosyal Yardım Bilgi Sistemi, social assistance data system

SP. Saadet Partisi (Felicity Party), Islamist

SYDGM. Sosyal Yardımlaşma ve Dayanışma Genel Müdürlüğü (General Directorate for Social Assistance and Solidarity)

SYDTF. Sosyal Yardımlaşma ve Dayanışmayı Teşvik Fonu (Social Aid and Solidarity Encouragement Fund)

SYDV. Sosyal Yardılaşma ve Dayanışma Vakıfları (Social Assistance and Solidarity Foundations)

TC. Türkiye Cumhuriyeti (Republic of Turkey)

TDP. Toplum destekli polislik (socially supported policing)

TL. Türk lirası (Turkish lira). Used to designate the official YTL, *yeni Türk lirası* (new Turkish lira)

TGRT. Türkiye Gazetesi Radyo ve Televizyonu (Turkey Newspaper, Radio, and Television), national privately owned conservative television channel

Acknowledgments

THIS BOOK WOULD NOT HAVE BEEN POSSIBLE WITHOUT THE HELP
of many friends and colleagues. I extend my thanks, first and foremost, to those
muhtars who generously agreed to talk with me and tolerated my being in their
midst. I am also grateful to my other interlocutors in Istanbul—residents, party
rank and file, party activists, municipal councillors, and members of municipal
teams. They willingly answered my questions and generously shared their time
and experiences with me. Most of them unfortunately will have to go unnamed,
as I have promised to guarantee their anonymity.

I wish to thank all my colleagues who have helped and supported me in carrying out this work. I am grateful to Gizem Aksümer, Ceren Ark, Başak Demires
Özkul, Sema Erder, Hamdi Gargın, Charlotte Joppien, Clémence Petit, Nilay
Özlü, Fikret Toksöz, and Cemal Yalçıntan. Many café conversations with fellow researchers of Turkey made the research experience most stimulating and
pleasant.

The initial input for this research came from a collective project funded
by the French Agence nationale de la recherche, which I had the honor of
coordinating during its four years of existence. The purpose of the program,
called "Order and Compromise: Government and Administration Practices in
Turkey from the Late Ottoman Empire to the Early 21st Century," was to develop
a sociohistorical perspective on patterns of government, and to offer a new
understanding of late Ottoman and Turkish public action. I am very much
indebted to the team who worked on this project for the endless debates and

stimulating discussions we produced, without which none of this work would have been possible. I wish to thank more especially the members who engaged directly with my work and who lent me unflagging support, gave me invaluable advice, and commented on preliminary versions of parts of this book. I express my sincere thanks to Marc Aymes, Benoît Fliche, Benjamin Gourisse, Noémi Lévy, Jean-François Pérouse, and Emmanuel Szurek.

I carried out most of the fieldwork during my time as a research fellow at the French Institute for Anatolian Studies in Istanbul. This wonderful research center provided an invaluable setting for exchange. I thank the institute team for providing a pleasant and stimulating work atmosphere. Many of the team members told me about their contrasting experiences with their muhtars, which helped me a lot in initially apprehending the institution, and in framing my work. After I came back to France, the CERI (Center for International Studies, Sciences Po, Paris) provided a perfect setting for scientific exchange and writing. I am very grateful to Miriam Périer, editorial manager at the CERI, for her insightful advice and great responsiveness over many years, and for supporting this project from the beginning to the end.

The academic framework—or pretext—under which I conducted this research was that of completing my Habilitation à diriger des recherches. I am greatly indebted to Jean-Louis Briquet from the National Center for Scientific Research, who consented to supervise it at the Paris Sorbonne University; I benefited greatly from his indispensable guidance and comparative insights. I also wish to thank deeply the members of the examining panel for their critical comments and invaluable input: Hamit Bozarslan, Béatrice Hibou, Yael Navaro-Yashin, Frédéric Sawicki, and Yasmine Siblot.

For their careful reading and comments, I am grateful to Assia Boutaleb and Sahar Saeidnia. Other colleagues, including Işıl Erdinç and Sümbül Kaya, helped me on specific points. I especially thank Jean-François Bayart for having inspired many reflections, and for greatly improving the French manuscript as I was preparing it for publication.

I had the opportunity to present parts of this work in numerous settings, and benefited from insightful feedback I received from several audiences. I am grateful to Bayram Balcı, the director of the French Institute of Anatolian Studies, and Sümbül Kaya, head of the Contemporary Studies Department there in 2019, for inviting me to present my research—and to Mine Eder for her numerous insightful comments and suggestions. I also thank Patrick Le Galès for inviting me to present my book at the City Is Back in Town research seminar at Sciences Po. I am very grateful to İpek Yosmaoğlu for providing the opportunity to present my work at Northwestern University. I thank Jihane Sfeir and Sahar Saeidnia for the opportunity to present my work at the Séminaire Mondes Arabes et Musulmans contemporains at Université libre de Bruxelles. The discussions and comments expressed on these occasions have been of immense help to me in thinking through many of my ideas and analyses.

Funding for the English translation was provided by the "Spaces, networks, circulations. The reconfigurations of the political in Turkey" research program funded as part of the Paris municipality's Emergences program (2015–19); and by the Research Division of Sciences Po.

For the punctilious English translation, around-the-clock responsiveness, and invaluable insights, I heartily thank Adrian Morfee. I am also much indebted to Renaldo Migaldi, whose meticulous and insightful editorial work has greatly contributed to the clarity and style of this book.

I would like to express my gratitude to the anonymous peer reviewers invited by my publisher, Stanford University Press, for their insightful comments, which greatly helped improve the manuscript.

I owe very special thanks to Kate Wahl and Caroline McKusick from Stanford University Press for their help in finalizing the manuscript and for their skillful advice. It was a pleasure working with them.

Finally, my heartfelt thanks go to my two wonderful children, Gabriel and Ariane, who have been a great source of joy and affection throughout the long process of researching and writing this book.

STREET-LEVEL GOVERNING

INTRODUCTION

SINCE BECOMING PRESIDENT OF TURKEY, TAYYIP ERDOĞAN HAS—TO general surprise—ushered the *muhtar*, a hitherto largely neglected figure, into the limelight. Each neighborhood or village elects a muhtar, or headman/head-woman: a low-level official with purely administrative prerogatives. In 2015, for the very first time in the country's history, the president started receiving muhtars in person. It even became habitual for hundreds of muhtars to travel to the president's palace from around the country to listen to Erdoğan deliver speeches about general policy. But why has the president suddenly turned to these minor and frequently scorned figures? Is this mere show, a typical move to stage power as close to the people? Arguably not.

Through this initiative, Erdoğan has sought to capitalize on one of Turkey's administrative specificities. This network of about fifty thousand low-level officials helps expand the reach of state institutions into citizens' daily lives, in every neighborhood and village in the country. Muhtars' ready access to local networks could thus make them a crucial instrument for spreading the message heard at the presidential palace.

But there is more to it than that. On one occasion, invoking the multiple threats the country faced, Erdoğan called on muhtars to keep a close eye on citizens and denounce any suspicious activities to the public authorities: "Is it possible that the muhtar, in his own village or neighborhood, doesn't know who lives in each house? He'll know. Is it a terrorist—is it possible he does not know? He knows. He will inform the nearest security forces [...]. For the step the muhtar will take at that moment will reinforce the state, and the strength of the state is imperative for the prosperity and tranquility of the people; we shall [inform the security forces], we are obliged to."[1] Here it must be borne in mind that most of the muhtars' prerogatives—identifying people, issuing certificates, or, more recently, ensuring that people with COVID stay at home for at least one week[2]—are based not so much on wielding bureaucratic power as on the muhtars' privileged access to the local population. Their work is grounded primarily in their direct knowledge of what is not necessarily written down in official registers—namely, individuals' daily lives, including such issues as unauthorized housing and off-the-record activities. These officials can therefore provide the state with a way of accessing private information that administrative rationales struggle to pick up. Does this mean that muhtars could potentially be used as a tool for widespread social control or even as a totalitarian surveillance device? A device that, in contrast to those used in recent history, would not work along bureaucratic lines but instead proceed from intimate knowledge?

A HYBRID POSITION

Any such interpretation needs nuancing straight away. Muhtars are not typical officials. They have a hybrid status. The *muhtarlık*—a word referring to the institution or office itself—does not fit into our ready-made categories. Instead, it is halfway between a state administration and a local elected body. The position is characterized by its fundamental ambiguity, primarily because muhtars are elected. While there are many similarities between muhtars and street-level bureaucrats, the way the former relate to those they administrate is wholly altered by the fact that these same people are their constituents. This has an indirect effect on how muhtars relate to institutions.

There are many kinds of elected administrators around the world, such as sheriffs or governors in the United States. In the case of muhtars, the tension between the two facets of their position–field administrator and elected official–is no doubt more palpable. First, this is because they do everything on their own, be it helping to maintain order, keeping the civil register, helping residents with administrative procedures, distributing social assistance, or countless other matters. Second, it is because they do all this at the very local level of the neighborhood or village, hence within a context rooted extensively in acquaintanceship. Muhtars are the outer edge of institutions. They embody a point of contact between state and society. They are limit-figures who operate where administrative and electoral rationales overlap, characterized by the very local nature of their direct contact with society. They provide a fascinating observation point for casting new light on the classic question of how social and political rationales intersect, and on the equally classic issue of the autonomy of the political realm–both in Turkey and elsewhere.

FROM A SOCIOLOGY OF THE STATE TO EXPLORING GOVERNMENT IN ACTION

Another reason why the limit-figure of the muhtar is intriguing is that it sheds light on how Turkish society and state intersect, revealing a picture at odds with dominant visions of the Turkish state. Traditionally, the Turkish state has been considered as a strong entity clearly differentiated from society.[3] Metin Heper went so far as to describe the Turkish state as "transcendental" (Heper 1992). In the words of Deniz Kadiyoti, "conventional social scientific analysis in Turkey has been strongly state- and institution-centered, focusing on policies and institutions as if these were acting upon a seemingly inert society" (Kandiyoti 2002, 2). Since the early 2000s, these representations of the Turkish state as clearly differentiated from society have been convincingly countered by historians of the early republican period (Akın 2007; Metinsoy 2011; Clayer 2015; Szurek 2015) and by political anthropologists (Alexander 2002; Navaro-Yashin 2002; Yoltar 2007; Babül 2017; Fırat 2019; Akarsu 2020). Interestingly, these criticisms have come primarily from analysts of society; representations of a state clearly separated from society have persisted much longer in political science. Only recently has political science begun to question this representation and to investigate the inner workings of the Turkish state and its practices of governing (Kayaalp 2013; Gourisse 2013; Aslan 2015).

Meanwhile, over recent decades the idea of a coherent state has been brought into question by several bodies of research in sociology and political science examining other countries. Enquiries influenced by sociology view the state as a complex institution, broken up into numerous loci and networks, where diverse social interests are repeatedly negotiated. Mention may be made, for example, of the analysis of organizations which since the 1980s has explored negotiated arrangements between local actors and administrative agents, particularly how they implement public policies.[4] In a collective research project, several colleagues and I sought to draw on these approaches to question the postulate of a strong, homogenous Turkish state autonomous from society.[5] This endeavor was consistent with Migdals' state-in-society approach (1994, 2001), which criticized the idea of the state as external to society, giving rise to several groundbreaking studies on Turkey (Watts 2009; Harris 2009; Belge 2013). It is within such a perspective that studying the figure of the muhtar takes on its full significance. For far from being classic bureaucrats, muhtars resemble institutionalized intermediaries. The fact that the office has continued to exist for so long, ever since the 1830s, as perhaps the oldest functioning public institution in Turkey, shows that indirect government and intermediation, far from being throwbacks to some distant past, have continued to play a role in the routine functioning of state, through the republican period right down to the present day. Therefore, muhtars complicate the persistent, dominant, and widespread idea of a general trend toward the "modernization" and "rationalization" of the Turkish state.

Due to their very role—namely, that of facilitating citizens' access to the state and, inversely, the state's access to citizens—muhtars provide a privileged viewing point of how the social and institutional spheres mesh. Being in certain respects part of the state, yet in others embedded in society, they call into question very specifically the idea that the state is sharply differentiated from society and endowed with clear limits. My initial research question was whether or not muhtars are part of the state, and whether they act as state officials or not. I changed my perspective in the wake of arguments by Timothy Mitchell, for whom the frontier between state and society, rather than being some ontological constant or given, is forever in play, continually constructed and contested (Mitchell 1991). My thoughts on this topic were inspired by Michel Foucault's change of focus when, setting aside the question of what the state might be, he considered what it does, looking at its concrete activities and the development of its constitutive apparatus—thus paving the way to many insightful works in political science and anthropology (Bierschenk and Sardan 2014).

My ideas have also drawn on Foucault's criticism of theories viewing the state as a centralized, unified, and sovereign power, which elevate it to a "primary, original, and already given object" (2007 [2004], 2), and lay down inherent constitutive properties. Foucault proceeds from exactly the opposite hypothesis:

"Maybe the state is only a composite reality and a mythicized abstraction" (2007 [2004], 109). Rather than studying the apparatus wielding power—that is to say, localizable legal and repressive institutions—he suggests analyzing the "mechanisms" underpinning the functioning of power. In this way of thinking, the activity of governing is not a monopoly of state, but something in which multiple agents partake, with power being exerted within society as a whole. This program has inspired many studies in terms of governmentality, emphasizing the multiple, varied, intermeshing, reticular, distributed, and localized nature of practices, technologies, and instruments of government (see Lascoumes and Le Galès 2005). It views the state from the vantage point of multiple practices, which are not all situated solely "in" what is commonly identified as the state (Foucault 2007 [2004], 112). It has also inspired scholarship on everyday politics, decentering the idea of a state authority and instead examining fragmented power practices as they actually occur.

But if we accept this idea of various fragmented power practices, at odds with the idea of a coherent state, then how are we to account for the idea of a coherent state functioning as a largely naturalized diffuse social norm—an idea that is particularly strong in Turkey (White 2013, 4)? Joel Migdal defines the state as "a field of power [...] shaped by (1) the image of a coherent, controlling organization in a territory, which is a representation of the people bounded by that territory, and (2) the actual practices of its multiple parts" (Migdal 2001, 15–16). Many works in the anthropology of the state have drawn on this approach to view the state not as a "distinct, fixed, unitary entity" (Sharma and Gupta 2006, 8) consisting of a set of rationales and institutions, but rather as a "phenomenological reality [...] produced through discourses and practices of power, produced in local encounters at the everyday level" (Aretxaga 2003, 398). For Gupta, anthropological studies of the state should focus first on the banal techniques of government and everyday practices of bureaucracies, and second, on the more abstract and translocal representation effects through which these practices become associated with the idea of an autonomous and impartial state (Gupta 1995). Abrams suggests we "abandon the state as a material object of study whether concrete or abstract while continuing to take the idea of the state extremely seriously" (Abrams 1998, 75). These studies of "the state" as something that is produced, reproduced, and contested through discourse and practice in everyday interactions with citizens led me to reformulate my initial question—that of knowing whether or not muhtars are part of the state—to instead focus on understanding in what contexts they refer to the state and draw on its legitimacy or authority. In short, how do they "make the state exist" through both their practices and their discourse?

A BOTTOM-UP APPROACH FOCUSING ON THE EVERYDAY LEVEL

These works suggest that we should pay particular attention to the loci where the state encounters society, among which we may immediately place the muhtarlık: "Instead of looking at the state as an entity 'from above,' we attempt to approach public authority 'from below,' from the variety of concrete encounters between forms of public authority and the more or less mundane practices of ordinary people" (Lund 2006, 674). For Gupta, "for the majority of [. . .] citizens, the most immediate context for encountering the state is provided by their relationships with government bureaucracies at the local level. [. . .] Because they give concrete shape and form to what would otherwise be an abstraction ('the state'), these everyday encounters provide one of the critical components through which the state comes to be constructed" (Gupta 1995, 378). It is through these routine practices and encounters that ordinary citizens experience the state, and the relationships between individuals and the otherwise abstract state take on material form (Siblot 2002). These relationships are largely structured by the concrete ties connecting citizens to the many different institutions embodying "the state." Recent works examining the state in Turkey have paid attention to concrete everyday government practices (Silverstein 2018) and more specifically encounters between citizens and the "state" (Alexander 2002; Navaro-Yashin 2002; Fliche 2005; Secor 2007; Yoltar 2007; Akarsu 2020). Many of these works focus on tense and contested settings: civil courthouses in poor urban neighborhoods (Koğacıoğlu 2008), criminal courts (Hakyemez 2018), women's shelters (Ekal 2015), Turkey's Kurdish southeast (Watts 2009), or policing in urban margins (Yonucu 2018).

By looking at muhtars, this book draws on this literature. But it differs from it in focusing on an ordinary and multifaceted institution with which citizens may come into contact, not only in specific situations (such as welfare distribution; see Yazıcı 2012) but for many different reasons, which may be conflictual or not–ranging from claiming social assistance or obtaining mundane paperwork to being searched for by the police. It analyzes how the practices of muhtars both underpin and undermine the image of a coherent and centralized state, where this image in turn constrains and shapes citizens' practice, along with that of officials. The question thus shifts from seeking to ascertain whether the Turkish state is strong, to revealing how it is produced on the ground and experienced on an everyday level through what is composed and played out around these encounters. It examines what specific "practical sense" of the state muhtars generate,[6] what ordinary relationships they engender with institutions, and what they produce in terms of socialization to the state and officialdom.

Such a perspective presupposes abandoning a top-down approach centered on national policies and institutions, in favor of a localized and socially anchored approach. It also implies shifting focus to look at what cannot be reduced to formalized, organized, and institutionalized forms of politics. This work is, in this respect, inspired by approaches in terms of low politics (Bayat 2009), infrapolitics (Scott 1990), vernacular politics (White 2002), and "politics from below" (Bayart 1981; Bayart 1992). These do not start from some a priori definition of what politics (or the state) might be, but instead view its contours as constructed in action, and as fluctuating (Bayart 1985). This requires attention to relatively broad practices anchored in their contexts. A further reason why this approach appealed to me is that my field observations shed light on the continuum between everyday life and the exercise of power, allowing for examination of the extent to which the political sphere might be autonomous from the social sphere.

This perspective additionally seeks to bring out the structuring role everyday practices play in forming the state and making practical sense of it. This entails turning away from an event-based approach to instead focus on the everyday level. The everyday refers to experienced practice—that is, practical knowledge and social experience (de Certeau 1984; Scott 1985). My approach is also inspired by German *Alltagsgeschichte*, which calls for understanding narrative "from below," as process and as product of how social actors appropriate meanings, events, and processes (Lüdtke 1995). It thus provides a way of emphasizing the role of "average people," on-the-ground public agents, and ordinary citizens.

THE SOCIOLOGY OF A POLITICAL JOB

These sources of inspiration led me to reformulate my object of study. My initial project of examining what muhtars are—state agents wielding institutional power, or representatives for neighborhood residents and their interests?—shifted to analyzing what they *do* and what this produces. This book examines how the muhtarlık as an institution actually functions. Looking at practices as they transpire in context enables us to gauge the practices of muhtars against the official rules–to which, as we shall see, they are far from conforming–and against other norms that inform how they go about their role, which may pertain to other registers (such as values, or moral obligation). Studying what muhtars do implies sketching a "sociology of work" akin to the sociology of political work (Fontaine and Le Bart 1994). This strong sociological focus differentiates this book from other, often more abstract and less sociologically grounded studies of governmental apparatus. The approach is manifold, drawing mainly on the sociology of organizations, the sociology of institutions, and interactionist sociology.

The work of subaltern public agents has become a topic for study, particularly in the sociology of organizations. This scholarship has shed light on their relative autonomy in implementing regulations, together with the extent to which their strategies seize upon zones of uncertainty, which exist in all organizations (Blau 1955; Crozier and Friedberg 1977). Lipsky has brought to light the influence wielded by street-level bureaucrats—that is, those who are in direct contact with the population. In carrying out their everyday work implementing regulations, they enjoy a certain power and hence capacity to significantly modify the sense of policies and how they are applied, via the practical choices they make in interpreting rules, selecting candidates, facilitating access to benefits, communicating or withholding "extra" information, and so on (Lipsky 1980). Many works in Lipsky's wake have emphasized the leeway available to subaltern public agents, due particularly to their capacity for dialogue and negotiation in their interactions with users (Warin 2002), and to a set of informal arrangement practices.

This book is less concerned with the leeway muhtars enjoy, or with how their actions modify the policies they are meant to apply, than with what their actions—particularly these arrangements and negotiations—produce in terms of governing. It focuses on understanding this mode of "government," considered as a "way of guiding the behavior of individuals and groups" (Bayart 2008 [1992], 28). This book analyzes the institution of the muhtarlık as one instance of an enactment of the "state, of political and administrative socialization" (Berger and Luckmann 1966), actualizing and producing relationships to institutions—both representations of the state and ways of "coping" with institutions.

From this point of view, recent alterations to the muhtarlık can shed new light on how government is undergoing transformation in Turkey. This "semi-formal" mode of government, indicative of the partial and indirect sway of institutions over entire swaths of social life, is being challenged as more impersonal and rationalized techniques of government are developed (Silverstein 2018). In an unexpected twist, the muhtarlık is not disappearing but is being reconfigured, and it continues to be used extensively by neighborhood residents. Personalized and informal government rationales coexist alongside impersonal and bureaucratized ones in present-day Turkey. Inspecting reconfigurations of the job of muhtar provides a way of investigating this composite form of government.

The question of the political effects of the muhtarlık can be framed in terms of domination and resistance: Does this institution provide a channel for pushing resident's interests, working around the institutional order or even subverting it? Or, on the contrary, does it enforce compliance to that order, as the executive probably expects? Over recent years, in an unprecedented move, the executive has become more involved with the muhtarlık and has subjected it to greater oversight, generating new dynamics in this respect. The muhtarlık is prone to working both with and around the institutional order, and its political effects are profoundly ambivalent. We ultimately shall see that micro-level modes of government display both social and territorial differentiation.

EXAMINING THE ROLES ACTORS TAKE

The sociology of institutions has shown that they only exist through the ways in which individuals take on institutional roles, hence the need to study the ways they do so (Lagroye and Offerlé 2010). One way of empirically tackling this question is therefore to study how they embody this role. A role-orientation approach is especially apposite, as the muhtarlık enjoys considerable "administrative autonomy"—or, put differently, limited obligation to comply with prescribed institutional practices (Dubois 2010, 5). There is far less hierarchical control over muhtars than over other bureaucrats. Consequently, muhtars may stray significantly from the official precepts supposedly guiding them in how they perform their role, and, by extension, in how they define it—hence my decision to examine very different muhtars and neighborhoods. We shall observe differing, socially situated ways of relating to this institution. As we will see, some muhtars behave in oppositional ways, while others engage with the institution as a way to enforce consent to the state order or even to act as a surveillance device. Two main sets of factors shape their contrasting ways of embodying this role: first, the differing constraints on their action, and second, the dispositions of individual muhtars.

From a relational perspective, the differing practices of muhtars need to be related to the sphere of constraints within which they act. In fact, the constraints on their action change over time and have increased in recent years; they also vary significantly from one context to another. This aspect takes on specific form here, since muhtars lie at the intersection of multiple spheres of constraint: institutional on the one hand, social on the other. Institutional constraints are increasing; and as we shall see, muhtars' relative autonomy from authorities and party politics—long a characteristic of that institution—is on the wane. We shall observe the effects this change has. The social constraints attendant upon the context in which muhtars work (the size of the neighborhood, salient social divides, and the types of requests made by residents) are in fact determinant. While the sociology of administrative relations has emphasized the significance of the setting in which counter staff interact with the public, muhtars not only officiate but also live amid the constituents whom they administer and who make incessant requests. The action of muhtars is significantly constrained by the fact that they live and carry out their functions in their own neighborhoods, a setting often marked by rumor, and in which they are acquainted with people to varying degrees. Study of the relationship between residents of a neighborhood and muhtars needs to be rooted in the larger set of neighborhood-level social relations in which they take on meaning (Siblot 2002, 80). How does this pronounced local anchoring influence—or even constrain—how muhtars do their job? For interactionist sociology, observing interaction in context is a way of linking contacts at the micro level to the political and social structures that govern them (Goffman 1959). The book thus studies interactions between muhtars and residents. By examining how muhtars "perform" and deal with interactions, we can further identify what representations they have of their role, and how they wish to be perceived. This, in turn, impacts on the representations of the state they produce.

Hence, paying attention to how muhtars assume their role raises the question of how citizens use the institution. The book analyzes not only the role as actualized by muhtars themselves, but also the practices of many different people who give it form. Users perhaps play an even greater part in defining this role than they do for "classic" administrations, given the muhtarlık's greater flexibility and its electoral dimension. This perspective echoes recent scholarship in Ottoman history, often inspired by subaltern studies, which emphasizes the degree of autonomy local populations enjoyed, and their capacity to negotiate with state actors (Petrov 2004; Quataert 2008). These works concur that nonstate actors—often disadvantaged ones—were capable of playing an active role in their relationship with the authorities, drawing on the leeway conferred by the law and its application (Lévy-Aksu 2012, 21). We shall observe that social differentiation appears crucial in the uses (or non-uses) citizens make of the institution. Generally speaking, those who are disadvantaged (in several meanings of the term) have recourse to the muhtarlık. However, it would be simplistic to reduce it to a straightforward "institution of the dominated."

This leads to the second dimension shaping their contrasting ways of embodying this role, namely the social dispositions of muhtars. Although this book examines an institution, it grants considerable importance to individual agents. This is for two reasons, the first of which is theoretical. Certain works inspired by Foucault, especially those analyzing disciplinary power, inquire into power mechanisms, with a tendency to overstate their coherence and effectiveness. Scott's analysis of the technical mechanisms enabling the state to apprehend a complex and fragmented world and act on nature, society, and space (Scott 1990, 1998) has been criticized for being disembodied, for lacking a sociological dimension, and for paying insufficient attention to the actual officials making use of these instruments (Herzfeld 1993). This raises the question of whether the practices of administrators are a direct application of some "state rationale." Sociologists of organizations, as well as those working in actor-network theory, have demonstrated the merits of focusing on actors in seeking to understand how political action actually functions (for Turkey, see Kayaalp 2013). For Bourdieu, "executive positions in large bureaucracies owe many of their most characteristic features, though these are never specified in any bureaucratic regulation or job description, to the dispositions officeholders bring to it at a given moment" (Bourdieu 1990, 88). Public officials draw on categories of perception that acquire meaning in the light of their social trajectory. This is especially true for muhtars, given that the institution has relatively little sway over them.

The second reason why this book accords considerable importance to individual agents is more pragmatic. Having no administrative apparatus, the muhtarlık is an extremely personalized institution. This dimension has increased over time, resulting in the gradual whittling away of any collegial dimension. The muhtarlık is composed of a muhtar supported by a council of elders (azas, or *ihtiyar heyeti*),[7] But it has been extensively "presidentialized." The councils of elders have become more and more marginalized in urban neighborhoods—largely because, since 1963, muhtars are directly elected by the residents, rather than indirectly by the councils. This is an ongoing trend, for generally it is muhtars who now decide on the ranking of their councillors, something previously determined by their constituents' preferential vote. One consequence of this personalization is that people say they are "going to the muhtar's" rather than "going to the muhtarlık." The institution is thus personalized and embodied to an unusual degree. Heeding agents implies placing their sociology at the center of analysis. This leads in turn to analyzing the social characteristics of muhtars and the conditions in which they are recruited, together with their trajectories and dispositions. This way, we can build up a satisfactory account of these agents who embody one specific but important contact between institutions and citizens on a daily basis. So this book sets out to analyze certain everyday practices of governing in Turkey, by appreciating who these officials are, where they come from, and how they make sense of what they do (see Babül 2017, 29).

A NEGLECTED FIGURE

This work fills a gap in the scholarship. The figure of the muhtar has been little studied, no doubt because it does not fit readily into classic categories. Even fewer works have looked at the muhtar in political terms. Political science in Turkey has never evinced any interest in this figure, who is generally considered to be infrapolitical, administrative, and in short insignificant. However, the very fact that muhtar elections are those around which most electoral violence–including death–is observed (mostly in villages) hints at the importance the candidates grant to this position.[8] The microlocal dimension probably goes some way to explaining the lack of scholarly interest. Political science about Turkey has rarely investigated how local political spheres function and are structured. There are few studies of local politics, and those that do exist are regarded as being of minor interest. Even the few benchmark studies about local politics make scant mention of muhtars.[9] In his book about local elections, Turan (2008) makes no reference to them. Only Joppien's recent book (2019) on municipal politics mentions muhtars, though without dwelling on them much. Since the 1980 coup they are no longer elected on party ticketa, and this seemingly has made the political dimension of their action an obsolete question, while maintaining the illusion of their neutrality with regard to politics. All in all, political science appears to have broadly assented to the "official" division of social activities: muhtars are no longer elected on party tickets, ergo they are outside the political realm. The presidential muhtar meetings have attracted some scholarly attention, but it has focused on other topics (populism, Denli 2017; the presidentialization of foreign policy, Ülgül 2018) rather than directly on muhtars.[10]

Although one strand of research has examined the political dimension of muhtars, it has looked only at muhtars in villages, not the ones in urban neighborhoods. The muhtarlık exists in both places,[11] but with greater means (its own budget) and prerogatives in villages. The studies in question were part of village sociology conducted in the 1960s and 1970s. Working within a developmentalist perspective drawing on theories of modernization prevalent at the time, they sought to pinpoint the dynamics of social change and integration in the nation, together with the role muhtars played in these processes (Yasa 1957; Kolars 1963, 87; Pierce 1964, 69, 85; Stirling 1965, 12, 270; Stycos 1965; Magnarella 1974). More recently, in her work about an Anatolian village, which focused on the symbolic dimension, Delaney (1991) viewed the muhtar as an important figure. These works are of limited interest for the approach taken here.

Most recent scholarship about urban muhtars views them from the perspective of administrative science. It mainly analyzes how they relate to other administrations, and the extent to which their means are adequate or inadequate for their missions. Much of it consists of master's dissertations, and often draws on questionnaire surveys. More recent works study the institution of the muhtarlık in the light of issues such as participation or local democracy. But these approaches fail to take local configurations into account, and generally seem shorn of context. Most studies of neighborhoods make little mention of the political dimension, and refer to muhtars only fleetingly.

Ultimately it is studies in related disciplines, particularly sociology and history, that are closest to the perspective taken here. Behar has written a precise study looking at the residents of an Ottoman neighborhood and the activity of its muhtars, drawing on a precious source, the notes of successive muhtars of an Istanbul neighborhood (Kasap İlyas) running back to the late nineteenth century, together with certain documents from the seventeenth and eighteenth centuries (Behar 2003). Several works of sociology about the outer neighborhoods of cities have also paid indirect attention to muhtars, depicting their role in local politics and in solving urban problems (Erder 1996; Erder 1997; Wedel 1999).

OBSERVING EVERYDAY STATE-SOCIETY RELATIONS

A further reason why there are few studies of muhtars is that working at a very micro level on daily activities that are fairly difficult to apprehend raises a certain number of methodological challenges. I had to combine different methods, sometimes in a makeshift manner.

There are few written sources. Official sources such as laws and regulations help build up the legal framework within which muhtars act, but they tell us virtually nothing about their practices. The archives of the prime minister's office contain mostly official reports and correspondence, and the available documents concerning muhtars cover the late 1930s to the late 1950s, but not systematically. These documents show how the central authorities thought about the *muhtarlıks*, especially those in villages, but they reveal only the official facet of their activity, relating to the central authorities. The Istanbul municipal archives cast light on the official written relationship between the municipality and the *muhtarlıks*, focusing on disputes over neighborhood boundaries. While these help us piece together certain debates and changes to the institution, they provide at best a very partial and fragmentary vision of the muhtars' activity. Written documents mainly take the form of letters, circulars, and instructions from the authorities to the muhtars, but the muhtars tend not to follow any standard archiving practices, and provide few written traces of their activity. When the muhtars do conserve documents, it is a matter of individual, fragmentary initiatives, and I did not always manage to gain access to them.

So most of the empirical material on which this work is based was collected during field research, I needed to select areas for empirical observation that were suited to localized analysis (Briquet and Sawicki 1989). I opted for the level of neighborhoods, and for a microanalytic approach to help bring out the intermeshing of social rationales (Revel 1996, 30–31). Insofar as I sought to apprehend the differing ways in which a single institution was actualized in varying contexts, I decided to select several neighborhoods. But which ones? Anthropological approaches to the state pay particular attention to its "margins," defined by Das and Poole as "sites of practice on which law and other state practices are colonized by other forms of regulation that emanate from the pressing needs of populations to secure economic and physical survival" (Das and Poole 2004, 8)—hence as places where "state law and order continually have to be re-established" (Asad 2004, 279). These approaches thus focus on specific technologies of power deployed by states to manage populations viewed as marginal (Yonucu 2018). Likewise, most works following Migdal's state-in-society approach look at sites of contest and opposition (Watts 2009; Harris 2009; Belge 2013). This is also the case for studies in "subaltern politics," which work on the assumption that subalterns practice specific forms of politics. Yet I believe this focus to be reductive, or even tautological, because the premises significantly shape the results obtained. I preferred, on the contrary, to conduct my investigations in contrasting neighborhoods with varying levels of wealth and marginality, so as to get an idea of the varying ways in which the institution is actualized, and thus analyze this mode of government in its diversity. For practical reasons I limited my enquiry to Istanbul, whose sheer size, diversity, and vibrant political environment allowed me to observe highly contrasting situations.

I did not have the luxury of choosing places to investigate based on the social properties of the muhtars or their neighborhoods. The first criterion was the possibility of building up a relationship of trust with a muhtar, which would enable me to gain lasting access to the field. My identity as a foreign researcher working for the French Ministry of Foreign and European Affairs did not fail to arouse suspicion about the "true purpose" of my research; it should not be forgotten that muhtars are also informers.

Additionally, it is important to stress that the period when I was conducting most of the survey (2013–14) was one of marked political tension: first, the Gezi Park protests and their violent repression (May to July 2013),[12] particularly in the very urban settings where my research was situated; the subsequent increasing conflict and visibility of urban issues in the public sphere; the scandal relating to accusations of government corruption (from December 2013); and the local elections during which the muhtars were elected (March 2014)–the first elections after the Gezi protests, adding to the conflict. The tensions caused by these episodes raised the stakes, fueled politicization, and compounded the sensitivity of urban issues. Consequently, muhtars were more exposed, making my research partners more suspicious and cautious. Yet this also made it easier for me to pinpoint what was at stake at their level. I left Turkey just before the executive launched several initiatives to reassert the value and role of muhtars and tried to tie them more firmly to state institutions. I made several follow-up trips until 2019, but could not analyze in-depth the impacts this policy had on the ground.

In any case, in conducting my research, trust was essential. It was down to the benevolence of individual muhtars whether they tolerated my presence and granted me access to less formatted discussions and scenes. I needed to be introduced to them, and so I approached muhtars who had had some contact with academia–because, for instance, one colleague lived in their neighborhood, and another had taught them or their children, or had met them at events organized to oppose urban renewal projects. It was then a matter of using their contacts to expand my base. In this way I managed to constitute a varied sample, which enabled me to observe muhtars and neighborhoods with sharply contrasting political and socioeconomic characteristics, and to highlight constants and salient differences in the conditions and ways in which each performed their job. Furthermore, at the time of my field study these neighborhoods belonged to five different district municipalities—three held by the AKP (Adalet ve Kalkınma Partisi, the Justice and Development Party), the conservative party with an Islamist background that has ruled the country since 2002, and two by the CHP (Cumhuriyet Halk Partisi, the Republican People's Party), the Kemalist opposition party. I did not seek representativity, but instead conceived of the exemplary character of social phenomena in other than rigorously statistical terms (Revel 1996, 31).

Of these six muhtars two, Bediz and Ebru, were women. Thus women were overrepresented in my sample, for after the 2014 elections women were just under 10 percent of muhtars in Istanbul, and 1.95 percent of neighborhood muhtars across the country.[13] To "individualize" all the muhtars while preserving their anonymity, I have assigned them first names starting with the letter used

The Neighborhoods Observed*

A is an old central neighborhood of middle- to lower-class residents (low-level employees, self-employed skilled manual workers, and small business owners) that is relatively well established.

B is an old central neighborhood undergoing gentrification, whose residents come from highly contrasting social backgrounds and include many disadvantaged people who have migrated from eastern provinces of Turkey since the 1960s.

C, next to B, is an old central neighborhood undergoing gentrification, with few residents and many businesses.

D is a sprawling, very disadvantaged outer neighborhood with a large population. It was built without authorization in the 1990s, and there were plans for an urban renewal project. The neighborhood's infrastructure is unfinished, with many dirt roads, and houses lacking water or electricity. Large numbers of internal migrants are still arriving there, and the neighborhood is socially and politically fragmented, thus sparking tensions.

E is a fairly central neighborhood dating from the 1950s. It is wealthy, with many luxury restaurants and shops.

F, an outer neighborhood built without authorization, sprang up in the 1960s. It is fairly deprived, but stable. All its infrastructure is in place, and no more internal migrants are arriving there.

*To preserve the anonymity of these neighborhoods, the press sources and sociological studies used for them are not referenced here. A table outlining the main characteristics of the neighborhoods and muhtars studied is included in the appendix.

to denote each muhtar's respective neighborhood: Ahmet for neighborhood A, Bediz for neighborhood B, and so on. I have kept women's names for women, and men's names for men. I conducted in-depth observations of how they performed their jobs, and visited them and their neighborhoods many times. By engaging with them over a lengthy period I was also able to note how contexts changed. In particular, observing them over many different periods–before and during elections; at Ramadan, an important period for social assistance; in troubled periods such as during and after the Gezi Park protests, and so on– enabled me to appreciate how political developments affected their activity.

I also encountered other muhtars on a less systematic basis. These interviews played a lesser role in building my analysis, but helped for examining specific dimensions in greater depth (the role muhtars play in urban renewal projects, the way post-Gezi urban citizenship activists considered and tried to build links with muhtars, and the role of muhtar associations). I have designated these "secondary" neighborhoods using lowercase letters (from g to k—without j, for I could find no male first name starting with that letter). Last, I sought to meet the main people with whom the muhtars were in contact. This of course included neighborhood residents, but also urbanists involved in urban initiatives and city planners, and party officials. It was harder to gain access to municipal and subprovincial department heads, and I met them less frequently.

The prime method I used was interviewing. In order to compare the muhtars' often self-glorifying declarations with what they actually did (and to understand which aspects they emphasized or downplayed), I needed to observe them at work. The angle taken in this study implied a praxeological approach, apprehending the muhtars' actions in context. Routine work cannot be observed in the laws and regulations framing these activities, or in what those who perform them have to say. Observation is the only way of apprehending in context the practical definitions agents have of their role, their moral judgements, the values they invoke, and the ways in which they conform to, deviate from, or resist the official order or the citizens' requests. Furthermore, observation is the only way to access how muhtars interact with the residents. Observation provides a way of apprehending the terms and forms of interaction, delivering better understanding of what is at stake in the relationships.

It was not easy, however, to observe muhtars, for they were unwilling to expose themselves to an outsider's gaze whenever this deviated from the image they wanted to present of themselves. However willing they were to answer at least some of my questions, I sensed that some were reluctant to let me observe them going about at least some of their activities. They retained control over our interaction, and often sought to get rid of me.

I adopted several techniques to overcome this difficulty. First, I used interviews as a "pretext" for observing. With few exceptions, I targeted exactly those moments when I supposed the muhtar would be busy or have lots of visitors. That obliged me to wait, and prevented me from asking questions, thus giving me a pretext to come back another time. The muhtars apologized for "having" to make me wait. But from my point of view this was often the most interesting part. It was when I was meant to be interviewing them but circumstances were unfavorable that I could begin observing their practices. In any case, the interviews rarely took place one-to-one, for neighborhood residents would phone or come in, repeatedly interrupting our conversation. The methodological differentiation between interviews and observation was somewhat artificial. Second, I asked the muhtars about what they were doing as they went about their work, to better apprehend their practices (Becker 1993). The muhtars seemed to be reassured by my interest in the material and factual aspects of their daily routine, which are to all appearances "not sensitive" and "apolitical." Third, I sought to "follow" these muhtars over time. I repeatedly visited them to build up trust and acquire greater understanding of their work. That enabled me to place what they said within the local configuration.

Observation enabled me to pick up on hesitations, uncertainty as to how to proceed, and the tensions produced by negotiation and adapting to various situations. Only observation makes it possible for one to apprehend posture, intonation, gestures, body language, and emotions, which are often more telling than what is said. The way muhtars act (talking to someone, or walking around the muhtarlık or neighborhood) counts just as much as what they say. I attached much importance to observing these trifling "details, little things, in short [...] what does not lend politics its nobility" (Hibou 2006, 16)—the modes of address, the banal conversations, the layout of the premises, and everything making up the "atmosphere." In this I followed the influence of Foucault's theories about the "hymn to small things" and "the political anatomy of detail" (1995 [1975], 139).

There were certain limitations to the observations I could conduct. I had access to the muhtars' "official" setting, the premises where they received visitors in their muhtarlık. But it would be reductive to suppose any "unity of place" to their activity, and this is one of the factors differentiating muhtars from street-level bureaucrats. Muhtars officiate in many other places and contexts, such as on the phone and in the street, for neighborhood residents, shopkeepers, and passersby are forever calling out to them. They officiate at home, for people go to visit them there. Or they officiate when they are out visiting, or taking part in all sorts of ceremonies and meetings. They officiate in practically all their social interactions, as well as with officials from the municipality, the subgovernor's office, or such-and-such a social center. On several occasions I tried to accompany them outside the muhtarlık. I asked them to let me know what meetings they would be attending, but they would "forget" to tell me, and would say later that the hour or day had changed several times, thus covering their tracks. They were skilled at "partitioning off" their settings and publics, so that my technique of just "being there waiting" was less effective. I only had limited access to most of these "other" settings, places, and times. In particular, I rarely managed to attend when muhtars were meeting official interlocutors from the subgovernor's office, the municipality, or political parties. I did not gain access to the muhtars' meetings with the district municipalities or the subgovernor's office. I only caught glimpses when these people (police officers, postmen, municipal administrators and councillors, staff from the subgovernor's office, or party cadres) visited or phoned the muhtar. These interactions gave me precious but limited indications. And this introduces a significant bias: "By focusing on public and formal scenes, observers abandon what goes on in the wings, the asides, the interstices where the crux of social exchange tends to be played out. [...] The main risk is of decontextualizing the procedure, in the light of the surrounding institutions, from the sphere of social relations in which it is placed, from the setting of parallel controversies adjacent to it" (Blondiaux and Fourniau 2011, 21).

One final limitation should be mentioned. Muhtars operate in a context of personalized acquaintanceship characterized by preexisting ties, in which neighborhood residents are not all equal. Whenever I observed an interaction between a muhtar and a given resident, though I could guess whether they were previously acquainted, I could not know in what their acquaintanceship consisted. Without prolonged immersion in this milieu, I could not access the implicit dimension shared by the protagonists, and it was often awkward or intrusive for me to ask afterward. I also did not know their reputations. This was a bit less true in neighborhoods B and C. Since I lived nearby, I often went to those neighborhoods and frequented certain shops. By dint of being greeted by me as I went past, they grew accustomed to my presence. I regularly went to chat over tea with the muhtars there about events in their neighborhood. But despite that, I do not claim long-term immersion in an acquaintanceship milieu.

This book is divided into four parts. Part 1 goes over the origins and main characteristics of the institution of the muhtarlık. It shows that the muhtarlık is not a classic administration, but a hybrid institution. It does not fit the dominant interpretation of Ottoman and Turkish history, viewed in terms of bureaucratization. Instead, I suggest, muhtars should be seen as institutionalized intermediaries. The institution is characterized by the voluntarily partial sway that state institutions exert over it. The activity of muhtars cannot strictly be said to be professionalized (chapter 1). The pronounced social anchoring of the muhtarlık has an impact on the social profiles of muhtars, meaning that they are comparable to notables (chapter 2). The resilience of this figure of indirect government, despite the institutional upheavals the country has been through, means that intermediation needs to be considered an integral part of the Turkish state's functioning.

Part 2 analyzes how the role of muhtar has been reconfigured by the arrival of databases which, from the perspective of rationalization, ought to have led to the muhtars' demise. The introduction of impersonal IT administrative mechanisms has led to their prerogatives being reduced. Yet, rather than disappearing, the muhtars' role has been reconfigured. Though they intervene less often and less directly, they continue to act as intermediaries and as means of redress, particularly for the distribution of social assistance (chapter 3). The coexistence of apparently opposed modes of government raises the question of what is specific to this institution. Members of the public make extensive use of it due to its proximity and familiarity. They present muhtars with all sorts of requests which exceed the official definition of their function. Muhtars find themselves caught between these demands, to which they are sensitive since they depend on their electorate, and institutional injunctions. Thus they seek to reconcile the two. But the public image they give is primarily one of being prompt to serve their constituents, thereby producing the image of a negotiable state (chapter 4).

Part 3 analyzes the ambivalent and contrasting political effects of this mode of government. Due to its familiarity, the muhtarlık makes the state accessible, and partakes in the administrative socialization of citizens. At the same time, due to the possibility of individualized treatment and accompanying arrangements, the muhtarlık embodies the possibility of prevailing upon the official order, thus feeding incessant suspicions of favoritism. The effect is to strip the state of its neutrality (chapter 5). A further ambivalent dimension to the institution's political effects relates to the fact that muhtars, with their extensive autonomy, inhabit their role in widely differing ways. At times they act as institutional relays, at others as a channel for residents' demands. The ways they embody this role are also linked to the neighborhood context, as well as to their very different personal trajectories (chapter 6).

Part 4 analyzes the muhtarlık's loss of autonomy over recent years. The ways in which muhtars assume their role cannot be dissociated from their relationship with institutions, which have a strong and ever-growing influence on the resources available to them. There is also an increasingly marked partisan political dimension to their relationship with institutions (chapter 7). The authorities have recently become more directly involved with the muhtarlık, thereby diminishing its autonomy. The municipalities are increasingly involved at the neighborhood level, thus marginalizing the muhtars. More proactive urban planning policies have led to an increased number of conflicts involving muhtarlıks. Lastly, since 2014 the executive has been seeking to bind the muhtarlıks ever more closely to it (chapter 8). The comparative autonomy from institutional and partisan political considerations that have long characterized this microlevel of government might well be coming to an end, thus suggesting a crucial transformation of patterns of government and state-society relations in Turkey.

Part 1

A HYBRID INSTITUTION ANCHORED
IN LOCAL SOCIETY

Chapter 1

AN INCOMPLETELY FORMED INSTITUTION

THE MUHTARLIK WAS INTRODUCED IN ISTANBUL IN 1829. IT WAS then generalized to the rest of the Ottoman Empire, before being systematized over the course of the following decades. The creation of this new institution was not an isolated event, for it took place at a time when the state was reconfiguring its hierarchies and powers, and introducing new bureaucratic procedures. Strictly speaking, the emblematic period of the *Tanzimat* ("reorganizations") only started in 1839, yet the previous decade was one of major administrative reform, also often described by historians as a process of "bureaucratization" and "centralization."[1] A similar perspective tends to be taken towards the creation of the muhtarlık.[2] But I believe it reductive to view the introduction of the muhtarlık in terms of bureaucratization and centralization—misleading, even. Any such interpretation tends to take muhtars as state agents; I believe it more appropriate to view them as intermediaries. This chapter argues that the main characteristic of the muhtarlık is its partial hold over its practitioners. It first recounts the developments of this intermediary institution, and then addresses its hybridity in the present day.

ORIGINS AND SUBSEQUENT DEVELOPMENTS
The Formation of a New Institution
It is worth briefly examining how the muhtarlık was formed over time. The literature suggests several causes. Let us look at the two main ones. First, the corps

of Janissaries, which had hitherto conducted municipal policing, was disbanded in 1826, and so another means was needed to ensure public order in cities (Çadırcı 1970, 411; Ortaylı 2000, 108). Second, stricter controls over population movements were introduced in reaction to the ever greater flow of people to the cities, particularly Istanbul. It was the imams who were in charge of issuing or refusing certificates of passage for their neighborhoods. It is worth pointing out that the religious hierarchy wielded extensive powers at that time, pertaining to civil status, judicial authority, and the apportionment of taxation. But the way the imams controlled population flow had its weaknesses, and there were numerous accusations of corruption, laxity, arbitrary decisions, and abuse of power (Ergin 1936, 121; Ortaylı 2000, 108). In 1829 two muhtars were appointed to assist the imams in each Istanbul neighborhood; they were granted the civil functions hitherto exerted by the imams.

The muhtarlık was rapidly expanded to the provinces, while the *derebey* ("valley lords," or regional potentates) were progressively removed from office.[3] The muhtarlık was first introduced in 1833, in Kastamonu, in the wake of a conflict between the population and a local notable in charge of tax collection. His excessive demands sparked a revolt supported by the *mütesellim* (the local lieutenant of the nonresident provincial governor, or even a provincial governor). The notable was stripped of office and two muhtars introduced in each village or neighborhood. Apparently the mütesellim boasted to the Sublime Porte that order had been reestablished and the population satisfied, as a result of which Sultan Mahmud II ordered the governors to generalize this system to all provinces between 1833 and 1835 (Çadırcı 1970, 412).[4]

Scholars have therefore suggested that the introduction of the muhtarlık was an attempt to rationalize and standardize ways of managing populations (Lévy-Aksu 2012, 222). More specifically, it has been interpreted as revealing broader tendencies—first, the secularization of the administration, and second, its bureaucratization and centralization. Regarding secularization, the new office sidelined the religious hierarchy from municipal and security affairs, eventually excluding it altogether. Until the first half of the nineteenth century, the religious dignitaries had been in charge of relations between a neighborhood and the outside world. The imams, appointed on the sultan's decision, were the local representatives of the *qadi*—the judges in Islamic courts, who also were part of the administrative hierarchy of the empire. Under Sultan Mahmut II (1808–39), qadis were relieved of their powers in matters of security and civil status.[5] The muhtars took over from the imams as the local intermediary between the state and populations.[6] However, this interpretation in terms of secularization needs nuancing. Although the local administration was no longer headed by clerics, the religious dimension continued to be a determining factor in how it was run, right up until the end of the empire. The 1864 Provincial Regulation (*Vilayet nizamnamesi*) stipulated that each neighborhood was to have two muhtars from different religious communities (apart from communities with less than twenty households). The council of elders was to have three members from each religious community and a maximum of twelve members. Imams and non-Muslim religious dignitaries were ex officio members (Aytaç 2009, 62).

The interpretation in terms of bureaucratization and centralization merits more detailed discussion. It is based on the fact that, from the outset, the position of muhtar had links to the state apparatus. The appointment of muhtars, like that of imams, was confirmed by the Porte, and they received a seal (*mühür*) produced by the Mint (Çadırcı 1970, 413).[7] This seal still acts as the symbol of the muhtar today. Muhtars were also part of the state apparatus by virtue of their salary. When in 1838 the Ottoman state started paying salaries to state agents— who previously had been remunerated primarily in kind and in tax exemptions (Güneş 2014, 42ss)—muhtars also started receiving remuneration, though only on an irregular basis (Ortaylı 2000, 110). There was no fixed rate of pay. Rather, it was negotiated on a case-by-case basis, depending on the number of inhabitants and the distance from administrative centers. It came from the budget of the *muhassıl*, a type of provincial governor in charge of collecting public revenue. But the level of public funding was insufficient (Çadırcı 1993, 8; Ortaylı, 2000, 110). In 1842, when the Istanbul government decided muhassıls would no longer oversee revenue collection, remuneration of the muhtars came to an end, as did that of many local officials. This led the muhtars to call for remuneration, something the authorities apparently refused, preferring to leave the matter to the discretion of the inhabitants, who made a contribution to pay the muhtars either in kind or via a tax surcharge (Güneş 2014, 49ss). Lastly, from an organizational point of view, the muhtars were associated with the state apparatus, though the authority they depended on was altered on numerous occasions. At times they were referred to as being placed under the supervision of registry controllers (*defter nazırları*), who in turn depended hierarchically on the Census

Ministry (Ceride nezareti). Elsewhere they were placed under the authority of provincial governors called mütesellims (Çadırcı 1970, 414–15; Çadırcı 1993, 7). The 1864 Provincial Regulation, which were progressively implemented in various provinces before being generalized in 1871 with the General Regulation for Provincial Administration, established an administrative hierarchy with an integrated pyramid of districts. Under these regulations, muhtars were usually placed under the authority of the police chiefs (*zabtiye amirleri*).

The 1864 Provincial Regulation and 1871 General Regulation did not just systematize the organization of muhtarlıks; they also set out the nature of the muhtars' duties. And significantly—given that it lends support to the interpretation in terms of bureaucratization and centralization—these duties related primarily to the executive functions of central government. The muhtars' main task was to ensure order and security in the neighborhood. They selected and commanded the night watchmen who were in charge of maintaining order (*bekçi* or *korucu*). It was the muhtars' duty to inform the authorities of any crimes committed in the neighborhood, and to help solve them. They also played an important role in monitoring population movements, being in charge of recording new arrivals; checking the certificates of passage and internal passports (*mürur tezkeresi*) required for moving around the empire; and issuing certificates of good behavior (*mühürlü pusula* or *ilmühaber*), which were required to obtain the internal passports that residents needed if they wished to leave the neighborhood.[8] In addition to this, the muhtars had to inform the local population about the law and any recently promulgated decrees and regulations. They also played a part in conscription (Çadırcı 1970, 414; Çadırcı 1993, 6–7). Furthermore, they were in charge of keeping the neighborhood accounts and, together with the council of elders, assisting the government in the apportionment of taxation—certain taxes being owed by the neighborhood as a whole—after consultation with the heads of family. They were also involved in the subsequent collection of those taxes. The muhtars had to maintain the civil register and transmit it to the registry controllers.[9] It was their role to inform the relevant authorities of any unauthorized buildings, and of any property with unclear tax status. Finally, they had to assist other institutions in the neighborhood. Thus, far from simply taking over the civil duties of imams, the muhtars rapidly assumed new spheres of competence. The Ottoman authorities implicitly expected the muhtars to control and be abreast of virtually everything that happened in their neighborhoods (Behar 2003, 165, 169).

Erbay Arıkboğa argues that the links between the muhtars and the state apparatus, and their powers pertaining to the state's executive functions, mean that the creation of the muhtarlık marked a significant step in the advent of a centralized state. For him, the muhtarlık was neither a local government body nor a devolved state organization, but a unit performing tasks that were regarded as obligatory and which needed to be carried out at first hand by a power going through the process of centralization (Arıkboğa 1998, 105; Arıkboğa 1999, 107). Likewise, writing in the 1930s, Musa Çadırcı described village muhtars as "executive government officials" (*hükümetin uygulama memurları*; 1993, 9).

Yet muhtars were not straightforward state agents, being in an intermediary position between the Ottoman executive and judicial authorities on the one hand and the local population on the other. Muhtars were elected, and the local authorities were barred from playing a role in who was appointed. They could also be stripped of their functions if neighborhood residents filed complaints against them (Güneş 2004, 53). Little is known about how they were elected, at least in the early years.[10] The Provincial Regulation clarified things by introducing an annual election with votes cast by taxpayers (Aytaç 2009, 63). Furthermore, muhtars acted as the legal guarantor of their neighborhoods, in whose name they could testify before a court—both collectively and, if necessary, individually. They were regularly called upon to act as mediators or to represent the neighborhood in dealings with the authorities (Çadırcı 1970, 414; Lévy-Aksu 2012, 222). Thus they could also transmit collective complaints and requests to the authorities, notably via petitions, which almost invariably bore the muhtar's seal. Thus, for instance, in the late nineteenth century the muhtar of the Kasap İlyas neighborhood in Istanbul became a community leader, probably more due to personal initiative or that of the population than to any regulatory provisions (Behar 2003, 79, 82).

Finally, it would appear that muhtars were invested with local powers. The 1864 and 1871 regulations granted village muhtars responsibility for local affairs including roads, cleaning, managing property bequeathed to the neighborhood community, supervising the construction of charitable buildings, settling disputes between local residents, and even trials on occasion. Although these texts do not refer to neighborhood muhtarlıks, certain authors consider the regulations to have applied to them too (Güneş 2014, 125). It is quite possible that the prior system for organizing local neighborhood affairs—such as waste collection and maintenance of order by neighborhood watchmen (*bekçi*)—went unchanged, though it was probably now supervised by the muhtars (Arıkboğa 1998, 102–4). At the same time the municipalities, which were going through a process of institutionalization, were granted extensive new powers under the 1871 regulation.[11] These partially overlapped with the local tasks being carried out by the muhtarlık, though without the limits of each being laid down. Two institutions thus coexisted with partially overlapping prerogatives, and without any hierarchical or codified link between the two.

The local powers invested in the muhtars, the fact that they were elected, and their status as representatives of the local population in dealings with the authorities mean that they are better viewed as intermediaries than as bureaucrats. Cem Behar thus describes the muhtars as "middlemen" (2003, 160). Noémi Lévy-Aksu also uses the term "intermediary" to refer to actors "assuming a particular role in managing public order, and thereby acting as privileged interlocutors with both the state and urban society. Community elites, local religious leaders, and muhtars are all categories which guaranteed that public order be upheld thanks to their functions and social status" (2012, 30). The muhtars may thus be considered as institutionalized intermediary figures, alongside the many other figures in the empire who have been extensively studied, such as local notables, whose names often figure in registries alongside the muhtars.

A Hybrid Institution with an Ambiguous Status

It is not easy to pin down developments to the muhtarlık in the wake of the political upheavals of the 1910s, including the Young Turk revolution, internal conflicts, World War I, and the subsequent transition to a republic. The muhtarlık was abolished for a while, before being reinstated in a form very similar to that of the Ottoman period, though now within a republican framework. In this very different context, its position within the local political and administrative system was complex and ill-defined.

The Law on Provincial Administration passed in 1913 by the Committee of Union and Progress abolished the Tanzimat regulations, and consequently those concerning the muhtarlık. It made no reference to the muhtarlık, but neither did it reattribute its powers to other institutions. It may thus be suggested that the neighborhood muhtarlık continued to function in the existing manner, at least in some of its former powers. This may well have been without any legal basis as set out in parliamentary acts, but with the blessing of the authorities (Türk Belediyecilik Derneği and Konrad Adenauer Vakfı 1998, 13). A circular dated 1918 informing governors' offices that they were to continue establishing neighborhood muhtarlıks lends support to this idea (Aytaç 2009, 65).

This silence continued during the period of Turkey's transition to a republic, before the muhtarlık was subsequently abolished. The 1924 Constitution does not refer to neighborhood muhtarlıks, nor does the 1929 Law on Provincial Administration. The 1930 Law on Municipalities mentions the delimitation of neighborhoods without referring to the muhtarlık. Over the course of the 1920s and 1930s, the new regime organized its local administration, introducing a stronger distinction between villages and neighborhood muhtarlıks.[12] The 1924 Law on Villages laid down regulations for village muhtarlıks, and for the first time defined muhtars as state officials (*devletin memuru*). But a 1933 law (no. 2295) explicitly abolished the neighborhood muhtarlık in places where there was a municipality, thereby confirming that the former had continued to exist in informal manner. The preamble to the 1933 law is revealing, for it justifies the need to abolish the muhtarlık on the grounds that no such thing existed anywhere else in the world.[13] It specifies that, since under the 1930 law drafted "in accordance with the most recent scientific bases" municipalities carried out the tasks previously performed by the neighborhood muhtarlık, the latter were now redundant (Arıkboğa 1998, 114). The abolition of neighborhood muhtarlıks was thus an outward sign of a form of normalization of the Turkish state, which sought to rationalize its operations. Most of the muhtars' powers were transferred to the municipalities. The 1934 application decree divided up their prerogatives and reallocated them to the municipal police, the gendarmerie, the neighborhood watchmen, and even on occasion to elected inhabitants.

No doubt the abolition of muhtars was a response to criticisms of how the muhtarlık functioned. According to Osman Nuri Ergin, a historian of local authorities who also taught at the police academy, "the muhtars and councils of elders did nothing but oppress and eat away at the people," providing no service without financial recompense. He notes that it was difficult to contact them even during opening hours, and criticizes the fact that while pretending to serve the population, they only looked after their own personal interests. According to Ergin, given that the muhtars were neither local nor government officials and had ties with "political organizations"—in all probability the single party, the CHP (Cumhuriyet Halk Partisi, the People's Republican Party)—it was apparently very difficult to sanction or dismiss them (1939 [1932], 92–93).[14] He thus criticizes their insubordination and the fact that they served themselves rather than the state or the population. The draft law abolishing neighborhood muhtarlıks was passed by the Turkish parliament with little debate (Arıkboğa 1999, 115).

But the lack of any reliable system to identify individuals soon caused problems (Aytaç 2009, 65). It would appear that municipalities opened neighborhood bureaus, allocating staff to work there, but did so without any legal basis or much success. After a few years of trial and error, some members of parliament suggested setting up a new organization for administering neighborhoods (Ergin 1939 [1932], 94–95). Finally, the neighborhood muhtarlık was officially reinstated in 1944. The preamble to the draft law states that the functions previously carried out by the muhtarlık were no longer being satisfactorily fulfilled, thus justifying their reintroduction on the grounds of an "administrative void" (*idare boşluğu*; Arıkboğa 1998, 117).

Analysis of the three draft laws drawn up in 1943 and 1944 together with the debates in parliament and parliamentary committees shows that there was no clear consensus about the status of the muhtarlık.[15] The provisions finally adopted therefore need to be considered as resulting from a series of fairly contingent compromises. It would be mistaken to attribute them with any hypothetical "rationality" or, a fortiori, any administrative rationale.

The 1944 Law on the Organization of Neighborhood Muhtars and Councils of Elders in the Towns and Cities (*Şehir ve kasabalarda mahalle muhtar ve ihtiyar heyetleri teşkiline dair kanun*), and an associated 1945 decree still in force today, did not significantly expand the muhtarlıks' realms of authority. Under these provisions, a muhtar continues to be supported by a council of elders (*ihtiyar meclisi*), elected at the same time to assist in certain tasks. Council members have subsequently tended to be referred to as azas. The muhtars' responsibilities, set out in the 1944 law, relate primarily to central power. The muhtarlık has to apply and enforce the center's instructions, inform security forces of suspicious or wanted people living in the neighborhood and identify

future conscripts, maintain the civil register and draw up the electoral lists, issue certificates and alert the administrative authorities to any epidemics. But
the muhtarlık no longer plays any role in the apportionment and collection of
taxes, since collective taxes no longer exist. Many subsequent laws not relating
directly to the muhtarlık entrusted them with new tasks, but did so on an ad
hoc basis and without any plan.[16] Erbay Arıkboğa regrets that the muhtarlık is
viewed as being apt to assume any task whatsoever (1998, 124; 2002), and is a
"stopgap" (boşluk doldurucu) to be exploited at will.

In the debates preceding passage of the 1944 law, certain members of parliament had suggested granting neighborhoods legal status and endowing them
with local authority like villages. But the idea was soon dropped. The 1937 constitution did not provide for any such administrative level, and attempting to
introduce it would have entailed a cumbersome and uncertain procedure. Debates also related to the links between the muhtarlık, the municipalities, and
second-tier administrative divisions such as subgovernor's offices.[17] The final
text did not attach the muhtarlık to municipalities, with which muhtars were
most closely involved, or to second-tier administrations. The law describes the
neighborhood muhtars as auxiliary to municipal services, while placing them
under the authority of the subgovernors' offices (Aytaç 2009, 65). Thus, the
muhtarlık was instituted as an autonomous unit with an indeterminate position within the administrative system (Palabıyık and Atak 2000, 154), placed
somewhere between municipal authorities and second-tier administrations
(Arıkboğa 1998, 117–22). The law establishes the muhtarlık as a means for assisting the public authorities in the provision of services to the local population
(Aldan 1956, 16). But despite this, it was not endowed with any local powers,
even on the smallest scale; those remained the prerogative of the municipality.

Let us look more closely at the ambiguity surrounding this status. From a
legal point of view, muhtars are considered "public agents" (kamu görevlileri),
and their rights and duties are governed by the law relating to state officials.
In practice they are widely considered as officials, particularly as most of their
responsibilities are associated with the central administration. The Council of
State (Danıştay) and the Supreme Court of Appeals (Yargıtay) have endorsed the
principle that muhtars are subject to the precepts of the law pertaining to trials
of officials (Palabıyık and Atak 2000, 152n8). Insofar as they are endowed with
legal authority, are associated with the law, and hold an institutional position

defined independently of their person, muhtars may be considered bureaucrats in the meaning developed by Max Weber (1978 [1921], 220 et seq.).

But in other respects they do not comply with Weber's definition of the rational-legal bureaucrat. First, their recruitment is not on the basis of skills and professional qualifications, attested by a diploma. The elective nature of the position debars any requirement of specialized skills, and contradicts the principle of permanence. Muhtars are not part of the administrative structure, and do not officially join the administration. There is no promotion on the basis of seniority. Muhtars themselves often rail against this ambiguous status. Thus, Duran regretted that "the muhtarlık is subject to law 657 [on state officials], he is a public agent, well supposedly. [. . . But] muhtars do not have the rights of public agents. [. . .][18] They are public agents, but they are not public agents; there are legal rights, but they do not enjoy these legal rights."

There is even more ambiguity surrounding the status of muhtars given that they are elected—in local elections held every five years since 1963, and hence at the same time as mayors, municipal councillors, general councillors, and metropolitan mayors.[19] Their position is therefore temporary. From this point of view, muhtars are more like local elected representatives. But they do not have the same status, since they are not legally vested with any power to represent the population.

The Shift Away from Party Affiliation

Another element setting muhtars apart from elected representatives is that, since the 1980 coup, they have not been allowed to have ties to political parties. In parallel to parties' growing hold over politics in republican Turkey, the muhtars had become linked to party politics with the advent of the one-party period. One decision of the 1927 CHP convention was that muhtars would only be appointed with the approval of party inspectors (*müfettiş*), as indeed was the case for officials in charge of social, political, economic, and cultural affairs (Payaslıoğlu 1964, 421). The CHP designated its candidates for the 1931 elections at its first-tier party conferences.[20] Any other candidates stood as independents, with little apparent chance of success.[21] These ties to the single party strengthened the muhtars' links to the state apparatus, together with the pressure the latter could exert on muhtars to be loyal to the CHP. The 1930 municipal elections were the first in which there were rival candidates, who stood for the very short-lived opposition, the SCF (Serbest Cumhuriyet Fırkası, the Free Republican Party). The bureaucratic hierarchy pushed muhtars to side with the CHP. In the town of Finike, in Antalya province, the subgovernor warned muhtars that they could not join any party other than the CHP, and that, were they to do so, they would be sentenced to death for reaction (*irtica*; Güçlü 1999, 19). In a village near Kemalpaşa, in Izmir province, a muhtar and a sergeant, acting on orders from the governor, apparently opened a ballot box and replaced vote slips for the SCF with slips for the CHP.[22]

The transition to a multiparty system in the late 1940s had direct implications on the selection of muhtars, for the position became a major political stake. CHP archives show that as of the late 1940s, the former single party viewed the muhtar election results predominantly in terms of party rivalry, which is not particularly surprising. But this was also true of the local and national press, indicating that the parties viewed both village and neighborhood muhtar elections as a test of their popularity. Many newspapers reported election results, village by village and neighborhood by neighborhood, in terms of the number of votes garnered by each party. This test was all the more precise and localized as these elections were held more frequently than other elections, and often not at the same time.[23] In 1965, the elections for muhtar were held one month before the legislative elections. As a local newspaper put it: "In this run-up to major elections, the leaders of the CHP and AP (Adalet Partisi, or Justice Party) provincial organizations have attached great importance to the muhtarlık elections. The two parties have gone to great lengths to turn the results of these votes, just before the major elections, into a show of strength."[24]

From the 1950s to the 1970s, many muhtars came from the parties' activist bases. In 1952, several delegates to the CHP's Erzurum central district conference were muhtars.[25] In 1977, to stand for the CHP, candidates first had to run for selection by the party,[26] as for other elected offices (as a municipal councillor or MP). This meant that the party preselected candidates, but also that it supported those it selected. Incumbent muhtars also took part in "pre-elections" held by the parties in the 1960s and 1970s to designate their candidates for legislative elections. These did not really correspond to primary elections, since only delegates, local leaders, and muhtars who were party members were entitled to vote, mainly because there were no reliable local party membership registers (Bektaş 1988, 122). The muhtars were thus involved in party-political procedures, including decision processes relating to the key issue of designating candidates (Cumhuriyet Halk Partisi 1968, 321–27).

Muhtars would thus appear to have been integrated into party dynamics at this period. Despite a lack of data, it can be hypothesized that these partisan political rationales generated specific muhtar career trajectories and profiles. This may be illustrated by the example of Ayhan Altuğ. Born in 1933 in Istanbul, Altuğ became involved in building housing cooperatives in the new upmarket Istanbul neighborhood of Etiler. In 1963 he was elected as muhtar on a CHP ticket, retaining this position until 1973. Far from remaining a "mere" muhtar, he was elected as head of the Istanbul muhtar association. In parallel to this, he climbed the political ladder. He was long a member of the CHP subprovincial executive board, ending up as its chairman. He was also a member of the provincial executive board, which he also chaired. He was then a CHP member of parliament from 1977 to 1980 (TBMM 2010, 1054). This trajectory is probably not typical, given how far Ayhan Aytuğ managed to rise. But it shows that the muhtarlık could serve as a springboard for a political career.

The little data available for this period suggests that muhtars apparently played an active role in the politicization dynamics characterizing the second half of the 1970s, and particularly as a local relay for political parties. Certain muhtars were actively involved in the violent confrontations between left and right, especially in the massacres targeting left-wing sympathizers and Alevis in several Central Anatolian small cities in the late 1970s. Several testimonies highlight the role played by various muhtars in exhorting the population to take part in the pogroms during the bloodiest episode, which took place in Kahramanmaraş in December 1978, leaving more than one hundred dead according to official figures.[27] On December 24, 1978, the attacks, which had started five days earlier, spread to new neighborhoods. According to several witnesses, "a group of assailants headed by the muhtar of the Namık Kemal neighborhood, armed and bearing a flag, and another man, attacked houses to cries of 'God, God, we're going to destroy the communists! Old or young, crush the communists' heads!'" (Gürel 2004, 121). Thus, together with many other officeholders, certain muhtars apparently acted primarily as party activists rather than as neutral officials.

There are also a few recorded cases of muhtars importing partisan political rationales into state institutions in a way comparable to that of other officials

(Gourisse 2010). A reformed MHP (Milliyetçi Hareket Partisi, or Nationalist Movement Party) activist describes in his memoirs how he was released after being arrested for a gun battle in Ankara:

> A search was being carried out in the cafés, and a weapon was found on a friend we called Hikmet the soldier [Asker Hikmet]. The police rounded us up and put us in a vehicle. Before getting in, Hikmet the soldier said to the café owner, who was the muhtar, "Tell Necati Paşa" [i.e., Necati Gültekin, the MHP general secretary]. They took us to the [...] police station. Two hours later they released us. (Tanlak 1996, 21; quoted by Gourisse 2010, 304).

This anchoring to political parties probably provided muhtars with resources and specific links to institutions, while also implying injunctions and constraints. The 1980 coup put an end to these ties between muhtars and political parties. On taking power in 1980, the junta removed the incumbent muhtars and nominated new ones—a step it also took for mayors. It was in 1983, with the return to a civilian regime, that the trajectory of muhtars started to diverge from that of other elected representatives. While the latter took up their partisan political affiliations once again, the 1984 Law on Local Elections stipulates that muhtars standing at either the village or the neighborhood level cannot run under a party banner.

Despite being held at the same time as other local elections, ballots for muhtars therefore have certain specificities. Candidates for the muhtarlık, unlike those for other elections, do not have to make a prior declaration to the body in charge of supervising elections, the Electoral Council, to obtain confirmation of their eligibility. The election of muhtars and their council of elders is thus not subject to an electoral calendar. Candidates may declare up until voting day. The only requirement for standing as a candidate is to place ballot papers in the voting stations on the day of the election. A candidate's eligibility is checked only after they have been elected. The results are not included in official electoral statistics (Arıkboğa 1998, 118n47). The electoral procedure is thus monitored significantly less tightly than those for other ballots.

While the ties that muhtars once had to political parties probably brought their position closer to that of other local elected representatives, the reduced sway of political parties since 1980 has reversed that trend. This shift away from party affiliation is an original phenomenon. Scholarship on the social history of politics in other European countries has inquired into the profiles of local elected representatives. In most cases, these profiles have changed as parties have extended their reach down to the most local levels. Officeholders have increasingly tended to have backgrounds in activism and party politics, rather than as "notables."[28] But the case of muhtars apparently bucks the trend toward professionalization in political activity that is observable in many other situations. Nowadays very few muhtars climb the political ladder toward other elective functions in political parties. On the contrary, local luminaries continue to dominate the muhtarlık, as will be noted in the following pages—a phenomenon which has no doubt increased since 1980. The office thus stands apart, due to the declining hold Turkish political parties have over microlocal politics.

The muhtars are thus neither really local state officials nor simply local elected representatives. Revealingly, they figure in the official protocol of subgovernors' offices as being in a "hybrid" position. They are placed well below prefectural officials, the local directors of public banks, the directors of provincial party organizations, and members of the municipal council. However, they appear before the directors of professional organizations, and the directors of foundations and associations of public utility. They are thus placed beneath the administrators, and figure between "classic" elected representatives and "civil society" representatives.[29] Muhtars regularly complain about their unclear status. According to Ebru, a graduate who is well informed about the texts governing the muhtarlık: "We are in fact everything. We are elected independently; there is no party or any other force behind us. But we have *bağ-kur* insurance, as if we were employers.[30] But in the event of a judicial enquiry we are held to be officials; we are judged and sanctioned as state officials. It is not clear what we are. That is why I ask what I am. A mayor? An official? I have no idea. The muhtar has to be autonomous, has to have revenues. If I am elected, I should have the status of an elected representative."

The muhtarlık has an ambiguous institutional position. It was set up to act as an intermediary in the imperial context, before being reintroduced in a similar form but within the republican institutional order, which was in many ways very different. There were numerous intermediaries in the days of empire, but it is often held—among scholars at least—that these disappeared in republican Turkey. Other institutionalized intermediary figures, such as the *derebey*, did indeed disappear under the republic. The muhtars are the only ones to have survived the regime change—though at the price of an ambiguous and subordinate status.

AN OFFICE WITH ONLY PARTIAL HOLD OVER ITS PRACTITIONERS

The muhtarlık is a hybrid institution with an uncertain position in the political and administrative system. As we have seen, it is not clearly anchored in any specific hierarchy, but instead combines elements of a local body with others of a second-tier administration. Furthermore, it is a largely subordinate part of the local political administrative system. This is true in several ways. First, it is excluded from official decision-making circuits. Second, it has few specific resources. This generates a dual form of dependency: the muhtarlık depends on other institutions, and muhtars depend on other resources to carry out their functions, especially personal resources. The position of muhtar is rarely the officeholder's sole or even principal sphere of activity. Due to the conditions in which muhtars operate, the position does not require any exclusive allegiance from them. Thus, institutional rationales exert limited sway over those who hold the office.

Exclusion from Decision-Making Circuits

Unlike Ottoman neighborhoods, and unlike village muhtarlıks which have a legal personality, a budget, and local responsibilities, the neighborhood muhtarlık does not have the official status of a local body, a budget, or an administration.[31] Consequently they do not have any decision-making power in their own right.

Furthermore, the muhtarlık is sidelined and sometimes excluded even from official decision-making circuits. Muhtars tend not to be integrated in decision making at the level of the municipality, the subgovernor's office, or the governor's office. They do not have a vote on the municipal or general council, or even a consultative voice. This exclusion from decision making even relates to issues pertaining to their neighborhoods, including the most decisive ones such as urban renewal programs, or those affecting the urban fabric more generally. Municipalities are under no obligation to consult with them on these issues, or even to inform them. [32] Muhtars generally declare, however, that they are informed of decisions and announcements by the municipality and subgovernor's office about issues pertaining to their neighborhoods. But this is not systematic, and it mostly occurs after the decisions have been taken (Şevran

2005, 116 et seq.). A muhtar sometimes learns of plans to construct a building only when asked to sign the certificate of vacancy (*boş yazısı*) needed to demolish a building. For the first time, however, the 2005 Law on Municipalities enjoins municipal authorities to consider the muhtarlık's opinion.[33] Article 9 states that the municipality "takes into account in its decisions the common desires of the neighborhood residents, and tries to ensure that its services are provided in accordance with neighborhood needs." It stipulates that muhtars are responsible for determining the collective needs of the residents, improving the quality of life in their neighborhoods, communicating with the municipal authorities and other institutions, and intervening in neighborhood affairs. It does not, however, specify how they are to intervene, nor does it introduce any such obligation. Hence, the authorities only rarely ask muhtars their opinion or solicit their prior feedback. Ebru, who has held her position since 2005, said she never took part in the meetings of the district municipal council, and did not see the mayor between 2010 and 2014. When the muhtars are involved in decisions, they do not decide the manner in which they intervene, but are solicited by the authorities when it is deemed necessary. Sometimes a muhtar protests to the authorities when the neighborhood residents urge them to act against an official decision, often after it has already been taken. They then need to take up the issue and fight hard to get their voice heard (see chapter 4).

Muhtars have no control over decisions relating to local urban development, and often criticize them. Gaffar heads an old central neighborhood, home primarily to self-employed skilled manual workers and small business owners. When a group of activists for participatory urban development came to see him, he explained that the major problem in the neighborhood was that it was earmarked for transformation into a tourist zone, despite the fact that the workers and business owners—Gaffar himself is an ironmonger—wished to stay. Although he was not certain that the neighborhood would be demolished, he feared that it might be, and he mentioned the possibility of expropriations. He also criticized another long-standing project to relocate the self-employed workers to a large site on the periphery of the city. On several occasions he criticized the government as well as the municipality, which in his opinion was failing to provide enough services. He suspected it meant to push the exasperated residents to leave of their own accord.

Muhtars complain about being excluded in this way. As Duran observed: "The muhtar cannot command, he cannot order that something be done. [...] He tells you about a problem, as if I was your employee and I said to the boss, 'Boss, this is missing here, that is missing there, can you do something about it?' He's like a spokesman, like an employee in fact." Duran expressed bitterness, denouncing a municipality that governed without consultation, which preferred not to involve the muhtars as it viewed them as being too attached to the wishes of the neighborhood residents.

In recent years, however, there has been a tendency to involve muhtars on certain consultative bodies. Since 2004 an elected representative of the muhtars sits on the boards of the Social Solidarity and Assistance Foundations (Sosyal Yardılaşma ve Dayanışma Vakıfları, SYDV), which are in charge of distributing assistance at the level of each subgovernorship. Some muhtars are members of city councils (*kent konseyi*), participatory bodies created in 2005 with the local implementation of Agenda 21.[34] These city councils are supposed to make recommendations to municipalities regarding development, projects, and budgeting priorities. But the muhtars with whom I spoke showed little interest in them. Some seemed ignorant of their purpose, while others denied having any interest in them. The muhtars who had reacted enthusiastically when the councils were set up, such as Fikret, soon lost their enthusiasm. This may be attributed to the uncertainty and lack of conviction that took hold once the councils were up and running. In any case, these consultative bodies involve not all the muhtars, but only those elected to represent them. These developments indicate a shift from the principle of intermediation to that of delegation. The muhtars are there not as intermediaries but as "grassroots" representatives of the neighborhood residents, perhaps to display that local concerns are being taken into account.

All in all, with its ambiguous status and functions, its few powers, and its lack of decision-making authority and institutional allies, the muhtarlık would appear to be an institution that can be easily circumvented or bent to the will of its partners.

Lack of Means

The second weakness the muhtarlık suffers from is a lack of means for carrying out its functions. As a result, the muhtars are in a comparatively precarious situation. This relates both to their available means for action, and to their income. Consequently, most muhtars continue to have outside activities and are dependent on third parties: the municipalities, and also the neighborhood residents via the fees they pay. This shortage of means and revenue limits the sway the muhtarlık can exert.

The 1944 law did not provide any budget, staff, or premises for the muhtarlık. This point was raised in debates about the law, with certain members of parliament fearing that it would hamper the action of the muhtarlık (Arıkboğa 1998, 122). It is not rare for muhtars to carry out their duties from premises they own or rent, or even from their homes. A questionnaire survey of muhtars conducted in Izmir in 1998 showed that 31.1 percent of respondents carried out their tasks in municipal premises, 30.2 percent in premises they owned, and 30.7 in premises they rented (Palabıyık and Atak 2000, 154, 167). Fikret, a building contractor and a muhtar from 1989 to 1994 and again from 1999 to 2019, carried out his duties until 2010 in a building he owned and had built himself. Cemil, a muhtar since 1994, long used the estate agency he rented. This lack of specific premises is indicative of the semiprivate nature of the office. Furthermore, many muhtars have to pay the operating costs (electricity, water, ink cartridges, telephone, etc.) out of their own pockets, something about which they often complain. Duran used premises provided by the municipality, but still had to cover his own operating costs: "We are the ones who pay for everything, the electricity, the water. Because the bills are in my name, not the muhtarlık's."

Over recent years, the municipalities—often district municipalities (neighborhoods A, D, E, F), but also sometimes metropolitan municipalities (as in the case of neighborhoods B and C)—have provided the muhtarlıks with premises and equipment. The district municipality covering neighborhood F set up several *semtevi* (neighborhood centers) in 2010, often with premises for the muhtarlıks. Providing premises in this manner is indicative of a trend towards attaching these institutions to municipalities, a phenomenon dating back to the 2000s (see chapter 8).

Muhtarlık E was based in private premises before being relocated to a municipal site in 2004. The district municipality allocated it part of a building, which had turned out to be too small to house a dispensary as had been initially planned. But it did not provide any funding for refurbishment. The muhtar called on the generosity of local businesses, the private clinic, hotel, and so on.

"A few of my uncle's friends helped, and the work was done," Ebru (the nephew of the muhtar in question) laconically explained.

This municipalization of the muhtarlıks is far from total. In Istanbul, many are housed in private premises, either because the municipality has no premises to provide or because it does not wish to provide any. Out of the twenty-three muhtarlıks in the district of neighborhood E, two or three still had no premises in 2014, in which case the municipality paid their rent. In a neighboring district, ten out of forty-five muhtarlıks had no institutional premises.

In addition to help with premises, the 2005 law encourages municipalities to cover certain of the muhtarlıks' expenses.'[35] Thus, the district municipality of neighborhood F has institutionalized the provision of equipment for the muhtarlıks (computers, printers, ink cartridges, furniture, and paper), and has undertaken to pay their electricity, water, gas, telephone, and Internet bills. This support may also include the cost of employing auxiliaries, requiring a larger budget, especially in populous neighborhoods where the muhtar cannot perform all tasks unaided. However, there is nothing obligatory about this assistance, and municipalities apply it unequally. Some, such as the district municipality of neighborhood A, provide no help. Others provide it on an ad hoc basis, or only help some muhtarlıks but not others, depending upon the relationship they have with them. The level of help is thus unequal and variable, and this can lead to contrasting and sometimes unstable situations.

Dependency on Other Sources of Income

This shortage of means generates forms of dependency, indicating that lawmakers have not sought the muhtar's exclusive allegiance to the state. First, the material dimension of the muhtarlık limits the sway it exerts over officeholders, for they usually have other sources of income and even other professional activities. Second, the lack of training means that muhtars are not specialized administrators, and import the socialization and routines they have acquired elsewhere into the way they carry out their duties.

Ever since the muhtarlık was set up, the issue of their remuneration has been problematic. The exact status of the payments introduced in 1838 was never resolved. Were they actual salaries, or just defrayal of expenses? That is why the fact that muhtars continued to have other professional activities and did not incur expenses linked to their muhtar activity (such as regular travel), was invoked as a reason for reducing the amount they were paid (Güneş 2004, 45 et seq.). The principle of payment itself was soon dropped. The 1944 law does not instigate any salary for muhtars, and this led to objections from some MPs who feared that "public services [would] be transformed into individual business" (Arıkboğa 1998, 123). It was only in 1977 that muhtars started being remunerated and provided with social security coverage, in the wake of a protest campaign by the muhtars' federation.[36] This payment is not a salary, but a remuneration (*ödenek*). It is not enough to live on. Until recently it was less than half the salary received by qualified high school staff, and less than the minimum wage.[37] Thus, in 2013 Duran said, "I started [in 2009] with TL280 [per month], now I earn TL420; but TL350 goes on the *bağ-kur*, leaving TL70."[38] This obligatory insurance therefore represented a sizeable portion of the muhtars' remuneration. In 2014 about a quarter of Istanbul muhtars were in arrears on their social security payments, according to the head of a muhtar association. It is only very recently that their remuneration was increased. It practically doubled to TL871 per month in early 2014—a bit more than the net minimum salary, which by then had risen to TL846. In early 2016 it rose again to TL1,300— rising more rapidly than, and even overtaking, the net minimum salary, which then stood at TL1,177. This may be interpreted as an attempt to bind the muhtars more closely to the state (see chapter 8). However, these increases also had to make up for the loss of other sources of income for the muhtars—namely, those related to issuing documents.

The muhtars' remuneration is only one part of their income. They also receive fees on certain documents they draw up, services for which the price is fixed each year by the governor's office. This income is meant at least partially to cover structural expenses such as rent and electricity, but any surplus constitutes additional income for the muhtars. The amount received is proportionate to the size of the neighborhood's population. But this varies enormously. In Istanbul in 2019, certain neighborhoods had fewer than one hundred inhabitants, thirty-seven had more than fifty thousand, and the most populous had more than ninety-three thousand. In the late 1990s an observer calculated that an Istanbul muhtar in a neighborhood with a population below seven or eight thousand could not get by without another source of income (Arıkboğa 1998, 146). A widespread belief has it that muhtars in very populous neighborhoods have very large incomes.[39] It is thought that they can earn a lot of money without doing much,[40] and that people in such neighborhoods become muhtars mainly for financial gain (Arıkboğa 1998, 140). Even Gaffar, who has been a muhtar since 1994 for never more than 250 inhabitants, reckoned that "before, being a muhtar provided a steady income. In populous neighborhoods the muhtar used to earn more than an MP."

However, muhtars in charge of very populous neighborhoods have difficulty completing their tasks and often must hire assistants, which diminishes their "profits." In his neighborhood of about fifty thousand inhabitants, Duran paid a secretary TL800—amounting to double his own remuneration up until 2014—and also paid for her meals, which according to him came to between TL1,000 and TL1,200 per month. As far as possible, muhtars try to avoid employing anyone. After her secretary quit to get married, Ebru, in charge of a neighborhood of about twelve thousand inhabitants, justified not replacing her: "Our budget means it is not possible to take on help. There's the insurance, the meals, we have to pay all of that; but in any case, what do we earn? I would give TL800 or TL900 and have to pay their insurance. That is why I didn't want to. Recently my brother-in-law [. . .] went bankrupt. He is alongside me as an aza. What needs doing, we do it with him." Ebru thus drew on family support, probably in exchange for some compensation. A similar strategy is to have the secretary elected as first aza, or to continue to get them to work without being paid. This is what Hikmet, himself first aza until 2014, had envisaged when he ran unsuccessfully for the muhtarlık.

The muhtars' income from issuing documents has decreased significantly since 2009, as many public services have become computerized and databases set up, so that fewer certificates are now issued by the muhtars. Neighborhood residents no longer have to go to the muhtarlık for certain administrative needs. This is particularly true of the civil register. Previously, moving to another neighborhood entailed getting a residency certificate from the muhtar and paying him a paperwork fee. But it is now also possible to obtain a residency certificate free of charge from the district population bureau or even from the internet. Most muhtars complain about this.

Duran, who ran a neighborhood of fifty thousand residents, said that during his first six months, which corresponded to the 2009 transition to the address-based system, these fees brought in between TL350 and TL450 per day.[41] He reckoned that his daily income decreased to between TL50 and TL70, or perhaps

TL100 on a good day. Multiplied by the number of days worked, that came to a maximum of TL2,000 in 2013, leaving only a modest sum once he deducted the expense of employing his secretary. He expressed his disillusionment: "In 2008 this 'address-based system' (see chapter 3) came out, but we didn't know. I was running as a candidate. Of course, [the money] is not why I ran (*buna güvenerek*) when I got involved in the process. But, well, once in position, you have to keep on the go." Ebru, who was in charge of a neighborhood of about twelve thousand people, kept accounts of her income, which varied from TL30 to TL102 per day. She reckoned that the income from these fees had dropped by about half. Yet she said she was satisfied with this change, which also diminished the amount of what she regarded as pointless paperwork. But the vast majority of muhtars complain—such as İlhan, who concluded, "It is not possible to do this job" (*yapılamaz iş*).

The position has thus become a lot less attractive. This is the case in neighborhood h, where the incumbent muhtar did not stand for reelection in 2014, preferring to return to his previous job in the textile industry. Hikmet, his former aza, explained: "He said the muhtarlık was no longer attractive. To tell the truth, there was a financial aspect to the muhtarlık before, which has disappeared." Gaffar's neighborhood only had around 150 people, and he has probably never made much money from issuing certificates; he complained that nearly all his remuneration went for phone bills and other expenses. He reckoned that the government "pacified" muhtars by increasing the remuneration in 2014 (see chapter 8). Yet in populous neighborhoods, the increases do not compensate for the loss of income from issuing documents prior to the reform.

All the muhtars who were interviewed denied drawing any substantial income from their position. They all emphasized the fact that it cost them more than it brought in financially. Thus, Fikret's son, in a neighborhood of about eight thousand people, declared that, though the district municipality provided the premises and a computer and paid for all his water, electricity, and even tea, "you spend overall; the muhtarlık does not bring in anything [financially]." Despite the size of his neighborhood of fifty thousand inhabitants, Duran was more vocal in his demands: "The papers brought in income; it was something substantial. I experienced it for six months. [...] Before, a hundred or so people came to get papers every day. That fell to ten people. Three of them come for a poverty certificate, which is free. Two are poor; you don't make them pay. You end up only getting five to pay." He complained that he had to pay for the office supplies and for ink cartridges.

Under these conditions, the muhtars' personal income can be very directly influenced by whether or not the municipalities pay certain running expenses. This shortage of means therefore makes the muhtars dependent—on the municipalities, the inhabitants, and other sources of income. This problem transpires in the case of Duran, whom the municipality did not help financially: "The state has not put a cent towards my computer [. . .]. I am also the one who had to do the interior of the office when I arrived; I paid TL3,000. I took over the computer of the former muhtar; there was a program on it. He tricked me at the time, as he said it was a new program, when in fact it was really old. I had to pay TL1,000 for the Office program."

All the muhtars reject the idea that they became muhtars out of financial interest, and some of them mention other motivations. Hikmet, the outgoing first aza and losing candidate in 2014, despite being aware of these financial limits and complaining about the scaling back of the muhtars' functions, mentioned less material reasons: "Let's not leave the place, at least let's not leave our neighborhood, to others. Let the neighborhood stay with us, so that there is a place you can go with your mind at rest." Duran had to explain why, in these conditions, he was standing for reelection in 2014: "Why should I carry on, since I spend so much money? There is no economic interest, fine, but the spiritual dimension is important (*hiç bir menfaat yok, maneviyatı çok*). I envisage another term in office, since there is this chaotic urban transformation. I envisage sacrificing another five years, so as to protect the rights of the poor." A few weeks later, he returned to this question: "I am convinced that we [the neighborhood] will run into very serious problems. I have acquired a certain amount of experience, documents, and knowledge [. . .] at least to take up a stand alongside the people. [. . .] So as not to leave the position empty, I will be standing for reelection." This discourse of disinterested behavior, and even of generosity and self-sacrifice, can be analyzed in the wake of Pierre Bourdieu in terms of the interest of disinterested behavior (1990). This myth of service and disinterest is a classic feature among elective representatives in many contexts (Fontaine and Le Bart 1994, 22). Writing about local elected representatives in France, Fontaine and Lebart note, "The job is characterized using a familiar, amicable, even a loving register, with a host of reciprocal gratifications, but is also made up of sacrifice and abnegation (in the name of superior interest)" (1994, 26). We are here dealing with recurrent motifs in what elected representatives have to say about themselves.

Nevertheless, the position of muhtar brings with it a certain number of advantages. Gaffar recognized that "there are advantages to being a muhtar. [. . .] There is a financial dimension; of course it means an income. [. . .] And then there is the firearm." Indeed, muhtars are entitled to bear a firearm for the rest of their lives, as part of their duty to help maintain order. For some, this seems to be a significant recompense, mentioned by several of those interviewed (but only men). The Istanbul metropolitan municipality has, furthermore, granted all muhtars certain material benefits, such as free public transport and free parking in municipal car parks.

Above all, the position provides certain, though not wholly official, opportunities for financial or material accumulation. First, certain documents issued by the muhtars may give rise to unofficial payments. This is the case for the inheritance card (*veraset kartı*) required to inherit real estate, which is filled out by the muhtar. Many muhtars request compensation for this service. All state they are reasonable in what they request. Bediz said she received very small sums—TL20 to TL30—but denounced the greed of "other muhtars" whom she suspected of asking TL500 or TL1,000. The situation is similar for the vacancy certificate required to demolish an empty building. Second, muhtars can ask payment for certain favors—and for bending the rules, a not uncommon practice. Until recently, enrolling a child in a school other than one normally assigned through one's residence entailed getting the muhtar to produce a slightly modified residency certificate—a practice that could give rise to bribes. Finally, muhtars may profit from the resources attendant upon their position. One such resource is their contacts with agents working in the municipality or subgovernor's office, who may be involved in awarding public service contracts, or in providing privileged access to information such as changes to the land-use plan, the status of plots of land, urban development plans, or upcoming amnesties for buildings erected without permission. Information is a crucial resource, given the high degree of legal insecurity in Turkey (Kuyucu 2014). This information, and privileged access to it, can be used to facilitate real estate procedures—for example, in obtaining a building permit or opening a shop. Furthermore, the position of muhtar has become more attractive in step with the rise in land value since the 1990s.[42] Thus, there were twice as many candidates for the muhtarlık in neighborhood h in 2014 as in 2009, no doubt due to the urban transformation plan that includes the demolition of housing cooperatives. Half of the candidates were building contractors or worked in real estate. Although it is hard to assess the revenue from these forms of accumulation, it is important to be aware that they exist.

Despite certain variations in time and space, it may be considered that the muhtarlık was instituted as a partially self-financed activity, with the subsistence of the muhtars being left to the contingencies of their locality. The fact that personal income is fluctuating and uncertain strongly influences the social profiles of muhtars. It was not always possible to obtain precise data about the income of those interviewed. However, many retained their links to external professions, either in tandem with their position or afterward. This shapes how they go about their functions. Thus, many muhtars, including those who have long held the position, consider it a sideline.

According to a survey of Istanbul muhtars carried out by a journalist in 1989, 37.8 percent had other jobs, and 37 percent received pensions; 3.6 percent had other jobs and also received pensions; and only 21.6 percent said they had no other source of revenue.[43] According to a survey carried out in Izmir in 1998, 74.6 percent of respondents were retired, and 22.9 percent had other jobs (Palabıyık and Atak 2000, 154). Those muhtars interviewed for this study confirmed this trend. Fikret continued to work as a building entrepreneur, and Cemil continued to work in real estate, even though it tended to be less lucrative than before. As for Duran, he no longer had much time to devote to his tire distribution franchise, and had temporarily handed it over to an associate while retaining his stake in it for afterward. He said he even financed his term as muhtar from other sources of income: "I spend a lot. At the moment I cannot finance the expenditures here [from what the activity brings in]. I try to finance this by outside business. [. . .] It's your other job that brings money in—if you have one. Otherwise you do it all the same, but you run up debts." Gaffar continued to work as an ironmonger, and İlhan received a pension. Ahmet was the only "professional" muhtar in my sample. He was elected in 1994, when he had just lost his job. He has subsequently made the muhtarlık his sole occupation and profession, becoming head of a muhtar association.

The women in my sample did not have any other source of income, but nor had they any prior to becoming muhtars. Being elected did not represent a change in career for them. Ebru, who had worked as a medical secretary, was looking for a job when she took up her position. While in office she has continued to study by correspondence. Bediz has never held any paying job. If these women have been able to become muhtars, it is also because they had no families to look after. Most female muhtars are middle-aged, and their children have grown. This was the case with Bediz, who was born in 1966 and had divorced by the time she ran for the muhtarlık, and whose two children both studied or worked. As for Ebru, born in 1979, she became a muhtar before getting married and becoming a mother.

The fact that it is virtually obligatory for a muhtar to have another source of income, yet without being able to work full-time, narrows the range of compatible professions. To be a muhtar, the person must be able to get by without a paid activity to live on (pensioners and women), or must be able to combine the position with a parallel professional activity from which they can free up some time. This constraint determines the outside careers of muhtars. It excludes employees, for instance. In the 1989 survey of Istanbul muhtars, over 89 percent of those with other jobs were self-employed skilled workers or small business owners.[44] In the Ümraniye neighborhood studied by Heidi Wedel, nine out of ten candidates in 1994 were small business owners or came from the liberal professions (Wedel 1999). Gaffar carried out his functions from his ironmongery. Since only about 150 people lived in his neighborhood, being a muhtar did not take up much of his time.

Apart from the issue of time compatibility, certain professional activities may be profitably combined with that of muhtar. One of the most frequent outside jobs is that of a building contractor, particularly in neighborhoods with predominantly unauthorized housing. This is not by chance. First, as we have seen, the privileged contacts with the municipality that come with being muhtar can provide building contractors with accumulation opportunities. Second, the building industry requires certain skills that can be readily deployed by a muhtar. Fikret, a building contractor, pointed out how his building experience benefited him: "As I am in real estate, I am abreast of the rules. [...] As I have had my own business since 1987, I know all about issues relating to land registry and title deeds. If I send a written request to the [municipality's] technical affairs department, I know exactly what I want."

Another job often combined with the position of muhtar is that of real estate agent. Advertisements are often pinned on the walls or windows of a muhtar's

FIGURE 1. A muhtarlık based in a real estate office. Istanbul, 2014. Photograph by the author.

premises (figure 1). For the past thirty years, Cemil has been a self-employed real estate agent. He long operated his muhtarlık from his real estate office. Since the office was destroyed in 2003, he has shared the premises of the muhtar of an adjacent neighborhood. Although he cannot display property advertisements in the windows of that office, he has continued to work by word of mouth. It can be hypothesized that the position of muhtar attracts a disproportionate number of people working in real estate and construction; these jobs are compatible with the office and may even be profitably combined with it.

In conjunction with the temporary nature of the office, the fact that most muhtars have other professional activities, even if they are not full-time jobs, and other sources of income means that their professional horizons transcend their role as muhtars. In the early 1990s a study of 222 Istanbul muhtars included the question "Which do you consider to be your profession, the muhtarlık or the other job you have?" Of the respondents, 70.7 percent answered, "My other job" (Horasan 1992, 71). In the 1989 survey of Istanbul muhtars, the proportion offering that response had been virtually identical: 70 percent.[45] The muhtarlık is often a secondary occupation in the eyes of its holders. Said İlhan, a muhtar from 1980 to 2019: "Personally, I do this job as a hobby. I am retired. Instead of sitting around at home, I sit around here." Gaffar, despite being a muhtar for twenty years, also explained that he did it as a hobby, declaring, "The muhtarlık does not speak to me." The position of muhtar is thus not the "sole or main profession" of its holders—a fact setting them apart from bureaucrats as defined by Max Weber.

It is revealing in this connection that the law does not stipulate the working hours for muhtars. Article 39 of the 1945 application decree simply states that they must be in the muhtarlık for as long as is required by their daily activities, and must inform the inhabitants and the subgovernor's office of their hours (Aytaç 2009, 130). That being said, many muhtars post extended "bureaucratic" hours of between seven and eight hours per day, though this is not systematic (figure 2).

However, the muhtars' practice of continuing to exercise other activities sometimes generates conflicts. Their function as muhtar and the availability it requires may threaten or lead them to neglect their other professional horizons. Ebru struggled to combine her duties with her correspondence studies, which were dragging on. She has had to interrupt them on several occasions. She eventually obtained her final diploma, and passed the entrance exam for a master's degree in human resources. However, she did not follow the master's course due to family health problems, and ended up re-enrolling for a curriculum in international relations. Her workload meant she could not devote much time to the latter studies, and this was a source of concern for her. As for Duran, he described his inability to look after his business, and the professional losses he has had to endure, while he spent much energy, and perhaps money on his muhtarlık.

Furthermore, active pursuit of other professional activity affects how muhtars carry out their functions. It can lead to them to invest insufficient time and energy in certain "optional" aspects of the job, or overinvest in others. Activists visiting Gaffar as part of the "Istanbul Belongs to All of Us" citizen participation initiative asked him whether he attended municipal council meetings. He answered: "I am not rich. I have to support my family. I pour all my time into that. [. . .] If I am not there [in the store], I also have a fish grill stand. But

FIGURE 2. The door of a muhtarlık, Istanbul, 2004. "Opening Hours: 10–12, 14–16. I am working at my job at the radio shop. Across from the church [address and telephone details]." "Registration of residency for workplaces and bachelor rooms is not performed. Note: no residency registration. Please do not ask." There are numerous spelling mistakes. Photograph by Jean-François Pérouse.

I don't go to meetings with the NGOs [sic]. It is only when you have an uncle [a support network] that you do that." Thus, having a main professional activity tends to dissuade certain muhtars from being zealous. Fikret justified the fact that he did not sit on the Social Solidarity and Assistance Foundation board, whose members include one muhtar per district: "I did not even run for office. I don't have enough time. It's those who have the time who go there. [. . .] You have to go there every Wednesday and spend the whole day. Personally, that's time I spend pouring concrete."

This underinvestment of time in the muhtarlık exposed Fikret to criticism, and to the suspicion that he viewed his other professional activity as having priority over his elected position. In 2012 the metropolitan municipality was threatening to destroy a park recently redeveloped by the district municipality in his neighborhood, on the grounds that it was illegal. It lay in a zone of public and mortmain lands where virtually all the buildings could be considered illegal. The neighborhood residents occupied the park to defend it, but Fikret did not support the protest movement or visit the park. Apparently he was spotted during his working hours at the district planning office, and the protesting residents publicly accused him of spending too much time looking after his private affairs, and of neglecting the neighborhood residents' concerns. They demanded that as their muhtar, he accord them his principal or sole allegiance. Actively working at another profession can generate criticism, if it is thought to infringe on the muhtar's time. The fact that the position only has a partial hold on muhtars, and that they retain outside interests and activities which may be their priority or at least influence how they relate to their functions, derives largely from the conditions in which they perform their duties. Nevertheless, it is something that neighborhood residents can hold against them.

Training is another dimension to this partial hold of the muhtarlık over its practitioners. Once elected, muhtars receive no specific training from any institution to get them to conform to standardized practices. Yet the muhtarlık requires administrative, technical, and even legal skills, as well as a certain amount of knowledge that cannot be made up on the hoof. Thus, Bediz noted that "you can be a computer whiz kid, but if you don't know the system you can't do anything." In 1996 a private publisher brought out a muhtar handbook written by a former governor and former head of local administration at the Ministry for the Interior, who has also written reference works and legal commentaries for local authorities (Aytaç 2009 [1996]). This handbook reproduces the most important legislation and regulations; it contains commentaries about the muhtarlık, elections, duties, and rights; and it reproduces the most common official forms, all with the aim of providing a basis for acting as muhtar. It is apparently distributed to recently elected muhtars by local administrative boards in governor's and subgovernor's offices. The book was republished in the wake of strong demand from these offices, first in 2004 and then again in 2009—that is to say, after each local election. It seems reasonable to think that the handbook is promoted by the district administration as a "guide," and thereby helps in training muhtars. Quite often, copies of the book—or of a few other sometimes older reference works—are lying around in muhtarlıks,[46] but not all the muhtars interviewed knew about them. When confronted with a complex situation, they start not by turning to a reference book, but by asking advice of a colleague.

Most of the muhtars said they had trained "on the job," picking up what they knew from diverse sources, though never from administrators or municipalities. Rather, they had learned from their peers, from their secretaries, from former azas, or from their own family circles in cases where the muhtarlık ran in the family. Ebru inherited her position when her father died. On being elected, she took over his azas. She also relied on her father's secretary, as well as on muhtars from adjacent neighborhoods: "[My father's secretary] knew everything, and helped me a lot. My muhtar friends also helped me a lot." She mentioned two or three muhtars from adjacent neighborhoods, and added that whenever she came across a question to which she did not know the answer, she immediately called them to ask what to do. She concluded, "That is how I matured (literally, "cooked," *piştim*)." But this is not the case for all muhtars. Bediz, whose predecessor handed nothing over to her—he had supported her rival in the election—benefited from the help of three other muhtars whose offices were adjacent to hers. She said she had learned a lot from her peers, in terms of technical skills and also contacts. These forms of transmission are not institutionalized. They require personal channels that vary from one situation to the next.

Trained in this way, muhtars have little choice but to refer to routines developed by their predecessors or by their predecessors' entourages. The latter teach them how to go about their tasks, giving advice and oral instructions. The fact that there is no legal or administrative training is thus compensated for by the incorporation of norms, and by acquiring "practical sense" that enables them to confront unexpected situations (Bourdieu 1977).

The lack of specialized training means that muhtars are not socialized in any specific way. Furthermore, there is no prospect of professionalization offered by working in the administration. The muhtars' prospects for moving on to electoral careers within political parties are also very slender. Since 1980 at least, it has been hard for muhtars to advance to partisan political elected office, and few have done so. Therefore, they do not fit in with analysis in terms of political professionalization—a phenomenon that in other contexts brings out how over time elected office has become a specialized career supporting its practitioners, who thus have increasingly moved away from the figure of the "notable" and become professional politicians instead (Offerlé 1999). One consequence of this lack of specialized training and professionalization is that muhtars do not constitute, or barely constitute, a group external to the social groups from which they issue, due to any specific ethos, functions, or specific interests. Indeed, muhtars remain firmly anchored in their own groups of origin. This sets them apart both from professional politicians and from administrators of the Weberian ideal type.

In addition to this, muhtars do not join together much as a group. Various associations and federations represent their interests (at the time of my field-work, the main federation was undergoing national restructuring). But though muhtars are all members of such organizations (membership is obligatory), few are actively involved in them or interested. Thus, Fikret admitted that the associations are useful insofar as they defend muhtars' rights and interests (electoral procedure, remuneration) and provide social support (particularly in the event of illness or bereavement). But he said he did not have enough time to attend their meetings: "I am not active. I've had enough." Apart from Ahmet, who long headed the Istanbul muhtar association, only Ebru appeared interested in the associations, and had just been elected to the district executive committee of the main muhtar association. She was also the interviewee to display the great-est ambition to enter politics.

It is rarely possible to live on income from the muhtarlık, and it does not require any specialized training. Hence, the position of muhtar has but a partial hold over practitioners. Muhtars pursue other professional activities and operate in other social spheres, due to their precarious status and shortage of means. One consequence is that muhtars remain firmly rooted "elsewhere," and retain their outside interests. Everything indicates that the lawmakers have not sought to turn the muhtarlık into the sole horizon of action for its office holders.

Chapter 2

HOW THE MUHTARLIK FUELS THE PRODUCTION OF NOTABLES

THE HYBRID STATUS OF MUHTARS AND THE RELATIVELY PRECARIOUS conditions in which they perform their duties mean they are close to and dependent on the electorate whom they administer—to such an extent that these ties are in fact constitutive of their role. Muhtars are socially embedded. There is hardly any "gap" between them and the people they administer—bearing in mind that distance is a characteristic of bureaucrats as defined by Max Weber. It thus seems worthwhile to view muhtars from a different angle and examine whether they correspond to what Max Weber referred to as "notables," defined as persons

> (1) whose economic position permits them to hold continuous policy-making and administrative positions in an organization without (more than nominal) remuneration; (2) who enjoy social prestige of whatever derivation in such a manner that they are likely to hold office by virtue of the member's confidence, which at first is freely given and then traditionally accorded. Most of all, the notable's position presupposes that the individual is able to live for politics without living from politics. He must hence be able to count on a certain level of provision from private sources (Weber 1978 [1921], 290).

The previous chapter showed that the first of these propositions applies to muhtars. This chapter inquires into the second dimension, that of social prestige opening the path to election. On what basis are muhtars elected?

This chapter starts by looking at the profiles of muhtars and their electoral campaigns, arguing that they are elected primarily on personal resources, not partisan-political or institutional ones. Their election also relies on the mobilization of groups assembled on different bases, as is studied in the second section of this chapter. The third section analyses muhtars' longevity in office, which is a supplementary aspect of their notabilization. On the basis of these three observations, the final section looks at the consequences of viewing muhtars as notables on historiography about Turkey, and on sociology of the state more generally.

THE RESOURCES DEPLOYED FOR ELECTION

What resources do candidates deploy to obtain the position of muhtar? It is not easy to answer this question, given the lack of systematic data. However, a certain number of constants do emerge. Not just anyone can stand for the office, much less be elected. The candidates' social profiles and the arguments put forward in their campaigns provide information about the resources they use to get elected, and hence about what constitutes their electability. The main specificity of muhtars in this regard is that, unlike all other categories of elected representatives in Turkey, they have been barred since 1980 from drawing on the support of political parties, even though officially they are no longer prevented from being party members (Aytaç 2009, 161). Their campaigns thus rely largely on personal resources like local anchoring, kinship, involvement in the neighborhood, money, and being well known. These resources preselect certain types of profiles, and to a certain extent differ from one neighborhood to another. Nevertheless, certain constants emerge.

"Being Well Known"

Given that the candidates are not selected by political parties, their reputations and the social and relational capital they can draw on are important for muhtarlık elections. When asked about electability, the first thing many muhtars mentioned was being well known (*tanınma*). As Duran put it: "If people don't know that you have lived here for years, if they don't know you, they won't vote for you in any case. What do they do? This person has lived here, he has had a small business in the neighborhood, I've seen him at school, he has his place here and there. But I vote intentionally for this person; I know him, I know his personality." Hikmet, who was a losing candidate, said, "In any case, it's

FIGURE 3. Banners for two muhtar candidates in the same Istanbul neighborhood, March 23, 2014. The slogan across the top of the first banner reads: "A reliable team, a reliable muhtar." The second banner simply announces that the candidate is running for the office. The candidates' names and photos apparently suffice to identify them. Photograph by the author.

pointless standing if you're not well known." He mentioned a candidate who had moved to the neighborhood two years before the elections, and who only got a few hundred votes: "Even though he spent loads of money and used his networks, people didn't vote for him, as they didn't know him." It is revealing that electoral banners often display only the name of the candidate, which is apparently sufficient to identify them, without any need to distribute pamphlets presenting them in greater detail (figure 3). The election takes place within a context of expanded acquaintanceship, in which voters are presumed to know the candidates. But what is being well known grounded in?

Being Local and Close to Voters
One dimension of electability is local anchoring. It is almost unthinkable for a muhtar to be parachuted in from outside. Officially, muhtars have to have resided in the neighborhood for at least six months upon being elected. But the

case mentioned above by Hikmet suggests that six months are not enough to build up a sufficiently strong local presence. It may thus be asserted that local anchoring is key to the muhtar's role. The social imaginary of local anchoring is so constitutive of the figure of the muhtar that it amounts to a precept. And indeed it is something candidates systematically emphasize, together with knowledge of the neighborhood.

Established families are clearly overrepresented among muhtars, in the meaning used by Elias and Scotson (1965) to designate respectable families who have long lived in a working-class neighborhood. In neighborhoods built by migrants from the rural exodus, muhtars—including a fair share of those currently in office—frequently come from founding families who were the first to settle there, often illegally on public land. Fikret, who arrived in Istanbul in 1961, said he was "the grandson of one of the first three *gecekondu* dwellers in the neighborhood."[1] His grandfather had migrated to Istanbul to work in a factory. Ebru's grandfather came from the Black Sea region and moved into the neighborhood a long time ago, when there were only fifty or so houses. The duration of residency in the neighborhood is thus an important factor for candidates' reputation and knowledge of the area, and is systematically emphasized in the biographies they circulate.

But these families have not just been present for a long time; they also often have a certain standing,[2] based on occupations that signal a certain status. The preponderance of small business owners among muhtars is not solely due to their jobs being compatible with the position's time demands. It also because their business brings them into contact with many neighborhood residents, who get to know them. Fikret explained, "My father was an *esnaf* [shopkeeper], and we are an important family in the neighborhood. My father had a grocery store and was a gas cylinder distributor. We are an old family and are well known. We welcomed everybody with open arms." Fikret is the "founding muhtar" (*kurucu muhtar*); in other words, the first to hold the position when the neighborhood was established as an administrative unit in 1989. He served until 2019, with a gap from 1994 to 1999. Likewise, the two main branches of Ebru's family run local businesses, and include a dentist, a former MP, "the" neighborhood florist, a chemist, and so on. As Ebru put it, "It's a bit as if we encompassed the entire neighborhood. [. . .] People, most of them, like us because we are the [family name]; the ties between us go back a very long way."

Another sector that apparently provides access to the position of muhtar is local building and real estate. In an old and upmarket neighborhood like E, Ebru's father and brother (who was muhtar in the 1960s) were both in the building trade. She related that her father, on becoming an aza in 1973, had looked after the muhtarlık, acted as a real estate agent, and worked in the building trade all at the same time. Her other uncles also had worked in the building trade, and had constructed buildings in the neighborhood. The activities of small localized contractors and real estate intermediaries bring them into contact with people.

A Family Concern

Another resource for being elected muhtar is kinship, with the position often being transmitted within a family. Two of the muhtars followed for this study had inherited the position from their fathers. The most patent case in my sample is Ebru. She was looking for work, having previously been a medical secretary, when her father, who had been muhtar for five years, was left in a vegetative state after a heart attack. When a muhtar cannot perform their duties, the law states that the first aza takes over. But Ebru short-circuited the aza, and set about working in the muhtarlık. According to her, the neighborhood residents assured her of their loyalty: "When I was in the muhtarlık, people often told me, 'Afterward you'll be our muhtar, we want to carry on with you, we really liked Emre Abi [literally "elder brother," meaning Ebru's father], we have a moral debt to him [vefa borcumuz var], we owe him a lot [onun bize hakkı çok geçmişti], we often ate his food and bread.'"

When Ebru's father died ten months later, early elections were held. She made her election appear natural on the basis of the privileged ties that existed between the neighborhood residents and her family. The residents were apparently "very loyal [vefalı]. There are lots of people who aren't ungrateful [iyiliğin karşılığını verecek cinsten insanlar]; they all said, 'We really like Emre, we really liked your father, we want you, we have a debt of loyalty, stand and we will vote for you.'" Ebru would probably not have been elected without her family background, since at the time she was twenty-six years old and a woman—factors that she admits were disadvantages in running against two substantially older men. Her father had to some extent prepared her for going into politics. First, he had given her a first name literally meaning "be elected," since she was born on a by-election day. Second, he had urged her to work with him. She referred to this legacy in these terms: "My father entrusted the muhtarlık to me."

Ebru's father, in turn, had inherited the position from his brother. As Ebru put it, "The muhtarlık came to us from the dynasty a bit." The first muhtar in the family, a distant uncle who served as a colonel during the 1960 coup, was elected in 1963. Since then, the position has remained within the family. When Ebru's uncle left the position in 1973, he handed it to his brother, Erhan. Ebru's father then became aza to his brother Erhan, and took over the position of muhtar when Erhan quit due to illness. He had already been working alongside him at times. "In any case," said Ebru, "in my uncle's day everyone viewed my father as the muhtar, since he was the one who tended to be in the muhtarlık." Elections sometimes turn into intrafamily rivalry due to this dimension. When Ebru ran to succeed her father in 2005, one of her rivals was her cousin, the son of her paternal uncle Erhan—and one of the other candidates, "the neighborhood photographer," also came from a well-established family. Ebru based her campaign on the arguments of continuity and her father's popularity, presenting herself on the election posters as "Ebru, daughter of the late muhtar Emre." She won the election hands down. In the next election her only rival was the photographer, whom she beat. In 2014 there were no longer any rival candidates. Her first aza was her sister's husband, who had already held the role under her father. And her second aza was her paternal uncle.

Far from being an exception, the trajectory of the muhtarlık in neighborhood E—even though it is upmarket and considered very "modern"—reveals how important kinship is in acquiring and transmitting the position. In addition to direct parent-child succession, many muhtars have a forebear who previously carried out the function. Cemil also inherited the position from his father. In neighborhood F, I observed the transition as it took place. Fikret was seeking to install his son as successor, by getting him to work with him as secretary at the muhtarlık (while also getting him to work in his building company). Officially it is forbidden to take a first-degree relative as aza. Transmission strategies thus consist of getting a relative to work as secretary to familiarize them with the role, and to leave other tasks to the azas, or even marginalize them.

Involvement in the Neighborhood

But not all muhtars inherit their position, nor do all come from influential families. Other resources can be mobilized which acquire particular significance when few of the aforementioned resources are available. One of these is neighborhood involvement, particularly previously-held positions of collective responsibility. Muhtars have very often been involved in *hemşehri* (hometown) organizations, indicating their strong anchorage in solidarity groups based on geographical origin.[3] These organizations often act as a trampoline to elected local positions generally (Wedel 1999; Kurtoğlu 2005). There are far greater levels of involvement in *hemşehri* organizations in unauthorized neighborhoods, most of whose residents are migrants from the rural exodus, than in the better established, more central neighborhoods. This would not seem to have been a factor in the elections of Ahmet, Cemil, and Ebru, for instance. Conversely, Duran, who "won" rather than inherited the muhtarlık in a recent migrant neighborhood, had been involved in several associations. He founded his village association in 1998, and was involved in running it for several years. Likewise, Fikret was one of the founders of a *hemşehri* association four years before he became muhtar, and was involved in running it for twenty or so years. He continues to be active there today. He was also a founding and active member of an association founded in 1992 to spruce up the neighborhood. Such organizations are another frequent route to the muhtarlık. Kadir, muhtar since 2014 of a very underprivileged neighborhood on the outskirts of Istanbul, chaired the neighborhood association from 2004 to 2008, and still sits on its board. Fikret, in a similar type of neighborhood, has also long been very active in neighborhood cooperatives, and has played a role in an association for building a mosque, though he has not held any positions of responsibility in it.

Being actively involved in serving constituents is something that can be leveraged to get elected as muhtar. Thus, Bediz was involved for ten years in helping the school in the adjacent neighborhood, particularly in the parent-teacher association: "I did a lot to help out with the school. . . . I was there every day, really every day. Lots of parents thought I was a teacher. And believe me, if there were 750 parents, at least 500 of them had my phone number. I told them they could call me whenever they wanted." She was well known and appreciated for her active involvement.

Money

Another personal resource that can be mobilized for election is money. The fact that candidates receive no financial support from parties for campaigning, coupled with the modest income the position provides, leads to a certain degree of selection by money. But though some muhtars are clearly wealthy—such as Ebru, who carries several of the latest smartphones—there are also muhtars from comparatively modest backgrounds.

The cost of campaigning can vary significantly from one neighborhood to another, depending on its size as well as the level of competition, which in turn is related to the opportunities for accumulation the muhtarlık provides. There tends to be less competition in campaigns in established neighborhoods (A, B, C, E) than in those on the city's outskirts (D and F). The scale of the financial and real estate stakes in the latter, especially in the event of urban renewal projects, is no doubt one explanatory factor, as is the neighborhoods' greater size. The structural expenses of a muhtarlık campaign are reasonable, arising from the cost of printing voting slips. In some cases—particularly for outgoing muhtars in small neighborhoods, where there is not much competition, as in neighborhood C and E—there is little in the way of campaigning, sometimes just a few banners. But in more populous neighborhoods, particularly if the competition is stiff, candidates rent premises, hire a minibus, have a campaign song composed, plaster the neighborhood with posters, and distribute handbills, pamphlets, and even food, tea, and sugar. According to estimates produced by the outdoor advertisers association, in 2004 a muhtarlık campaign cost on average between US$3,000 and US$5,000, only one-tenth of he cost of a campaign for an urban-district mayoralty.[4] Hikmet, a butcher by trade, who in 2014 stood for the muhtarlık in an educated middle-class neighborhood with about fourteen thousand inhabitants, said he spent TL10,000 (about US$4,500), and reckoned that it was the structural minimum. But he suspects that a rival, whose main resource was money, spent about TL200,000 (about US$91,800). These campaigns are not always financed solely by the candidates, who draw on various forms of support, including financial contributions, from their "sponsors."

The main resources used in muhtarlık elections must not be considered independently, but in combination with each other, and in relation to the neighborhood, its socioeconomic level, and its salient social divisions.

GATHERING SUPPORT: THE COLLECTIVE BASES FOR MOBILIZATION

Still, muhtarlık elections are not as "personal" as they might appear. They are also based on building localized coalitions and mobilizing groups on various bases. The two main forms of collective support are derived, first, from political parties, and second, from assembling a list of councillors.

Party Resources?

Does the fact that muhtarlık candidates have no official party label disqualify all forms of party resource from the electoral contest? The situation is in fact more nuanced, especially as muhtarlık elections take place at the same time as other local elections, thus tending to blur any distinction between them. Parties do indeed intervene in the election of muhtars, but under certain conditions and in specific ways.

At election time, parties frequently try to present themselves as being close to the acting muhtar. Candidates, especially for local elections, frequently appear alongside the muhtar, or even muhtarlık candidates. Thus, muhtars are forever being invited to ceremonies to publicly announce candidates standing for party selection. In 2014, Adem Göktaş stood for selection as the AKP candidate to be Maltepe urban district mayor. At the ceremony when he announced his candidacy, he was flanked by his supporters, party officials, municipal councilors, and NGO managers, as well as many current and former muhtars.[5] For candidates this is a matter of displaying the level of support they enjoy in the race. Candidates seek the support of opinion leaders such as muhtars and religious leaders (Ark 2015, 233). They also often pay them visits. They get to know them, ask for information about the neighborhoods and their problems, promise to work to solve them if elected, present their projects, and hold out the prospect of fruitful cooperation, asking the muhtars to support them. Ebru said that ahead of elections, candidates running for municipal positions would visit the muhtars, note their requests and complaints, and profess that they valued them. But, she said, they did not show up after the elections, and nothing changed. She denounced these visits as attempts to use the muhtars for electoral purposes. "Their thing is to ask for votes," she said—or even to "hijack" them for their advantage.

If muhtars are courted at election time, it is because they are generally held to be able to get voters to turn out (Aytaç 2009, 115). Certain candidates and parties pressure incumbent muhtars into working for them, or at least into abstaining from supporting their rivals. At a meeting of a CHP neighborhood committee during a local election campaign in Adana in 2009, a muhtar complained about a candidate for metropolitan mayor putting "pressure" on muhtars. The CHP provincial secretary reckoned that this sort of work by muhtars was effective, because "what the muhtars say matters."

So parties and candidates court incumbent muhtars, as presumed opinion leaders, during local and at times national elections. But to what extent do parties intervene in the election of muhtars? Frequently parties and candidates, especially for the position of mayor, support certain candidates for the muhtarlık. In the 2014 local elections, a member of the Istanbul CHP provincial executive board claimed that the party supported candidates for the muhtarlık. Likewise, a CHP municipal councillor in Beyoğlu, citing various examples, stated that whenever the incumbent muhtar was pro-AKP, the CHP supported rival candidates. It may be a matter of supporting an individual with whom the party hopes to cooperate closely. Thus, in 2014, in neighborhood h, a candidate ran with explicit backing from the SP (Saadet Partisi, the Islamist Felicity Party) after the party's local organization decided to support him. Still, given that it is forbidden to stand with party support, and given that muhtars are supposed to be neutral in their duties, such ties to political parties are fairly illegitimate. Thus Hikmet, one of the rivals, was quick to point out: "That's to say there are no party candidates, muhtars don't have a party, for when the muhtar is elected he doesn't perform his duties as someone with ties to party A or party B; he performs his duties generally."

In the event of a party backing a candidate for the muhtarlık, what form does that support take? Nobody I spoke with mentioned a party giving material support to a muhtar's campaign, though it is not impossible. Support tends to take the form of campaigning groundwork. During the 2014 local elections, activists from the HDP (Halkların Demokratik Partisi, the pro-minority and left-wing People's Democratic Party) in the Mahmut Şevket Paşa neighborhood (in the district of Şişli) explicitly supported a candidate for the muhtarlık, keeping her pamphlets on their premises and saying they distributed them when they were out canvassing. Ahead of the 2014 elections in neighborhood D, there were rumors that the AKP-controlled municipal authority and the party itself had promised financial recompense for any candidate who managed to beat Duran.

Party support can also take the form of mutual back-scratching, in which a muhtarlık candidate and a party, or a candidate for another office, support each other's campaigns. In the Şahintepe neighborhood in the district of Başakşehir, the AKP openly supported the outgoing muhtar in 2014. Speaking at a public meeting, a prominent local AKP activist apparently said she intended to continue doing a lot to help the neighborhood, and would be better able to do so with the incumbent muhtar. The person chairing the meeting reportedly then declared that the people present could ask what they wanted of the muhtar. In exchange for this, the muhtar and his azas, some of whom were openly AKP activists, apparently did a lot to help the party. As part of his campaign, the incumbent muhtar reportedly relayed the AKP position on locally important issues, such as a controversial planned urban renewal project, which had the backing of the AKP municipality. For instance, he said at a public meeting, "Don't believe anyone who tells you that Şahintepe will be demolished. They said a lot of things when we renovated the primary school. But now look, we have a new school" (Ark 2015, 382). One of his rivals for the position of Şahintepe muhtar was both the former muhtar of the nearby neighborhood of Kayabaşı (1995–99) and a former CHP Başakşehir municipal councillor (2009–14), who came from a well-known and respected family. This rival openly supported a specific candidate in the CHP primaries, and campaigned with him (Ark 2015, 285). At times a muhtarlık candidate and someone standing for another local office will not only call for mutual support but even campaign together. One such case involving the CHP occurred in 2009 at Başıbüyük in the Maltepe district (see chapter 8).

Parties do not, however, systematically support muhtarlık candidates, and indeed it is fairly rare for them to do so. In neighborhood h in 2014, only one party, the SP, clearly supported a candidate. As Hikmet—one of that candidate's main rivals—explained, he had previously held positions in the Refah Party,[6] and visited people at home, a bit like a local party leader. Hikmet then said that most SP supporters voted for him. But the other parties, which did not have "their" own people running, did not support any particular candidate. Despite there being another candidate who had headed the AKP youth branch, the AKP did not support her, perhaps because several other candidates in the race were also fairly pro-AKP.

Hence, party officials often consider it to be in their best interest not to support muhtarlık candidates. In the 2009 local campaign in Adana, the CHP ran into a problem in the town that Ali—who was heading the party's candidate list for the municipal council of the provincial capital—originally came from.

There were two candidates for the muhtarlık in this CHP stronghold, both of whom had close ties to the party: one of Ali's relatives, and another man. During a CHP public meeting there, Ali called on his relative to speak, but did not invite the other muhtarlık candidate to do the same. However, party officials did not want the party to be associated with one candidate to the detriment of the other. The provincial secretary criticized what Ali had done, saying to an activist: "What business is it of his? The muhtarlık is something separate." A few days later, the party held another meeting in town. The party's subprovincial chairman took the floor and declared that both candidates for the muhtarlık were the party's candidates. The next day, in an aside, the party's provincial chairman criticized Ali, stating that, as the CHP candidate, he should not have taken sides with his relative. He complained that the party had had to set up the second meeting to correct this mistake. The CHP officials wanted to prevent the party from coming across as being taken over by one of the two muhtarlık candidates, or by the divisions within the village, probably so as to avoid losing votes from the other camp in the municipal elections, which were viewed by party officials as having priority over muhtarlık elections.

Party officials view alliances with muhtars or muhtarlık candidates as bringing certain constraints. A few days earlier, at a CHP neighborhood committee meeting in one of the party's strongholds, the head of the committee said that the party had to avoid becoming involved in muhtarlık affairs. Likewise, the provincial secretary general said, "Once you start working with muhtars you can't get out of it; it creates problems for the party, we risk losing votes, it's difficult to manage." He reckoned that inhabitants do not vote for muhtars on the basis of political leaning: "Most of the time, people don't know which political side muhtarlık candidates are on. And even if they do know, what counts above all is their personality, people that they like or don't like, people that they can trust or otherwise." Thus, party officials would seem to consider it not necessarily in their interest to lend their support to any one candidate, for it entails risks.

The party dimension can be difficult to handle for muhtarlık candidates too, depending upon local power relationships. Many candidates have had party ties of varying strength at some stage in their career. Such was the case for Bediz, who had been head of the AKP neighborhood women's branch for two years, a nonofficial but nevertheless important role in interacting with the electorate. Some candidates seek to renew or emphasize these ties, while others seek to downplay them. Thus Hikmet, a former aza and losing muhtarlık candidate in 2014, said that people identified him with the AKP, which caused him problems: "Personally, I didn't [have any past AKP activity], but my brothers and sisters did. My younger brother, my elder sister, and my younger sister used to be involved in the party. My elder sister headed the women's branch in the neighborhood. My brother ran the youth branch. But personally I never had any role in the party. People knew that. [. . .] It had effects, and it also caused [negative] reactions." He said he had not presented himself as being aligned with any party, nor had he approached the (AKP) district mayor, who had nevertheless attended the opening of his butcher shop two years previously. He explained: "If you are close to one side, you can't get votes from the other side. [. . .] I tried not to emphasize my political leanings. Emphasizing your political colors can be beneficial, but then you can't benefit from the other colors." The risk to a candidate was to lose on one side any votes they gain on the other, especially in the event of clearly divided political sympathies. Besides, the AKP had come in for criticism in the wake of a planned urban renewal project that had been supported by the outgoing muhtar, for whom Hikmet had acted as first aza.

To what extent do citizens know the candidates' political leanings? This information would appear to be semipublic and socially differentiated. In Hikmet's terms, "Those who know, know (*bilen biliyor*); they know what party I come from, what party I support. [. . .] But there are a lot of undecided people who have only recently come to the neighborhood. You can't go and see them and introduce yourself saying, 'I am from such-and-such party.' Still, when I went out canvassing a lot of people asked us which party I was from. 'Aunt [a respectful form of address for an older woman], I am a muhtar; a muhtar doesn't have any party, the muhtar helps each and every person.' But they insist. In general, I didn't say what party I am from. It wouldn't be ethical." This reticence to align with any given party was no doubt particularly pronounced in Hikmet's case, for he was still aza at the time of the campaign, and thus bound by an image of neutrality.

At times, muhtarlık candidates drop hints about their party affiliation, using ambiguous terms that will be understood by some voters but not others, in order to connect with sympathizers without those "external" to the party noticing. That would appear to have been the case in 2014 for a muhtarlık candidate in the Mahmut Şevket Paşa neighborhood. This candidate had HDP backing, as

FIGURE 4. Election poster for a muhtarlık candidate, Istanbul, 2014. Her unofficial party affiliation is signified by the color code, which resembles that of HDP election posters. Photograph by the author.

confirmed by activists, and to a certain extent her campaign posters borrowed the design and color code used on HDP posters (figure 4). This visual connotation might have gone unnoticed by those not in the know, but the ties existed in practice. Though they were not wholly concealed in the campaign, they were only expressed indirectly.

Similarly, other candidates take their inspiration from a party slogan and slightly modify it, thereby expressing their party sympathies (such as "Everything for such-and-such a neighborhood," clearly alluding to the 2007 and 2011 AKP slogan, "Everything for Turkey"). Maintaining ambiguity is a way to avoid breaking the law, but it also generates a degree of latitude enabling the candidate to assert their party links—or, on the contrary, conceal or deny them, depending upon the situation.

So despite being officially banned, party rationales are at times caught up in elections for muhtar. Muhtarlık candidates and parties alike can view this as being in or against their interests. This is closely bound up with their assessment of the local political situation and the balance of power. Candidates can encounter difficulties in invoking party sympathies, just as parties can encounter difficulties in supporting candidates. Thus, muhtarlık elections exhibit rationales that are partly independent of the partisan political realm. This can explain why Fikret, who stood to be an AKP municipal councillor in 2014, and whose ties to the AKP have been known since then (and probably earlier), has since 1989 been muhtar for a neighborhood that votes mainly for the CHP (which receives on average over 40 percent of the vote, in comparison to about 30 percent for the AKP). This type of mismatch between the dominant political support in a neighborhood and the political inclinations of the muhtar is frequent. While it is tricky and fairly uncommon to explicitly invoke political parties for collective mobilization when running for muhtar, other forms of local coalitions are more common.

Compiling Councillors' Lists

The other main basis for local coalitions is frequent, and even virtually systematic. Candidates for muhtar do not run unaided, but put together support teams, generally comprising family members, their prospective azas, and people from various other horizons. Families thus play a role in building support for their election. Bediz said that her two campaigns were financed, for relatively modest sums, by her nephew, who paid for her voting slips and the printing of posters. "They were all there with me to distribute voting slips—my children, my daughter, my son, and all my nephews," she said. "There were also my friends, my pals, and my azas by my side." Ebru was helped during her first campaign by her sisters, brother-in-law, mother, and uncle, as well as some friends. Relatives' circles of acquaintances can also provide assistance. Hikmet mentioned that he received help from his sister, who had headed the AKP neighborhood women's branch. He recounted that she and his mother-in-law did a lot, especially in suggesting that he or someone from the campaign pay visits to this or that person.

The advisers (or azas) play a lead role in building up support beyond the family circle. Muhtars are elected with a list of azas (four titular and four stand-in members). It is the muhtarlık candidates who choose their azas, for it does not seem to be a particularly valued position and brings no financial recompense. What criteria are used? A distinction needs to be made between the first aza, who has a special status, and the others.[7] The first aza is a sort of substitute for the muhtar. In particular, the first aza can sign in the muhtar's stead if the latter is absent or unable to do so, and therefore has to be someone the muhtar trusts. Ebru appointed her brother-in-law as her first aza. "If there is a meeting I have to attend, my brother-in-law has to take over the muhtarlık; in any case he knows everything about the [IT] system, he doesn't send visitors away, he helps them, he knows how to draw up the certificates, and he calls me if need be," she observed. "He is always available, he has the time. [...] When my father was ill, he was the one who signed for him; he knows the procedures, everything, he doesn't have any problems, nor do I." Ebru said she would not leave her "business" to anyone other than him, including her other azas.

The other azas do not perform many tasks associated with the muhtarlık. Despite this, the 1944 law lists those among the muhtar's responsibilities that require the assent of the majority of the azas. These comprise the most important responsibilities, such as approval of applications to have lost identity papers reissued, most responsibilities relating to the military draft, and the issuing of poverty and residence certificates.[8] But in fact, muhtars do not really involve the azas in these procedures, and give them little to do. They all told me that the azas have little if any importance. Said Ebru, "To tell the truth, the azas don't have many tasks." Similarly, Duran said that "the azas don't do much." Bediz confirmed that "they don't have any activity, it's only the first two who are important; [...] they're the ones who look after [your work] when you're not there. And their signature is required for conscripts to receive their salary. Other than that, azas don't have any real purpose." Hikmet said that according to the procedures, azas do have work: they are supposed to oversee several streets to monitor any issues, and to hold meetings with the muhtar each month. But he recognized that he had never witnessed that happening when he was first aza, from 2009 to 2014. Duran was the only muhtar in my sample to mention having got the azas to countersign applications for identity papers. Ebru explained why she did not involve her azas: "In any case, the other [azas] can't come. They are all busy at work with their tasks; they are all shopkeepers. They can't say, 'I'm shutting up shop, I'm going to go help Ebru, [...] I'm on duty at the muhtarlık.' [...] They don't know [how to run the muhtarlık]; I would have to explain it to them. They would have to reply to those who come, but would they be able to give a satisfactory answer to their questions? It's a bit of a risk. That's why I don't take that risk."

And so, aside than the first, azas are not chosen as stand-ins for the muhtar. What are their duties, and how are they selected? Certain muhtars, such as Ebru and Duran, indicated that it is important to have a shared vision, and to choose friends with whom you can work. But the azas' main duty appears to be acting as a bridge with different groups, channeling information, and building up electoral support. When I asked Fikret how he chose his azas, he explained: "There's a political side to it. You know there are Alevis and Sunnis. I drew up a list that could appeal to [people from] all regional backgrounds [*memleket*], which would represent everybody. [. . .] I can't go everywhere. That is how I stay informed; in each street there is someone close to me—for that matter, not necessarily an aza. That's how I share it out. I take those who are close to me." Duran, too, said that azas were needed to act as a bridge between the muhtar and various groups: "If someone is unable to pass on a problem to me, maybe he considers that X is closer to him. . . . So he can tell X, who then passes it on to me."

Azas are selected largely for their presumed "vote potential." When asked about his criteria for selecting azas, Fikret admitted he looked at what forces they could draw upon (*arkasındaki güç*). This helps to explain why the election posters for certain muhtarlık candidates display more aza candidates than there are positions. There was the case of a muhtar standing for a third term with twelve candidates displayed for eight aza positions (figure 5). When I asked about this, one of the aza candidates answered scornfully: "You do anything to hoodwink voters [*baş döndürmek*; literally, make someone's head spin]." On the official voting slip, there were only eight names. According to the incumbent muhtar, the reason for displaying more candidates on election posters was to get people to identify strongly with the list.

The elections in this neighborhood were keenly contested, with six lists in all. Hikmet, the former first aza who subsequently ran for election as muhtar, had not carried over the former aza team to his list. He explained that they would vote for him anyway, and that he preferred bringing in new aza candidates to maximize votes. The principle governing the selection of these azas was not therefore proximity, but the idea of garnering votes from other circles.

So while azas are not much involved in office, they play an important role in the campaign. Hikmet said he conferred every evening with his prospective azas, and asked them to suggest places they should go. He assigned them a role in linking with voters: "You can't do much to convince people you don't know.

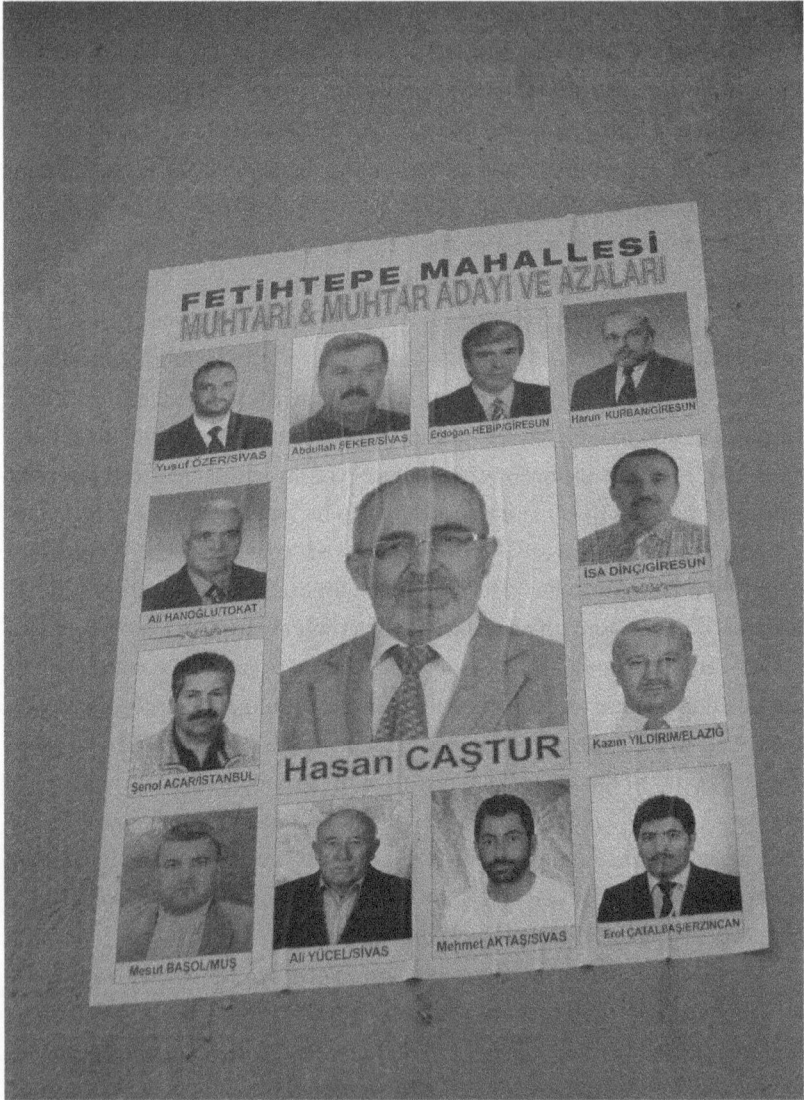

FIGURE 5. Election poster for a muhtarlık candidate, incorporating the portraits of twelve other men said to be aza candidates. Istanbul, March 24, 2014. Photograph by the author.

It's only the people you know, the circles you know. [...] There's a reason why there are azas. Each looks after their own circles [*çevre*]."

What does this recurrent term mean? The places azas come from are systematically indicated on election handbills, pamphlets, and posters (see figure 5) in neighborhoods inhabited by migrants from the rural exodus, where geographical provenance is often considered a prime criterion for classifying the population. Duran claimed that his neighborhood was home to people from almost every province in the country, and explained that he sought to build up good contacts with them on the basis of the provinces they came from, especially those with the largest number of migrants: "When I take this aza, I ought to be able to communicate more rapidly with these people, with this region [*yöre*]." Each aza on Duran's 2009 list came from a different province, mainly those from the largest migrant groups in the neighborhood. Hikmet, the unsuccessful candidate, confirmed the importance of this factor:

> For us, there is a sort of solidarity based on coming from the same region [*memleketçilik*]. If there is a candidate from Adıyaman, people from Adıyaman try to vote for him. [...] First, you try to take azas from provinces that the largest number of people came from. [...] As there are a lot of people from Erzurum, I took two azas. As there are a lot of people from the Black Sea, I took someone from Trabzon. [...] When you go out canvassing, you do it with the azas. Say that this aza lives in that street, where there is a majority of people from such a region in, say, road X. Well, when you go canvassing in that road you go there with this aza, as he knows the place well. [...] Unfortunately, I didn't manage to have anyone from Malatya. We went to see several people and asked them. They promised their support, but refused [to be placed on the list of azas] as they had their own muhtarlık candidate. [...] As there was a candidate from Malatya, most people weren't for it.

The situation was the same for people from Isparta, who supported "their" candidate from the same province. The person in question stood a good chance, having already been muhtar, and having monopolized the "from Isparta" resource, as it were. Nobody from Isparta consented to appear on the aza list of any other candidate. Thus, in putting together their lists, muhtars base their selection on types of belonging—especially geographical provenance and religious denomination—that are widely viewed as electoral bases. Candidates see each geographical provenance in terms of a "voting potential" that they gauge fairly accurately.

Certain *hemşehri* groups, constituted either as associations or as less formal groupings, therefore present themselves as vote intermediaries. In certain cases it is the *hemşehri* associations who designate members likely to accept being placed on aza lists. On occasion these groups make decisions about whom to support. Hikmet said there was an association from Malatya that decided to support its own candidate. Associations active in local, housing, and cooperative issues can act in similar manner, yet others do not. This type of procedure is akin to an informal primary system. In 1994, in an outlying neighborhood of Ümraniye that was home to several tens of thousand inhabitants, there were ten or so candidates. Certain origin-based groups, some of which were organized as associations, held primaries in order to avoid diluting their votes (Wedel 1999).

There is a similar type of balancing act regarding political parties, though it is less explicit. It is not unusual for people with experience in party activism, especially former neighborhood representatives, to figure on aza lists. Hikmet, who, as seen earlier, had problems with his pro-AKP reputation, listed one person with AKP ties, one person with MHP ties, and two with ties to the CHP. He explained his choice in the following terms: "If you take someone with a background in the MHP, the CHP, or the AKP, at least you try to take their votes." However, he did not have anyone with ties to the SP, for his main rival was seen as pro-SP and was considered by Hikmet to monopolize this resource. This sort of balancing act can generate lists combining different party tendencies. The purpose is to attract voters from different groups without excluding anybody and without appearing to be under the thumb of any one party. In neighborhood h only one party, the SP, clearly supported a candidate who openly displayed this affiliation, and all other candidates had azas close to different parties. Hikmet claimed that the votes of the parties other than the SP were dispersed.

In addition to this blending, Hikmet was careful not to choose established activists. He distinguished between being *partili* (a partisan) and *parti kökenli* (having a party background), designating past or informal—thus less pronounced—party affiliation: "As it's going to trigger rejection, you can't take partisans [*partili*] from other parties, say the MHP or CHP. That's why, in general, I didn't take [. . .] people who could be described as extreme [*uç*]; that is to say, people employed by a party." Listing azas from different groups may arise from a wish to establish or maintain links with various components in the neighborhood population, based on geographical, political, and denominational lines.

Within these groups, a certain number of individual qualities are valued when choosing azas, primarily being known and recognized. Hikmet explained, "The muhtarlık […] is to some extent a matter of reputation [*tanınmışlık*], of being liked in the neighborhood. […] For example, who among people from Adıyaman do people listen to? X. I go see X and try to take him as aza. […] First, he is elderly; and second, he was one of the first people in the neighborhood." Local leaders are thus valued, as Fikret confirmed: "He has to be a father, a head of family, worthy. People have to listen to him. He needs to have an entourage and be appreciated." So especially in recent neighborhoods such as D and F, the azas are nearly all middle-aged men. There are few women azas, overall. Fikret noted: "There are leading people [*önde*] from each region [*bölge*]. I definitely appoint azas from these regions. From each area [*yöre*]. Cultivated, honest, self-confident people whose word is respected, who attended high school or university."

Fikret here emphasized education as a criterion. But a closer look at azas' jobs, which are frequently indicated on posters, shows once again that the preferred occupations are those which bring people into contact with the residents, with shopkeepers doing well. That would appear to be true for all types of neighborhoods, irrespective of size or socioeconomic level. In 2009, six of Duran's eight azas were shopkeepers or small business owners [*esnaf*], one was retired, and one ran a textile business. In her slightly better-off neighborhood, Bediz said she had preferred to appoint people who were known in the neighborhood, especially shopkeepers people liked, who made up almost half the azas on her list. Even in an upmarket, long-established neighborhood, Ebru admitted she chose her azas from among shopkeepers or small business owners "who people see face-to-face, who people know." Acquaintanceship is thus a key idea.

It would be reductive to limit the number of factors in compiling the lists to just one or two. Azas are often chosen for a combination of reasons, with each person presenting several desirable characteristics that balance with those of other prospective azas. At times, the lists also result from compromises. When there are a large number of candidates, certain ones pool their strengths and form a single list so as to increase their chances. Thus, Duran was elected in 2009 over the incumbent muhtar thanks to an alliance with another candidate with whom he blended lists. Likewise, in 2009 Hikmet agreed not to stand as muhtar, and to instead be first aza on another candidate's list, with the promise that they would swap roles in the next election. But when Hikmet then sought to rally his rivals in 2014, he found that "whoever I went to see, everybody had declared themselves muhtar." His 2014 election bid was unsuccessful. It would appear difficult to negotiate alliances, given that there is only a position for one muhtar in a neighborhood. The run-up to an election is a period of great fluidity, marked by attempts to form alliances, and their attendant negotiations and reversals.

Supporters are also mobilized on election day. Elections for muhtar are much less closely monitored than are other elections. The ballot papers for muhtar and aza candidates are printed and distributed not by the electoral authorities but by the candidates themselves, who therefore must ensure that their ballot papers are available throughout election day. In every polling station there is a big, open table with the ballot papers for the other local elections, and polling station officials are present. But the ballot papers for muhtars and azas are not on the table; they are inside each voting booth, in a space that is closed and secret. A classic maneuver feared by all those interviewed consists of a muhtar candidate's supporters either removing the ballot papers for rival candidates, or stacking ballot papers for their own candidate on top to conceal them. Unlike political parties, muhtar candidates do not have official election clerks. Instead, they try to place someone in each polling station to check that the vote runs properly and that their own ballot papers are available in each voting booth all day. This requires considerable organization in large neighborhoods, which can have up to several dozen polling stations.

The same problem arises when the votes are counted. Elections for muhtar take place on the same day as several other local elections. The voting slips for muhtar have to be placed in separate envelopes and ballot boxes. But the envelopes are often found to contain voting slips for one or more of the local elections in addition to those for the muhtarlık. According to a report by an association overseeing the electoral process, this sort of mix-up occurred in 66 percent of polling stations in the 2014 local elections, and was the largest "defect," as a normative perspective would put it. The regulations explicitly stipulate that slips for muhtarlık should be in a separate envelope, and not in the same envelope as the slips for the other local elections; and that the slips placed erroneously in a single envelope should be considered as spoiled. However, only 79 percent of electoral committees counted the "mixed" slips as spoiled, with 20 percent counting them as valid (Oy ve ötesi 2014: 14–15). Given the scale of these confusions, candidates for muhtar consider it crucial to have a representative in polling stations when the votes are counted, to ensure that their interests are not adversely affected. This requires the support of many people.

The election thus often involves building localized coalitions on various bases. Although the party dimension does play a role, nonparty and even nonpolitical bases are preponderant. This is an important factor in the relative degree of autonomy the muhtarlık has from the partisan political sphere. The coalitions created for the election mean that, once elected, muhtars are indebted towards the groups and individuals who supported them.

ELECTORAL CONSOLIDATION: LONGEVITY IN OFFICE
AND A BOOST FOR INCUMBENTS

Muhtars seem to remain in office for long periods of time, considerably more than those in other types of offices. This, however, is hard to quantify in the absence of electoral statistics. In a study of Izmir muhtars carried out in the early 2000s, 35 percent of respondents were in their second term of office, and 30 percent were in at least their fourth (Palabıyık and Atak 2000, 155). A cadre at the Istanbul muhtar association reckons that only about 10 percent of the muhtarlıks in Istanbul change hands at each election, although this figure was markedly higher in the 2014 elections. It is rare for an incumbent muhtar to be beaten. When a new muhtar is elected, it is usually because the incumbent did not stand for reelection. Bediz was elected when the incumbent muhtar stood down in 2009. Former muhtars are sometimes even reelected after a break, as was the case for Fikret after an interruption of one term (1994–99). So rather than giving rise to classical political professionalization (since serving as muhtar would not appear to be a springboard to partisan political careers), the muhtarlık appears to generate forms of electoral consolidation. This speaks for interpreting the muhtarlık as a position creating and reinforcing notability.

Several things can be deduced from a muhtar's longevity in office. First, those who hold the position remain fairly strongly attracted to it. Second, the position would appear to be a major source of influence for incumbent muhtars, whose capital of networks, personal ties, and experience can be used as an electoral resource. When incumbent muhtars do not stand for reelection, they tend to sponsor successors. Frequently they train a successor by handing over the office in mid-term, especially when the successor is a relative, thus enabling them to build up networks and influence before seeking electoral backing. Muhtars who commence in mid-term tend to win the next election.

A Significant Incumbency Advantage

What does this incumbency advantage consist of? There are various ways in which the outgoing muhtar can consolidate their position. The fact of carrying out the function enables them to increase their personal and personalizable resources. Three factors can be distinguished here. First, the incumbent has privileged access to institutional interlocutors. Second, carrying out the function generates notability. Third, the role played by the incumbent muhtar in the election process itself confers an advantage.

First, acting as muhtar grants access to major administrative and positional resources. The incumbent muhtar can consolidate their networks within the political and administrative apparatus. Their access to various authorities means they can benefit from the resources they distribute—namely, information and privileged access to public services. These all act as symbolic and concrete evidence of the incumbents' capacity. Mobilizing the confidence and satisfaction capital muhtars have accumulated enables them to consolidate their electoral hold. For instance, Bediz based her second campaign on services rendered. She said her record spoke in her favor, claiming it was clear that she had worked well.

Second, the position of muhtar generates notability. A thirty-eight-year-old divorcee and mother of two children, Bediz was born in Ağrı, in eastern Turkey, to a Kurdish-speaking father and an Arabic-speaking mother. The social image associated with her marital situation was compounded by her not wearing a veil, especially as she was candidate in a conservative neighborhood. In addition to this, some on her family sought to dissuade her from standing for election, judging it unseemly. She boasted about the esteem she enjoyed since becoming muhtar, five years after her divorce: "Everybody is sitting in the cafe, and when I pass by, men stand up and greet me: 'Hello, muhtar.' It makes me really happy." She attributes the respect to her position, "perhaps because I am muhtar. Perhaps because of the services I have rendered since becoming muhtar, perhaps because they like me a lot."

Furthermore, acting as muhtar consolidates local anchoring, since it involves acting as a notable. Several muhtars said they "had to" attend burials and other private ceremonies. For instance, Bediz claimed that she was invited to funerals and attended as the muhtar. She claimed that she never failed to present her condolences. She told me, "If someone from the neighborhood is buried in the local mosque, I certainly try to attend. [...] Since becoming muhtar, I do that more than before—that's to say, before being muhtar I didn't attend for everybody's losses. Well, I'm not going to lie; I went if it was a close neighbor, but since becoming muhtar I go without fail." She reckons that attending burials and weddings is part of the muhtar's role. "I go; that's to say, in my opinion, it's something you have to do. At the end of the day it's your people, your neighborhood; you have to reach out to citizens." Duran said he was solicited because of his position: "In people's eyes you are elected, you are the head [*amir*] of the neighborhood." These events are opportunities to interact with citizens and generate links that are not solely political and administrative. As seen earlier, reputation is a major resource for being elected as muhtar, and from this point of view, incumbent muhtars are automatically privileged, since they are known by the neighborhood residents. However, this notability takes different forms, depending upon the neighborhood. For instance, Ebru, a young woman in a very upmarket and progressive neighborhood, recalls attending only three funerals in the six years she was muhtar. She stated that she was rarely informed about them, and only went when they were held close to her home.

Since they are well-known, incumbent muhtars often campaign less than their rivals. Thus, in talking about the 2014 campaign in which five people were running against him, Fikret, who had already served four terms of office, claimed that he did not campaign because he did not need to. He said he did not put up any posters or hand out photos, while the other candidates campaigned in order to get themselves known. The ten banners he had set up in the neighborhood simply read: "Fikret, muhtar and your candidate for the position of muhtar."

And so, when incumbent muhtars stand for reelection, the elections often go undisputed. Thus, in 2014 no rivals ran against Bediz, who had been muhtar since 2009; against Ebru, muhtar since 2005; or against Cemil, since 1994. They all seemed firmly established in the office. As Ebru progressively consolidated her position, she reduced her campaigning. In her first campaign, in 2005, she had two rivals and had gone out canvassing; she had handbills and pamphlets of various sizes printed and had placed them on car windshields, shop windows, and walls. In 2009 she only had one rival, and claims she barely campaigned, only setting up ten or so banners in strategic neighborhood spots (avenues and crossroads) to announce that she was running. In 2014 she had no rivals and simply put up a dozen banners, only to inform voters that she was running. It was as if her rank as incumbent muhtar spoke for itself, and prevented her from campaigning in too visible a manner: "To me it seems a bit . . . printing pamphlets, canvassing, I think that . . . it's as if there were things that weren't going right if you promote yourself like that, . . . trying to drum up votes." Among the incumbent muhtars, Duran was the only one to conduct a genuine campaign in 2014, handing out tracts and pamphlets and going out to meet the voters. But he presided over a very large neighborhood of about fifty thousand people, was a controversial figure, and had many rivals. The campaign was very tense. He was finally reelected by a small margin.

Both Judge and Party to the Election Process

If muhtars remain in office for a long time, it is also because of the role they play in the election process. They play an active role in organizing the ballot, a role that can present a certain number of possibilities for influencing the vote. The institutional advantage of incumbent muhtars transpires primarily at two moments: first, in checking the electoral registers, and second, in the distribution of "voter cards" (*seçim kağıtları*). These two occasions provide many opportunities for the muhtar to interact with citizens, kindle or renew their allegiance, and remind them that it is important to vote.

Electoral registers are displayed in the muhtarlık eight weeks before the vote. Voters have two weeks to check that their names are on them and, if not, to apply for registration or to modify the constituency for which they are registered. Checking the electoral register might seem trivial, but many voters find it hard to find their name there, and must ask the muhtar for help.

But the advantage of distributing "voter cards" is even greater. These cards are not required of voters, an identity document being sufficient to be able to vote. The card is purely informative, indicating which polling station each voter is registered at. However, many voters think they need the card to be able to vote. Indeed, the vast majority bring their voter cards to the polling station.[9]

Voter cards are distributed in two ways. They can be sent out by mail, or distributed by the muhtar. The electoral committee of each subprovince decides on a case-by-case basis which method will be used. For the 2014 local elections, in all the constituencies studied, it was the muhtars who distributed the voter cards—the preferred method of the Turkey Muhtar Association. Postal distribution can cause problems, given that many dwellings lack mailboxes and public services are often suspected of being politicized and "infiltrated." There are plentiful rumors of voter cards being destroyed or siphoned off by mail carriers. Muhtars are particularly active in peddling these rumors, presenting themselves as the best-positioned and most trustworthy people to distribute the cards. In response to the many visitors who were surprised that voter cards were not being sent out by mail in 2014, Fikret opportunely pointed out that "last time, sacks of voter cards were found in the forest; the postman had got rid of them." One resident who happened to be in the muhtarlık retorted: "Clearly, it is the surest institution [*en garanti kurum*]. Who else can give out voter cards? The muhtar, of course!"

Distributing voter cards, a job for which muhtars are paid, provides them with an opportunity to come into contact with voters, campaigning "without appearing to do so" (Legall, Offerlé, and Ploux 2013). A few days before the election, Fikret, who was standing for reelection, called out after a neighborhood resident who had come to get some certificates, asking if he had taken his registration card. The resident answered that his uncle had taken it. When the resident, having obtained the papers he needed, got ready to leave, Fikret said, "Let's use our voice. Let's take hold of our ballot." Here, (non)distribution of the voter card provided Fikret with an opportunity for personal interaction—with use of the intimate second-person singular form of address, *sen*, and reference to a relative of the resident, whom Fikret also knew. As in other contexts, "in places with fairly small populations, simple interpersonal contact is enough to 'remind' people that it is important to vote, and this exhortation to vote reactivates allegiances requiring no explanation, given that it is so self-evident who to vote for" (Le Bohec 1994, 191). Likewise, when a man came to ask for papers, Fikret asked if he had picked up his voter card, and the man confirmed that he had. The muhtar replied, "There's no need for me to tell you about the muhtarlık?" This observation is redolent with unspoken meaning, suggesting presumed allegiance.

Muhtars recognize that distributing voter cards brings electoral advantage. As Ebru confessed, "You see people face-to-face, you're in contact with them, and you say 'I'm standing, I'll be at the ballot'; and that way, you call on people to vote." Exhortations to civic duty combine with electoral tactics. Though Fikret complained about the extra work involved in distributing about eight thousand voter cards in a sprawling, hilly neighborhood, he also expressed his satisfaction: "We talk face-to-face with voters. [. . .] At first I was angry, but in the end it was good. You hear what voters think about the neighborhood, you offer them tea or coffee. You end up controlling voters." He added, "It's good, the citizens came to me [literally, to my feet; *vatandaş ayağımıza gelmiş oluyor*]. Those who didn't know me also came."

For muhtars, distributing voter cards makes their campaign seem more natural. They are not (solely) in the embarrassing position of a self-promoting candidate asking for votes, but in the more comfortable one of an official providing information or a document. Some muhtars wait until they receive the voter cards before starting to solicit people. This was the case for Bediz, despite receiving criticisms she recounted thus: "'There are only fifteen or twenty days left [. . .]; why don't you go out canvassing? Why aren't you at work? Don't be so self-assured.' I answered, 'So I'm going to ring doorbells: "Hello, here I am!" No, I can't do that. I'm going to wait until the voter cards arrive, and I'll take them to people: "Here's your voter registration card, my friend, and by the way, I'm running again. Here's your voter card, and here, take my voting slip."'"

There is no clear distinction between distributing voter cards and campaigning, and many muhtars seek to benefit from this ambiguity. They frequently hand out election handbills together with voter cards, and even with their voting slips. If people are not at home, the muhtars often leave their election handbills in mailboxes along with the voter cards (figure 6).

Distribution of voter cards is an opportunity to inform people that the muhtar is standing for reelection, to provide information about the context, and possibly even to justify the candidacy. In muhtarlık F two weeks before the election, a man came to get his voter card and said to Fikret that he had heard he was perhaps not going to stand. Fikret replied, "Yes, I had thought of packing it all in and going back to being a normal citizen. But then I received an offer to stand as an AKP municipal councillor, and I saw that that wasn't the job for me. And finally I reckoned that I had put in so much effort until now that, well, I'd

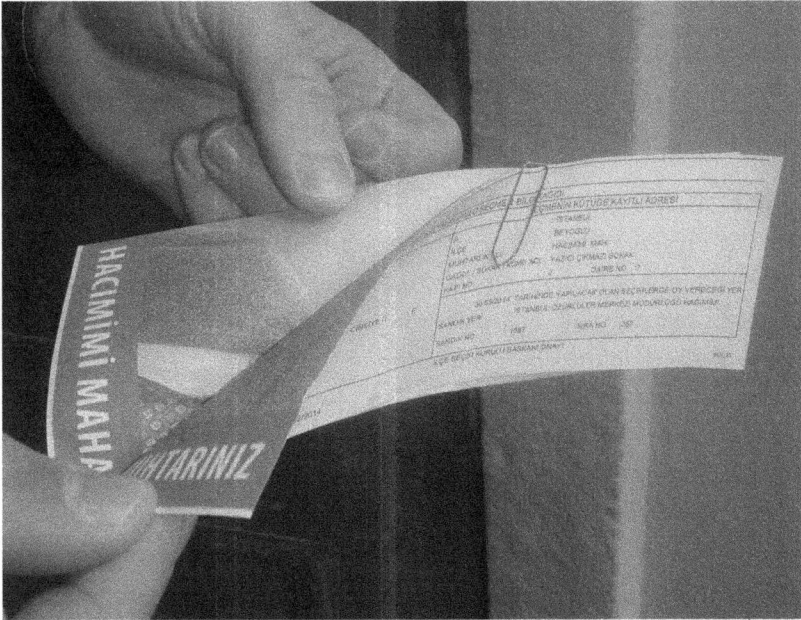

FIGURE 6. A "voter card" left in a stairwell together with the incumbent muhtar's election handbill. Istanbul, March 2014. Photograph by the author.

carry on." Fikret not only confirmed that he was running but also justified his hesitations. After having unsuccessfully sought selection as an AKP candidate for municipal councillor, he was standing again for the muhtarlık. No doubt anticipating that this could give rise to criticism, he presented it in a way that precluded its being interpreted as a fallback choice.

Handing out any remaining voter cards also provides muhtars with an opportunity to stand outside polling stations on voting day. Cemil said he spent the whole election day outside the polls in his neighborhood, handing out voter registration cards to people who had not yet received them. So while muhtars play no official role on election day, they nevertheless are almost systematically present. As in other contexts, "the presence of municipal elected representatives, as though officiating at the ritual, is an opportune reminder to inhabitants of the collective or private services rendered" (Le Bohec 1994, 191).

The incumbency advantage is therefore particularly significant for muhtars, and it takes various aspects. The length of time they have held the position is a major factor. It would appear to indicate a sort of electoral consolidation, though perhaps not political professionalization in the strict meaning of the term—a phenomenon which can also be described in terms of consolidation as a notable.

AN INSTITUTIONALIZED INTERMEDIARY

The first chapter of this book explored the genealogy of the muhtarlık, viewing the position as a continuation of the role of Ottoman intermediaries. The muhtarlık was suspended when the new republic was being consolidated, and was reinstituted in virtually identical form a few years later, despite profound changes to the political and institutional context. But the defining characteristics of Ottoman intermediaries still broadly applied. For though muhtars' powers relate primarily to governing, they are elected officials, with a hybrid status and precarious means, who are only partially under the sway of state rationales. The muhtarlık is rarely their sole or main activity, much less their sole horizon of action. There is very little in the way of political professionalization in the strict meaning of the term, and even less in the wake of the separation between political parties and the muhtarlık. Instead, the muhtars' role as notables has been consolidated. Finally, elections for muhtar are based on and regenerate personal resources and strong localized social anchoring.

In the wake of the various points set out thus far, is the term "notable" of use for describing contemporary muhtars? In historical sociology, the term has been used to emphasize the social and professional origins of holders of elective office, characterized by their social status in local society. This may be assessed via certain empirical indicators, such as how old their family is; its "reputation"; and the muhtars' socio-professional situation, prestige, renown, relational networks, and so on (Garraud 1994, 29). The merit of this term as used by Weber and in historical sociology is the emphasis placed on the social anchoring of elective positions, and on how social qualities are institutionally recognized. The Ottoman term "muhtar" comes from the Arabic and means "elected" or "chosen," in the sense of distinguished or esteemed.[10] It was used as an honorary title to refer to respected people who sometimes acted as intermediaries between populations and institutions, prior to the position being institutionalized (Güneş 2014, 14, 17–18).[11] When the position was established in the 1830s, the official texts indicated that muhtars had to be upright individuals with a certain authority (Güneş 2014, 24).

Historical sociology has shown that the social status of notables enabled them to hold elected office as a secondary activity, largely unfashioned by political organizations. Changes to notable figures, and their subsequent decline or even disappearance in places such as France, have been analyzed in the light of certain sociological shifts: first, the emergence of local "activist" elected officials, characterized not by their personal resources but by their ties to national political parties; and second, the increasingly technical aspect of the tasks carried out by local elected officials, which require specific skills. These changes that marked "the end of notables" in France have affected Turkey too—though not muhtars, or at least to a far lesser extent. It may be argued that the disappearance of party affiliation since 1980 has hampered the emergence of "activist" profiles, which in turn may have led to the marginalization of "notables." On the contrary, it can be posited that these developments led to the re-notabilization of the profile of muhtars. Nevertheless, this dynamic is not without parallels elsewhere, and similar processes of re-notabilization can be observed in other places, such as Iran (Adelkhah 2017).

The sociology of organizations has highlighted a second aspect to the term "notable," defining them via their function as mediators between local populations and central state agents (Grémion 1976). It is precisely this aspect that has been accentuated by the "notables paradigms" or "politics of notables" advocated by certain Ottomanist historians, who define notables as "those who play a certain political role as intermediaries between the government and population," among whom muhtars can be included (Hourani 1968, 48). They are agents of the central state, but also embedded in their local society. Their role is precisely to articulate these two levels. This acquires particular significance in the light of historiography about Turkey in terms of modernization, which holds that intermediary figures were limited to the Ottoman period and archaic modes of government (Massicard 2004). My perspective on muhtars coincides with and builds on the conclusions of Michael Meeker, for whom intermediaries did not disappear with the formation of the Turkish Republic, but instead lasted into the 1960s at least. It can be said that such intermediary figures still exist today. Discussing French municipal politics, Mattina (2004b) speaks of the institutional legitimization of the mediating role played by notables. But we can go further and, in the case of muhtars, argue that institutions produce notables. The institutional order, including that under the republic, has been based on and has fueled notabilization processes, and thus the production of notables.

Studying muhtars from this perspective leads to the issue of the institutionalization of social anchoring. The point is to emphasize that muhtars are embedded in different social orders simultaneously, and that their role issues from acting as intermediaries between them. As Michael Meeker notes about provincial elites, they are "both inside and outside the official class" (Meeker 2002, 147). Rather than being some zero-sum process, it is the muhtar's social role—the fact that they are known, recognized, and respected, and are able to forge a social coalition in the neighborhood—that makes them electable and reinforces their role for institutions. In return, their official role as a link to institutions reinforces their social role in a positive feedback. This perspective brings out how the state connects with society and society connects with the state (Meeker 2002). In sum, they are a figure in the mutual constitution of state and society. The muhtar acts as a figure spanning the official order, which is itself complex and shifting, and the local society.

The official attributes of muhtars presuppose that they are anchored in their local society. Identifying suspicious individuals, reticent conscripts, and the needy requires firsthand experience of the neighborhood, based on being embedded there. This militates against any interpretation that views state institutions as purely rational-legal phenomena, with social anchoring being a regrettable necessity, or even a form of parasitism. The institutional field partially interconnects with the social field. It organizes, frames, and institutionalizes this interconnection, though without controlling all the effects. The legislative, in fashioning the social anchoring constitutive of the muhtarlık, did not seek to bind muhtars in exclusive allegiance to state institutions. The sway institutions exert over muhtars is only partial, leaving considerable room for external rationales. The issue of the "limits" of the state thus takes on an additional dimension. The figure of the muhtar leads us to question our very idea of the state as being by definition a rational-legal entity—at least in ideal terms, or in the claims it may make (irrespective of any "deviance" in practice). Yet equally, we need to recognize how powerful a construct the idea of the rational-legal claims of the state is, and to conceive of the coexistence of these two phenomena (Mitchell 1991).

Part 2

A FAMILIAR INSTITUTION IN THE TIME OF DATABASES

Chapter 3

THE MUHTARS' CHANGING ROLE

URBAN MUHTARS MIGHT SEEM ARCHAIC, USELESS, AND DESTINED to disappear. There have been numerous calls for the muhtarlık to be abolished, a topic that has resurfaced in public debate over recent decades, especially in the wake of public administration reforms in the 2000s.[1] These reforms converged with larger trends to promote the rationalization and digitalization of data about citizens. As Silverstein argues, "Institutions [and] practices [...] are reformed through technical adjustments ostensibly designed to collect better data. New requirements on producing and reporting quantitative data generate new ways of capturing information by new entities, in new formats, at new intervals, and for new purposes. [...] These changes may seem arcane or technical and far from the political arena, but in fact they are part and parcel of how the political is being reformulated" (Silverstein 2018, 332). How has the rationalization of governmental technologies impacted the role of muhtars? Has it spelled their end? While the figure of the muhtar has been taken up in cultural productions over recent years—in TV series, for example—it has been in a stylized and largely romanticized form.[2]

Admittedly, these reforms have led to a scaling back in muhtars' prerogatives, and has diminished their position. However, the issue is less one of survival than one of coexistence. Their role complements and has been altered by rationalized forms of government. These two distinct repertoires of governmental rationales, based on different "regimes of power/knowledge," coexist and shape each other. On the one hand, muhtars are called upon to make up for the imperfections of incomplete rationalization—including by institutions themselves. On the other, citizens turn to them as a means of redress and to circumvent these new procedures, which are often confusing and inaccessible.

THE MUHTAR'S REDUCED ROLE AS GUARANTOR

The muhtarlık is based on the use of experiential knowledge, of which muhtars have less in the wake of recent administrative reforms. Faced with growing difficulties in carrying out their functions, muhtars sometimes opt to withdraw in various ways, thereby weakening their office.

Embedded Governing

The muhtarlık is grounded in experiential knowledge,[3] rooted mainly in the experience of living in the neighborhood on a daily basis. This knowledge is neither official nor set down on paper, and pertains to phenomena that are not necessarily documented. The muhtarlık enables public authorities to access and draw on this locally grounded experiential knowledge. In other words, muhtars' social anchoring in a web of acquaintanceships underpins their official functions; this is what I am calling "embedded governing."

Such government grounded in experiential knowledge predates the official creation of muhtarlıks. In the classical Ottoman period, the neighborhood was institutionalized as an administrative unit where certain rights and duties were exercised collectively. The neighborhood had collective responsibility in two areas. First, certain taxes were collected and payable by the neighborhood as a whole (Güneş 2014, 2–3). Second, the neighborhood qua collective entity could be held liable, and its inhabitants held collectively responsible for crimes committed in its public spaces (Tamdoğan-Abel 2004, 168). Jurists argued that it was not the state but the inhabitants who were morally responsible for making these spaces safe—first, because it was they who used them, and second, because they could intervene directly in any incident (Lévy-Aksu 2012, 221). The inhabitants also had obligations toward each other. Thus, any person wishing to move into the neighborhood had to have a local guarantor (Bayramoğlu Alada 2008, 151 et seq.). These obligations cultivated a sense of responsibility but also of mutual control, at times going as far as denunciation (Güneş 2014, 69). Since the classical Ottoman period, the *mahalle* has thus been both an administrative unit and, to a certain extent, a sphere of collective responsibilities and mutual obligations. Behar has pointed out that the neighborhood "was always both a *basic urban administrative unit* and a *social and economic entity.* [. . .] The *mahalle* was essentially a basic urban community defined by a dense network of relationships, before being a 'ward,' a local administrative unit" (italics in the original; Behar 2003, 6, 9). At the end of the Ottoman period the neighborhood would appear to have been the most significant level in the daily life of a city's inhabitants—socially, economically, and relationally (Lévy-Aksu 2012, 220). It often generated a powerful sense of community.[4]

Thus in setting up the muhtarlık in the 1830s, the Ottoman authorities did not create a level of government from scratch. Rather, it took its place amid already functioning social units, to which the authorities strengthened their administrative links. For instance, from the outset the muhtar was in charge of apportioning taxes between households based on his knowledge of the inhabitants' income. Being socially embedded in a neighborhood that is both a small-scale administrative unit and a dense local society has always been a constitutive part of the muhtar's role. Their mission is based on their capacity to translate their experiential knowledge into a form that institutions can use—and vice versa. It is because of their daily experience that muhtars are supposed to be able to detect draft dodgers, and the forces of law and order elicit their help when seeking suspects.

It is also because they are socially embedded that muhtars are entrusted with the role of guarantor, giving their experiential knowledge an official dimension. This function is embodied in one of their principal powers, namely the issuing of certificates pertaining to various fields such as, until recently, good conduct, and still including residency and poverty. Under the Ottoman Empire, the muhtar certified the marital status of a person to authorize a wedding: "This semi-official written statement from the leader of a similar neighborhood [. . .] carried with it greater credibility than a simple declaration by a private person" (Behar 2004, 554). Even nowadays, the role of the muhtar in producing certificates is not to check against other documents. It is they who produce an official document based on their experiential knowledge of a situation, and who verify *de visu* the declared situation, as attested by Bediz: "When bedridden people need a certificate, I go to their home to check that they actually live there and that they are bedridden. If that is the case, I provide the documents, but I don't give one without checking." Because of their alleged knowledge of neighborhood residents' daily life, muhtars are sometimes even approached by private individuals to act as personal guarantor.[5]

This experiential knowledge also underpins the production of identity documents. In the late Ottoman period, the muhtar's testimony was of greater identificatory force than identity papers (Behar 2003, 164). Nowadays, though most civil registry procedures can be carried out at the population bureau, anyone making a first application for ID papers or who has lost them must first get their identity authenticated by the muhtar.

The muhtarlık thus makes the population more legible—legibility being "the capacity to locate citizens uniquely and unambiguously" (Scott, Tehranian, and Mathias 2002, 10)—by producing knowledge that institutions can use to govern or exert control. Analysis of how population legibility is produced in different settings has primarily focused on onomastic, documentary, and statistical techniques, associated with writing practices (Das and Poole 2004b, 9–10). Yet what underpins the muhtars' role in making inhabitants legible is their embodied experience and knowledge. It is this knowledge which enables them to find an address when the streets are problematically named, or when two numbering systems exist in tandem—thus, when written knowledge is of little help, or is only loosely linked to reality.

Why is this form of "embedded government," based not only on writing practices but primarily on forms of experiential knowledge, found in Turkey? It is arguably linked to the volume and scale of phenomena falling outside the official order. In Turkey there is a fair degree of uncertainty about the identification of citizens (Massicard 2013; Fliche 2015), and unregistered activities (work, building, etc.) are far from marginal occurrences. According to this somewhat functionalist interpretation, institutions governing certain largely undocumented dimensions of social life need to draw on intermediaries who may provide knowledge based on their direct experience. From this perspective, which ties in with theories of modernization, it could be thought that drawing on embedded and experiential knowledge is merely a transitory phase of government. Reforms to rationalize the administration may be viewed as enhancing ways to consign things in writing, and would thus seem to threaten the type of "embedded governing" that muhtars embody. However, this is not exactly what happens.

Diminished Experiential Knowledge

Muhtars' experiential knowledge about the population lies at the heart of many of their missions. Improvements to rationalized and disembodied state knowledge about the population thus sideline them. This diminishes their knowledge of their constituents, making it more difficult for them to retain their position as an intermediaries and guarantors, and leading them to withdraw in various ways.

Imperfect Knowledge

To appreciate how muhtars' knowledge is diminished, it is useful to look at how they actually "apprehend" the population. Their knowledge is far from perfect, being both unequal and contextual. First, it is important not to reify the neighborhood as a closed, homogenous, coherent unit. Studies of Muslim cities have long held their "neighborhoods"—considered by those studies as closed, homogenous, coherent units, —to epitomize a fragmented and immobile "Islamic" form of city.[6] Furthermore, it was mainly due to the idea of neighborhoods with closed barriers at night that Max Weber excluded the socially and politically fragmented "Islamic city" from his ideal type of the city (1986 [1921]). But since the 1970s, works on urban history have questioned this vision.[7] Several studies have shown that the degree of homogeneity within neighborhoods was frequently overestimated. In particular, Behar has shown that most Ottoman neighborhoods in the nineteenth century were home to various social strata. It is important to move beyond the vision of neighborhoods as virtually homogenous entities where everyone knew each other.

Furthermore, areas of belonging do not always map exactly onto administrative entities (Lévy-Aksu 2012, 217–22). The administrative boundaries of neighborhoods have been redrawn on several occasions, most recently in 2009, when the small neighborhoods in the historical center of Istanbul were regrouped, compounding the mismatch between administrative boundaries and social boundaries, which are neither clear-cut nor stable (Behar 2003, 14). In addition to this, the density of social ties is not the same in a neighborhood with only a few hundred inhabitants as in one that is home to several tens of thousands. Nowadays, the historic and central neighborhoods of Istanbul like A, B, and C are markedly smaller (in both spatial and population terms) than more recent neighborhoods on its outskirts like F or, even more markedly, D. Lastly, the high degree of residential mobility characterizing many Turkish cities means that it would be wrong to postulate stability, which differs from one neighborhood to the next (Özelçi Eceral and Uğurlar 2017). Some neighborhoods have a relatively stable population (such as F, with little population movement and few tenants), while others experience significant levels of demographic churn (B and C undergoing gentrification, D with high levels of immigration from various provinces, and A with significant immigration from Syria). There is thus no way muhtars can identify and know all the residents of their neighborhood. Instead, they rely on extended acquaintanceship; that is, they can get information about any individual fairly quickly, using a limited and manageable number of intermediaries. The knowledge muhtars have of their constituents is variable, depending on various factors including the extent and configuration of their relational network. Fikret claimed he could draw on a trusted network of intermediaries: "I have a man in each street. If I don't know personally, I'll get him to ask a few questions." A few weeks earlier, his son said: "Our intelligence [*istihbarat*] is very effective. There is trust [*samimiyet*]."[8]

A Resource for Carrying Out Function

This experiential knowledge is of major use to muhtars in carrying out their functions. Their legitimacy, particularly with their institutional interlocutors, is grounded in their "mastery of the field." They are proud to display their knowledge of the neighborhood. According to Bediz, who has lived in her vicinity since the early 1980s, "If you have been living here for thirty-five years, you end up by more or less figuring out [*iyi kötü çözüyorsun*] everybody's situation." Fikret boasts of knowing 99 percent of the 8,500 residents of his neighborhood, though he no doubt tends to exaggerate. In answer to my question about how he issued poverty certificates, his son responded, "We use our memory. We know everybody, except tenants. The muhtar knows everything. We are the oldest family in the neighborhood." Fikret claims that his knowledge even encompasses the inhabitants' health and personal lives: "I know the private life [*iç hayatı*] of most people. I know who has cancer, who is ill. [. . .] I have the phone number of 90 percent of the people in the neighborhood. […] I can get in touch with anybody."

Muhtars continually acquire, maintain, and expand this precious knowledge. In simply carrying out their functions, they build up information about everyone's life, including certain private aspects. Administrative interactions constitute opportunities to exchange information about the situation generating the request. One day, when a resident entered muhtarlık E, Ebru guessed that he needed a residency certificate. She seemed abreast of why he was there. He was planning to open a shop. Ebru asked him what he was going to sell. He answered, and even told her all the things he had sold in his life. Sociability at the muhtarlık often involves sharing news. Equally, postmen leave official notifications and summons they are unable to deliver to their addressee with the muhtar–meaning that the latter is abreast of residents' fines, debts, recoveries, and court summons. Lastly, the muhtars' mediation and intervention in private conflicts provides them with opportunities to build up sometimes intimate knowledge about certain residents (relating to alcoholism, family or health problems, domestic violence, etc.).

While officiating, muhtars gather information about their neighborhood inhabitants, including information in spheres outside their official powers. Shortly before the elections, a woman came to fetch her voter card in muhtarlık F. Fikret asked her how things stood with her husband's voter card, as her husband had clearly not come to fetch it. The woman answered that he had left their home. Fikret asked what had happened. The woman answered that he had not come back; so Fikret now knew about a separation. Some muhtars even try to make the most of such interactions to gather information. Bediz said that she asked everybody registering with her for their phone numbers. As for Ahmet, since assuming office in 1994 he has been building up a personal computerized database that is far more detailed than the official database; it contains the numbers for telephone landlines and mobile phones together with the residents' blood types, and information on whether they rent or own their dwellings.

Dwindling Knowledge

Administrative reforms introduced during the 2000s have meant that muhtars now gather less knowledge about the population. The MERNİS database (Merkezi Nüfus İdare Sistemi, central population administration system) was introduced in 2004. It allocates each citizen a "Republic of Turkey identity number" [*TC kimlik numarası*] to be used as their unique administrative identifier. The purpose of this system is to rationalize the identification of individuals, and to eliminate incoherencies and duplicate entries (Topal 2005, 85). In the second half of the decade it was backed up by the introduction of an address-based registration system. Whereas previously only muhtars issued residency certificates (for a modest fee), citizens can now also obtain the certificates free of charge from the population bureau, and even electronically. For school enrollments, parents previously had to go to the school with a residency certificate drawn up by the muhtar; but now, the education authorities automatically allocate pupils to schools using their registered addresses.

This change in registration procedures has reduced the number of visits to the muhtars, and with it the knowledge that the latter have of their neighborhood residents. In her wealthy neighborhood of about twelve thousand inhabitants, characterized by fairly high levels of residential mobility and scant relations between neighbors, Ebru admitted that newcomers rarely came to her, and she did not really know them. She regretted that they registered with the population bureau and no longer needed to come see the muhtar. This change has affected her knowledge of newcomers. "That causes me some problems," she said. "Before, I used to receive the residency registration fee. 'Ah hello, welcome, how many of you are there?' I would look at their identity card, chat a bit, and do the registration. That's all over now." Ebru said she knew between 40 and 60 percent of the neighborhood inhabitants to varying degrees. She claimed to have a bond particularly with the older residents, but said that she did not know the newcomers, not even the disabled. Fikret also admitted that he had better access to inhabitants who were long established in the neighborhood than those who had moved there recently or were passing through.

Bediz regretted not knowing all the people in her neighborhood. "To my mind, the muhtar ought to know everyone." She felt it was newcomers who did not come to present themselves who were responsible for the situation, and she mimed an imaginary dialogue: "Someone who has never come loses their identity card after a while and comes to see me: 'My muhtar, I live in your neighborhood.' 'How can I know that you live in my neighborhood? How many years have you lived here?' 'Five years.' 'And why have you never come?'"

Forms of Withdrawal

Muhtars are solicited to attest to situations about which they know less and less. This shortfall places them in a difficult position, especially for the production of identity papers—one of the domains the administration controls most stringently. Muhtars have often learned this at their own expense. One day, a man Bediz did not know came to have some lost papers redone. When drawing up an application for the renewal of identity papers, muhtars must be shown another identity document with a photo on it, authenticating the individual. But this man did not have any other identity document with a photo on it. In that case, the official procedure is to send the applicant to the police—but it is long and complicated. However, that is not what Bediz did. Upon noting that his name was recorded in the computer system, she asked questions based on information in her database, which was the same what had been on the lost identity card, to check whether the man was indeed who he said he was. He answered all the questions, and she approved the application. A year and a half later the man was arrested, and it turned out that he had stolen the identity. Since Bediz had drawn up the application, she was called in for questioning. She argued that she had acted in good faith. The neighborhood policemen, with whom she regularly interacted, believed her, and no legal steps were taken. "They said, 'My muhtar, if it had been another muhtar or a male muhtar, we would have thought that it was for the money; but as we have known you for two years, we know you would never do such a thing for the money.'" Thanks to the policemen's testimony, Bediz did not end up in trouble.

After being confronted with a comparable situation—a similar request presented by a child, backed up solely by a blurry photocopy and no other identity document—Cemil was put on trial, and acquitted. Faced with such a request, muhtars have to choose between trusting the applicant—potentially exposing themselves to sanctions—and applying the administrative rule, which protects them but disappoints the applicant. All the muhtars in my sample seemed inclined, at least in their early days in office, to trust people. Over time, realizing the sanctions they risked incurring, they often became more cautious, like Bediz. However, Bediz only rarely sent an applicant she did not know to the police. She said that in such cases she called upon someone she knew who also knew the person in question, and thus relied on acquaintanceship.

Duran experienced a similar episode. An inhabitant he did not know wanted to get his documents redone, but was unable to present a document with a photo on it. As the person was registered in his neighborhood, Duran asked the applicant a few questions. On obtaining the right answers, he approved the application—just as Bediz had done. At the next stage, the official at the population bureau asked more questions to authenticate the applicant. Unlike the muhtar, this official had access to the entire civil registry, including sections not figuring on identity cards. This time, the man was unable to reply. It turned out that he was trying to steal someone's identity. Having approved the application, Duran, accused of producing false papers, had to defend himself before the prosecutors. He told me he had argued in his defense that it was impossible to know each person individually in a neighborhood with fifty thousand inhabitants. He also underlined how difficult it was to resist inhabitants' requests, and the existence of pressures and threats, including physical ones: "If you go to Ataköy or Bahçeşehir [educated middle-class neighborhoods], the people are cultivated, but in my neighborhood people say, 'Muhtar, do you think you're a sultan, or what?' and they grab you by the collar, they break your nose or jaw, or pull out a knife. [...] They say, 'You'll see, I'm going to destroy you. You're going to give it to me, brother, you have to. I am a citizen of the Republic of Turkey. I am registered here. I have lived here for x years.' [...] They kick up a fuss. [...] From time to time you call the police. They take some time to arrive, even though they're just next door."

What Duran emphasized here was the public authorities' inability to provide effective protection—together, implicitly, with the inability of the official order to impose itself, and his own inability to impose it unaided. Duran told me that this episode had made him wary. He said that if he knew an applicant's parents, he gave the document without any problem; but that if he did not know the person, he fell back on the official procedure, to the discontent of applicants who generally wanted their papers rapidly. Duran concluded, "Identity papers are a nightmare for us. [...] If the person wanting his papers has committed an offense, [...] the muhtar stands trial for complicity." Duran's predecessor had been tried before a criminal court for a similar affair. This procedure is scheduled to end with the introduction of identity smartcards. Duran was relieved about this: "Muhtars will run into fewer troubles. Ah, it means TL5 less for certificates to change identity papers, but personally I'm glad. It's an enormous responsibility."

Muhtars face the same type of problem when asked to issue poverty certificates—declarations certifying that an individual is needy. This presupposes that they know the economic circumstances of their neighborhood residents, which is not always the case.[9] In her upmarket neighborhood, Ebru tended to adopt an attitude of withdrawal. She said she issued poverty certificates to anyone who requested one, based exclusively on declarations by the person concerned: "You give them in the light of declarations by the person, of the sort: 'Do you work?' 'I don't work.' You write, 'He declares that he does not work,' [. . .] and beneath it you write in any case that it is issued on declaration. I cannot know if he has social insurance, if he owns a building, if he has assets. That is why we take down the person's declarations, and then the institution to which they address their request validates it or does not. That's their responsibility. [. . .] In any case, you can't check anything. If I go to the land register and ask if X owns a building, they won't reply in any case, as I am a third party, and they can only give that information to the person concerned." Despite sidestepping her mission to act as guarantor, she said she carried out her duties: "Ultimately, our laws entrust us with the power of issuing poverty certificates, and when we consider it to be necessary, we grant them on the basis of their declaration."

Similarly, Duran stepped back from his role as guarantor by recording solely what people declared. Duran said that he would give a poverty certificate to anyone who asked, even to someone "with a seven-story building," because he did not have the capacity to investigate their property. He justified this attitude on the grounds of institutional malfunction and insufficient means of verification: "Normally, legally speaking, the muhtar is guilty. But I don't conduct any observations or investigations. I cannot. The day the subgovernor's office gives me an employee, I will do so. But as they do not, this is what I do. At the bottom of the poverty certificates I write: 'No observations made, certificate issued on request,' and then I put my stamp." Both Duran and Ebru justified this form of withdrawal—attesting not to a situation but merely to a declaration—by the shortfall between the powers invested in them and the means at their disposal.

Muhtars may also be called to testify due to their supposed knowledge of situations. But this places them in an awkward situation, and they sometimes refuse to do so. Ebru had been summoned by a judge as a witness in a case about former spouses living in separate flats in the same building. She had been asked to clarify whether they were indeed separated, for they were suspected of benefit fraud. She said she had refused to testify about the private life of inhabitants: "I cannot say anything, it's people's private life. [...] I told them that I knew the person as an inhabitant of the neighborhood, but that his private life was none of my concern." When I asked if it was normal procedure to ask muhtars this kind of thing, she answered: "I don't know. In my opinion it's not normal. I'm muhtar of a neighborhood with between ten thousand and eleven thousand people. I'm not interested in who is married to whom, who is divorced, who goes to visit whom. Not personally, and even less as muhtar. I'm not there for people's private lives." Her account emphasizes two interesting elements: first, a conflict over what the muhtars' role consists of, with certain authorities assigning them the role of "informant," asking them to relate facts which, to Ebru's mind, pertained to citizens' private lives, and thus was outside her official role; and second, the fact that she did not know whether this request was a standard or legal way of proceeding. Ebru was the only university graduate in my sample, and was well informed about the regulations defining her powers. Her account shows how "unclear" the role of muhtar is, and the extent to which interpretations may diverge.

Ebru was also reticent when various institutions–she mentioned the police and the MİT (Milli İstihbarat Teşkilatı, or National Intelligence Agency)— requested information about residents, for she feared being held liable for her declarations: "You don't know the details of why they're asking questions. Sometimes they're making an enquiry about someone they're thinking of employing; they ask me if I know him. But things like that, for the very long-standing residents, okay, I can provide that for people I've known a very long while, but to what extent can you know everyone? That's why the answer I give"—she paused to choose her words carefully—"must not be binding. That is, if I say, 'Yes, I know Ayşe, she is very good, very aboveboard,' then tomorrow, if there is a problem with her, they must not be able to turn that against me. [...] I gave her address, [...] but our relationship is 'Hello, my muhtar.' How are you?' 'I'm fine.' The person takes their papers and leaves, that's all. That is why the answers must not engage my liability." When I asked whether in the event of problems, institutions could take legal action against her, she answered, "I have no idea! And what if they did? Ultimately, you made a declaration. They asked the neighborhood *mülki amir*."[10] Ebru thus refused to be held responsible for information she might give about inhabitants. Once again, the situation appeared unclear, and she did not know exactly what risks she incurred.

Due to the conditions in which they carry out their functions, many muhtars are reluctant to officially attest to situations they know less and less about. Because the computerized collection of information sidelines them, it is increasingly difficult for muhtars to assume their role as providers of information, certifiers, and guarantors. They tend to withdraw from these roles, perhaps hastening their own marginalization. Does this mean that the knowledge they have of their neighborhood has become redundant? Is their continuing presence merely a stay of execution? Not really. Improvements to the state's increasing rationalized knowledge and the attendant forms of government may have sidelined the muhtars, but they have not rendered their cooperation superfluous.

FORMS OF COMPLEMENTARITY

In practice, the certifying role of muhtars has not disappeared. Rather, it has changed: in many ways, it complements rationalized forms of knowledge. Two forms of complementarity may be observed: first, as this rationalization is often incomplete, muhtars are still solicited to "make up for" mistakes and imperfections in rationalized procedures. Whereas they previously played a central role, they now play an auxiliary one, checking and intervening in the event of problems. Second, the imperfectly rationalized procedures are often confusing, for citizens and the authorities alike. In this context, muhtars act as a fallback resource when citizens endeavor to circumvent these procedures.

Verifying and Making Good

The experiential knowledge of muhtars has not been shorn of all pertinence for institutions, but now provides a way of making up for shortcomings in standardized computerized knowledge. Muhtars check databases, make good the errors generated in them, and indicate what they fail to capture. In 2005, according to a brochure produced by the population directorate, there were still problems with the residency database, with many citizens being registered as living at the wrong address (Topal 2005, 87–88, 93). Furthermore, whenever a citizen registers as living at a given address, this automatically leads to all other citizens being removed from that address and from the electoral register, without them being informed of this. This generates many errors, especially because in some places the numbering system for buildings and flats is approximate or duplicated.

Muhtars may intervene at the request of neighborhood residents to correct errors in the databases. When residents find they have been struck off registers, they turn to muhtars, who try to understand why their residency registrations have been annulled, and to "make good" the administrative records. Thus, muhtars act as a resource for citizens when rationalized processes malfunction. Furthermore, certain muhtars endeavor to remedy shortcomings in the databases. Thus, Bediz said she had taken the initiative to inform the electoral committee of voters on the electoral roll who were in fact deceased or on military service. Finally, even other government officials approach muhtars for help in making up for insufficiencies in the databases. Each month, the district population bureaus send lists of people who have declared that they have moved, for countersigning by the muhtars. The population bureaus do not rely solely on what has been recorded by the administration, but require verification by eyewitnesses. Certain muhtars note the irony of the situation: though no longer the sole authority for changes of address, they still have to check where people live.

Indeed, computerized databases are frequently unable to locate citizens. Municipal police officers requested Ahmet's help to deliver bills for prison meals to recently released ex-detainees. To find a citizen in the MERNİS database, you need their identity number, something the police did not have. Ahmet thus used the database he had built up himself, in which he could do searches by address. He managed to locate half of the people the officers were looking for. To find one of them, he called his uncle on the telephone. To find another, he phoned a former neighbor. The police were able to locate these individuals only by calling on the muhtar's local knowledge. So, though sidelined, this embodied knowledge is nevertheless used on a daily basis, including by officials.

Identifying the "Needy": A Crucial Yet Sidelined Role
One sphere allowing for better analysis of the interplay between rationalized knowledge and muhtars' experiential knowledge is that of social assistance.

Muhtars have long played a central role in this domain. Recently they have been sidelined by the computerization of data about citizens, and the introduction of new procedures. However, they are extensively called upon to remedy and help circumvent these new and often confusing procedures.

Under the Ottoman Empire, social assistance was primarily composed of individual aids given on request on a case-by-case basis—and this is still largely the case today. Those distributing public and private social assistance have long called on the help of muhtars to identify the needy,[11] because of what network analysis would call their "positional centrality." The consultative and guiding role of muhtars in this field has multiple aspects: they know what is available, point people towards aid, tell them when and where to apply, issue poverty certificates, intercede and register people on lists of the needy, and sometimes distribute aid. Even if muhtars have never been the only ones involved in distributing social assistance, they have long played a pivotal role.

An important aspect of muhtars' role here is that of issuing poverty certificates (*fakir ilm-ü haberi* or *fakirlik belgesi*). The existence of such documents is attested for the nineteenth century, but its origins are probably older, though hard to trace. Poverty certificates may be used in various situations for a wide range of public and private institutions (figure 7)—thus reinforcing muhtars' crucial role. They may, for instance, exempt holders from paying for certain public services, such as legal defense fees. In the nineteenth century, holders received health treatment either free or at modest rates (Behar 2003). In the 1960s, people without social security coverage needed poverty certificates to receive free hospital treatment (Günal 2008, 26–27).

Yet while the poverty certificate has long been a prerequisite for obtaining aid, it rarely suffices. First, other documents are also needed to obtain certain aids; second, even when the poverty certificate is the only documentation required, it does not automatically grant rights. Thus, in the 1960s a poverty certificate did not in itself guarantee that its holder would receive free treatment in public hospitals; it was the head of each hospital department who decided who was exempted from payment (Buğra 2013, 168).

Muhtars enjoy discretion in deciding whether to issue a certificate, and they exercise that discretion on a case-by-case basis. Access to divisible aid is granted on the basis of their certification. In other words, individuals access benefits through the muhtars, who act as gatekeepers (Behar 2003, 161–64). Unlike counter staff in welfare offices in most Western countries, who check

FIGURE 7. Handwritten sign at the entrance to a mosque: "People wishing to receive a Ramadan food parcel must obtain a 'poverty certificate' from the muhtar." Istanbul, 2004. Photograph by Jean-François Pérouse.

whether claimants are in possession of documents issued by other administrations and whether they meet the criteria for receiving aid, muhtars have the power to grant poverty certificates to "those in need" without "poverty" being legally defined.[12] The lack of clarity, and the nonexistence even of attribution criteria and hence of clearly established rights, means the muhtars can act as they see fit. Furthermore, muhtars base their judgement on their supposed experiential knowledge of individuals' daily living conditions. They assess each individual case on the basis of their appraisal of the overall situation in the light of a broad swath of criteria. The issuing of certificates is, therefore, far from being a mere formality. In arriving at a judgement, the muhtars' interaction with applicants can play an important role, thus making the applicants' ability to plead their cause an important factor.

Today, however, muhtars' pivotal role in distributing social aid is being undermined. The first public social assistance reform confirmed their central role. After the emergence of new forms of poverty in the 1980s, associated with the opening up and deregulation of the Turkish economy and the subsequent dwindling of stable protected employment, the public authorities became more involved in social assistance. In certain precise situations, the rights to assistance were institutionalized on the basis of status and clear rules pertaining to health situations (being disabled or bedridden), and to certain family situations (being an orphan, a widow, or a breadwinner drafted into the military). It was muhtars who were asked to testify in most of these situations.

Other than for these specific situations, the situation did not change much for general social welfare. In 1986 the SYDTF (Sosyal Yardımlaşma ve Dayanışmayı Teşvik Fonu, or Social Aid and Solidarity Encouragement Fund) was set up to oversee the many local foundations in charge of distributing assistance, the SYDVs (Sosyal Yardılaşma ve Dayanışma Vakıfları, or Social Aid and Solidarity Foundations). Yet this institutional change was not accompanied by any fundamental shift in the philosophy of social welfare. This law did not introduce automatic procedures for assistance, which continued to depend on individual initiatives, with aid accorded on charitable grounds and not as a matter of entitlement by right. Applicants were unable to lay claim to any right to assistance given that the 1986 law did not introduce any precise criteria for poverty, instead defining the poor as those without social security coverage and "in a state of destitution and neediness" (*fakruzaruret ve muhtaçlık*).[13] In her analysis on the practices of assistance provision, Dodurka convincingly shows that given this lack of clarity, decisions continued to be discretionary. Furthermore, she observed that given the lack of reliable data about population, land ownership, social security, and taxation, the SYDVs were unable to check applicants' declarations and situations. They had little funding and few staff (who rarely had any specialized training), and were only occasionally able to carry out home visits. In practice, when examining an application they tended to follow the opinion of the muhtar, considered as best informed about the inhabitants' situation (Dodurka 2014, 119–21). Therefore, muhtars still helped the SYDV boards of trustees assess applications and decide on the amount of welfare.

Thus, this first stage in the institutionalization of public welfare did not question the centrality of the muhtars' role in guiding and assessing. Things changed in the 2000s, however, during the second stage of institutionalization of social assistance, transforming the muhtar's role. The economic crisis of 2001, the most severe economic downturn in the history of Turkey, led to employment becoming far more precarious, generating new forms of poverty. Combating poverty rose on the government's agenda. In 2004 the SYDTF became the SYDGM (Sosyal Yardımlaşma ve Dayanışma Genel Müdürlüğü, or General Directorate for Social Assistance and Solidarity), directly linked to the prime minister's office, with a marked increase in powers and budget.[14] In parallel with the quantitative increase in aid programs, there was a trend toward computerizing data and setting up systematized procedures to target beneficiaries. With the increase in regular cash transfers distributed by the SYDVs, identifying the poor became a major concern. Furthermore, the lack of any reliable mechanism for targeting beneficiaries led to the opposition parties raising suspicions about the arbitrariness, partisan favoritism, and clientelism of decisions. These criticisms pushed the government to institutionalize more systematic and less questionable mechanisms for identifying beneficiaries (Dodurka 2014, 86).

The first regular cash assistance programs were introduced as part of a project launched in 2001 in cooperation with the World Bank, which was heavily involved in managing the economic crisis. To target the poorest people, the bank recommended assessing their resources, which required data on income, property ownership, and so on. As official data was unreliable and covered only a small fraction of the population, the World Bank set up an indicator-based formula for assessing revenue, and drove the development of such databases (Dodurka 2014, 121). In 2009 the SYDGM launched an integrated database called SOYBİS (Sosyal Yardım Bilgi Sistemi, or Social Assistance Data System), containing information pooled from fourteen institutions.[15] This integrated database now underpins the SYDVs' assessment of applications for assistance (Dodurka 2014, 94).[16] Most SYDVs back this up with a home visit to the applicant, to assess their living conditions *de visu*. They may also ask the opinion of eyewitnesses of the applicant's daily life, such as the muhtar, the school principal, or teachers (Hacımahmutoğlu 2009, 158).

Does the use of databases to assess situations make the muhtars superfluous in identifying the needy? Do they still have a role to play, and if so, what is it? Muhtars still intervene, but in a different manner. First, only some of the assistance programs are "rationalized," and muhtars continue to play an important role in certifying poverty in the context of multiple assistance providers. Second, as in other fields, "informal channels continue to be important in what is supposed to be an increasingly technical system" (Silverstein 2018, 336). Despite this systematization, intercession continues to be central. There are thus two coexisting "regimes of power and knowledge," two ways of identifying beneficiaries: one using computerized official data, the other based on experiential knowledge of people's daily situation, embodied by the muhtars. Do these two approaches vie with each other? How do they interact?

This systematization is incomplete. This is true at the level of the SYDVs, and elsewhere too, for there are many assistance programs, dispensed by numerous providers using multiple procedures. In this complex landscape, muhtars continue to act as guides, and continue also to intercede.

The institutionalization of SYDV welfare procedures did not eradicate all suspicion of lack of neutrality. In the late 2000s, several audits and internal administrative reports highlighted the lack of objective and standardized criteria for measuring poverty, and the failure to apply mechanisms for gauging resources. This resulted in marked variation from one SYDV to another in how welfare was distributed, and even how each defined the poor. These reports called for greater standardization and institutionalization in granting assistance. In 2006 and again in 2009, the State Supervisory Council (Devlet Denetleme Kurulu) criticized the welfare system for its lack of oversight, making it vulnerable to populist strategies by the government.[17] In particular, ahead of the 2007 general elections and 2009 local elections, the SYDVs were accused of corruption in distributing welfare, which was frequently denounced by the opposition as an instrument in the government's hands.[18]

How are we to account for this situation? The high levels of undeclared work—and undeclared revenue more generally—complicate the assessment of poverty on formal criteria. In 2020, the Statistics Institute reckoned the proportion of undeclared work to stand at 28.7 percent (TÜİK 2020). By definition, this work eluding official registration is not recorded in databases. SYDV staff interviewed by Dodurka said that some flexibility had to be maintained in assessing revenue, without which it would be impossible to reliably identify the "truly" needy. Social workers conducting home visits observed a significant mismatch between directives and circulars on the one hand, and the realities they encountered on the other. They sought to make up for this by such arrangements as recording fictitious questionnaire answers. However, neither the gauging of revenue using databases nor observations made during home visits made it possible to arrive at a decision. Dodurka shows that applications often generated debate, and that the final decision on who benefited, how much they were to receive, and for how long lay with the SYDV board of trustees, which often found it hard to reach an incontrovertible decision. There was thus extensive scope for subjective and arbitrary decisions, creating leeway for intercession and influence (Dodurka 2014, 134, 169). Even though the provision of social assistance is presented as relying on objective measures like means testing, the way SYDVs grant welfare remains a conflictual process, only partly governed by the numerical "objectivity" of databases. As Kayaalp notes in another context, "Beyond the seemingly bureaucratic rationalization logic, there lies a messy world governed by uncertainties" (2013, 481). Various zones of uncertainty and influence remain, or continue to be carved out. It may be imagined that certain actors resist the complete rationalization of social assistance specifically to retain some latitude, thereby preserving the possibility of wielding influence. In this context, muhtars are probably just one category of actors who are able to wield influence.

While the opposition suspects that social assistance is used by the governing party and local authorities for top-down political ends as part of a coherent hegemonic project, other more localized and fragmented usages are probably underestimated—including influence by other actors, including muhtars. The 2004 reform not only increased the powers and funding of the SYDVs bu also modified the composition of their boards of trustees. Since then, their members also include two NGO representatives and two individual donors, together with a muhtar elected by his peers in the district. And there is fierce competition over the election of the muhtar to the SYDV board, indicating that this position is considered desirable. Duran explained that he had been a candidate, and had received as many votes as his main rival in the first round of voting. He put forward a highly political interpretation of the second round: "Apparently there were phone calls from upstairs: 'Whatever you do, don't let Duran become a board member.' They played politics with muhtar affairs. Apparently MPs called up my fellow muhtars. Because they're afraid of me. I don't let anything unfair get through." Duran's account illustrates the importance of this position. This importance converges with the above statement that decisions, at the end of the day, are made by SYDV boards of trustees, allowing their members to wield influence, yet also providing incentives to connive with underhanded practice. Furthermore, systematic targeting only concerns certain institutions and forms of welfare, not all, being most systematic at the level of subgovernors' offices, which dispense various forms of welfare. Though they do not all follow the same procedures, all now seem to use the SOYBİS database and are largely outside the muhtars' influence. Duran said that until 2009 the subgovernor's office distributed coal via the muhtars, leaving it to their initiative; but that since then, muhtars have no longer had any say in it. Fikret also said that the subgovernor's office now looked after coal distribution. He said it had asked the muhtars to update the lists of poor families, but had recently stopped doing even that.

However, the subgovernor's offices are far from being the sole dispensers of assistance. After the 2001 crisis, many organizations became involved in social action, particularly municipalities and many NGOs. And while there are plans for the SOYBİS database eventually to be made available to these other actors to assess all applications, that is not yet the case. In other words, social assistance dispensers are fragmented and do not designate all beneficiaries using databases. To varying degrees, they end up calling on the muhtars to assist.

District municipalities have become heavily involved in social assistance, driven in particular by the RP (Refah Partisi, or Islamist Welfare Party), which has been notable for its charitable activism since the 1990s, when it came to municipal office (Buğra and Keyder 2005). The AKP further institutionalized and developed municipal welfare. The 2005 law no. 5393 obliges municipalities to provide social assistance, and allows them to collect private donations for that purpose. There are grounds for thinking that municipal social expenditure has increased since the 2000s, though this is difficult to document, given the lack of data (Buğra and Adar 2008). Municipalities do not have access to SOYBİS, and each draws up its own targeting procedures, with the resultant lack of criteria and transparency feeding suspicions of arbitrary decisions and clientelism (Hacımahmutoğlu 2009, 165).

Many municipalities have set up beneficiary identification schemes that have sidelined the muhtars. Fikret commented on his exclusion: "The municipality arrives with prepaid cards without asking any muhtar for their opinion." Duran and Ebru said that muhtars are not involved in apportioning the schooling grants provided by certain district municipalities. Municipal authorities also oversee a certain number of distributions previously carried out by the muhtars. Ebru explained:

> When [. . .] we used to give lists with names of people, fifty or a hundred food parcels would arrive and we would distribute them to the needy in the neighborhood. And then [. . .] there was a rumor that muhtars did not carry out the distribution, that they took the parcels for themselves or distributed them to people they knew. I don't know how true that is. When this type of rumor appeared, the municipality said, "Give us the list; we will get our own staff to distribute it." After that, I gave names; [. . .] I sent food parcels to a few janitors, to two or three old ladies. And then that stopped too, and the municipality conducted its own investigations to know who was poor and who was not. They went over the lists and ranked them name by name, [. . .] and distributed food parcels to the people they had designated. [. . .] It got tougher after 2009; the district municipality started to do it itself, designating the needy itself [. . .], and I have not distributed any more food parcels.

However, many municipalities continue to involve muhtars indirectly or on a case-by-case basis. An official in a recently created outlying municipality run by an opposition party asserted that the municipality still habitually called on muhtars to designate beneficiaries. Most muhtars say they enjoy a certain capacity to influence the municipal schemes. Fikret said that the municipality sometimes called him to ask which residents needed help, even though it had a resident revenue database and carried out checks. He also said that in the event of a mismatch between the existence of a poverty certificate and the revenue recorded or a home visit by municipal teams, the municipality would call him to know why the mismatch existed. In neighborhood B, an employee in the municipal social affairs department was tasked with conducting home visits. Yet Bediz said the municipality also wanted to know the muhtar's opinion. She said that in certain cases—for example, when a man works but cannot feed his family—she alerts the social affairs department employee and asks him to come and check the situation at home, thus correcting the database verdict.

The muhtars' capacity to wield influence by recommending recipients or proposing lists of names seems to count primarily for in-kind or one-off assistance programs, which are less closely monitored. Fikret claimed to play a role in distributing municipal welfare: "Normally the municipality tends to give to those who are close to the party. But I have good one-to-one relationships [*ikili*]. I can suggest a few people. For instance, I put forward twenty or thirty people, and follow things up. For example, yesterday there was a meeting to talk about upcoming assistance for Ramadan. [. . .] We had handed in lists a long while ago, and went over them together, and brought them up to date." Regarding food parcels, he said, "I give the names of sixty to seventy families. And anyway, people go directly there and ask. Then the municipality asks me or conducts its own enquiry." He said that about two hundred families in his neighborhood received municipal food parcels, based on a list of beneficiaries he has drawn up. The role of muhtars in the allocation of municipal welfare varies from one district municipality to another, and from one muhtar to another.

In addition to this, most metropolitan municipalities have set up welfare programs. Once again, the way they target beneficiaries is not as standardized as for the SYDV programs. The Ankara metropolitan municipality has introduced various in-kind schemes for food and coal. It requires beneficiaries to have a poverty certificate, and certificates attesting that they do not own any real estate or vehicle. It checks whether the applicants have social insurance, and assesses their standard of living by conducting home visits (Hacımahmutoğlu 2009, 137). In addition to its women's coordination center, which hands out periodic food assistance, the Istanbul metropolitan municipality has set up a fund that pays out cash assistance twice per year. Applicants must have a poverty certificate backed up by a letter setting out their situation. Then the municipal employees conduct an inquiry, visiting the applicant's home and sounding out neighbors, shopkeepers, and the muhtar, and on occasion comparing this information with social security documents or inquiry reports from the women's coordination center. About one hundred people in neighborhood F receive this type of assistance. Fikret said that he helped channel its distribution by suggesting families, and that afterward the metropolitan municipality conducted its home enquiries and applied its revenue test. He said he was able to intercede: "I have good relations with this authority. I call them up; I have influence."

In parallel with this, many NGOs distribute assistance. Their targeting procedures and the role played by muhtars differ even more widely than for municipal authorities. Charities have to demonstrate their probity and display transparency and accountability if they are to generate confidence and collect donations.[19] Some have set up highly codified targeting mechanisms—such as the Islamic Deniz Feneri Association (Lighthouse Association), which has introduced a nationwide standardized database backed up by home visits to examine living conditions. But most organizations are not in a position to conduct such rationalization, and many call on the muhtars to identify beneficiaries. Thus, when the semipublic Red Crescent organization wished to hand out clothing to twenty or thirty children, or distribute meat during Ramadan in neighborhood B, they turned to Bediz for her help in finding beneficiaries.

Lastly, private donations are still sizeable. Individuals or businessmen wishing to perform good deeds often contact muhtars—but since the 2005 law, they also increasingly contact municipalities. Fikret said that associations of businessmen wanting to give financial assistance to fifteen or thirty families, or food aid to fifty families, ask him for a list of those in need. Likewise, Duran recounted that some people, rather than sacrifice a sheep during Ramadan or the Sacrifice Feast, prefered to give assistance to a few people. "Of course, they come now and again, and I take notes about people who are very needy." Such donors rarely have the means to set up other forms of targeting, and in general call on the muhtars to do it for them.

Some, such as Fikret, justify their role in designating beneficiaries by assessing requests on a case-by-case basis: "Someone who is doing well but then goes bankrupt—of course I will help him at that time. Life can be like that." He thereby legitimized his margin of appreciation as a way of circumventing rigid and sometimes inappropriate criteria. Yet muhtars back down if the database shows that a request they have relayed is unfounded. Bediz recognized that she did not know everything and might take wrong decisions. She recalled that one day a woman had asked her why she had not given her any coal. That woman had a tiny studio flat. Bediz said she had immediately called the head of welfare at the subgovernor's office, Burak. After checking his database, Burak had told her this woman received a pension, as did a girl living in her family. Besides, there was a young adult in the same family. He had added that this woman's daughter also worked. That made four incomes in total. Bediz had said she did not know, and apologized.

Despite long acting as pivotal gatekeepers in this domain, muhtars have never exerted a monopoly on identifying beneficiaries. Nowadays they are increasingly just one actor among many. Their scope for direct intervention is declining, as are the resources they can distribute at their discretion. While the muhtars are sometimes involved in designating beneficiaries, their word no longer suffices in most cases. It is now normally double-checked against databases or home visits, thus reducing its arbitrariness.

This context of partial rationalization and uncertainty is key to understanding the issues at stake in the distribution of assistance, and the strategies of the actors involved. The muhtars' diminished role has refocused on two points: guiding applicants, and providing means of support and redress. This complex landscape increases the need for guidance: it is difficult for applicants to find their way through the many various assistance programs, providers, and procedures. This is especially true given that the landscape is unclear and is always shifting. Even many public forms of aid are one-off, with no guarantee that they will last or be regular. Thanks to their versatility and "multipositionality," muhtars are still resource people for accessing information about welfare services. When asked by a woman for information about food parcels, Ebru replied: "It is the [district] municipality that hands out food parcels, but it's not certain that they'll give any this year; last year they didn't hand any out. Neither food parcels, nor checks to pay for shopping. I don't know if they'll do any this year; there's no program for the time being. Before, they used to ask us for lists, but normally you should approach the municipality directly." Thus, Ebru has been comparatively excluded from the process. On being approached for information, she admitted she was poorly informed. Despite that, she presented herself as a mediator who could guide the person. This guiding role is not exclusive, however. Over recent years, a significant partisan political dimension has emerged. Since the AKP came to power nationally and in the great majority of local authorities, its neighborhood cadres have played a significant mediating role, particularly for the distribution of institutionalized welfare by municipalities and subgovernors' offices. More broadly, they have acted as brokers, bringing the problems of citizens—probably at least in part along partisan political lines—to public institutions, and assisting them in their dealings with bureaucrats. Therefore, because of its specific government patterns and especially its very extensive brokerage activities, the AKP has sidelined the muhtars—at least where its members hold political office.

The second dimension to the role of muhtar in this new landscape is in acting as a means of support and redress. We shall look at two aspects of this: first, in granting poverty certificates that have limited direct effect but offer a way of showing support for a request; and second, as relays to help circumvent rules in uncertain situations.

The great majority of assistance providers require applicants to have a poverty certificate, the issuing of which remains a monopoly of the muhtars. During the "people's assembly"—a meeting when inhabitants publicly present their grievances to a member of the district municipal council, assisted by the muhtars—all applicants are advised to obtain a poverty certificate from their muhtar before applying to the local authorities who dispense welfare. This document is all but indispensable for requesting assistance, even if for most providers it is not sufficient, particularly because it is one of the least reliable elements.

Some assistance providers view the poverty certificate as being of dubious worth. In his "muhtar manual," Aytaç argues that since poverty certificates are not based on any inquiry but only on declarations by the applicant, they are unreliable and of questionable legal value (Aytaç 2009, 205). Likewise, certain providers do not place much faith in the testimony of muhtars, whom they regard as untrustworthy. Damla Işık shows that even though the Deniz Feneri Association requires a poverty certificate for each application, with certain applicants adding a letter of support from their muhtar, these are not taken into account in decisions about assistance (2012, 63). Said one data-entry worker she interviewed in her study of private poor relief in Turkey, "We don't trust muhtar documents. Muhtars know the families, and they may not be entirely truthful, [in order] to get [families] some money or other assistance from us and so win the favors of their future constituents" (Işık 2012, 64). This worker thus questioned the reliability of muhtars due to the stakes at play in their relationship with neighborhood residents. For the same reason, when the association conducted a neighborhood inquiry, it privileged what the neighbors and grocer had to say rather than the muhtar. Işık shows that poverty certificates issued by muhtars are often considered of questionable worth.

So why continue issuing such documents if they are ineffective? The fact of making a recommendation is perhaps as important as knowing it to be effective. By providing a certificate, even one explicitly "on request," and even without knowing whether it will be of any use, the muhtar shows his or her support for the applicant. In his study of municipal clientelism in Marseille, France, Cesare Mattina has shown that while local politicians' power to distribute resources (mainly social housing and jobs) has been eroded, clientelist practices and habits remain firmly in place. Thus, local politicians continue to receive requests from residents and to write recommendations and letters of support. They display great willingness to listen to these requests, and do what they can to help. Yet such initiatives are increasingly ineffective, and certain more cautious politicians no longer promise applicants anything. Thus, while politicians continue to intercede personally, in the great majority of cases this produces no concrete results (Mattina 2004a, 151–52): "[This] has a symbolic meaning, however, explained by the need to maintain a certain level of hope and expectation among citizens regarding the role and possibilities politicians have to respond to their requests" (Mattina 2004a: 154). This leads to a generalized system of "false" letters of recommendation, whose "sole objective is to show symbolically to a voter that someone is looking after him" (Mattina 2004a: 152–53). Equally, the muhtars' power to distribute assistance is being eroded, but poverty certificates are still used extensively. In issuing one, the muhtar shows that they have done what they can to help the applicant, even though they are not sure whether much will come of it. This helps explain why many muhtars issue poverty certificates to anyone who asks for one. Issuing this type of document forms part of the relationship between an applicant and the muhtar, in which the latter can openly display that they support the requests of their constituents (see next chapter).

Similarly, when a sick old man came to see Ahmet to complain that his SYDV welfare had not been renewed because he was absent when the yearly inspection took place, and that he could not get through to the SYDV, Ahmet answered, "Don't go there! Come see me." He phoned someone with whom he was on good terms at the SYDV, and said, "Do you know Mehmet from my neighborhood?" He then explained the situation, and easily got the SYDV person to agree to renew the welfare. Thus even though he played no part in the decision, Ahmet managed to unblock the situation and figure as an effective means of support for the old man.

The uncertainty characterizing the complex landscape of assistance also fuels demands for support and intercession. Yoltar shows this very convincingly in her analysis of the implementation of the "green card" scheme introduced in 1992, which was replaced in the late 2000s by universal health coverage. The green card scheme guaranteed free access to health services for the poor under legally specified criteria. However, Yoltar shows that most of the eligibility criteria had to be specified by each provincial health directorate, and thereby became ambivalent. The complex procedure to check revenue meant that obtaining a green card was an uncertain process (Yoltar 2007, 55–100). First, various sources of revenue were used to calculate poverty. But it was often impossible for administrators to check applicants' declarations. Given that there was no SOYBİS database at the time, they could not access official data about applicants' income. It was hard to know whether an applicant received other forms of public welfare, for most of these were not granted on a regular basis, and each institution kept tabs only on its own beneficiaries, if at all. The green card bureau required applicants to document the information themselves. Thus, applicants had to get their declarations certified by the muhtar, the population bureau, the tax office, the land registry, and the municipality. Local administrators of the green card scheme could never be sure they had obtained all the information about applicants' income, for they did not trust information provided by other public institutions, and because they were concerned about the existence of undocumented income. They sought to ensure that beneficiaries "really" did meet the criteria. Their suspicion of fraud led them to instigate multiple police checks, despite these officially being made only for specific cases. The police officers in charge of the investigations sometimes carried out home visits, and tended to question eyewitnesses such as neighbors or the muhtar about the household's living conditions. There were cases when an applicant had no registered property, but a neighbor or the muhtar told the police that the applicant received income from a property registered under a relative's name, or that a member of the family had a well-paid job, thereby disqualifying the application. At the end of the day, these checks were insufficient to verify the existence of unofficial income, or to decide on eligibility.

The uncertainty was further fueled by the fact that not everyone meeting the criteria obtained a green card. The number of cards issued was in fact not indexed on the number of needy people, but dictated by other rationales. Senior officials at the Ministry of Health exerted pressure to curb the number of beneficiaries in each constituency, without specifying any criteria. Thus, in 2007 local administrators for the province of Adıyaman apparently only obtained twenty thousand green cards out of the one hundred thousand requested. The attribution criteria were thus inoperative, since the number of cards issued was not indexed on them. Under these conditions, local administrators applied their own criteria—not always exempt of all moral judgement—to "eliminate" applications that did in fact meet the criteria. In 2004 they apparently put an end to the green cards of certain Alevis rumored to have converted to Christianity.

Das and Poole have emphasized the often confusing nature of state documents and practices, both for those subject to these practices and for the officials in charge of applying them, blurring any clear-cut dividing line between legality and illegality (Das, Poole 2004b, 10). In the case of the green card scheme, Yoltar shows that these uncertainties fueled the applicants' impression of arbitrary decisions, generating suspicion and the feeling that things were unforeseeable. Applicants endeavored to maximize their chances by employing various tactics to ensure they obtained the card, even if it meant circumventing the official rules. Thus, certain applicants sought to obtain false attestations, including those generated by databases. Some people strove to make their tax and real estate data fit the criteria, drawing on the complicity of people they knew who worked in the local administrations involved.[20]

This type of tactic entails drawing on personal ties. Muhtars are among the figures people may turn to for this type of initiative. Thus, muhtars are solicited by applicants to support their attempts to influence a procedure. An example of this is the case of a man who sought to obtain a green card for his second wife, to whom he thus was by definition not officially married, and who was recorded under the household of her father, who was too wealthy for a green card. On several occasions the man asked the muhtar to testify to this situation when he went to the green card bureau, or to see a lawyer to get him certify that he had three children with his second wife. The muhtar thus supported this man in his attempt to circumvent the regulations.

The fact that the rules are confusing generates uncertainty, which prevents their being implemented in a predictable manner. This uncertainty impacts the experience citizens have of the "state," with a general feeling that things do not follow procedures, thus fueling suspicion. This drives a demand or longing for the state, together with attempts to circumvent its functioning by arrangements, intercession, and workarounds. And so, even though the objective power of the muhtars in distributing assistance has diminished, they are still involved as an accessible means of support and redress. What matters is not so much any real capacity for influence, as belief in their capacity to support attempts to broker an arrangement.

Embodied experiential knowledge, the crux of the muhtars' function, is being sidelined and rivaled by improvements in another type of state knowledge, namely databases. These two types of knowledge and government are not mutually exclusive. In another context, Akarsu shows that personalization can go hand-in-hand with the digitalization of many administrative procedures (2020, 32) in what in Turkey is called *e-devlet* ("e-state"). A vision in terms of modernization would tend to suggest that the rationalization and digitalization are destined to eclipse the personalized forms of government. Yet in fact they coexist and interact. Following the partial systematization of techniques to register citizens, the muhtars' objective role has diminished and been substantively altered. They are increasingly dependent on institutions to grant resources. Their role is increasingly indirect, providing support and guidance for inhabitants in their dealings with the authorities. But they also act as a means of redress and source of help to circumvent official procedures.

The coexistence of different procedures to perform the same functions expands the leeway available to muhtars, who may choose to assume certain prerogatives that are no longer exclusively theirs. Yet rather than wishing to defend their "turf" come what may, many muhtars opt to withdraw from certain prerogatives that could potentially expose them to risks, given the conditions in which they operate. The coexistence of several procedures to perform the same functions also increases leeway for citizens, who may select their interlocutors, choose their procedures, and decide to a certain extent how they interact with the state, opting to address the muhtar, a party, or a more impersonal administration. What parameters govern these choices? In this complex setup, why do some people in some situations view muhtars as more appealing than other institutions?

Chapter 4

THE RESIDENTS' CHAMPION

THE MUHTARLIK IS ONE OF THE INSTITUTIONS THROUGH WHICH
Turkish citizens experience the state. And given that muhtars carry out various
functions, there are many opportunities for coming into contact with them. Yet
muhtars' exclusive prerogatives are on the decline, and citizens can increasingly
do without them. What are the specificities of the muhtarlık in comparison to
other, more "bureaucratic" administrations? Which citizens use them? Why?
And in what ways?

The muhtarlık is a familiar institution. It is more accessible and less impersonal than other administrations, due to the proximity of muhtars and the
type of relationship they have with neighborhood residents. Citizens thus make
extensive use of muhtars, calling on them, for example, to act in matters that
fall far outside their official powers. Interestingly, muhtars tend to accept these
extensive uses, and to position themselves as residents' champions, sometimes
even against public policies. However, this is only part of the picture, this image being first and foremost a performance. Beyond that image, the muhtars'
position, caught between social demands and institutional constraints, is much
more diverse and context-dependent.

A FAMILIAR INSTITUTION

Muhtarlıks come across as being more accessible than other administrations. In
her work about certain local-level institutions in France, such as post offices or

social centers, Siblot has put forward the notion of "familiar institutions." This term refers to multipurpose institutions serving a socially varied public, with specific relational practices set in a local environment and grounded in the uses people make of them (Siblot 2006, 124, 203). This familiarity implies proximity, even connivance, between street-level public workers and local residents. It is based on activating sociable relations, and leads flexibility in providing services. All three aspects apply to muhtarlıks too. This familiarity stands in sharp contrast to the dominant social imaginary of the state in Turkey. Babül convincingly shows that since the early republican period, the state has been widely viewed as the agent of modernization, and thus as having a civilizing duty: "The social imaginary that shaped the bureaucratic realm in Turkey was informed by a long-standing distinction between the governor and the governed" (Babül 2017, 43). She further argues that "bureaucratic authority and governmental legitimacy depended on the distinction of government workers from *halk* (the common people). This distinction was based on the bureaucrat's ability to embody and channel the state [. . .] mainly due to their high level of education and proper institutional enculturation" (Babül 2017, 42).

Conversely, this familiarity is grounded in specific routine practices, and transpires in the everyday relationship between muhtars and their inhabitants. This is particularly visible in the comparative proximity between muhtars and residents, and in the limited level of institutional domination. The muhtarlık is not solely an administrative entity. Rather, it is very much situated within local social relations, often acquaintanceship. This influences how citizens relate to it.

Reduced Social Distance

First, the muhtarlık is the institution that is closest to the population in geographical and social terms. This proximity is what sets the muhtar apart from the Weberian ideal-type bureaucrat characterized by distance from those administered. Consequently, muhtars and citizens relate to each other with greater proximity than in a classic administrative situation.

In terms of geography, a muhtar must have lived for at least six months in the neighborhood, though most have resided there for far longer. This local anchoring clearly distinguishes muhtars from "street-level" public agents who tend to be external to the society they administer. The police administration even prohibits officers from serving in their hometowns, because it considers it suspect "if an officer [is] invested too much in one locale, suggesting a possible case of corruption of disloyalty to the *teşkilat* [organization]" (Akarsu 2020: 29). In other cases, even when "street-level" public agents such as teachers or imams happen to live in the neighborhoods where they work, this anchoring does not form an integral part of their role.

To some extent, this proximity is also social. Muhtars tend to be minor notables from the upper social categories in the neighborhood, though this is not systematic. In well-off (E) or highly stratified neighborhoods—for example, those undergoing gentrification (B and C)—they are not necessarily from the upper social echelons. Still, among elected representatives and officials overall, they are the closest to inhabitants. This is all the more important bearing in mind that Turkey's bureaucrats have traditionally based their claims to governmental legitimacy on standing above the people–what Babül calls "bureaucratic distinction" (2017, 42–43). Muhtars in working-class neighborhoods might figure among those who have done fairly well for themselves, though their immediate entourage still includes people with limited resources and little education. It is rare for muhtars to treat these disadvantaged populations scornfully or condescendingly–a common occurrence in certain other administrations.

An important factor reducing the social distance between muhtars and inhabitants is the former's level of education. From the time of the Ottoman reforms to the early Republican period, education formed the backbone of this "bureaucratic distinction" (Babül 2017, 45). It is still a precondition for working as a public-facing official to have completed secondary schooling, while primary schooling is required to be a municipal or provincial councillor. But the only requirement for being a muhtar is knowing how to read and write Turkish.[1] A 2004 study carried out in Çankaya, a predominantly upper-middle-class and educated central district of Ankara, established that 27.4 percent of the muhtars held primary school qualifications, 21.6 percent held middle school qualifications, 35.3 percent high school qualifications, and 15.7 percent university qualifications (Şevran 2005, 102). Purely for comparison, in 1989 11.8 percent of Istanbul metropolitan municipal councillors held primary school qualifications, 13.8 percent held middle school qualifications, 17.6 percent high school qualifications, 5.9 percent vocational school qualifications, 47.1 percent undergraduate qualifications, and 3.9 percent postgraduate qualifications (Erder and İncioğlu 2008, 77).[2] Figure 2, in chapter 1 of this book, attests to a shaky grasp of spelling. Ebru was the only one of the muhtars I followed to have attended university; Duran held only primary school qualifications. In both geographical and social terms, muhtars are closer to their inhabitants than any other category of officials.

Several studies have shown administrative relations to be characterized by extensive social domination, particularly towards the lower classes. In 1950s Britain, families from disadvantaged working-class neighborhoods had an awkward relation to institutions, leading them to cast public administrations and their officials as "them," from the same world as bosses and notables (Hoggart 1957). As Babül (2017) argues, this "bureaucratic distinction" is particularly strong in Turkey. Yet people often consider the muhtar as one of their own (*sır katibi*), highlighting the specificity of this figure (Arıkboğa 1998, 162).

One final dimension to social proximity is acquaintanceship. Babül notes that "bureaucratic authority is linked to the bureaucratic subject's distinction from the governed. This distinction requires government workers to disengage themselves from the community as much as possible, and prohibits them from undertaking the sorts of mundane activity that might put them in contact or on an equal footing with the people whom they govern" (2017: 47). This, again, clearly distinguishes the muhtars from other officials. Relationships with the muhtar may overlap with acquaintanceships built up over time within the complexities of local society. Once again, this is not systematic. Acquaintanceship is very unequally distributed, and less relevant in very populous neighborhoods with high levels of residential mobility. Acquaintanceship produces social obligations, influencing how people relate to the muhtar. In this respect, the muhtarlık relies on familiarity and even intimacy to a greater extent than any other political or administrative post (Yildirim, Ucaray-Mangitli, and Tas 2017, 669).[3] When administrative relations are entwined with acquaintanceships, this tends to foster a degree of flexibility in how inhabitants relate to the muhtar. All these forms of familiarity reduce the distance within the administrative interaction. More generally, the muhtarlık collapses the assumed social distance between the "state" and the residents.

Semibureaucratic Interactions

How does this familiarity with the muhtarlık transpire in the way people use and interact with their muhtar? Muhtarlıks constitute in-between spaces which blur any strict distinction between public and private (Yildirim, Ucaray-Mangitli, and Tas 2017, 665). Buildings and the physical arrangements through which institutions materialize partially mold proper behavior and shape legitimate uses (Dubois 2010, 37). Babül argues that "government spaces such as courtrooms and factories, which house encounters between ordinary people and government workers, are imagined as educational environments where the latter guide the former about the proper ways of conduct" (2017, 47). We shall see that, on the contrary, the layout of muhtarlıks and the way they are used are not solely bureaucratic, but also lend themselves to conviviality.

Muhtarlıks are physically set within the social life of the neighborhood, as can be seen in their layout. Certain muhtars—such as Gaffar, Ahmet until 1997, and Cemil until 2001—carried out their tasks in a private or professional space not specifically dedicated to that purpose. When there are dedicated premises, these are often adjacent to a place that is part of neighborhood life, such as a park, square, or cafe. Premises provided by municipalities are often part of

FIGURE 8. Several muhtarlık premises provided by a district municipality and grouped around a cafe. Istanbul, 2013. Photograph by the author.

larger complexes (as is the case for muhtarlıks B, C, E, and F).[4] In neighborhood D, a problem area, the muhtarlık backs onto a municipal park and the police station. In neighborhood E the muhtarlık is next to the post office and a common room where inhabitants, especially elderly ones, come and sit, drink tea, chat, and watch television.

Being embedded in local life contributes to the central multipurpose nature of muhtarlıks. Relations in muhtarlıks are not limited to bureaucratic interaction centered on administrative proceedings; they extend to other areas. This transpires both in the forms of interaction and sociability, and in the wide-ranging and diverse uses inhabitants make of the institution.

In material terms, a muhtarlık is halfway between an administrative office and a lounge. The premises are arranged in such a way that several people may sit there, with several chairs, a sofa, or a bench. If someone enters while a conversation is underway, they wait in the room and listen to what is going on, sometimes taking part in the conversation. Unlike in a conventional government office where members of the public line up at a counter, there is no material barrier or line demarcating a confidentiality zone, and both physically and symbolically separating the muhtar from the public. The status of the place is not self-evident, and often needs to be spelled out or negotiated. In neighborhood F, an outlying neighborhood dating from the 1960s that is home to people from the rural exodus, an old woman wearing a headscarf and clearly from a modest background entered the muhtarlık. Fikret's office looked comparatively modern and administrative, with a computer. The visitors' chairs were placed on a kilim. The woman asked if she should take off her shoes, as one would do in a house. Fikret answered no, but without mocking her question or appearing surprised by it. This contrasts with Koğacıoğlu's analysis of courtrooms, where the judges and the prosecutors considered it their mission—and a natural outcome of their position—to "educate" people in how to participate in the culture of the state (2008).

Relations within the muhtarlık differ from those in a classic administration. In most muhtarlıks, distant administrative interaction is not the norm. The way people are received in muhtarlıks is only partly codified according to specifically administrative procedures distinct from other forms of social activity. Relations in the muhtarlıks reproduce other forms of sociability pertaining outside the realm of politics and the administration. Certain inhabitants stop off for a chat when in the vicinity of muhtarlık. In muhtarlık E, a man arrived accompanied by his daughter, who was about twelve. He said he had come from the post office, where the situation was chaotic. Ebru answered, "Yes, apparently the [IT] system is down." The man did not appear to have anything specific to ask. He spoke of Ebru's father, whose portrait was on display in the muhtarlık office, and cited him as an example of father-daughter relations. He proffered some spiritual religious words, to which Ebru answered "*amin*" (amen) before leaving. It is possible that this man had come to make some request but had decided not to do so in my presence. Still, this type of visit without any precise or declared purpose occurs frequently, and does not seem anomalous. "Visits" are an important form of sociability outside politics, and are performed in the event of bereavements, births, and celebrations, or simply as a mark of courtesy. They draw on general repertoires of social relations such as friendship, sympathy, lending a hand, and recognition. They bring to light the existence of interpersonal ties "naturally" extending to a political dimension (Briquet 2005, 34). As studied elsewhere, intimization is the transmission of anything associated with the private realm, such as family or friends, into the public-political sphere. Through intimization, actors transmit their experiences into the public political sphere via specific roles and relations "inherent" to the private domestic sphere (Yildirim, Ucaray-Mangitli, and Tas 2017, 664). Depending upon the context, Ebru described the people who came to see her as *sakin* (inhabitants) or *vatandaş* (citizens), but also at times as *misafir* (guests or visitors).

In most cases, muhtars welcome their visitors and take care to be convivial in how they relate to residents. This is especially the case when they know them. "Welcome, Mehmet; take a seat," Fikret called out on seeing him arrive on his premises. Even when she did not know her visitors, Ebru, in her upmarket and well-educated neighborhood, tended to greet them with a cordial, "Come in, welcome" (*Buyurun hoş geldiniz*).

Even when there is no prior acquaintanceship, impersonal and formal terms of address are comparatively rare in muhtarlıks. Muhtars and their "guests" often use terms from the register of fictive kinship.[5] When an elderly man entered Bediz's premises, whom she clearly could not immediately place, she called him *amca* (uncle, a term frequently used when speaking to an older man). Because she was young, many visitors called Ebru *kızım* (my daughter). Fictive kinship brings about ties, together with moral obligations working both ways: "Familial metaphors serve to strengthen ties between person and firm and, by extension, the state" (Alexander 2002, 227). This shapes the relationship along personal and affective lines, rather than in a neutral and anonymous register promoting an abstract idea of civic citizenship. Various "tie signs" between protagonists– hugs, familiar modes of address, the use of first names, hearty greetings, and so on–often indicate the personal nature of the relationship (Goffmann 1959). They turn friendship, sympathy, solidarity, loyalty, and solicitude into acts. To this extent, the muhtar differs from the figure of the anonymous, impersonal bureaucrat relating to citizens on the basis of "bureaucratic indifference," a characteristic trait of bureaucracies. Unlike the bureaucrat, muhtars do not become humorless robots even when sitting behind their desks. They do not lose their identity or become "nonhuman," nor do they reject anyone who does not fit into their categories (Herzfeld 1993, 1).

Muhtars often offer their visitors tea. This may occur in other administra- tions when a visitor is received by someone in charge, but that happens far less often. In muhtarlıks, the offer of tea is not systematic. It happens either when the muhtar knows the citizen personally, when someone is kept wait- ing, or when other people in the room have been offered tea and a new visitor arrives. Offering tea is a mark of conviviality, and it turns the interaction into a reception. When a man Fikret clearly knew arrived in his office, though the office was full, Fikret said, "Sit down; drink your tea." During her first election campaign, Bediz used an argument based on conviviality, thus implementing an "intimization" strategy (Yildirim, Ucaray-Mangitli, and Tas 2017, 673). Since it is often women who come to get official documents, she emphasized that they would be more comfortable with a woman muhtar and could drink their tea: "They say, 'Ah, my muhtar, we voted for you on purpose. Look, we come to see you and drink your tea and coffee. But if we went to see a male muhtar, we would not enter the room and would leave as soon as we got our papers. We wouldn't be able to smoke a cigarette and drink tea.'" With the time taken to prepare it—Turkish tea needs to be left to brew for at least ten minutes—and then drink it, tea implies a lengthy interaction during which people chat. Offer- ing tea may also be a way for the muhtar to try to prolong the interaction, strike up a conversation, or place their visitor under an obligation. This differs from the situation Lipsky describes for street-level bureaucrats, who need to limit their number of "clients" and keep interactions brief due to their heavy workload.

When the muhtar and visitor know one another–and sometimes, though not systematically, when they do not–the simple fact of requesting administrative documents often leads the applicant to explain the circumstances behind the request. A man arrived in muhtarlık F who clearly knew Fikret, addressing him with the familiar pronoun *sen*.[6] He explained that he had come because he had found work and needed certificates to draw up the contract. Fikret issued the papers and asked for more information about the man's new job. Of his own accord, the man told him what his salary would be. Muhtars find out about many aspects of their constituents' private lives through this sort of conversation.

Often the encounter generates an exchange of more general information not necessarily relating to why the visitor is there. Sometimes this is instigated by the resident. An elderly man entered muhtarlık F when two other residents were already sitting there. Fikret's son made fun of him for having half elec-trocuted himself while doing some home repair, and the old man related the incident in detail, to the others' amusement. He then initiated an exchange of information, asking Fikret: "And what are you up to?" Often it is the muhtar who asks after visitors. Another day, when a man entered the muhtarlık, Fikret asked him how his family was, using the familiar pronoun. Evidently somebody in the man's family was ill. Conversations touch on numerous topics, with gossip commonplace, thus placing the muhtarlıks within the register of local sociabil-ity. Everyday sociability, administrative dealings, and requests for assistance or electoral backing are not separate dimensions, but are continually mixed together in discussions.

Acquaintanceship creates obligations. It is also something that both par-ties actively sustain. A woman came to ask Fikret for her identity card. Fikret spoke to her using the familiar pronoun, asking after someone they both knew who was ill. He almost apologized for not visiting: "We drive past, but we don't stop. I hope she gets better." As she was leaving, Fikret asked her to pass on his greetings, and promised he would come by. This exchange shows how visiting the sick is an obligation which Fikret had clearly not performed. In muhtarlık E, an elderly woman came to get a residency certificate for a relative. Pretending she never passed by the office, she apologized for not coming often enough. She and Ebru exchanged news, and the conversation turned to the betrothal of one of the woman's female relatives. The woman's excuse shows that ac-quaintanceship obliges the inhabitants to visit fairly consistently, especially as it is comparatively easy to go and see the muhtar. This woman could have gone to the population bureau for her residency certificate. But perhaps the fact of knowing Ebru encouraged her to go to the muhtar instead. For people in the muhtar's circle, it is deemed good form to go and get certificates from them, so as to nurture ties.

Muhtars are one of various embodiments of "the state." They humanize the relationship between the rulers and the ruled, which is often characterized elsewhere by impersonal relations. Due to the ties built up between muhtars and citizens, either previously or during the interaction, the relation is not purely bureaucratic. The muhtarlık is close: friendlier than a classic administration. Often it is a personalized institution. People mostly say not that they go to the muhtarlık, but that they go to the muhtar. The muhtarlık is a place where people talk and explain their individual circumstances, and this further sustains its familiarity.

Attenuated Institutional Dominance

To what extent does this familiarity attenuate the domination within administrative relations (Siblot 2006, 200, 228)? Do people go to the muhtar as they would visit an acquaintance? Despite this familiarity, muhtars, like any other officials, still exert domination over neighborhood residents through their status, power, prerogatives, and relational capital. However, the institutional domination muhtars exert is attenuated in comparison to that exerted by other officials. This is in part due to their reduced social distance—but mainly to their dependence on residents.

A significant aspect of this reduced institutional domination pertains to how citizens—and muhtars, as residents—relate to the law. In neighborhoods of squatter settlements, inhabitants often have an ambivalent relationship to the legal order. And the muhtars tend to have lived in such unauthorized dwellings (*gecekondu*) at odds with legal requirements. Fikret, rather than seeking justification, asserted with some pride: "I have always lived in a *gecekondu*. Even if the building has five floors it is *kaçak* (illegal)." This shared experience of illegality produces a degree of connivance that would be far harder to establish with an official who by definition represents the "law." Even in better-established neighborhoods, muhtars often have a distant relationship with the law. In Cemil's muhtarlık, as in most official places, a big official poster reminds visitors that it is forbidden to smoke, and indicates the amount of the fine. Cemil usually covers this poster with other material and openly makes fun of it when smoking with visitors in his office.

However, the main reason why the institutional domination exerted by the muhtars differs from that wielded by street-level officials is that they are elected. Muhtars depend on voters for reelection. This clearly distinguishes their relationship with neighborhood residents from that which administrators may have. To a certain extent, this dependency may even reverse the institutional domination. Two weeks before local elections, a man came to Fikret's muhtarlık to collect his voter card. Fikret's son received him in the secretary's office. But instead of letting his son manage this basic paperwork as he usually would, Fikret, who heard him from his office, came out and engaged the man in conversation. Using the familiar pronoun *sen*, he asked him if he had retired. The man answered he was waiting to do so. By way of reply, Fikret said he was running for election: "I am a candidate, as you know. I think well of you, but I don't know what you think." The man replied hesitantly: "I have not given it any thought yet. Good luck. We used to have a lot of votes, but now—well, I'll be off." Fikret was implicitly requesting that the man vote for him. This sheds light on a relation of mutual interdependence, in which the neighborhood resident is not the only one asking for favors. This relation is much more symmetrical than a classic administrative relation. The muhtarlık is the only administration in which citizens exert a certain power over the person sitting behind the desk–and one vote to be elected muhtar is of greater weight than one to be elected mayor or president. This implies a relation of mutual yet unequal dependency. The specific power relation between muhtars and inhabitants means that the muhtarlık is an institution–perhaps the only one–in which the average neighborhood resident can legitimately ask for something.

WIDE-RANGING USES OF THE MUHTARLIK

What effects does this specific relation have on how inhabitants relate to their muhtar, and the uses they make of him or her? There is no doubt a link between the institution's familiarity, the specific power relation, and the fact that residents make very extensive uses of the muhtarlık. They go to the muhtar for many different reasons: to ask for information, for individual or collective services, or to make all kinds of requests. They turn to them for specific types of help, often approaching them for advice or to plead their cause, or else to request personalized help or intercession on their behalf. Let us briefly go over the four main types of use, going from those which are closest to the muhtar's official prerogatives to those which are furthest removed: requests for services and administrative help, personalized demands, requests for help in finding work or housing, and requests to mediate in conflicts.

Requests for Services and Administrative Help

First of all, residents approach muhtars with numerous requests for public services. This phenomenon in fact predated the 2005 Law on Municipalities granting muhtars responsibility for determining residents' collective needs and communicating them to institutions. Back in the nineteenth century, muhtars forwarded requests about public services from residents to the authorities. Requests and petitions addressed by subjects to the Porte nearly always bore the stamps of muhtars, often alongside those of imams and notables (Güneş 2014, 113–14; Lafi 2011; Lévy-Aksu, 2012, 302).

In a 1995 questionnaire study on involvement with local authorities in Turkish cities,[7] respondents reported how weary they were with local authorities, and how remote they felt from them. Still, muhtars topped the ranking of those deemed able to solve neighborhood problems, and city problems too. Overall, 36 percent of respondents placed them ahead of mayors, whom they rated at 32 percent. This rating of muhtars rose to 38 percent in *gecekondus* and 39 percent in more modest milieus. According to another study carried out ten years later in Ankara, when residents had a problem relating to their neighborhood they turned to muhtars first (62.1 percent of the time), far more than to municipal councillors (24.2 percent; Şevran 2005, 132). İlhan, the muhtar of an old upper-class neighborhood for thirty-five years, said, "When they have a complaint, inhabitants come to me, because they trust me. But I tell them to also go directly to the municipal building." A municipal official spontaneously admitted, "For citizens, the municipality and bureaucracy may be problematic. . . . It is only as a last resort that citizens come [to the district municipality]." To cite but one instance I witnessed, an elderly woman came in and explained to Ebru that she was there because her electricity was not working, adding that garbage in the bin on her streetcorner had not been collected for a week: "I've come to see you as you look after things, nobody else can solve that."

Requests relate to many different matters. Duran said, "I look after all sorts of matters here. If there is lots of mud on the road, I look after it. If the tarmac is in a bad way, I look after it. If the mains burst, I look after it." Bediz said that she took care of such varied matters as rubbish collection, extermination, cleaning, public lighting, street furniture, parks, electricity transformers, and refuse containers. Said Ebru, "We are intermediaries between citizens and the state. When I say state, [...] that might be the municipality or subgovernor's office. That is to say, we are there for the problems they haven't been able to solve." It may also be a matter of relaying requests to open a post office or school.

Residents go to see the muhtar with requests concerning defective public services and infrastructure, hoping that they will relay them to the public authorities. Although certain studies have portrayed such uses as specific to poorly equipped outlying neighborhoods (Wedel 1999, 190–91), they also occur in wealthier neighborhoods, even though needs are less pressing there. Thus, Ebru explained that she had "got a police station built." Her neighborhood depended on a comparatively distant police station, something residents complained about. She explained that she had gotten things rolling with the district municipality and the district head of security, who apparently granted her request.

Shortly after being elected in 2014, the mayor of the district to which neighborhood E was attached asked the muhtars to tell him of any neighborhood problems. Ebru drew up and passed on a list of twenty or so problems: stray animals (issues of cleanliness, and the need for setting up an animal pound); pavements taken up by restaurants and their delivery bikes, blocking pedestrians and making it impossible for residents to park their cars; the neighborhood park's dangerous state of disrepair, and so on. Ebru said she had "prepared this document based on complaints made to me, things I've heard about, that people talk about the whole time." The role of muhtars is thus primarily that of responding to the complaints and requests they receive.

This channel enables inhabitants to exert a degree of control over public bodies. In muhtarlık F, a man who clearly knew Fikret–they used the familiar pronoun when talking to each other–complained about the local water board. When the workers came to repair the mains, they damaged a staircase and left without repairing it. An individual resident probably would not be able to do much about such a situation. But this sort of denunciation carries more weight if it passes through an official intermediary. Fikret immediately called the head of the local water board, an acquaintance, to tell him about the situation and ask him to sort it out. Residents thus resort to the muhtar to relay requests for collective services, but also to defend their interests before the public authorities, particularly in the event of negligence. In a way, the muhtarlık is an institution that defends the residents—more so than it defends, say, those who merely work in the neighborhood.

Second, many residents go to the muhtar to get certain administrative tasks performed with their help of the muhtar—to get forms filled, to ask for social assistance, or to get help with any kind of procedure. This includes matters unrelated to the muhtars' official prerogatives. The muhtarlık premises are often equipped with faxes and printers, which many residents ask to use. One day, a woman arrived in muhtarlık E and asked permission to print out a two-page resumé. Ebru was fairly cold and reticent: "That is what Internet cafes are for!" "I couldn't find one," the woman replied. Ebru answered, "There is one two roads away. [. . .] Okay this time, but I don't want to do it for everybody." Ebru printed out the resumé and glanced over it. The woman asked if she owed her anything. Ebru hesitated for a second, then replied, "No, it's fine." The woman thanked her and left. A few moments later, an old woman came in and said she wanted to send a money transfer. Ebru told her the post office was just next door, but explained to her what to do. The old lady thanked her, placed a form in front of her, and using the familiar pronoun asked if she could check that she had not made any mistakes. Ebru graciously replied that she had never sent money herself, but nevertheless went over the form and said: "It's fine; you have filled it out completely." The woman left satisfied. The muhtarlık is used as an open office for all sorts of paperwork. This type of use is very common, as shown by scenes observed even in the most educated and wealthiest neighborhood in my sample.

Individual, Even Personal Requests

Second, residents also approach their muhtar with private requests that sometimes have nothing to do with the muhtars' perogatives. Bediz explained:

> They say, "My muhtar, can you help us write our request?" and I write it. Or they arrive and say, "My muhtar, I have to go there, can you tell me the way?" Or else,

"We're going to get assistance; can you tell us who to go see?" They come for all that. [...] It will be for [social] assistance, or the hospital, or someone whose prepaid card has been canceled. "Can you write a request?" Or else someone who doesn't have insurance and comes to get one. [...] Or someone who comes: "My mother is bedridden; can you help her get disability benefit?" So I help. [...] I say, "Go to the hospital, ask for a disability report, and come back here; I will help you with the whole thing."

This is also true for simple things that only take a phone call. Even Ebru, in her wealthy district, said, "We are the front line between the citizen and the state when they have been unable to make contact. [...] You have an old man who calls: 'My little Ebru, my daughter, my pretty daughter, the electricity has been cut off at my home. Can you try to find out why?.'" Studies have examined the way personal requests are part of the job of local elected officials in other contexts: "Personal applications, recommendations, and 'string-pulling' are an integral part of the job of an elected official. [...] Elected officials are constantly approached by citizens requesting their help" (Mattina 2004a, 132).

These requests are based on the idea that calling on the muhtar will increase the likelihood of success, because the muhtar knows how to formulate the requests and to whom to address them. Thus, it is common for inhabitants to ask the muhtar to get them a hospital bed, thinking that if the muhtar handles the request it will be given priority treatment. This is why inhabitants request that muhtars oversee their applications, for example, if a request for social assistance has been turned down. Duran explained: "Of course sometimes I may see that someone has not been treated fairly [*mağdur*], and I chase up their case. (...) I approached an institution, I drew up your requests, and included the necessary paperwork. [...] If you get a negative response, you tell me and I will intervene again. Or else I will write to someone else as well. [...] In that case, I pick up the phone and ask [the institution] again. I ask, 'Why didn't you proceed with that?' Of course, when it comes to assistance some citizens may be right, others may be wrong. If an injustice has been committed you can be sure I'll sort it out; that's to say I've helped lots of people." Duran thus presented himself as a means of redress.

People go to the muhtar for help in unblocking a situation, or to ask them to intercede. I was present when Bediz was trying to get a request for free health treatment accepted. She phoned the municipal employee in charge of social assistance and explained the applicant's situation, insisting on their financial difficulties. The employee asked her to send the person around, and promised to look after the matter. This did not guarantee that the request would be successful, but the application was no longer just another anonymous request and would now be processed, perhaps with a bit more attention. Bediz presented the matter as one of obligation: the municipal employee promised Bediz that the application would be processed, just as Bediz had promised the resident that she would look into it.

The boundary between requests for information, advice, intercession, or even circumvention of the rules is often not clear-cut. As Ebru observed: "About schools, [...] people ask, 'My son or daughter is about to start school. Where should we enroll them, what school would you recommend, what is school X like? Apparently you know someone in that school; can we arrange it, can we get them enrolled?'" This blurring of boundaries is also visible in the way inhabitants tend to present requests for intercession or circumvention of rules as requests for information.

Requests to Act as a Real Estate and Employment Agency

But requests to muhtars do not relate solely to public services and dealings with public bodies. Third, many neighborhood residents turn to muhtars as intermediaries–for example, when looking for a job, or for housing. Even muhtars who are not real estate agents by profession frequently receive and transmit requests and offers of accommodation. I saw Ahmet and Bediz do so. Certain landlords even insist that the tenancy agreement be signed at the muhtarlık.

People also turn to muhtars for help finding a job even in an upmarket district like Ebru's. People drop by to drop off their resumés, or to ask if any jobs are available. These requests concern not only the public sector but also private companies or individuals, particularly domestic services (Horasan 1992, 89–90). Potential employers also approach the muhtars; Bediz mentioned hotel managers and police officers looking for unskilled workers, people to clean and make tea. Fikret received a phone call from a man looking for work in the private sector, and said to him straight out, "You have to be a party member"—clearly referring to the AKP. The man answered that he was a member. Fikret went on:

"Fine; in that case there's no problem. It's the [AKP] neighborhood head who's handling it." Fikret gave the caller his name and phone number. Though he did not handle the work application himself, he explained to the caller what to do.

The reason muhtars are approached by neighborhood residents looking for jobs or accommodations is that they are well informed, and also that they are likely to intercede on an applicant's behalf or recommend somebody. One day, a woman whom Ebru knew called her looking for a job. Ebru told her that she knew a woman who was looking for a child minder, and asked what her conditions were. She then phoned the potential employer and identified herself as the muhtar. She explained the circumstances of her acquaintance, presenting her in a good light. She was careful to mention the woman's experience in looking after children, and also said that her elder sister knew the person well. Thus, she provided a guarantee of sorts. Ebru put the two women in contact, drawing on an affective register: "I'm sure you will like her (*seveceksiniz eminim*)."

Muhtars do not simply bring job seekers and potential employers into contact, but often also recommend someone looking for a job, or act as guarantors, relying on their reputation. However, this does not always suffice to get an application accepted; Fikret was unable to get his brother employed by an employer he knew indirectly.

Requests for Social Mediation

Fourth, and finally, thanks to their status, muhtars have an aura of officialdom, enjoy privileged contact with institutions, and are also generally viewed as reliable and bound to neutrality. In particular, inhabitants often turn to muhtars to act as mediators or arbitrators in family or neighborhood disputes (Şevran 2005, 140).

Bediz and Cemil, who run neighborhoods undergoing gentrification where there are bars and restaurants close to family dwellings, handled numerous complaints about noise. When the noise was caused by young people who had had too much to drink, Bediz and Cemil got the police to intervene. But they might also intervene directly, drawing on their moral authority. On receiving complaints about excessive noise from a restaurant, Bediz went in person to see whether to pass the complaints on to the authorities. In one case she was convinced that the restaurant owner had rectified the situation when he showed her the soundproofing he had installed, and so she did not pass the complaints on.

Furthermore, people frequently approach muhtars to act as mediators in family disputes (Erder 1996, 75–79). Women contacted Bediz for help with marital problems, or when their husband did not bring any money in. Calling on a muhtar—especially a woman—for help in this way is understandable given women's reticence to file police complaints for family matters, particularly for domestic violence, for fear of being considered in the wrong or sent back to their husbands. Although laws against domestic violence exist, this does not translate directly into a feeling of being protected by the legal system, especially in working-class circles (Secor 2007, 44–45). Fikret, for instance, said that inhabitants came to him with marital disputes—particularly women beaten by their husbands, or husbands seeking to get rid of their wives. Duran had also handed this type of problem, especially with women or children: "He turns his child out, or his father has beaten him, or he has run away. The child doesn't have any resources; he is hungry and comes to see you. You take him in, you look after him as if he were your own child. First you fill his stomach, perhaps you give him a bit of pocket money, then you take him back home. 'Look, it's your child.' You get involved in this type of problem. Or else two young people fall in love, [. . .] the families don't want them [to marry], they run away. One of the families is from the west, the other from the east. [. . .]. They come: 'come on, my muhtar, sort this out or reconcile our two families' [. . .]. You go to these families: 'Look, they like each other; don't separate people who love one another, come on.' You tell them and try to convince them—if it's possible, of course. And if you don't manage, there is the law."

Muhtars may turn to official bodies: the police or the judiciary. Duran said he had pointed certain people in difficult situations toward a psychologist who worked in the local social center, or else begged a lawyer to take on their case: "Lots of lawyers—my thanks to them—I can beg them to give an hour of their time to someone I send." But in certain cases, muhtars try to sort out the conflict themselves. It can even extend to employing physical violence. Fikret mentioned a case in which he had personally given a violent husband a physical pummeling, as a lesson.

The wide range of these cases shows that inhabitants view the muhtar as a multipurpose resource person who should be capable of providing solutions to all types of problems, be they public, private, or personal. They expect the muhtar to relay their requests and also, often, to accompany, support, or intercede with institutions on their behalf. The "familiar" aspect of the institution and the fact that muhtars depend on residents for reelection are two factors explaining these wide-ranging uses of the muhtar's services. The muhtars' field of activity thus expands far beyond their official duties. It also reinforces the muhtar's embeddedness in neighborhood society.

SERVING AND CARING FOR NEIGHBORHOOD RESIDENTS

There is only partial overlap between the muhtars' tasks as officially defined and inhabitants' expectations and uses of them. How do muhtars react to these numerous requests that go far beyond their official duties? In general, muhtars consider responding to collective or individual requests to be an integral part of their role even when it exceeds their official tasks and substantively alters how they perform their occupation. Not only do they accept solicitations; they are careful to present themselves as serving their constituents, or even acting as their advocates. They do this in two main ways: by displaying their accessibility, and by adapting their function to serve inhabitants. But how far do muhtars go in defending their residents' interests?

Viewing Requests Kindly

Most muhtars refuse to view their role as merely issuing documents, and make it a point of honor to distance themselves from any purely administrative rationale. They claim to care deeply about satisfying inhabitants' requests. The public expects the muhtar to look after matters referred to them, and to ensure that residents' complaints are addressed. As a middle-class youngster interviewed by Anna Secor said: "When you go to the muhtar, he is supposed to do something, because he is your muhtar" (Secor 2007, 38).

In private, however, some muhtars complain about certain requests they deem exaggerated. Hikmet, serving in a predominantly middle-class educated neighborhood, criticized people's lack of autonomy, and denounced certain usages he felt inappropriate or improper: "Even someone with a headache comes to see the muhtar. 'Muhtar, I have a headache.' When someone's electricity is cut off, even though the state has set up . . . 155 to call the police, 187 the gas company, if you call 110 the firemen come . . . people don't do it. 'The electricity has been cut.' 'Call 187!' [. . .] What does it have to do with the muhtar? So the muhtar is going to call 187. Our people [*milletimiz*] are a bit . . . what? . . . There's a problem with a tap. . . . Is it the muhtar who is going to repair the tap?" Bediz used the word "chore" (*angaria*) to describe the reason for certain visits, before withdrawing it as "perhaps a bit strong." Still, that does not stop her from receiving inhabitants affably. Though muhtars sometimes perceive the extensive uses people make of them as being improper or burdensome, they make it a point of honor to publicly express and display their devotion to their residents and to provide individualized responses.

Duran said, "Until the evening, whatever happens to people, you can be sure you will try to find solutions. For things I don't know, I try calling institutions to get information and point them in the right direction." Bediz said proudly that she took individual interest in everyone. Although she was in a privileged neighborhood, Ebru–the youngest and most educated muhtar in my sample– noted that "people have problems relating to their private life but nobody to tell them to, so they come and say: 'You are my daughter, I would like to share this with you.' [. . .] They've been through negative stuff; they come and want to get it off their chest. My population tends to be middle-aged. I have very few young people. [. . .] You know, old people, after a certain time, are always talking and conversing, so they come and we chat. They can easily tell me all their problems, for [. . .] they don't think of me as their muhtar, but as their daughter [*sen muhtar değil sen bizim kızımızsın*]. They view me as a member of their household. It's very flattering; it makes me happy." Far from disapproving of being prescribed this role, Ebru proudly expressed the affective gratification it gave her.

Duran also emphasized his capacity to hear private matters in confidence: "Here we even share family secrets. Someone comes who is in distress, perhaps they are about to commit suicide and haven't found anybody else to go and see. [. . .] At the same time, the muhtar is a neighborhood psychologist." Fikret also emphasized that people could entrust personal problems in confidence: "We share all manner of private things. In other words, there is trust." Muhtars cultivate a caring image.

Arrangements

In addition to listening with a kindly ear to all manner of requests and things entrusted in confidence, a prime way muhtars show empathy is in adapting their role on a daily basis to better serve their residents. Thus Ebru keeps official summons left by the postmen for residents longer than the legal three-month period because people sometimes come to collect them later; she thereby displays a form of zeal in serving her constituents. Ahmet goes so far as to phone individuals when he knows they have not come to collect official papers, for a fine is increased if not paid on time. Equally, when postmen cannot find people for whom they have a registered delivery, Ahmet checks the addresses and looks up their telephone numbers, or even keeps the mail until residents come to collect it, to prevent it from being returned. He said this was not his job, but that he did it to "help."

When asked to provide information or fill out forms, muhtars generally comply with good grace: "Of course I fill them out. If they are due to receive something more [a benefit] of any kind, I'm the one who does it," Bediz said. They do a lot more than explain the procedures to residents: they help them with their applications, and even carry them out in their stead. One day, a resident phoned muhtarlık E and requested a paper for a member of his family. Ebru told the resident he had to get it at the population bureau, and explained where it was. She not only advised the resident to contact the relevant institution directly, but got additional information. She called her contact at the population bureau, using their first name, to request confirmation that the constituent could go and get papers for someone else. The constituent called back, and Ebru told him that the applicant had to go in person. Whenever they act as administrative intermediaries, give advice, or help residents with official procedures, muhtars exceed their official job definition.

This availability also transpires in their opening times. Although most muhtarlıks post fixed working hours, muhtars are flexible in how they apply them. Duran said he was required to be open eight hours per day, "but none of the muhtars I know do that. This phone is open twenty-four hours per day. Because at eight o'clock something is going to happen to a citizen. There'll be some business at the police station, they'll call, and you go to the station. Or there's a fire, and you rush over." He also mentioned cases of flooding or snow when he was up till the middle of the night. "After five o'clock I'm not obliged to pick up the phone, but [...] public institutions call you from time to time. [...] For example, they've received a tipoff about some accommodation, and the prosecutor's office decides to send out an inspection. [...] In certain situations the muhtar has to be present. So here, the muhtar does not in fact really have opening times. Especially with the population, in any case, there are things to be sorted out twenty-four hours a day." After telling visitors several times that inhabitants called on him at six in the morning, Fikret boasted that people liked him, explaining it in the following terms: "Because my door is open day and night, people can come at any time–and they know it–for any reason." Although certain muhtars, such as Ahmet and Ebru, seem less flexible about their opening times, all regularly made exceptions. Thus Bediz said, "Normally I am here until five o'clock. Sometimes they call and say, 'My muhtar, I'll come at five-thirty, can you wait?' I say, 'Of course,' and wait." The limits to muhtars' work are unclear, and are always up for negotiation. Certain inhabitants phone with requests for certificates. Others ask Bediz to drop off their papers on her way home, something she said she does with good grace: "I've taken papers to a lot of people's homes, and not a single one can say they've given me money."

Muhtars make it a point of honor to be reachable at any moment. Many hand out their mobile phone numbers. Bediz said she gives hers to everyone and tells them to call if necessary. I saw her almost tell someone off for not having her phone number. Muhtars allow business to spill over beyond official hours. As they are also the neighbors of those they administer, there are numerous interferences with their life outside work. Bediz expressed this in the following terms: "[When there are] discussions about the muhtarlık on the way there or back, you can't say, 'Ah, it's over, come back tomorrow.'"

Muhtars live in their neighborhoods. This means their availability is not limited in time and space to office business. It extends to all their daily behavior, including neighborhood relationships. One corollary of muhtars' acting within a dense web of comparative acquaintanceship, fed by questions of reputation and fueled by rumor, is the importance of maintaining a good image through their daily behavior. In his observations about notables, Weber emphasized the importance of "style of life" (*Lebensführung*) conferring prestige and destining them for domination: giving (resulting in moral debts), benevolence (a source of the "social esteem" accorded to notables), and forms of "honor behavior" whereby they enact their status (Weber 1978 [1921], vol. 1, 305–6). This helps explain why muhtars say they feel obliged to engage in certain practices and ways of being that validate their position and guarantee that their prestige is recognized. Fikret expressed things in these terms: "Votes [for the] muhtarlık go to you as a person. [...] Lifestyle is important."

The Rhetoric of Service

Why do muhtars accept these requests and role prescriptions in such a kindly manner? They have far more daily contact with their constituents than with officials. They are anchored in local society, with little administrative socialization and little hierarchical control. Therefore, the norms and practices underpinning their action resemble those of their constituents. As Duran emphasized, acceding to this type of request draws on widespread values of mutual help, assistance, and solidarity, which are shared by the muhtar, especially in the case of acquaintanceship. Ahmet expressed his feeling of obligation in the following terms: "I know everybody, it's as if everyone had brought me up [*herkesin elinde büyüdüm*], as if I had brought up their children [*onların çocukları benim elimde büyüdü*]. You become very close, you know them all well, you can't say no."

However, their alacrity is not wholly altruistic. Muhtars are in a relationship of dependency on those they administer, for it is the latter who elect them. This leads them to exceed their official obligations and try to satisfy their voting public. "Elected officials [. . .] know they cannot ignore or 'snub' someone who has come to ask them to intervene" (Mattina 2004a, 132). Like most elected officials, including those in other contexts, muhtars portray themselves as the population's servants. They deny all ambition or personal interest. They thus tend to say they owe their position to having yielded to the insistence of their constituents. They always present their initiative for running for office as coming from the population. Fikret explained: "People put pressure. I declared that I was a candidate twenty or twenty-five days before the election. For there weren't any strong candidates." His running thus "saved" the neighborhood from the prospect of a mediocre muhtar. Under these conditions, running becomes a "duty." Ebru, who took over her position when her father died, said the initiative had nothing to do with her: "The muhtarlık was not part of my plans. It was because they [the neighborhood residents] asked me to, the fact that they guided me, and because of what happened to my father. As so many people asked, I agreed." In this way, muhtars present their position as a matter of serving their neighborhoods.

The alacrity with which muhtars place themselves at the service of inhabitants transpires in the frequency with which they use the word *hizmet* (service)–featuring, for example in Duran's election slogan: "East, West, North, South, hand in hand to serve together! [*Doğusuyla, batısıyla, güneyiyle kuzeyle hep birlikte hizmet için elele!*]" It is an important term in Turkish political discourse (Copeaux 1996), and has also acquired a central place in AKP discourse, appearing in many of its slogans.[8] This rhetoric of service is not specific to muhtars, nor even to Turkey. "All elected officials, irrespective of whether their position is their livelihood, declare that they are the 'servants' of their fellow citizens" (Fontaine and Le Bart, 1994, 22). Bediz boasted that in her second election, the neighborhood residents voted for her because of the services she had rendered: "In fact it's hizmet; that is to say that if during my first term of office I hadn't done anything, they wouldn't have voted for me now, and I didn't waste anybody's vote [*kimsenin oyunu boşa harcadığım yok*]." She presented the votes given as a form of recompense for service rendered. Hizmet is a moral obligation for the giver, and it places an equal obligation on the recipient. This shared value thus justifies the requests inhabitants make of their muhtar, and the alacrity with which they respond.

Muhtars emphasize the qualities associated with hizmet, presenting themselves as hardworking, taking personal initiatives, and doing the utmost to obtain what they wish for their inhabitants. Fikret claimed that if residents had a matter to sort out with a public institution, he phoned and it was sorted out. He also boasted that residents knew this, and that he kicked up a fuss to make things happen. He even claimed nothing was impossible to obtain: "Sometimes it took time. [. . .] But if your style [*tarz*] is right, [. . .] you put pressure, you follow up . . . if you play things well, [. . .] that is to say, that if your attitude is being on the people's side, it works."

Backing Complaints about Public Policy

To some extent, muhtars side with their inhabitants' collective complaints against certain public policies. Some muhtars go so far as to provide inhabitants with resources for their protest, particularly in the form of contacts and information. Ebru expressed a feeling of obligation to support complaints and requests made by inhabitants against the authorities:

> As muhtar, I can't say I'm not supporting them. One way or another, you help. [. . .] You can't say, "'Go ahead and I'll support you from behind," or "Go ahead, but no one can see me." [. . .] The muhtar has to be wherever there is a problem. That's to say that we are here, in a way, to defend citizens' rights. [. . .] You are the

muhtar of a neighborhood, you were elected—well, you have to lend support. At the end of the day, people don't elect you just to be an intermediary with the state. They also elect you to share their unhappiness about lots of problems.

Muhtars do not systematically support all demands against official regulations. They do so only under certain conditions. First, they more readily become involved in this type of action when there is a consensus among neighborhood residents about the cause in question. They use various techniques to assess the support for a given request. Thus, Ebru at times used petitions to gauge residents' support, "for otherwise there is one person who wants it, and another who doesn't want it—how am I to know?" The level of support influences the way she defends a request before the authorities. Ebru sometimes advised inhabitants to use a petition. One day, she suggested to residents requesting a cat shelter that they collect signatures of those in favor of it, so that she could present it that way to the municipality. She thus used petitions not simply as a way to assess support, but also to give greater visibility to a demand with broad backing—and even, by helping to gather signatures, to boosting support and giving the demand greater weight. Muhtars may thus even play a leading role in mobilizing inhabitants.

However, it would seem that muhtars lend public support to their constituents' protests against institutions when it is a matter of fighting measures that harm residents and trigger widespread discontent. Two cases in which muhtars were involved in winning protests against public authorities help bring out the constraints and rationales at work. The first case concerned a protest by residents against changes to school zoning in neighborhood B in autumn 2013. There was no consultation about this top-down reform. Whereas schoolchildren in neighborhood B had previously attended a primary school with a very good reputation in a more upmarket neighborhood nearby, under this change they were sent to a relatively distant school with a poorer reputation. Bediz had been actively involved with the parent-teacher association of the well-reputed school for ten years. She took very much to heart this matter for which she knew she could obtain widespread support, even though it entailed placing herself in a difficult position vis-à-vis the public authorities. The fact that she asked me to stop recording when we spoke about this episode confirms the sensitive nature of her account.

She told of how she had openly disapproved of the change and warned the education officials that families would find a way to enroll their children in the old school without hesitating to use false proofs of residency. For her part, she had performed a kind of civil disobedience, accompanying all the families to enroll their children in the old school, with the support of the muhtar of the upmarket neighborhood. This way, nearly two hundred families managed to enroll their children in the old school, to the extent that the authorities, on receiving requests for exemptions, apparently told applicants to consult Bediz. Faced with this opposition, the subgovernor's office finally backed down and accepted to re-accept pupils into their old school. Bediz said that many inhabitants thanked her, mentioning this episode ahead of elections when stating their intention to vote for her.

It is difficult to assess what part Bediz played in the success of this protest. Far from being the only person protesting, she acted in concert with two other muhtars and the main hometown association in the neighborhood for people from the province of Siirt, together with Bedirhan, an AKP municipal councillor, who also originated from that province. Apparently the matter reached the ears of the prime minister, probably via this channel, since his wife also came from Siirt. Be that as it may, Bediz opposed the implementation of this measure by systematizing and even openly asserting how she got around the rules—a practice normally conducted discreetly and on a small scale.

Ebru, too, supported a protest by residents of her neighborhood, this time against a change to the traffic flow. The metropolitan municipality, in charge of the main thoroughfares, modified the traffic layout without consultation, transforming two previously calm and highly desirable roads into access roads for a bridge over the Bosporus—a plan that would have resulted in very heavy traffic, and in parking being forbidden. Residents set up a committee and tried various actions, including letters of complaint to the municipality and metropolitan municipality and a petition, but to no avail. They then hung banners at their windows criticizing changes to the traffic flow. Finally, Ebru explained she had called some friends at the television channel TGRT,[9] made it newsworthy, and it had appeared on TV. She recounted, "Once it went public, our voice was better heard. Afterward, things happened very quickly." Shortly afterward, the head of the municipal transport department finally accepted to meet the committee, and the old layout was reinstated. Ebru was not behind the initiative, but its instigators requested her support. She then cooperated with the committee, suggesting ideas and actions. She openly described the municipal plan as inept. She summed up her involvement in this protest: "As muhtar, I was the flag bearer." However, she did not claim that it had happened because of her, for there were twenty or thirty people actively involved.

These two neighborhood resident protests supported by muhtars were a matter of righting wrongs. Muhtars lend such initiatives legitimacy, and provide a certain number of resources, notably information, contacts, and experience. By underwriting the legitimacy of the initiative, they may also enable it to grow, expanding into new and hitherto unrelated circles. They thereby act as a conduit for relaying and supporting demands, for which there is no other institutionalized channel. Although not very visible, in certain cases this channel makes it possible to transmit microlocal preoccupations upward, and even to get the public authorities to back down.

In lending their support, muhtars privilege protests for which there is consensus among residents, and especially those not associated with any particular political alignment. An episode in neighborhood F in September 2012 provides an example of a muhtar not channeling a divisive local demand. Several dozen neighborhood residents were occupying a park due to be destroyed. This park was in the upper part of the neighborhood, which was strongly left-wing and had mainly Alevi residents. It had recently been upgraded by the district municipality (CHP). A few months later, the metropolitan municipality (AKP) undertook to raze it on the grounds that it was illegal, as indeed were nearly all the constructions in the sector, which was historically a squatter area. The occupiers said they had the backing of the district mayor, and the head of the local CHP branch publicly supported the protest. But Fikret did not show himself, and the protesters accused him of ignoring the residents' concerns. The muhtar from an adjacent neighborhood supported the occupiers, making Fikret's absence even more keenly felt. He expressed embarrassment about certain protests with a "political" dimension: "You take sides. The thing becomes political. About one single side. It becomes such-and-such a party."

As a matter of fact, the neighborhood was divided politically. This episode may be interpreted as articulating a divide between the inhabitants "from the top" (mainly Alevi and left-wing) and those "from the bottom" (who were mainly Sunni and closer to the AKP). It may also be seen as a confrontation between the district municipality and metropolitan municipality, coinciding with a party conflict between the CHP (which provided a service to residents "from the top") and the AKP (with little presence in the "upper" parts of the neighborhood). In this neighborhood where geographical, denominational, and political divides partly overlap, it was difficult for Fikret to explicitly support one side when a problem was associated with these divides–especially if he was not close to the side in question. It was also difficult for him, an AKP sympathizer, to oppose an institution controlled by this party. On occasion he also took up the defense of the "top" of his neighborhood, but in less politically marked situations (cf. chapter 9). It is not clear whether Fikret held back because only part of the population was protesting, or because this episode could be interpreted as a conflict between two institutions, or as a conflict between parties. It raises questions about the limits to the muhtar's support for residents and their demands.

It is clear that, in structural terms, muhtars do not operate as patented administrators. Any postulation that it is in their interest to strictly apply government orders is invalid. Consequently, their action is not defined solely by "state rationales."

ARBITRATING AND PERFORMING

Muhtars are thus generally swift to respond to inhabitants' requests. But it would be misguided to portray them as serving all their inhabitants' concerns, constantly defending their interests, including against the public authorities, as many local representatives do. For this is only one side of the coin. Muhtars are not really, or not just, local elected representatives representing their constituents' interests. They are also public agents acting as relays for the public authorities, including in sensitive issues like maintaining order. They are thus at the intersection of ascending and descending rationales.

Between Ascending and Descending Rationales

The history behind the creation of the May 1 / Mustafa Kemal neighborhood on the edge of the Ümraniye district on the outskirts of Istanbul may serve to illustrate how institutions and inhabitants project different functions onto the muhtarlık. This is one of various neighborhoods to have resulted from rural migrants settling on public lands in the 1960s and building unauthorized dwellings. In the 1970s the neighborhood was dominated by various left-wing organizations. A "people's committee" took control of the real estate market and changed the name of the neighborhood to May 1. It nurtured hopes of getting various public services provided, but encountered a legal void. Just like the committee itself, this unauthorized neighborhood had no legal status, being considered by the authorities as a rural zone. The "people's committee" set up a "committee of elders" who relayed residents' demands to the local authorities, and sought to obtain public services and facilities. Since this committee was anchored in the neighborhood, it was able to enter into negotiations with the public authorities, winning recognition as their interlocutor, and reinforcing its control over the zone. In 1978–79, the committee managed to get a cooperative, school, and health center opened. It then shifted its priority to obtaining the status of a muhtarlık, equating to official recognition, in order to facilitate its dealings with the authorities and obtain services (Aslan 2013 [2004], 159).

Shortly afterward, this neighborhood did obtain the status of muhtarlık, though in wholly different manner. The attempts by the committee were interrupted by the 1980 coup. One of the first measures the junta took was to institutionalize unauthorized neighborhoods without any legal existence, establish muhtarlıks, and make it obligatory to transmit a residency register to military command—all with a view to providing the authorities with more detailed knowledge of the population, so as to exert closer control over them. After changing the name of the neighborhood to Mustafa Kemal, military command then designated a muhtar. The latter, a former village muhtar from Erzincan province in the east of the country, had settled in the neighborhood with his children. He was a member of the neighborhood committee of elders, but was not involved in politics (Aslan 2013 [2004], 179). Various interests thus converged around the creation of the muhtarlık, emanating from radical activists attempting to obtain public services and a junta wishing to increase its control over the population.

When obliged to take sides, how to muhtars arbitrate? They try as far as possible not to arbitrate; that is, they seek to reconcile inhabitants' requests and injunctions from the authorities, thus positioning themselves as mediators. One situation in which it is difficult for them to straddle the divide is when municipalities raze illegal dwellings, particularly in neighborhoods where tension regularly sparks confrontations, such as neighborhood D. Most rural migrants who settled on the outskirts of Istanbul did so by building illegal dwellings.

These are often tolerated, but there are regular campaigns to raze them. These became more frequent once the AKP came to power in 2002, implementing a more proactive approach to reduce pockets of illegality. But during election campaigns, illegal building is often tolerated. Thus, ahead of the 2009 local elections about three thousand illegal dwellings were built in neighborhood D without anybody intervening. But two months after being reelected, the district municipality had the buildings razed. This led to violent clashes between police forces and residents, lasting ten or so hours. Duran explained that he had sought to reconcile the two sides.

> I got up on the tank. The subgovernor and the head of the District Directorate of Security ordered me to put an end to the disturbance.... It was especially me they called. The subgovernor promised that they would not destroy any more, as did the mayor. I got the people to sit down by telling them I had obtained a promise from the mayor, from the subgovernor, and from the chief of police that no more buildings would be razed. I tried to calm things down. [...] They gave me a megaphone. [...] I told them to disperse. But there were groups of masked troublemakers who had a go at me when they realized I was managing to convince people; they tried to knock me down. [...] They were throwing stones directly at the police officers and taking me as their target, [...] when all that people wanted was for their house not to be destroyed. [...] We held a meeting with the subgovernor that lasted until evening. I offered to make an announcement via the mosques telling people to go home.

Duran presented himself as a mediator, tasked by the authorities with calming the situation and relaying the inhabitants' demands. He said he sought to show the legitimacy of these demands (people fighting to save the roof over their heads), while calling on the demonstrators to display calm. He portrayed those who dug in their heels after his initial attempt at reconciliation as dangerous radicals. He reported having obtained concessions from both sides, and gave himself the credit for halting the violence, thus burnishing his image as a successful mediator between the authorities and the people.

More generally, muhtars are beholden to multiple and sometimes contradictory parties, being answerable both to inhabitants and to their institutional interlocutors, with each imposing expectations on them that point in different directions. They may also run into genuine dilemmas. These contrasting expectations projected onto the institution by inhabitants and the authorities raise the question of muhtars' loyalty. This is not a new question. During the late Ottoman period, certain measures sought to guarantee that muhtars' first loyalty went to state interests. With the Tanzimat, muhtars, like other state agents, had to sign a written oath proclaiming loyalty to the sultan on taking office. They undertook to make all their declarations in accordance with the facts, to not accept bribes, to distribute taxation honestly, to not misappropriate money (notably when collecting taxes), and to report people sought by the authorities. In the event of financial misappropriation, the population was deemed to be jointly responsible. Furthermore, muhtars were meant to report any irregularities they witnessed to the authorities, something which for a certain time was encouraged by incentives in the form of indemnities or tax reductions (Güneş 2014, 63 et seq., 83–85, 94, 104, 116). These measures show that muhtars did not systematically report irregularities.

The authorities have often viewed the issue of loyalty as problematic. During the troubles of the 1930s in majority-Kurdish regions, certain inspectorate generals were concerned about the difficulty of maintaining state authority and overseeing agents on the lower echelons, who operated within networks of social trust: "Another source of concern is base-level public agents, [village] muhtars, and guardians. These categories hail from the local population. They often have some sort of connection with one or various notables or tribal chiefs. This makes it difficult to keep confidential any measures taken by the government, and facilitates actions by rebel groups."[10] Likewise, in the 1950s nobody wanted to be village muhtar because the position as mediator between villages and institutions was difficult: given how unpopular public policies were, there was a risk of incurring everybody's wrath (Scott 1968).

Despite these concerns about muhtars' loyalty, measures seeking to ensure their loyalty to state interests no longer exist. But does that mean they are nowadays simply residents' advocates? How far do they take their devotion to residents' interests? Since muhtars are also subject to orders from institutions, how do they cope with these different and at times contradictory prescriptions, and the tensions they may cause?

Context-Dependent Definitions

It is hard to answer this question in general terms, given that muhtars' reactions are varied and context-dependent. First, what do muhtars say about themselves, about what they represent? On being asked, the muhtars in my sample gave varied answers. In what they say, muhtars declare themselves to be primarily on the people's side, and sometimes portray themselves as mediators between residents and the state. Only under particular circumstances do they claim to be representatives of the state or to act on its behalf.

As one might expect, most muhtars in my sample said they represented the "people." Duran, running a difficult neighborhood with people from modest social backgrounds, said he was "really one of the people. When they elected me, they didn't think of me as different. [...] I am part of this people. I am the true popular will." When telling the media how he opposed the municipality's raising real estate tax values, he explained: "What pushed me to act was that people paid so much tax because of these amounts. [...] It was going to represent a heavy cost for the neighborhood. I've lived here for twenty-two years. I have to think of my people." This statement needs to be viewed in the light of how Duran positions himself in general as a righter of wrongs, opposed to the municipality and to authorities oppressing the people. But it also needs to be referred back to the context in which he uttered it: he had just talked about his legal crusade against the municipality, which he described as not really caring about the residents' interests. In a far better-off neighborhood, Ebru, too, said she positioned herself as the voice of the people in their dealings with the authorities: "I represent the people [halk]. That is to say, at each meeting, whether with the [district] municipality, the metropolitan municipality, or the subgovernor's office, I always ask for what the people want, what they desire. I am their voice. [...] It is my duty to serve the people, to pass on the people's problems." The context was also important here, since Ebru had just criticized the mayor for not listening to muhtars. This type of statement is a way of legitimizing positions that criticize certain institutions–in this case, voiced by two muhtars criticizing their district municipality and the government.

In their pronouncements, muhtars do not place themselves on one side of some normative dualism (citizens or state), but rather as bridging the divide between state and society. They therefore invoke various repertoires rarely expressed in opposing terms. As Duran said, "The muhtar is a bridge between the people [halk] and institutions [kurum]." Fikret observed: "You represent the people and the state at one and the same time. [...] You pay visits when someone is born or someone dies. But when someone's house is being searched, the muhtar has to be there as civilian authority [mülki amir]." Later on, he said

that "the muhtar represents all the people living here. [...] It is an official institution, but the one closest to the people. It creates a link between the people
and the state. It's a mediator." This type of midpoint definition is very common,
and provides a way to avoid opting for one side over the other.

Do muhtars invoke "the state" in their pronouncements? Those in my sample
never told me they acted on behalf of the state. In some circumstances, however, they did lay claim to its authority. They sometimes referred to the state to
stress the importance of their status, their official responsibility. They thereby
endowed their self-presentation with an official quality and enhanced their
status with markers of hierarchy. On several occasions Fikret placed the muhtar
in the following chain of command: "state, subgovernor, muhtar" or "prime
minister, governor, subgovernor, muhtar." Duran, who presented himself as
one of the people when it was a matter of asserting that he represented his
constituents' interests, invoked the state to assert that, as the representative of
public order, he was vested with a mission to enforce the official order. Muhtars
therefore refer to the state to create, maintain, and manage social hierarchies
(Alexander 2002).

It is interesting that surveys reveal that residents and muhtars have differing
representations of their function, with marked differences in the importance
attached to the various components of their activity. In a *gecekondu* neighborhood in the 1990s, many inhabitants viewed the muhtar as their political representative in dealings with the district municipality, not as a representative
of the state (Wedel 1999, 190–91). This coincides with a questionnaire survey
carried out in 2004 in Çankaya, a privileged central district of Ankara: 47.6 percent of respondents reckoned that muhtars chiefly represented the neighborhood; 27.4 percent said muhtars represented the inhabitants *and* the state;
19.4 percent the inhabitants *and* the municipality; but only 3.2 percent the
state, and none the municipality (Şevran 2005, 105). According to the same survey, 66.7 percent of the muhtars who responded said they represented primarily the neighborhood inhabitants, with 25.5 percent of them reckoning that the
muhtarlık represented primarily the state, and 5.8 percent declaring that they
represented the municipality (Şevran 2005, 146). This study shows that muhtars
say they feel clearly more on the side of inhabitants than of the state. Nevertheless, comparing the results of the two questionnaires reveals that, though
both inhabitants and muhtars consider the latter to primarily represent the

inhabitants rather than institutions, more muhtars than inhabitants emphasize this point. In other words, muhtars say they do more to represent inhabitants than the inhabitants say, thus echoing the importance muhtars attach to fashioning their image.

Indeed, it is important not to consider these declarations in the abstract, but to relate them back to the context in which they were uttered, together with the purpose of such statements. More generally, it is crucial to compare how muhtars define their role in the abstract with how they position themselves in their interactions with interlocutors. It is to this that we shall now turn.

Portraying Themselves as the Residents' Champion

Beyond what they say, how do muhtars act? They do not–and cannot–always act as their constituents' champion. However, they often appear in such a light, partly because they carefully conceal any awkward choices that might tarnish this image. The idea that muhtars side with their constituents and are ready to serve them is not wrong. However, it is only one part of the story, since it also results from an image they construct in their own daily behavior. The way they shape their actions is also a performance–that is, a set of practices through which they present themselves and their activity in public interactions, producing impressions on an audience: mostly, on those they administer. Muhtars are thus constantly working to produce an image through their behavior, as well as through what they say about their actions. By presenting their actions in certain ways, they seek to control how these are interpreted. The office thus requires skill in controlling and modifying one's self-presentation, not only in front of field researchers (Goffman 1959). Especially in situations where inhabitants oppose the authorities, this image is a stake in the contest, as Bediz explained about the school zoning episode. When relating how she had fought against the zoning change, she dwelled on the matter of her image. The head of education apparently told families that the decision to redraw the zones had been taken in concert with muhtars, and that the latter had thanked him. This assertion may have sought to legitimize the rezoning to inhabitants, but a further effect was to delegitimize muhtars in residents' eyes. Bediz vigorously denied this assertion, repeating what she claimed she had said to the local head of education in front of the subgovernor: "How dare you set my people against me? [*Sen beni nasıl halkımla karşı karşı getiriyorsun?*]" This account indicates the importance Bediz attached to protecting her image as her inhabitants' champion.

This image is particularly difficult to uphold in the field of public order, for muhtars are statutorily obliged to lend their support to law enforcement agencies, for example, to help the police arrest someone at their home, to produce reports for the authorities about security issues, and even to denounce individuals. Bediz told of how she had accompanied policemen to arrest a man suspected of drug dealing: "I said to myself that the man was going to think the muhtar had denounced him. I took his hand and said to him: 'By Allah, I am not the one who brought them here, they are the ones who brought me.'" Bediz refused to come across as someone likely to denounce her constituents. She denied all initiative and responsibility in this arrest. While muhtars are supposed to have "public-spirited" intentions for the greater good of sustaining security and public order, it is even harder for them to assume their role in maintaining order in the event of acquaintanceship.

The police suspected a young man from neighborhood B of having committed murder, and asked Bediz for her help in taking him into custody. But the young man was the son of one of her childhood friends. She was convinced that he was innocent, but was unable to persuade the police of this. They ordered her not to warn the family of the imminent police raid, fearing that the man might take flight. She recounted it thus: "I said to them: [...] 'What is said inside the muhtarlık stays inside; nothing relating to the muhtarlık should transpire outside. The mother is my friend; but believe me, I will not inform her.' And, indeed, I did not inform her." She thus said she had prioritized her office over her personal ties, and had said as much to the police officers. The young man was taken into custody, then cleared of guilt and released. After this, his mother apparently asked Bediz to justify her behavior. Why had she not informed them? Bediz reportedly explained that, as she was convinced the woman's son could not have been the murderer, she had preferred not to warn the family, so as to not worry them unduly. She claimed the police had ordered that what happened in the muhtarlık should not transpire outside–thus attributing to the police the words she had attributed to herself, throwing light on the work to shape her self-presentation. This episode shows that muhtars do not present themselves in the same way to officials as to those they administer. Rather, they adapt their image, depending on their interlocutors. In some instances, muhtars also perform various attributes of statehood such as grandiosity, reverence, or strength in order to get respect from their constituents, or when they appear in official meetings.

Displaying Responsibilities, Concealing Refusals

Most of the time, however, muhtars act as the residents' champions. This implies overrating their achievements in some cases, and exaggerating the limits of their power in others. Faced with consitituents' expectation that the muhtars care for and serve them, they promote the part they have played in obtaining any services rendered. Many muhtars give themselves credit for things accomplished in their neighborhood, provided they have played some part in it, however small, even if it simply consisted of passing on a request. Fikret emphasized: "I did very well at providing services, especially during my first term of office. When I arrived here there was nothing. [. . .] I got a school built. Before, at the bottom [of the neighborhood], I did a three-story building. Over there, I opened a post office." Likewise, Duran took the credit for a free clinic that had opened, even though it was a collective initiative he was far from unaided in pushing through. Mattina has analyzed the importance of "managing to grant oneself the credit for an initiative [. . .] which must be imputable to personal action" (2004a, 135). When a request is granted, this enhances the muhtar's reputed efficiency as a mediator who achieves goals. Bediz told of how people thanked the district mayor when new container bins were installed, but also thanked her too: "All those who call by say, 'My muhtar, whenever we look over there, we think of you.'" By presenting themselves as effective mediators, and by even exaggerating the role they play in obtaining services, they help sustain what citizens expect of them in terms of service.

Yet muhtars are often approached about matters for which they can provide no solution. And, just as they seek to take the credit when a request is successful, they tend to blame some third party when it fails. One day, a middle-aged man came to the muhtarlık and told Ebru that his son, an electrician, would soon be back from military service. He would be looking for a job, and the man asked whether the district municipality was hiring. Ebru answered that he should tell his son to send her his resumé when he got back, but that she did not think they were hiring at that moment. The man insisted, saying, "You are the one in charge [*sen başkansın*]; you have a say [*sözün geçer*]!" Ebru replied, "No, I don't have a say [*sözüm geçmez*]! Tell him to come, do his resumé, give references, and I'll pass on his application." When the man insisted, she said, "The municipality is not hiring. I, too, told them to let me know if there were any job openings, for I receive requests. If it doesn't work, we could also call his former boss." When muhtars cannot provide solutions, or refuse to accede to inhabitants' requests, they invoke their lack of resources and emphasize the limits to their power.

Ebru also lamented that she could not satisfy all requests for employment. But despite that, she showed that she was looking after people's cases: "The two parties have to come to an agreement, or else you don't find anyone to hire, which is a bit of a problem. But, well, I write, I take notes. I say OK; I say that if ever I hear of something, I'll call them." When they cannot help residents, muhtars show solidarity and display forms of empathetic regret, even compassion. For instance, İlhan, the muhtar of an old upmarket neighborhood, admitted that he was unable to do anything about the pavements being overrun by parked cars and cafe terraces, something about which he received many complaints. "They brought out a circular, but everybody knows someone who can pull strings, and the municipal police can't do their job. I'm friends with the head of the municipal police, but that changes nothing; his hands are tied." He defended the residents and voiced his anger. He thereby showed that he was supporting their requests, even though he could not make anything happen. Muhtars thus handle requests, particularly those they are unable to satisfy, by listening and offering compassionate support. In this way, even if they do not provide what the residents wish, they maintain their image as their servants.

Muhtars sometimes side against or decide against their constituents, especially when the latter try to obtain through the muhtar some benefit or service to which they are not in fact entitled. In such cases, they deploy a certain number of tactics to keep their choice out of sight or render it more acceptable. Some provide poverty certificates to whomever asks for one, including people whom they judge as not being entitled to them. But some, being reluctant to put themselves at odds with the authorities, then call the subgovernor's office to give their true opinion about the individuals in question, while others employ deliberately ambiguous language in their correspondence, signifying that the certificates were unwarranted (Buğra, Keyder 2005, 30–31, 40). The compartmentalization of procedures makes such duplicitous approaches possible.

However, for other procedures it is harder. For instance, not only must any request for a conscript salary be countersigned by the muhtar,[11] but the latter must also openly state their "conscientious belief" (*vicdani kanaat*). In this way, the public authorities place demands on their conscience. Bediz related a matter of conscience and how she dealt with it. A woman came to request a conscript salary, but Bediz reckoned that the woman did not need this assistance, since she owned a car. She did not know what to write in the "conscientious belief" section. "If I say the family is needy," she said, "I won't have an easy conscience; if I say the family is not needy, the woman will take it badly." As she had to hand the form back to the applicant once she had filled it out, she could not screen what she had written. She emphasized how awkward the situation was: "I sat there and ended up writing some nonsense [*saçma*] I was instantly aware of: 'The family states that they are needy.' To tell the truth, now that I think about it, it makes me feel sick." Bediz did not assume her negative opinion in front of the applicant, but expressed her uneasiness. She admits using little strategies to avoid assuming open responsibility whenever she turns down a request for a poverty certificate: "To some I say that the [IT] system is down and that I can't issue one. They're little white lies." She gave a confidential laugh.

Being placed in a halfway situation leaves muhtars exposed to conflicting demands they cannot reconcile. But they often try to turn this to their advantage. In particular, they invoke officialdom to guard against requests they cannot or do not wish to grant, or to avoid openly acknowledging a refusal. Another tactic Bediz used to avoid explicit refusal was to warn that her accounts would be checked against other databases. "To some people I also say, 'If I give you a poverty certificate now, they will then enter your ID number, and if they see that you have a house, a job, a position, they won't give you [any social assistance]. So you'll have gone to all that effort for nothing.' Then they say, 'Well, OK,' and leave." By invoking a check using a procedure over which she has no control, Bediz is able to set limits to her power in granting assistance. This enables her to ward off situations in which she would be at odds with the authorities, and so guard against pressure from constituents. Fikret also acknowledged invoking officialdom against requests he felt were unjustified. His son said they did not give poverty certificates to everyone. He said that whenever they reckoned the circumstances did not warrant the request, they asked the people to provide official papers proving that they were poor. Requesting papers that are lengthy and difficult to obtain enables muhtars to stall without actually refusing. In so doing, Fikret's son shifts responsibility, denying his own autonomy in assessing the applicant's economic circumstances. Muhtars invoke administrative reasons to assert that there are limits to what they can do, particularly to protect themselves from certain welfare requests.

Displaying the limits of their power is also a way for a muhtar to try to get someone to accept a refusal. In muhtarlık F, an old woman asked for a poverty certificate, explaining that she intended to go to the municipality to request assistance. Fikret refused, saying that the municipality would not give her anything at that time. The woman insisted, and Fikret repeated that there was no point in trying at the municipality. The woman retorted, "Give me the paper so I can go." But Fikret continued to refuse, blaming it on the municipality: "They won't give you anything, I'm telling you straight. Everything they're doing at the moment is geared toward the elections." Fikret did not assume responsibility for his refusal, but instead pinned the blame on the municipality.

As far as possible, muhtars position themselves as mediators between the state and their constituents. They are attentive to requests from neighborhood residents, but without being in thrall to them. At the same time, they are careful to maintain an image of serving residents, and present themselves as their spokesperson. This image they produce, of championing their constituents, is intended to reinforce their legitimacy and popularity. But it does not mean that muhtars systematically side with their constituents. Indeed, in certain situations they cannot do so, due both to their status and to the constraints weighing on them (see chapter 7). By receiving and overseeing multifarious requests on a daily basis, by not accepting responsibility when they side with institutions or do not endorse constituents' demands, muhtars enhance their image as problem solvers. They help legitimize the extensive social use that residents make of them. They thereby reinforce their image as interlocutors who are available to be called upon for specific goals, together with the belief that personalized intercession is an important factor that can be effective in dealing with institutions.

Part 3

CONTRASTING POLITICAL EFFECTS

Chapter 5

AMBIVALENT INTERFACE WITH THE OFFICIAL ORDER

THE INSTITUTION OF THE MUHTARLIK, BY VIRTUE OF ITS STATUS and the uses made of it, allows for many concessions to social rationales. The familiarity that is its principle generates specific usages. Institutions produce civic competence, and generate relationships to the state. What does this familiar institution, in which requests are legitimate, beget in terms of government and relations to the state? Its effects are ambivalent.

On the one hand, it facilitates access to administrations, plays a part in administrative socialization, and partakes in the production of citizenship. Additionally, it furthers the two-way process of integration between local societies and the institutional order, especially via assistance for the needy and help with problem situations. It thus produces the image of an administration that is close, accessible, and attentive to inhabitants' needs. That is the topic of the first section of this chapter.

On the other hand, this familiarity potentially leads to arrangements. It thus places the institutional relationship outside the realm of rules and neutrality. This deobjectivization of the state, be it real or latent, paves the way to preferential treatment, thus feeding suspicions of favoritism. The way inhabitants and muhtars perceive and engage with the muhtarlık cultivates the representation of a state with which one may negotiate, encouraging requests for intercession and even rule bending. And in turn, this representation induces contrasting ways of relating to the institution. That is discussed in the second section of this chapter.

THE STATIZATION OF SOCIETY

The first facet of the muhtarlık's political effects can be described as integrative. The muhtarlık helps integrate socially marginalized individuals, renders the state accessible and intelligible to citizens, partakes in their administrative socialization, and enjoins people to civic behavior. In short, in Foucauldian terms, it contributes to the statization of society (Foucault 2008 [2004], 77).

An Integrative Dimension

To throw light on the integrative dimension of the muhtarlık, it is important to examine the differentiated social uses of it. In the preceding chapter, I dwelled on the wide-ranging uses citizens make of muhtars. However, I have not addressed the question of whether all citizens use the muhtarlık in the same way. They absolutely do not. There is no public quantitative data on how many or how often people solicit their muhtar. However, observation shows that the uses inhabitants make of the muhtarlık vary in the light of certain social parameters. Being able to call upon a personalized intermediary is far more important for certain sectors of the population than for others. It is groups who are disadvantaged—in the various meanings of the term, economic, social, or cultural—who solicit muhtars more frequently. It is in disadvantaged neighborhoods—particularly *gecekondus* and those built recently—that inhabitants use the muhtarlık most extensively. In the 1990s, muhtars of Ümraniye reported that they spent ten to twelve hours per day carrying out tasks that were not officially theirs, and that their offices were never empty. The numerous shortcomings of public facilities and institutions in recently settled areas, together with their distance from administrative centers, may go some way toward explaining this (Erder 1996, 75). In established neighborhoods with facilities and comparatively wealthy and educated inhabitants, the muhtarlık is used less. Thus, Ebru sometimes found time to read or watch television during office hours.

Within a given neighborhood, there may also be differences in the use inhabitants make of the muhtarlık depending on their socioeconomic status, which can differ markedly (Arıkboğa 1998, 128). Educated groups with a fairly stable or established economic and social position rarely solicit the muhtar. This is also true of people who work, as their working hours are the same as the muhtarlık's opening hours. When they have the choice, those with access to the directly relevant institutions rarely bother with visiting the muhtar. Says Duran, "Someone with a certain level of culture knows that the muhtar won't be able to do anything. They know it is not their job, and won't go and knock on their door. They'll go directly to the [relevant] institution, open that door without any problems, and get what they want. They know how public procedures work. In any case, they don't know the muhtar very well, and they don't come." Nearly all the educated people I spoke with reckoned that muhtars do not have any power or importance. They rarely go to the muhtarlık, and have a distanced relation to it. A thirty-three-year-old graduate who spoke several languages and lived in a middle-class neighborhood of Istanbul told me that muhtars were of no use unless you had something to sort out with military service. He said he never went there, and did not even know for which muhtar candidate he had voted a year earlier, despite having studied political science. But this distanced relation is also a way of asserting one's distance from a figure perceived as archaic and on the way out, and from political practices commonly associated with disadvantaged groups. In her wealthy neighborhood, Ebru said that it was rare for citizens to come in person, and that they tended to send their porters. In comparatively wealthy neighborhoods with blocks of flats and gated communities, caretakers are the main interlocutors with the muhtar, who has little direct contact with wealthy citizens.

Another factor in the use made of muhtars is village origin (Horasan 1992, 83–84). In a village, the muhtarlık is often the only public institution, and has greater powers than in an urban neighborhood. People who have lived in a village know more about the muhtarlık than they do about the municipality, for example; and once in town, they tend to turn to the muhtar (Wedel 1999, 190–91). Since urban muhtars share the same title and are similar to the village muhtars, people who spent part of their life in the countryside use them a lot for matters where they have no official authority.

All the muhtars to whom I spoke to said that disadvantaged groups came more frequently to their offices. The relation with the muhtar is of greater importance for people with few resources, particularly because material stakes are involved, such as obtaining social assistance. A revealing illustration of this is where people choose to request residency certificates. They are available from the muhtar in exchange for a few liras, or free of charge either from the population bureau (since 2009), or, more recently, directly over the Internet. Counterintuitively, it is the disadvantaged groups who tend to get their papers from the muhtar, while wealthy and educated groups tend to get theirs from the population bureau. Why is this? Neighborhood B is only a few hundred meters away from the population bureau, which is easy for all residents to reach. Bediz explained that poor people still come to her to draw up their certificates—but that she exempts them from payment. Wealthy people, on the other hand, whom she probably would not exempt, go to the population bureau for the same task. This choice is also linked to their literacy and administrative skills.

Another factor mentioned by Bediz that affects whether people come to the muhtarlık is that of "having problems": "Those in need come a lot. Otherwise, those with problems come—those with marital problems." In addition to income level, Duran insisted on the social and cultural dimension, together with how people relate to institutions and procedures: "If they go directly to the [relevant] institution [. . .], it's busy, and they have no chance of having the procedure explained to them, or pleading their case, or trying to convince someone. [. . .] Ultimately, here, it's the people who don't know how to go about things." Duran thus established a link between the level of education or administrative skill and the means used to contact the administration. In other contexts, too, for illiterate or uneducated people, taking up their pen to write to an administration or fill out a form is far from being self-evident (Dubois 2010, 27). The muhtar thus acts as a face-to-face intermediary for setting things down on paper.

This is notably the case for women—particularly elderly women. Women are often those in the family who go to the administration, or at least to the muhtar. As fewer of them work, they have more time to go to the muhtarlık during its opening hours. They are also less literate. Moreover, it is often women who request social assistance, since unemployed able-bodied men are often ashamed to ask (Buğra and Keyder 2005, 27).

There is a striking parallel to Behar's study of the Istanbul neighborhood of Kasap İlyas in the late nineteenth century. At that time, the muhtar significantly overstepped his legal prerogatives, acting as witness, public scribe, writer of petitions, guarantor, and intermediary to assist his flock in their official dealings. He also acted as an unofficial notary, in that many inhabitants called on him to act as witness and to register their legal and business transactions, even if it was not his job. But there was already a clear social factor determining whether people resorted to the muhtar. The leading local families never figure in the muhtar's registers. For Behar, illiteracy, poverty, and ignorance of rights were among the reasons for having recourse to the muhtar (2003, 161–70).

It would further appear that those who go most frequently to the muhtar are people who know them personally. When an activist for a participatory urban planning scheme asked İlhan who came to see him most frequently, he answered, "Those who know me come, of course, and I help them."

It would be simplistic but not completely untrue to conclude that the main users of the muhtarlık are the "dominated," given their multiple and not always overlapping characteristics: those seeking social assistance, the illiterate, people with a distant relation to the administration, those in a legally awkward position, women, the elderly, people from a rural background, people with health problems, and those who know the muhtar personally. Other groups, however, have few or no links to the muhtar—in particular, upper and educated middle classes, and people who have caretakers or live in gated communities, who draw on other intermediaries. People thus access the state in socially differentiated ways. Muhtars are, to a certain extent, oversolicited by the most disadvantaged.

Given this, the muhtarlık has integrative effects. It contributes to the social integration of individuals, particularly the needy, in several ways. First, it is a multipurpose institution where the general public can obtain routine certificates. At the same time, some of the muhtar's work involves looking after the cases of the needy (welfare claimants) and of marginal people (in matters relating to public order, and in looking after problem situations), but not in a separate place or in a different way. Because of this multifaceted nature of their office, muhtars commonly handle problem situations, and this is not stigmatizing for those who turn to them; in this regard, the muhtarlık tends to "normalize" the handling of problem situations and people.

Second, muhtars alert institutions to problem situations, so that the institutions can then take charge and provide for them, thus facilitating the integration of needy or marginal people into the institutional order. To help turn around a homeless alcoholic who was visibly getting worse, Bediz obtained papers for him and managed to get him a place in a rehabilitation facility, and then in a shelter for the homeless. She also obtained free social protection for him, and convinced the municipality to give him a cart so that he could work as a ragman. Of course, this was a success story Bediz liked recounting, and not all marginal people are looked after in this way. Still, the possibility of personalizing care by pinpointing needs on a case-by-case basis can smooth the integration of individuals in socially difficult situations.

Because the muhtarlık is familiar, it can play a role in steering toward other institutions people with certain problems they would be reluctant to present in bureaucratic administrations that are viewed as less "approachable." This transpired, for instance, during the "people's assembly" (halk meclisi) sessions introduced by several AKP district municipalities after the 2014 local elections. During these public hearings, residents were received by a municipal councillor in charge of a segment of the district, accompanied by the muhtars concerned and a few municipal employees. Most claims concerned welfare assistance. Muhtars channeled some problems they were aware of, thus making it easier for municipal bodies to look after them. One day, one of the two muhtars present at such a meeting received a phone call. "Why didn't you come? I told you to come," the muhtar said to the caller. "No, there's nobody—there's Bedirhan [the municipal councillor], another muhtar, and me, that's all." The muhtar did not mention my presence at the meeting, or that of the municipality public relations officer. "Why are you ashamed?" he asked the caller. "You've told your story to me two or three times, and to [Bediz] too. Go on, come around, we're waiting for you." He hung up. A few moments later, the woman who had called him arrived with her daughter, and set out her case. She explained that after the recent death of her husband and son, she was unable to pay a debt. She clearly found it hard to present her situation, and apologized: "We're not used to this." She shed a few tears. The two muhtars and the municipal councillor reassured her that her request was legitimate and reacted empathetically: "It's life, it can happen to anyone." The municipal councillor told her what she needed to do, gave her his calling card, and told her to go to the subgovernor's office and phone him from there.

Clearly, this woman would not have dared to explain her case directly to the municipal councillor or some official she did not know, despite having already presented it in some degree of confidentiality to two muhtars with whom she was acquainted. She was intimidated by the public nature of this hearing. It was the muhtar who encouraged her and no doubt enabled her to present her problem to the municipal councillor, thus making it possible for the public authorities to look after it.

Administrative Socialization

A second dimension to the statization of society is that muhtars, by spending their days explaining all types of procedures, help make the state intelligible to citizens, thus contributing to their socialization to institutions. One day, a man came to Ebru to get identification papers for his father, and asked her whether he could go and collect them himself from the population bureau, or his father had to go in person. Ebru told him that normally they could require the applicant's presence. She called her contact at the population bureau and asked the question. While on the phone, she asked the man if his father was mobile. The man nodded. "Then he has to go there himself." What is important here is that despite knowing the rule, Ebru did not just tell him what it was, but personally asked confirmation from the head of the relevant service in the presence of her resident. By explaining procedures and helping citizens navigate the administration, even in upmarket neighborhoods, muhtars contribute to their administrative socialization—that is, help them to learn the rules governing how public institutions function, to acquire the practical knowledge required for administrative procedures, and to interiorize institutional norms.

Writing in the mid-1990s, Sema Erder reckoned that the role of muhtars in pointing people in the right direction was specific to deprived neighborhoods, where many of the inhabitants were illiterate and had little administrative knowledge (Erder 1996, 77). But as this excerpt shows, Ebru routinely assumed this role in an upmarket district in central Istanbul. Nevertheless, this role in educating citizens is no doubt more prominent for less educated groups, who know little about how institutions function or how to access them–just the sort of people who predominantly go to see the muhtar.

Going to see someone face-to-face provides a way around the difficulties of writing, and a means to mobilize resources for verbal exchange (Siblot 2006, 63). Additionally, it enables a direct and at times interpersonal relationship with street-level officials. Thus, residents can solicit the muhtar to help allevi-ate bureaucratic constraints. Many citizens have a strained relationship with

Turkish administration, marked by feelings of insecurity and inhibition. In the 2000s, Alevis from central Anatolian villages viewed the state with distrust and incomprehension. Their representation of the state was one of pernickety and burdensome procedures being enforced by officials widely perceived as incompetent, prone to corruption, and shirking of responsibility (Fliche 2005). From this point of view, muhtars can be considered as administrative brokers, like those studied by Blundo in Senegal: "To increase their capacity to negotiate with an arbitrary and unpredictable administration, users need to embark on a journey of initiation into how the system really functions so as to make it intelligible. Initiation in how to use the local bureaucracy is often performed via the intermediary of veritable administrative brokers (such as duty officers, secretaries, clerks, customs informants, volunteers, and interpreters)" (Blundo 2001, 82; Bierschenk, Chauveau, and Olivier de Sardan 2000). Inhabitants harboring such feelings of incompetence may value face-to-face encounters, which allow them to "cope" better when dealing with administrative officials, as a way of overcoming a certain number of difficulties in how they relate to them.

Interestingly, this may also apply the other way around. Officials may also value face-to-face contact, especially as a means to produce consent or compliance with the official order. A few days before the municipal election, an elderly woman wearing a headscarf came to muhtarlık F to collect voter cards. Fikret took out his register and asked her if she knew how to sign. The woman answered suspiciously, "Sign what? Not something bad . . . [*Ne imzası, kötü bir şey olmasın*]. The other day they delivered coal and made me sign, and then the debts arrived." She explained in detail, clearly feeling she had been tricked, but without understanding how. "The scoundrels! [*Şerefsiz!*]" Fikret cursed. He reassured her, and she signed. Shortly afterward, another elderly woman in a headscarf came to get voter cards. Again, Fikret asked if she knew how to sign. She reluctantly answered that she would rather not sign. Fikret insisted, and forced her slightly. She tried to write. It was very laborious and very slow. He told her reproachfully that the municipality ran literacy courses. In both cases, Fikret managed to overcome the women's initial reluctance–apparently rooted in a combination of incompetence and mistrust–and, through speaking gently with them, obtained the administrative act of getting them to sign. With the first woman he was kind; he commiserated with her and condemned the ruse, thus siding with her. He thereby gained her trust and obtained her signature.

With the second woman he adopted a paternalistic attitude, informing her of a public service that could be relevant to her.

Enjoinders to Civic Behavior

Muhtars also help produce citizens, in that they issue a certain number of enjoinders to comply with the official order and behave public-spiritedly. Several muhtars said they had played a role in getting inhabitants to register officially. Fikret, for instance, said he had worked to ensure that inhabitants registered in the place where they really lived, as opposed to their previous place of residence or village of origin.[1] Registration is a particularly important issue in self-built neighborhoods, some of which are home to families that have fled conflict in the southeast of the country. The number of unregistered inhabitants in neighborhood D is thought to number several thousand, many of whom are registered elsewhere. Whenever Bediz encountered unregistered residents, she warned them that there was a fine for false declaration of address, and urged them to declare their new address if they had moved recently. This enjoinder was also intended to ensure that her official responsibilities were in line with her means of action, for muhtars have no official hold over those not registered in their neighborhood. It also makes sense as part of their election work. Yet it is equally an enjoinder to comply with the official order. Whenever muhtars issue it, they do not do so in terms of denunciation or remonstrance, but as a friendly warning.

Muhtars also assume the role of providing guidance about elections, one of their official duties.[2] They explain how to register as a voter, where polling stations are, the election process, and so forth. During the period when voter lists are on display, certain muhtars (such as Ahmet) check to see that their visitors are registered, even if they have come to the muhtarlık for some other purpose and have not asked him to check. Additionally, muhtars often call on people to vote in elections, especially when distributing voter cards. During local elections, it is in the muhtar's interest—as both umpire and contestant—that voters turn out. As Bediz put it, "You are in front of voters, you are in contact with them, you can say, 'I'm standing, I hope to see you at the polling station,' and so you call on them to vote. In any case it's very important; we want everyone to vote." A few weeks after the local election, a middle-aged woman wearing a headscarf arrived in muhtarlık B. She was from the neighboring district and needed a document; but her muhtar, whose office was next door, was out. Bediz said she would look after the matter, and wrote down the woman's cellphone number. The woman explained that she lived next to her mother's home, where her voter card had normally arrived until then, but that this time it had not arrived—so she could not vote. Bediz lectured her a bit: "The lists are displayed two months before elections; you can go and see." The woman appeared to feel the need to justify her behavior: "I didn't pay any attention to it; I only noticed later. But I encouraged lots of people to go and vote. I took them to the polling station." Bediz replied, "I always say to people to go and vote. They vote for whomever they want, but they have to go and vote. Anyway, fine—I'll look after it." The role muhtars play in electoral processes thus pushes them to remind residents of their civic duties.

By helping and giving advice, muhtars provide personalized assistance, something which is especially important for those with few administrative skills. Yet the very existence of this possibility feeds the idea that personalized assistance or intermediation is always possible, thus fueling citizens' expectations and making the acquisition of such skills superfluous. The familiar and accessible dimension of the muhtarlık thus has the effect of facilitating relations between inhabitants and the administration, making the state more intelligible and accessible, and teaching or reminding people of their civic duties. To a certain extent, the muhtarlık may thus be said to reinforce the statization of society and strengthen the institutional order's hold over it.

ADJUSTING THE INSTITUTIONAL ORDER

Yet the familiarity of the institution also has other consequences in terms of governing. The imperative to serve their inhabitants can incite muhtars to routinely adjust the rules. In conjunction with the personalization of relations, such arrangements feed the register of favors and even favoritism. This potential for arrangements has deobjectivizing effects. It influences how inhabitants view the institution and relate to it.

From Arrangements to Infringement

As seen in the preceding chapter, muhtars tend to find arrangements. They spare their inhabitants administrative "hassle" or facilitate procedures, by drawing up paperwork over the phone, for example, or handing a document to a third party–even in an upmarket neighborhood like E. One day, a man in that district wanted to get his identity papers renewed, but did not have a photo. Ebru plainly knew him, and was clearly accommodating: "If you come back to see me with a photo, I'll do that. You don't even need to come yourself. You can send someone; I'll give it to them." A woman entered muhtarlık E with her son to get identity papers for him. She handed over her identity card to Ebru, but she had forgotten her son's. She rang her husband to ask him for the identification number on the latter's card, but he did not answer. Ebru then said, "We'll sort that out [*hallederiz*]." She called the population bureau and gave the mother's identification number and her son's name. The person she was talking to indicated the requisite identification number, and Ebru drew up the application. When seeking to find solutions for their residents, muhtars take shortcuts to avoid bureaucratic red tape, and often stretch the rules. Voluntary little displays of consideration by muhtars help ease relations and facilitate procedures for the public. In a way, residents consider muhtars a way of accessing the state less hampered by unnecessary rules and formalities. Akarsu has noted that people want everyday officials who can bypass tedious procedures while performing official work (Akarsu 2020, 35). This is a role muhtars are happy to perform.

Muhtars sometimes take this accommodating attitude to the point of turning a blind eye when a requisite is missing, or giving their inhabitants "tips" on how to dodge rules, and especially sanctions. One day, a man phoned Ahmet. They clearly knew each other, and swapped news. Ahmet told him that two official notices had arrived for him. Over the phone, the man asked him to open the letters, which Ahmet did. One was a reminder about a bank debt, the other a reminder for an unpaid electricity bill. The man seemed surprised by the electricity bill, which he said he had paid. Ahmet advised him to check with his electricity supplier, but to not exceed the date. He told him what he needed to do. Then he said that the next omnibus law would include a debt amnesty, but he did not know if it would apply to electricity debts. He promised he would find out from his "friends who work in the electricity department." Even when they are not acquainted with the people concerned, muhtars may try to protect inhabitants from sanctions. This was also the case of educated Ebru, in her upmarket neighborhood. A woman arrived in muhtarlık E to register her new address, though it was several months since she had moved, because another person had now registered at her former address, meaning that her own registration had been canceled. Ebru did not tell the woman off, but warned her that late declaration of change of address was subject to a sizable fine. Without solicitation, she added: "But don't say anything before they ask you; maybe they won't debit the fine." Thus, muhtars often ease and even alter the administrative order. These arrangements can extend to flirting with illegality, and even infringements against the institutional order, as when a muhtar registers someone under a false address for school enrollment, or divulges supposedly confidential information. Muhtars thus do much more than just help residents cope with administrative red tape.

Indeed, muhtars sometimes "adapt" the official order to residents' demands and needs–and sometimes manage to stretch the rules for their benefit. Many muhtars claim that it is wholly legitimate to "cover" activities which, though no doubt illegal, enable people to get by. Bediz proudly said she had broken the official rules to help someone in difficulty. She told of how she had helped a homeless alcoholic who did not have any papers: "I acted as if he lived in my neighborhood, and had an identity card made for him." This enabled her to get him a place in a shelter, and free social protection. She thus presented herself as a righter of wrongs, using public resources to defend those most in need. She thereby vested her action with moral purpose, even though it broke the law. Positioning themselves as siding with residents can thus include bending the official order to their ends. İlhan, in charge of an old middle-class neighborhood, was also at ease with bending the official order to serve residents' interests: "People cannot choose the school where they enroll their children. So what do they do? They cheat; they look for someone who lives near where they want to enroll their child. They get false documents made. They have to." He did not condemn this, but implied that people had no choice. He did not conceal the fact that he granted their requests, which he apparently viewed as a way of defending their legitimate interests, thus condoning strategies to get around the law.

As we have seen, muhtars often deem it legitimate to defend their constituents' interests against an official order widely perceived even by them as unfair. Likewise, Ebru proudly explained that she had helped a young man whose cart–which he used to prepare and sell meatballs during football matches–was confiscated by the municipal police. Peddling is forbidden but tolerated during football matches and concerts. Ebru pleaded the young man's case with the municipal police, who consented to give him back his cart while enjoining him to be more careful in the future. Ebru expressed her satisfaction:

> It makes me very happy because he got his cart back, and since that day he regularly calls and asks how I am. He comes with his mother, with his father, they come to thank me. [...] And I, for example, I do what I can to help them, for they're not the sort of people who turn their back on you when you do something for them; they're people who remember for ten years things you've done for them. [...] They are very virtuous [*temiz*], very good people. That is why what I did was very good. I'm very happy to have done it.

The image this conveys is of a muhtar who does good, listens to the poor, and willingly breaks the rules if this will enable "ordinary people" to get on. Ebru expressed her expectation of moral recognition, and her satisfaction on obtaining this recognition—something she presented as gratifying.

In African contexts where the system of state norms does not coincide with the system of popular norms, Blundo states that "the boundaries between the licit and the illicit became blurred and could be shifted in the light of circumstances, both by users and by state officials caught between the duties inherent to their status and the pressure of social, identity, and political networks" (Blundo 2001, 80).

Indeed, the fact that muhtars can and are prone to adapt or even infringe the rule may be considered their true "added value" in comparison to that of an impersonal administration. It is in muhtars' interest to allow themselves and their inhabitants slight deviations from institutional norms. Lipsky has shown that street-level bureaucrats cannot just strictly apply regulations; they arrange the rules, exploiting their room for maneuvering and applying rules in the light of their own interests. This easing of rules which is observable among street-level bureaucrats is also found among muhtars–perhaps to an even greater extent, due to their electoral dependency on those they administer, the value of mutual help which they share extensively with them, and the role prescriptions that residents place on them. Getting around or bending the rules thus does not amount to isolated marginal practice, but forms part of a system of institutionalized dispensations.

These arrangements are not the preserve of just a few muhtars, but are common to all. And there is nothing new about this. Back in the nineteenth century, the muhtar of the Kasap İlyas neighborhood, despite taking his role very seriously, routinely issued papers to people in irregular situations (Behar 2003, 123–28). Archives from the Tanzimat period are full of examples of muhtars keeping quiet about young men meant to be drafted into the military, declaring that they were dead, altering their birth dates in the registers, or even substituting other people in their stead. Equally, there are many examples of muhtars falsely declaring that certain people were unsupported to enable them to receive assistance (Güneş 2014, 82–83). In the nineteenth century, the muhtar and imam of the Kasap İlyas neighborhood prevented matrimonial decisions which, though legal, would have been unpopular locally. They adopted a pragmatic approach and facilitated matrimonial arrangements that were formally open to criticism—choosing to ignore cases of adultery, for instance. Far from applying the letter of the law, they found ways of bending it to local expectations, stability and harmony being their main preoccupation (Behar 2004, 555).

Institutionalized Favors

While all muhtars apparently adopt an accommodating attitude, it is important to stress that they do not do so systematically, nor toward everyone indifferently. Bediz said, "Sometimes they call over the weekend and say, 'My muhtar, may we come round today for a residency certificate?' [. . .] Sometimes I tell them to come, but I also sometimes tell them not to." Bediz may allow it, but on a "case-by-case" basis. An arrangement may be envisaged, but it is not systematic. Strict application of the rules coexists with arrangements and other more accommodating attitudes. A given muhtar may successively adopt bureaucratic and then accommodating behavior. Arrangements do not form part of a general attitude. Rather, they are a widely acknowledged possibility. And since they seem to be decided in a discretionary way, they come across to applicants as being favors.

In what situations do muhtars act in an accommodating way? It is difficult to provide objective and systematic analysis of favors, for they leave little trace, taking place orally in face-to-face interaction. One favor that may be frequently observed relates to the tax paid on certificates–despite a fixed-rate "stamp tax" being set by the governor's office each year. The official notice indicating these tariffs is on display in all muhtarlık premises (figure 9). Despite this, citizens rarely pay the official price. During election campaigns certain candidates, particularly those from the radical left, promise to issue free certificates. This

İSTANBUL MUHTARLAR
FEDERASYONU
Akşemsettin Mh. Safran Sk. No. 22 Fatih / İSTANBUL Tel. 0216 499 34 54

MÜHÜR TASDİK ÜCRETİ

İSTANBUL VALİLİĞİ İL İDARE KURULUNCA 4541 SAYILI YASANIN 20. MADDESİ
GEREĞİNCE 2015 YILI MUHTAR EVRAK HARÇ ÜCRET TARİFESİDİR.

1. İkametgâh ve Yerleşim Yeri Belgesi ....6,50 TL

2. Nüfus Cüzdan Sureti ....6,50 TL

3. Nüfus Cüzdanı Talep Belgesi ....6,50 TL

4. Aile Cüzdanı Talep Belgesi ....6,50 TL

T.C.
İÇİŞLERİ BAKANLIĞI
Mahalli İdareler Genel Müdürlüğü
Nüfus ve Vatandaşlık İşleri Genel Müdürlüğü'nün 03/08/2008 tarih ve 51184 sayılı yazısı
Yerleşim Yeri ve Diğer Adres Belgesi'nin yalnızca sisteme bağlı muhtarlıklarca elektronik ortamda
verilebileceği, Köy ve Mahalle Muhtarının ödeneklerinin ödenme usulü, Köy ve Mahalle Muhtarları
ve İhtiyar Heyetleri tarafından verilecek resmi evrak ile Mahalle Muhtarlarının harç tahsilat
ve paylarının ödenme biçimi hakkında yönetmelik hükümlerinin geçerli olduğu bildirilmiştir.

İstanbul Valiliği İl İdare Kurulunun 07/01/2015 tarih - 2 Sayılı Kararıdır.

Kadir DELİBALTA
İstanbul Muhtarlar Federasyonu
Genel Başkanı

Akif AK
İstanbul Muhtarlar Federasyonu
Başkan Vekili

Bülent Abdullah ÖZEN
İstanbul Muhtarlar Federasyonu
Genel Sekreteri

FIGURE 9. Notice announcing the prices for payable documents issued by muhtars in 2015: residency certificate, civil registry excerpt, certificate of application for identification papers, and certificate of application for family record book. Istanbul, June 2015. Photograph by the author.

FIGURE 10. Election poster promising "free stamp, signature, and residency certificate." Istanbul, March 2014. Photograph by the author.

was the case, for example, of a candidate from the alternative pro-Kurdish left, supported by the HDP, in a turbulent neighborhood (figure 10).

In practice, I did not encounter any muhtars who systematically exempted inhabitants from payments. Muhtars often asked the official stamping price, particularly in purely administrative interactions. Thus, Fikret asked a woman who had come with her adult children for three documents to pay the official price, after a very formal conversation in which he told them how to obtain a medical certificate. Likewise, he asked a man who had just found a job for which he would earn the minimum wage for the official price. On occasion, Ebru asked even people she knew personally to pay the regulatory fee, even after having swapped news with them.

Yet none of the muhtars I observed systematically collected this tax—not even highly educated Ebru, in her middle- to upper-middle-class neighborhood. They all assessed situations on a case-by-case basis. The 1945 regulations (article 37) stipulate that the poor may be exempted from paying this tax, though without defining who counts as "poor." It is thus up to the muhtars to assess each situation. Yet the case-by-case assessments muhtars make are far from limited to instances of poverty.

Many muhtars boast of exempting certain categories of the population from paying this tax, invoking the principle of exempting the poor. Officiating in a fairly poor neighborhood, Fikret's son told me that they only took money from those who were well off, and that about twenty people came each day, but they only made five of them pay. Bediz, similarly working in a modest neighborhood, started by stating the official criterion, namely the social situation of the claimant: "It's my sixth year, and until now I have not received the tax from a single student, despite the notice on display that we are entitled to receive money on official papers. This money goes directly to the muhtar. I have not collected it from a single student or unemployed person. I say, 'Find a job first, and some money, and then come back.'" She thereby highlighted the gap between her economic interests, on the one hand, backed up by what she regarded as her right, and her practice on the other. By proudly emphasizing her generous interpretation of "poverty," Bediz advanced the principle of social justice, thereby displaying her disinterestedness and selflessness. But she went further, declaring: "It is only very rarely that I collect money. In fact, [these past five months] I have not collected five cents"—indicating that she also provided exemptions wholly independently of the poverty criterion.

Besides, observation of muhtars in action reveals a certain number of gaps between what they say and what they actually do. A young man asked for an excerpt from the civil register and a residency certificate. Bediz asked him what street he lived on, and his identification number. She issued the two documents, and he asked how much he owed her. Without asking whether he was a student, Bediz hesitated and then replied: "Normally it's TL12, but this time it'll be TL5." Was this because she knew he was hard up? It was not at all clear that she knew him, since their exchange had been purely administrative, and Bediz did not know his address. Why did Bediz reduce the sum, rather than exempting him or letting him pay the official price? The law provides for exemption of payment, but not for reduction in payment. However, observation shows that reduction is at least as frequent as exemption. Case-by-case arrangements are thus not merely a matter of exemptions for the poor, as stipulated by the regulations. The muhtar may adjust the fee above and beyond what the rules stipulate. Not paying the tax is thus a stake in just that interaction between muhtars and residents in which there would appear to be nothing in play—namely, the issuing of administrative documents. During this interaction the visitor may seek to be exempted, for instance, by signaling their poverty, or by seeking to place the encounter on a personal register; but I never saw anyone explicitly trying to negotiate the price.

Is it simply a matter of muhtars putting into action what they say about being disinterested? Arguably not. In the exchange between Bediz and the young man, what mattered more than the reduction of the fee itself was her hesitation, emphasizing uncertainty and hence choice, and then the "favor" that her words made explicit ("normally . . . but this time"). By highlighting the favor she was granting, Bediz placed the man under an obligation. Equally, though it was a very minor favor, she pointed it out explicitly ("will do"). On the same day, another man came in and asked if he could send a fax. After hesitating a moment, Ebru accepted. The man thanked her and went out. A few minutes later he came back and said he had forgotten to pay. She answered "TL2 will do," indicating that she was doing him a favor. Muhtars thus give the impression of granting little favors—not systematically (otherwise there is no favor), but regularly enough for people to come to expect it.

Bourdieu states that

> the choice to potentially make an exception to the rule is one of the commonest and most effective means of acquiring "personal power," that is to say a particular form of bureaucratic charisma acquired when a person distances themself from the bureaucratic definition of their function. The bureaucrat sets himself up as a notable, endowed with a degree of notoriety within a territorial jurisdiction and acquaintanceship group. He does so by securing a symbolic capital of gratitude. This is generated by a wholly particular form of exchange, found in all societies, that generates "big men." The principal "currency" is, in this particular case, quite simply exceptions to the rule, or accommodations with the regulation, granted or offered as a "service" to a user (Bourdieu 1990a, 89).

It is precisely because it suspends the possibility of purely and simply applying the rule that an exemption granted becomes a service rendered, hence a resource that may be exchanged, entering a circuit of symbolic exchanges underpinning the muhtars' social and symbolic capital. These little favors do not cost the muhtars much. However, they are profitable in that they place their recipient under obligation (Siblot 2006, 175). Thus, there is nothing residual about bending the rules.

Bending the rules fulfils a political and social function, making it possible to build up and maintain ties of obligation. Tolerance granted to a particular individual reinforces a muhtar's credit with them, and with those they administer more generally. This credit is personal; it is accorded to the person who, by authorizing an exception to the rule, stakes out their individual freedom instead of behaving as an impersonal figure identified wholly with the rules they meekly apply (Bourdieu 1990a, 89, 91). This credit is all the more personal as any tax received goes to them personally. Waiving it is thus a form of gift. The possibility of exempting is a matter for the muhtar's magnanimity. The muhtars' auxiliaries or secretaries—such as Ebru's brother-in-law and Fikret's son—apply the official price virtually systematically.

By positioning themselves as facilitators for procedures, and by authorizing or even triggering the negotiation of the relationship—or creating an obligation out of a simple administrative transaction—muhtars fuel and even help legitimize the register of personalized requests, and of favors.

Differential Treatment?

The prevalence of favors, together with the fact that they are not systematic, raises the question of whether people are treated differently, and if so, on what basis. Not everyone necessarily benefits from these arrangements, or at least not to the same degree. A "bureaucracy with a human face" is also one of favoritism. For a muhtar, with a specific social position in their neighborhood, one inhabitant does not always equal another.

Are there principles that govern the granting of favors by muhtars? And if so, what are they? It is hard to know without knowing the relations they have with each constituent. However, observations suggest certain elements. First, assessing the financial situation is not the sole criterion for exempting or reducing the amount of tax paid. For example, the inheritance card (*veraset kartı*) needed to inherit a good is officially free, but many muhtars charge for issuing it. The amount charged may be openly negotiated, and apparently the financial situation of the applicant is not the only factor considered. Bediz recalled, "Someone came to see me two months ago and I did a lot of work for him; I had to go and consult very old files. Besides, he doesn't live in the neighborhood, [... but] the deceased was registered in my neighborhood. I said to him: 'Look, these are two enormous buildings. Normally I charge TL20 each, but for you it will be TL50 per building, making TL100. Initially I'd said TL200, but he didn't accept, so I dropped to TL100, and he said OK." Here Bediz set out some principles guiding her action. She put forward certain "aggravating" criteria justifying her "greed": the principle of proportionality, whereby the greater the value, the higher the charge; the amount of work required; and finally, the fact that the person was from outside the neighborhood, meaning that there was no proximity or electoral dimension that could justify favored treatment. Implicitly, geographical proximity was invoked as the criterion facilitating favorable treatment.

Likewise, acquaintanceship and friendship would appear to be grounds for exemption. For instance, fraudulent practices by Ottoman muhtars, such as issuing unwarranted certificates, "could be associated with recompense, but this was not always the case; they were often grounded in the desire to protect someone they knew well" (Güneş 2014, 82–83). Ebru, officiating in a very well-off neighborhood, seemed little inclined to grant exemptions. After having spontaneously helped to transmit an application in which a required item was missing, and without the visitor asking her how much he owed, she asked the official price. However, Ebru had already done the person a favor by forwarding an incomplete application. A few minutes later, a man she knew came in and used the familiar second-person form of address. He requested a residency certificate to open a shop. He asked if it cost anything—which, in comparison to saying, "How much do I owe you?" is an implicit way of encouraging the muhtar to decline payment. And indeed, Ebru answered, "No, it's fine." Then, a friend whom she clearly had studied with came to ask for an excerpt from the civil register and a residency certificate. Ebru did not make this person pay anything, either. Thus, being on friendly terms with the muhtar may well reduce administrative constraints. Bediz even explicitly mentioned not just friendship but also acquaintanceship as a reason for exemption: "I have never collected tax from anyone who did not have a [good financial] situation, or from anyone I know."

Negotiating Ties and the Stakes Involved

The ways in which taxes are negotiated vary from one person to another and from one situation to the next. More generally, however, a personalized relationship may facilitate an arrangement or favor. The importance of creating this kind of personalized relationship or obligation can be understood in the light of citizens' "practical sense" of the state. Secor has shown that in Istanbul in the 2000s, there was a widespread representation of a state in which nothing worked according to the rules, and where the average user was sent endlessly traipsing from one counter to the next. The predominant opinion was that bending the rules, in the form of bribery or through knowing people, was important or even necessary for receiving public services. The state was thus experienced as unequal and unfair. People who had access to the state, however slight, were viewed as privileged (Secor 2007, 41, 47). In a similar way, in the early 2000s, Alevi villagers from central Anatolia developed a perception of the administration in which rigid application alternated with bending the rules. The incessant switching from an official to an unscripted register, from the incorruptible to the bribable, generated anxiety among users, who were forever uncertain of the outcome of their dealings with the administration. They sought other types of interface than those laid down by the legal framework, drawing on "other" connections, mostly informal, which were more effective than a depersonalized administrative relationship (Fliche 2005). Similar phenomena occur in many other countries. In Senegal, for instance, citizens' representations of the administration were strongly marked by distrust and uncertainty. There was a widespread belief that the administration functioned on the basis of who you knew, and that it was necessary to be equipped against possible blockages and prevarication. Citizens therefore sought to personalize their administrative relations. Before approaching an official behind the counter, they tried to find out about any real or fictitious ties that could be mentioned to pave the way to their official request. Personalizing administrative procedures reassured citizens who were facing what they imagined to be an all-powerful administration (Blundo 2001, 81, 89). Similarly, establishing privileged ties is a major stake in interactions between muhtars and inhabitants. Even when there is no prior acquaintanceship, one of the stakes in the interaction may be to create or negotiate a personalized tie.

Are such favors and attempts to personalize relations specific to the muhtarlık, or do they also exist in other administrations? Several works on Turkish administrations suggest that citizens with personal relationships to state officials may pass behind the counter and chat and drink tea with them while asking a favor, while other people have to wait their turn. Yoltar has shown that when a relative, colleague, or acquaintance of an official asks them to go around an official rule or alter the habitual functioning of the institution, the official may seek to respond to this request out of respect for the mutual responsibility entailed by these close ties (Yoltar 2007, 100). Therefore, the existence of favors and the search for privileged relations is not specific to the muhtarlık, and may be observed in other, often more bureaucratic administrations. However, one of the specificities of the muhtarlık resides in the comparative ease with which an obligation may be created or negotiated, for it is always possible to find a common acquaintance, and equally easy to promise a few votes for a muhtar.

For residents, personalizing relations with the muhtar is often a way of leaving bureaucratic interaction behind, generally to give greater weight to a request by trying to create an obligation and incite an arrangement. However, because of the specific relation of dependency between muhtars and residents, it also happens that muhtars try to personalize relationships. The underlying reasons for personalizing relations are not necessarily the same for muhtars as for residents. Muhtars tend to personalize interactions during electoral periods. A few weeks before the local election, Fikret sought to establish a personalized tie with an unknown constituent when requesting his support. A young man, whom Fikret clearly did not know, entered the muhtarlık and asked for his voter card. Fikret welcomed him, saying, "Let my compatriot come in [*Gelsin hemşehrim*]! What is your name?" The young man said his name was Tolga. Fikret ran off the names of some people he knew with that surname: "Which of the Tolgas do you come from? [*kimlerdensin*?]" The man answered, and Fikret replied, "Ah, right! You can take their voter cards, they're there! What job do you do?" The man answered that he worked in security. Fikret replied, "Very good! I'm standing for the muhtarlık. A vote is a vote." They spoke about the region the young man was from. Bringing the conversation to a close, Fikret reminded Tolga of a common acquaintance: "X knows me. Tell him I say hello." Fikret had begun the exchange by postulating a fictitious shared geographical origin, calling the young man "a compatriot." In cities, invoking a shared geographical origin is one of the main ways of establishing a tie with a stranger (Erder 1999). He had then gone over the people he knew, to find a common acquaintance.

However, it is not only in the context of elections that muhtars personalize relations with their residents. Personalization may also help them obtain assent more readily, for example, when getting someone to accept a refusal. Let us go back to the old woman asking Fikret for a poverty certificate, at the end of previous chapter. When Fikret turned down her request, he used a familiar form of address and insisted that there was no point trying to get assistance from the municipality, linking this to her geographical origins and denomination: "You come from Sivas, don't you?" The woman said she did. Fikret added, "Fadil [the municipal employee in charge of assistance] isn't interested in you; your ID card says Sarkışla [a subprovince in Sivas province where mainly Sunnis come from] [...]. I'm telling you straight. [...]. They won't give you anything. Everything they're doing at the moment is geared toward the elections." The woman then replied, "What have they done for us in any case?" Fikret answered, "Exactly, nothing." Fikret did not grant her request, but he personalized the relation, mentioning the woman's geographic origin and religious denomination, and "taking sides" with her by denouncing alleged discrimination by the municipality, whom he blamed for his own refusal. This display of solidarity was perhaps a way of getting her to accept the refusal. In some situations, muhtars are prone to personalize relations with their residents, due to the specific relationship they have with them. They are certainly more susceptible than other officials to entertaining personalized relations with residents.

Producing Complicity through Shared Identification

As the above encounter shows, personalization is not carried out only by direct or indirect acquaintanceship. More frequently, it occurs via identification to a shared group. There are several possible bases for this, of which the most frequent is origin. This is the case in neighborhoods inhabited mainly by migrants from the rural exodus. Thus Duran said, "There is a prejudice in 70 percent of the population, the image that 'He's not my muhtar, I don't vote for him.' [...] If I'm from Tokat, an inhabitant who comes from elsewhere will say, 'He's not my muhtar.'" For her part, Bediz explained that she tried to gather votes by playing on group identifications:

> In my neighborhood in general, most people are from Bitlis and Siirt. [...]
> Siirt is Arab, and Bitlis is Kurdish. [... During my first election] I went and rang
> everyone's bell. [...] When I rang at people from Bitlis, I said, "I'm Kurdish too,"
> for they are Kurds. When I rang at people from Siirt, I said, "I'm Arab, my mother

is Arab." When I rang at people from the Black Sea, I said, "I too am one of yours, as I am from Turkey [*Türkiyeliyim* ...]." That is how I gathered so many votes.

In these declarations, votes are interpreted in terms of identifying with groups of origin, an identification that can generate a form of solidarity and even mutual obligation. This suggests that muhtars are considered to have differential relationships with their inhabitants, and that this variation follows a principle of regional, ethnic, religious, or political identification or proximity.

This is an important aspect in representations of the muhtarlık. In a survey conducted by Secor in Istanbul at the turn of the 2000s, 80 percent of respondents said they were discriminated against in their daily life, and expressed a feeling of inequality and injustice. They apparently thought that others were better treated and enjoyed better access to state services. On this basis, Secor argues that the imagined relation between the state and citizens is mediated by collective identities. The dominant idea was thus that different groups enjoyed differential access to institutions. Among the groups to feel most discriminated against were the Kurds, who reported that they always felt they were the object of general suspicion. This was also the case for working-class groups and, though no doubt less so nowadays, those who were devoutly religious. In previous research I have observed that Alevis felt widely discriminated against by institutions. Secor has shown that these groups believe they encounter discrimination based on signs of collective identification such as name, place of birth, accent, clothing (headscarf), and facial hair. Many of them avoided contact with certain institutions such as the police (Secor 2007, 44–46).

These powerful collective identifications also influence representations of proximity with the muhtar. People who identify with their muhtar on the basis of regional, religious, or political affiliation tend to turn to them more frequently. In neighborhood D, when the government, metropolitan municipality, and district municipality were controlled by the AKP, the fact that Duran was Alevi no doubt meant he was one of the sole institutional channels used by Alevis.

Another basis for establishing or maintaining privileged ties in interactions is political orientation. This too may serve to create a tie and an alliance. One day, I came with activists from an urban citizenship initiative to visit İlhan as part of a series of visits to muhtars. Although it was the first time these activists had met İlhan, a state of complicity developed. It was clear that the activists, from the Gezi Park movement, were opposed to the government. Put at ease, İlhan said, "My friends often tell me to shut up, but I am not Tayyipçi [a supporter of Tayyip Erdoğan]. I can't be. When he appears on TV, I turn it off or switch to a sports channel. [...] I don't go to the Istanbul Metropolitan Municipality [then in the hands of AKP], as I don't like them. I don't even go to their *iftar*. I say I'm not available. [...] Sometimes they come from the municipality when there's something to do. Whenever I can, I send them packing." When they were about to leave, the activists promised to lend İlhan their support without specifying what form it would take—which is a way of departing on good terms. He replied, "I too will help you, always. But AKP supporters can't expect anything from me." Certain of the activists appeared disconcerted by this declaration of party preference and biased behavior. A discussion followed. İlhan felt obliged to justify himself: "Anyone who comes as an AKP supporter, who presents himself as an AKP supporter–they can't expect anything from me." İlhan established complicity by declaring his support and explicitly asserting that, on political grounds, he did not grant it to everyone. He no doubt supposed that his interlocutors, who like him were opposed to the government, would appreciate this statement. But it implied political bias in performing his functions, which shocked his interlocutors, who were activists for an "alternative" and universalist form of urban citizenship.

This brings us to one of the central paradoxes in the muhtar's job, which occurs when the importance of establishing complicity and privileged ties runs up against another integral component of their role: the expectation that they behave impartially. This neutrality is officially prescribed, but is also an imperative upheld by certain citizens, such as these activists, as well as by most of those without close ties to their muhtars.

Private Complicity, Public Neutrality
Independently of these representations, does muhtars' behavior really make a distinction between groups? It is hard to detect such practices, given how hushed up they are. But such practices are frequently suspected to exist, and are often denounced. For example, Ark reports that the muhtar of the Şahintepe neighborhood (in the Başakşehir district), a Sunni AKP supporter, did not inform Alevis that the municipality dispensed education grants, and thereby excluded them from applying for them (Ark 2015, 190). But while this type of

differential treatment can be detected here and there, it is hard to gauge precisely. Besides, it does not transpire in all places in the same form, or toward the same groups. From this point of view, the muhtarlık may well generate territorial fragmentation, as it produces unequal access to favors, with different groups enjoying preferential access in different neighborhoods.

Whether or not it is actually observed, the perceived prevalence of favors means that muhtars are continually suspected of granting certain residents preferential treatment (Buğra and Keyder 2005, 47). This transpires particularly in the realm where they have greatest room to maneuver, namely the distribution of welfare assistance. The impartiality of muhtars is a recurrent ground for suspicion and criticism, particularly in outlying neighborhoods with more acute social and identity divides, where large volumes of assistance are handed out.

Establishing personalized ties–or even potentially personalizable ones– may feed relations based on obligation, and facilitate access to the administration. Yet personalization may also have a negative impact on administrative relationships. Writing about Argentina, Auyero has shown that the existence– even supposed existence–of people with close relations to power implies the existence of an outer circle deprived of such access. Those in this outer circle denounce bias, and have more a negative view of this personalized and supposedly exclusive manner of doing politics (Auyero 1999, 302 et seq.). For those who do not benefit from these alleged arrangements, going to the muhtarlık may be like going to an ordinary administrative service, or may even produce a feeling of exclusion. A passerby of whom I asked directions in neighborhood F accompanied me for a few hundred meters, then suddenly blurted out that Fikret would not be reelected because he discriminated. Like this person, certain inhabitants feel less privileged by their muhtar than others, or even slighted. Some avoid contact with the muhtar, who is viewed as championing "others." This is particularly true in strongly polarized contexts. Likewise, a context of acquaintanceship brings with it instances of dislike and rancor, often heightened by the electoral dimension, for the elected muhtar has beaten rivals and their entourages. In certain cases, suspicion of favoritism may drive avoidance. A fifty-year-old housewife from the Black Sea explained that, after conflicts in her village fifteen years earlier over land boundaries, in which the muhtar had played an important role, a certain number of families no longer spoke to him. Such phenomena may lead to reluctance to request something of a muhtar one does not want to deal with, so as to avoid having to present one's case or risk a refusal (Siblot 2006, 91).

The social embeddedness of the muhtarlık leads to certain preexisting aspects of social relations in the neighborhood being imported into the institution, such as divides or modes of identification. Additionally, the intrusiveness of this institution may fuel avoidance of the muhtar. The muhtarlık intervenes in certain areas relating to residents' private lives. As seen earlier, muhtars are often informed of many events that can be considered private, such as illness, infidelity, and marital violence. This is reinforced by their role in transmitting official notifications and summons should the mail carrier not manage to deliver them in person, such as court summons, debt recoveries, and letters from the tax authorities or from notaries. Most muthars seem not to be really concerned with privacy protection. For someone who is acquainted with their muhtar, it can be awkward or embarrassing to ask for a document without explaining why. But even when one is not acquainted with the muhtar, one may not want to tell them about a situation. Some people refrain from visiting the muhtarlık, such as a colleague of mine who told me she did not go because she thought she would be profiled. One day, a woman with a young child entered Fikret's office and asked him whether an official paper had arrived for her, since she had been away for a week. Fikret asked if a notification had been left on her door.[3] The woman answered, "No, but where we live they get torn up."[4] After asking her name, Fikret checked the official papers left with him and said, "It doesn't ring a bell. What kind of paper are you expecting?" The woman was silent. He asked again, but she dodged the question. She clearly preferred not to say what the paper was about, and slipped out discreetly when someone else arrived. Dislike and rancor may be harder to overcome than lack of a relationship. In that case, administrative coldness may be sought as a guarantee of neutrality.

Muhtars deny through words and deeds any form of favoritism, seeking at all times an image of neutrality in public. A first dimension to this image resides in denying any favoritism based on close ties such as kinship or friendship. Thus, in talking about social assistance, Fikret said, "Personally, I don't serve my pals." Equally, Bediz said she designated recipients not on grounds of friendship, but on criteria of need: "I did not do this favor because he is my friend. If he is truly in difficulty [*mağdur*], I put him on the list. [...] For example, my aunt's daughter no longer has a job, but when I put her on the school list [for social assistance], I put her right at the bottom, in case there was room for everyone. If there is none left, the neediest come first." Bediz said she had a clear conscience.

A second dimension of this image of neutrality resides in muhtars asserting that they have no privileged ties to any identity or political group. While all mention the groups of belonging which they say form the structure of the electorate, they boast of gathering votes from different groups. Thus, Fikret's son said that people vote by region, but that "they"—Fikret and his team—garnered votes from all the citizens living there. Fikret himself, who comes from the Black Sea region, said the same thing: "Here [. . .] there are denominations, there are various formations, there are Alevis and Sunnis, there is a block from the east, Kurdish citizens. They are a separate formation. But I get votes from all, from all three groups. I am in contact with everybody. Ah, I get votes from everybody, maybe a few more from the Black Sea. I have azas from these three groups [Sunnis, Alevis, and Kurds]. [. . .] I behave with equal distance." The fact that the various components of the population are represented among the azas is put forward as proof of neutrality, of not siding solely with one group. Bediz said she had gathered votes from all groups to deny the idea that she represented only one part of the population. On our first encounter, Duran said:

> My slogan is "East, West, North, and South, hand in hand to serve together!" [*Doğusuyla, batısıyla, güneyiyle kuzeyle hep birlikte hizmet için elele*]. I am from Tokat—Alevi. The former muhtar was from Kastamonu, Sunni. There is a large Kurdish community too. [. . .] I have applied that not just in words, but in deeds too. I said that I would do away with regionalism [*yörecilik*]. [. . .] Why should I look at people and distinguish on the basis of their dress and their religion? [. . .] There are twenty-five [hometown] associations in this neighborhood, and I managed to bring them together. [. . .] We are going to act together on what unites us: our roads, our tarmac, the stones, our land, our houses, our zoning, our park. [. . .] No section of the population can look at me with prejudice, and each says, "This man is my brother."

In the same way, when talking with Fikret, a CHP municipal councillor stated: "You cannot be the muhtar of a region." Fikret admitted that "they say that I give to my region." He denied this accusation, presenting as proof a file full of handwritten lists of welfare recipients dating back to 2004. A bit earlier, Fikret's son had said that the municipality showed favoritism in services, but that he personally did not make any distinction.

Similarly, all muhtars very frequently say they have no party ties. Since the 1980 coup and the prohibition of running under a party banner, the action of muhtars "would not appear to legitimately take place within the purposes, rules, and ways of doing associated with the specialized political order. Subsequently, the intrusion of preoccupations and objectives relating to politics, that is, usually espoused by specialized political actors and organizations, is perceived as a danger for properly preforming these activities. [. . .] It engenders worry, indignation, and refusal" (Lagroye 2005, 365). The muhtars' action is meant to take place in conditions that set it apart from party politics, occurring within a context limited to the circumscribed stakes of the locality, and foreign to the ideological conflicts dividing political parties (Lagroye 2005, 364). Certain muhtars claim a pragmatic approach in avoiding political leanings and weighing things impartially. Thus, Ebru said she did not consider her work "political": "As I am not prepared for a political position, I do not regard [my work] as politics. That is to say, I don't do politics here. Here, personally, I try to sort out people's problems and troubles." Muhtars commonly say things like, "The muhtar does not have a party [*Muhtarın partisi olmaz*]," or "The muhtar is from the people's party [*halkın partisinden*]." Ebru expressed this in terms of neutrality of action: "Of course, as muhtar I keep an equal distance from all parties." An avowed party tie opens the way to suspicions of favoritism, lack of neutrality, and even deviation from stated intentions, leading to loss of legitimacy. A muhtar who acts in the light of political affiliation is, by definition, not attentive to all the residents, listening to some more than others, and thus no longer guaranteeing the general local interest. By distancing themselves from party politics, muhtars vouch for their preoccupation with the general interest, showing that they place local devotion and the "common good" above partisan political causes. Displaying an image of political neutrality may be considered a way for muhtars to preserve their moral authority and legitimacy.

Such an image may also be considered as a way for muhtars to safeguard their heterogeneous social support. Two days after the 2015 general elections, Bediz and another muhtar from an adjacent neighborhood were commenting on the results in their respective neighborhoods, noting that they had gotten more votes than each of the parties. Bediz concluded not only that they had greater "democratic" legitimacy than parties, but also that they had won over voters from several parties. In fact, many muhtars get votes from across the political spectrum–Fikret got more votes than the winning party in 2014–and they feel they have to accommodate electors from different political backgrounds, as seen in chapter 2. The frequent claims of political neutrality may also enable muhtars to stay on good terms with people from different political tendencies. In spring 2014, Fikret campaigned to be selected as an AKP candidate for municipal councillor. This episode was a sort of political coming-out, in which he abandoned the habitual limitations of being a muhtar. During the few months before the election, Fikret's Facebook page included "likes" of politically oriented pages,[5] admittedly visible only to his "friends"—thus, in a context in which he controlled how public they were. When he was not selected as a candidate by the AKP, he ran to be reelected as a muhtar, and deleted the "likes." Shortly after the 2014 local elections, a man came to Fikret to request a residency certificate. He and Fikret clearly knew each other. The man admitted he had "block voted" for the MHP in the local elections, but implied that he had supported Fikret in the muhtar election. Fikret responded, "There's no problem between us; we can think differently." The two men reaffirmed an alliance despite their presumed political divergence.

Informed inhabitants generally know the political inclinations of their muhtar—or at least think they know, and speculate about it. In this sense, one may speak of a "public secret" among informed local configurations (Vannetzel 2010). Therefore, broaching the topic of party allegiance often generates a certain embarrassment amongst muhtars, especially when visitors presume the muhtar is close to some party. When an inhabitant asked Fikret if the AKP government corruption scandal that became public in late 2013 might affect him, Fikret explained that as a state official he was tied to no party, and so had nothing to worry about–despite having sought selection as an AKP candidate for municipal councillor a few weeks earlier. Similarly, when asked by a visitor about support he had supposedly received from the head of the local CHP branch, Duran vigorously denied it:

> I have no problem with the AKP base. Really, we get on very well. I also get on
> well with the MHP. I get on very well with Saadet and the CHP. A muhtar can't

have a political party. People say I am from the CHP. The [AKP] municipality, in particular, has insisted on this a lot. I answered as follows: "If having an honorable stance is being from the CHP, then yes, I am from the CHP. And if it is being from the MHP, then I am from the MHP." Of course, as an individual, I have a political opinion and I have a vote. But I haven't received anything here; I haven't asked anyone for any support. [. . .] I get on well with [names of the heads of the local party branches]. I get on well with the SP, and with the BDP too.[6] I get on very well with the AKP base, but not with their head. Because I don't enter politics [ben siyasete girmem]. I am not a politician. I am a muhtar."

So, even though certain muhtars enjoy privileged ties with parties or act in a politically oriented manner, they are careful not to show it—or do so only within controlled situations of interaction among like-minded people. I overheard a phone conversation in which Fikret implied that he treated the voter cards of MHP sympathizers in a specific manner. He hurriedly cut short the conversation which had suggested action guided by a partisan political perspective. Likewise, just after telling me that she had run the AKP women's branch in the neighborhood and had been extensively helped in her activities by an AKP municipal councillor, Bediz asked me to stop recording, and said: "I am muhtar, and a muhtar cannot have a party. That is why I don't want to mention my party here." In so doing, she stated that she "had a party." But she immediately nuanced this, stating that all political tendencies were represented in her family: the AKP, the BDP, the MHP, and "even" the CHP. She also said that her family included several party officials, mentioning her aunt's son, who had held important leadership positions in the MHP, together with her nephew, a board member of the Istanbul AKP Federation. Mentioning these various party ties in her family seemed to be a way of countering the party affiliation she denied. In fact, in daily practice Bediz had close ties to the AKP–except that she did presented things not in such terms, but as ties to the municipality. One day, the director of the neighborhood center phoned Bediz,[7] and asked her to provide the names of people who might be willing to become actively involved in the AKP women's branch in the neighborhood. Bediz justified this request to me on the grounds of her "local knowledge": "I know people; I know who is close to the AKP." She immediately "neutralized" this avowal of party ties, referring to her "more general" knowledge as muhtar: "That's to say, I can know who is from what party, who can work actively for what party. The muhtar knows that." She said she also received this type of request from other parties: "If there was someone who came to see me from the CHP and said, 'My muhtar, we want someone to play a role in the women's branch or in the municipality, if ever anyone in the district is looking for that, let us know.' [. . .] Or else, for example, there are women and young people who come and say, 'My muhtar, I would like to take up a place in the AKP or CHP women's branch.'" She finally justified her ties and help on the grounds of friendship: "Hülya [the director of the center in question] is someone I like a lot. I've always told her that if there's anything I can do for her, I'll be by her side. But I say that to all party friends. Whatever I can do, I do. If someone needs something, if someone wants something, I help."

Bediz is careful to deny any party ties in public. It is only when surrounded by fellow party supporters that she emphasizes her ties to the AKP. She adjusts the weight of the partisan political dimension according to whom she is talking with. She told me that during the June 2015 general election she had gotten the municipality to transport disabled people to the polling station. She had also insisted that invalids who could not reach upstairs polling stations in buildings without elevators could vote in the courtyards, which in fact infringed electoral law. She explained that she had had to go up against the polling station chairmen. Bediz recounted these episodes with pride, emphasizing her capacity to bend a rule for a just cause. However, when recounting this episode to Bedirhan, an AKP municipal councillor to whom she was very close, Bediz added a detail she had not shared with me: "There were reactions. People asked who I was working for, for the voters I helped were all old women with headscarves [*hep çarşaflı teyzelerimiz*]. 'You work for the AKP,' they said."

It is possible that Bediz's prior support for the AKP, which was fairly well known in the neighborhood, was brought up in certain situations to discredit her action. One may also consider that during elections, any act that interfered with voting would be interpreted along party lines, especially as these elections took place in a climate of great tension, and amid suspicion that the ruling party was not respecting procedures. When I, a foreign observer, was present, Bediz emphasized how her action was a civic act: increasing turnout, and combating discrimination against the disabled. When talking to an elected party councillor, she presented the same episode as a party act, perhaps to show that she acted to further the party's interests, even though this party behavior exposed her to criticism.

Managing the Presence of Various People

To sum up, in public muhtars produce an image of neutrality. But they also need to discreetly lead everyone to understand that they may grant them favors. Under these circumstances, the possibility of segmenting publics and establishing side spaces is important. In the muhtarlık, the presence and placing of people is more diverse and open than at a counter. Whereas a counter restricts the scope for exploiting such possibilities, muhtarlıks are open reception areas where anybody can come in without warning. Certain things may be said or asked in the presence of others, but other things may not. Muhtars endeavor to exert control over the confidential nature of discussions by applying a series of techniques to manage the simultaneous presence of various people.

Many muhtars have introduced surveillance techniques of varying degrees of sophistication. Ebru installed a bell that rang when someone opened the door to the entrance of the building where she worked. Whenever it rang, though she could not identify who it was, she knew a visitor had entered and could get ready. Muhtarlık F is composed of two rooms: a little outer room used as the secretary's office, often occupied by Fikret's son, and a larger room for the muhtar, containing his desk and computer. But Fikret only used the computer as a closed-circuit television screen to see who was approaching the building. On this topic he said, "You never know when your enemy might arrive." When asked to explain, he said, "Some people come to ask for money to buy bread, for example." Most of the time, the door between the two rooms was open. But on occasion, Fikret shut it to create confidentiality, or his son skillfully delayed a visitor or researcher to leave his father alone with an important guest. In general, "routine administration" was conducted in the secretary's office, whereas important matters such as favors and things said in confidence were carried out behind closed doors. In the division of labor, muhtars tend to delegate purely administrative tasks (the routine issuing of certificates) to their assistants (secretary, family member, or first aza); but they personally perform tasks requiring more negotiation, social skills, or decision-making themselves. In Duran's muhtarlık, the secretary received and filtered visitors, handling all current affairs without bothering Duran.

While the muhtar's office is where people are received, muhtars manage to have various less public "annexes," such as a kitchens or backrooms, where visitors are not allowed to enter unless invited to do so. At several moments during our talks, Ebru went off to another room she used as a kitchen. She could phone from there, or receive visitors without fear of being bothered by anyone else. These annexes make it possible to have confidential talks. Muhtars signal to certain visitors whether it is the right moment or not, depending on who is present. They similarly control their phone conversations ("There are people here; I'll call you back"). In muhtarlık F, a "director" (in Fikret's words) put his head round the door, saw the office was full, and said: "I was just calling in to say hello." Fikret implied that he should come back later: "It's busy now. We'll talk another time." The man responded in veiled terms: "I'll carry on as I'm going, is that okay?" To which Fikret answered, "Yes, carry on without changing anything." It was an election period, and they had confidential things to say to one another.

For the muhtar, it is not simply a matter of managing their schedule or workload. It is also a matter of creating semiconfidential spaces in which some things can be said and negotiated, and of maintaining the possibility for complicity despite the public nature of the place. Controlling the public nature of situations is a major issue in interactions, reflecting a central issue in the muhtar's work: namely, partitioning. Favoritism or bending the rules has to be recognized by one group or beneficiary while being concealed from those excluded from it. Thus, muhtars strive to come across as "everyone's muhtar." Yet they also let it be understood on the side that they are particularly close to each interlocutor taken separately. But this image of neutrality remains fragile, and is often brought into question.

The familiar nature of the muhtarlık thus produces ambivalent political effects. First, the muhtarlık has integrative effects that are especially useful in helping public institutions tend to the disadvantaged. Muhtars facilitate relations with administrations, helping to make them less distant and alien, and thus contributing to the public's institutional socialization, even inculcating citizenship. While transmitting knowledge about and skills in administrative matters to citizens, muhtars also act as a resource to fall back on for those without such know-how. At the same time, however, the personalization of the institution leads to its deobjectivization. Arrangements, a core dimension to the role of muhtar, feed the image of an amenable institutional order that tolerates and even encourages favors and rule bending. The fact that public officials may act in accordance with their close ties or are suspected of doing so–a very common feature, as far as muhtars are concerned–tends to question the existence of a neutral state existing outside society (Secor 2007, 49). The predominance of the register of favors may give each individual the impression or hope of being favored, but it also nurtures suspicions of favoritism. While this may facilitate the relationship certain residents have with the institution, it may also at the same time complicate that of other residents, thus triggering avoidance.

Chapter 6

ENACTING CONTEXT-DEPENDENT ROLES

ANOTHER WAY OF APPREHENDING THE POLITICAL EFFECTS OF THE muhtarlık lies in studying how muhtars engage with their role. This enables us to examine the extent to which the muhtarlık may provide a channel for working around the institutional order or, conversely, may help enforce compliance to that order. Like many other local officials, muhtars carry out a large number of different tasks. "As for the 1001 facets of an elected local official's activities, while a source of delight for the interested parties, thus spared from routine, they are a source of despair for political scientists, discountenanced by such dispersal that it discourages any attempts at modelling" (Fontaine, Le Bart 1994, 11). The diverse fields in which muhtars intervene mean that the very contours of their job are hard to pin down precisely.

The body of existing legislation is of limited help for grasping these activities. Fethi Aytaç, a former governor and head of local authorities at the Ministry of the Interior, notes with regret that the laws detailing the muhtars' missions are dated and dispersed, and concludes: "Nowadays it is virtually impossible to arrive at a clear, precise idea about the responsibilities, spheres of competence, and missions of neighborhood muhtars" (Aytaç 2009, 6). Additionally, due to the misalignment between muhtars' numerous prerogatives as set out in the regulations and the meager means at their disposal, they do not perform all the missions officially attributed to them. Research conducted between 1967 and 1971 by the Ministry of the Interior counted 143 prerogatives attributed to muhtars by various legal texts, finding that 47 percent of these were carried out and 52.9 percent were not (Arıkboğa 1998, 126). No doubt this method flattens out complex phenomena. However, though dated, this simple observation sheds light on the extent to which muhtars' official attributions fail to match their practice. Since then, things have become even murkier, for many of the muhtarlıks' functions have been transferred to other administrations without any clarification of the exact division of powers. Despite its functions being specified in many laws and regulations, the position of muhtar remains "vague" (Jeannot 2011).

Additionally, there is little standardization regarding the position due to weak administrative oversight. State administrations and institutions have little hierarchical power over muhtars' work. As Ebru explained,

> There are no checks or anything of that sort. Because in any case, I don't have any activity [*zaten bir faaliyetim yok*]. What could they check anyway, the number of documents I issue per day? Or are they going to control how I converse with people? I don't pay any taxes, I don't issue any invoices, I don't have anything that could be checked. Ah, the only thing that could happen would be if I behave very disrespectfully toward a citizen; then he could go and complain about me at the subgovernor's office, and they could then ask me to draw up a report. Afterward, it would depend on the situation. If the subgovernor reckons that the muhtar might well have done that, [. . .] an investigation is opened, and you are acquitted or sanctioned. It can even go as far as having your stamp withdrawn. But I've never heard of any such case. [. . .] We are an institution it is impossible to check up on.

Even for matters relating to the civil registry or the falsification of identification papers (see chapter 3), muhtars are only rarely stripped of their functions.[1]

The muhtarlık thus enjoys a fairly high degree of "administrative autonomy"—that is, only limited compliance with institutionally prescribed practices (Dubois 2010, 5). The muhtarlık may be viewed as a particularly flexible institution (Siblot 2006, 194). Because of this administrative autonomy, there are divergences in how muhtars follow the principles meant to guide how they perform their role, and even further, in how they define it. Some muhtars, such as Duran, engage with the institution as a means of opposition. Others, like

Ahmet, engage with it as a way to enforce consent to the state order, or even as a surveillance device. Likewise, some are heavily involved in distributing assistance, the clearest example in our account being Bediz; while still others, such as Cemil or Ebru, are markedly less so. The sociology of institutions has brought out how institutions only exist through the ways officeholders perform the roles incumbent on them, and through how they use these roles. These usages alter the institution (Lagroye, Offerlé 2010, 17 et seq.). Agents enjoy room to maneuver, as do an institution's users. The institution is transformed by the practices of muhtars and residents alike. By accepting or declining to satisfy the expectations of the various people with whom they come into contact, and by assigning differing weights to these role prescriptions, muhtars inhabit their role and transform the institution. Hence, the ambiguity of the statutes, the diversity of the fields in which muhtars intervene, and the lack of administrative oversight affords them extensive leeway to determine their own manner of performing their functions.

DIFFERENT WAYS OF BEING A MUHTAR

The extensive margin of appraisal muhtars enjoy raises the question of what factors determine their practices. If we are to go beyond interpreting the disparity in muhtars' attitudes as stemming from arbitrary causes, we need to bring out the determining factors affecting how they engage with and perform their role. The context in which they exercise it is an important determinant—particularly the municipal policies in place, together with the number of inhabitants and social makeup of the neighborhood, both of which influence the requests they receive.

But these differing enactments also stem from the ways in which officeholders assume their role as muhtar. Bourdieu has demonstrated that the way the law is enforced depends on the dispositions and interests of those applying it. In particular, he has emphasized the importance of their social backgrounds and schemes of perception (Bourdieu 1990a, 86–96). This is thus linked in the first instance to the selection of muhtars, for candidates with different profiles are elected in different types of neighborhoods. Given the absence of any standardized training or shared administrative culture, we need to attach even greater weight to muhtars' personal backgrounds in explaining the ways they assume their role.

This chapter examines the diverse ways in which muhtars assume their role by looking at how they perform the distributive aspect of their function, one of the areas in which they enjoy greatest discretion. There are virtually no rules governing how they issue certificates, designate welfare beneficiaries, or intercede. In legal terms, discretionary power designates the sphere of autonomy within which public agents may take different positions while still complying with the law (Beaud 1994, 474). It thus designates the room for maneuvering that is open to subaltern agents in applying rules and regulations. Discretionary power may be viewed as the possibility, accommodated by lawmakers, that the conditions in which the law is applied may be influenced by factors other than the law.

Basing Exchanges on Ties of Obligation

This distributive dimension is in fact closely linked to inhabitants' requests. Like other elected officials, muhtars feel obliged to satisfy their voters' demands in order to win election. This type of political tie has often been analyzed using the concept of clientelism. Many studies on clientelism show that a vote may be cast in recompense or anticipation of advantages the local official has granted or promised to certain voters (Briquet 2005, 31). Viewed in such terms, this exchange may provide certain voters with a way of compelling an elected official to grant them satisfaction, for they may wield their vote as a promise or as a threat of sanction. Muhtars and neighborhood residents alike may voice this exchange explicitly. Thus, when Ahmet handed over a poverty certificate to a man come for that reason, the latter declared, unsolicited: "I have two votes, and I have given them to you." Bediz told of how a man she had helped said he had voted for her: "During my first term, a man [. . .] came to see me several times and I helped him; very simple things, it wasn't anything especially serious. Then this man moved, but—he owns his own home—he continued to register as living here. A few months before elections, he called me. He was living in Kocaeli [about sixty miles from Istanbul], and apparently told my aza that he had not even voted in the municipal elections, and had come solely to vote for me."

When talking about elections, as well as more generally, residents regularly disclose who they have voted for. A young man, come to collect eleven voter cards at muhtarlık F, said to Fikret: "Our eleven votes are yours." It is common to express electoral support for a muhtar, including on election day. Ebru talked about conversations in the polling station: "There were always voters who met me at the door, or who met my mother or one of my sisters, and said: 'Don't worry, we voted for Ebru.'" Openly stating how they voted establishes the muhtar-resident relationship as a form of exchange. The effect of this can be to reassert a tie, or to try to place the other under an obligation. Thus, various attitudes muhtars display, like pronouncements about their availability and the idea of exchanging votes for services, may be considered consistent with clientelism.

If considered in terms of clientelism, the distributive dimension does not seem prone to variation. Thus, Mattina reckons that the power of local officials in Marseille stems from their capacity to distribute municipal jobs and housing in exchange for recognition of their status as elected officials. He argues that the crux consists of their "presenting themselves to the population as relays to get public resources assigned to them on particular and personalized grounds" (Mattina 2004a, 131). Writing about Peronist district leaders in Argentina, Auyero likewise states that "their control over upper-level resources (goods and services) determines the sum of lower-level resources (people) that they control" (2000, 98). It could be reckoned that it is, by definition, in the muhtars' interest to distribute as many goods and services as possible, so as to consolidate their social support as translated into votes.

And indeed, certain muhtars issue certificates to whoever asks for one, including to those they don't consider to be entitled. Apparently, muhtars are often overly generous, being reluctant to refuse a bit of extra help. Such practices can be interpreted as a way of expanding their circle of support among the voters they administer.[2] In the 1960s, when a poverty certificate gave access to free hospital treatment, one doctor reckoned that the overwhelming majority of patients paid nothing, for muhtars issued the certificate to anyone who asked (Goodman et al. 1964). From this perspective, it would be in muhtars' interest to try to maximize the benefits they distribute.

Yet, interestingly, I observed major differences between the distribution practices of muhtars. Some are heavily involved, others less so, while still others even avoid it altogether. Not all the muhtars I observed systematically sought to increase the resources they distributed. Certain ones were very active in distribution practices, whereas others did not prioritize it, or even neglected it. None of the muhtars interviewed in the study by Buğra and Keyder expressed any wish to have greater authority in distributing assistance. Alongside certain overly generous muhtars, others protect public resources most zealously (Buğra and Keyder 2005, 30–31, 40). I also saw Ahmet and Fikret turning down requests for poverty certificates. It may thus be said that while muhtars are certainly sensitive to the matter of reelection, it does not constitute their sole reason for action, nor does it compel them to satisfy all requests presented by constituents. So how are we to understand the diverse ways in which they perceive and carry out the distributive dimension of their function?

Localized studies of political sociology have criticized instrumentalist analyses of clientelism, instead emphasizing the moral dimension or the symbolic and personal relationships built up in this type of exchange (Briquet 1997). They draw on the notion of moral economy introduced by E. P. Thompson (1971) and defined by James Scott as a system of values underlying the principles of legitimacy which govern exchanges (1976, 158). This perspective draws attention to the principles determining how these exchanges are perceived and appreciated: they are viewed not as purely instrumental, but as grounded in a sense of justice (Combes and Vommaro 2015). Clientelism is grounded in a moral economy of political ties, made up of reciprocal obligations and moral bonds which are themselves constitutive of fairly structured political loyalties (Grignon and Passeron 1989). Thus, rather than making any precise material promise, officials undertake to be receptive to voters' needs. Satisfying voters' private interests is not necessarily undertaken immediately, and instead remains latent within a relation perceived as a long-term commitment creating reciprocal obligations.

These studies emphasize how "patrons," though dominant, are bound by obligations to their "clients." For the elected official, one of these obligations is to "render service" to his or her voters. This explains why the officials display their availability and devotion, as analyzed above. For voters, it includes the obligation of responding to this service with political and electoral loyalty. The political exchange is thus transformed into a moral duty of reciprocity (Briquet 2005, 36, 38). This transpires around the very widespread term hizmet (service). Hizmet places both a moral obligation on the giver and an equal obligation on the recipient. This shared value of hizmet thus justifies the requests inhabitants make of their muhtar, and the alacrity with which the muhtar responds. This helps explain why both muhtars and residents, far from hiding these exchanges or being ashamed of them, talk about them with pride. When Bediz talked openly about residents saying they had voted for her, she spoke with great satisfaction: "It is a very fine thing. I really like it." It is not just services and material goods that are exchanged, but also symbolic recognition, consideration, and gratitude.

Hence, the exchange of obligations between residents and muhtars often takes place as part of a broader and long-lasting relationship, combining administrative work, service, and solicitude, without any precise divide between those things. Residents and muhtar alike sustain dynamics based on obligation and counter-obligation. One day, a fairly old man entered muhtarlık B and said, "I've come to thank you for what you did." His comment was about his roof, which had been redone by the municipality after a fire. He thanked Bediz warmly. Then he took out a list of his relatives drawn up by his own village muhtar, and asked Bediz if she could remove from the register one who had moved out of the village. Here he was asking not for a favor, but for a routine administrative act. While Bediz was doing this, he reiterated his gratitude: "They prayed for you. You did better than a man." While Bediz was busy on her computer, the man talked about his health problems, and thanked her for her part in getting the municipality to repair the fire damage to his roof. He thereby formulated her intervention as a favor, and acted as one under an obligation. He established, or maintained, a relation of obligation. Factoring in the moral dimension to these exchanges helps "complexify" the tie, which is not purely an instrumental matter of a vote in exchange for a service, but is also comprised of values and obligations.

Moral Judgments

To what extent does the moral dimension help explain differences in how muhtars assume their distributive function? Moral judgments and values are also at work in muhtars' distribution practices, which may not simply be meant to maximize distribution. In the early 2000s, a directive from the local welfare fund introduced public benefits for the unemployed for the first time in Turkish history. Applications had to be made via the muhtar. But the muhtars did not simply apply this measure and allocate the benefit. Many tended to despise requests for assistance, considered them dishonorable, and even suggested that applicants turn to their relatives for support (Buğra and Keyder 2005, 40, 45). Yet from an instrumental perspective it would have been in the muhtars' interest to distribute as much assistance as possible—especially as they were urged by the institutions to satisfy citizens' demands, thereby allowing the muhtars to present themselves as resource providers to their constituents, and as effective relays to their institutional partners.

So how are we to explain the muhtars' reluctance? Moral judgments shaped their practices. Buğra and Keyder show that, in accordance with dominant representations of poverty, many muhtars considered unemployment a matter of individual responsibility, justifying not public welfare but, at most, family solidarity. They tended to disdain such applications, and even to shame applicants. The muhtars were guided by broader representations pertaining to individual responsibility and family support, or to values such as honor. Thus, they tended to short-circuit the delivery of social policies running counter to such representations (Buğra and Keyder 2005). In a way, because of their embeddedness in mostly conservative popular worldviews, muhtars hampered or even impeded the implementation of reformist policies. Hence, they fueled social conformity and political conservatism, not because of their political orientation but because of their social position. Nowadays, the same kind of representations sometimes deter muhtars from "maximizing" distribution, thus causing them to abstain from dispensing resources.

For example, Bediz and other officials channeled benefits, or refrained from so doing, on the basis of certain moral judgments. A visibly very poor woman with a dark complexion arrived with her baby at a public meeting of the "people's assembly." It was obvious she was Romany, of whom there were many in the neighborhood. The municipal public relations officer said to her, "There you are; we were waiting for you." All those present glanced knowingly at one another. As they explained to me later, this woman came every week and seemed to get on their nerves. She complained that she had no welfare card.[3] Bediz, who generally intervened empathetically in favor of applicants, spoke with her and mentioned a police raid, implying that her son was involved in drug trafficking. The woman refuted this, claiming that, were she involved in drug trafficking, she would not be in such circumstances. She appealed to Bediz, saying, "Bediz is well aware of the conditions in which I live." But Bediz did not take this up, nor did she seek to help this woman, whom she probably considered undeserving. She did, however, adopt a less severe attitude toward her than the other officials had. In this case, which deviated from the norms of social and family merit, the officials adopted a distant attitude. Bediz's dedication to serving her residents and her distributive zeal were held in check by her personal judgment about the behavior of applicants in the light of certain moral considerations. The influence of moral values and judgments also extends to the form of distribution. In Bediz's words, "Among the families to whom I channel assistance for schooling, there is a mother and son. The mother is bedridden, and it is the son who looks after her. Many people told me he gambled. And, without hesitating, I told one of the teachers, 'Let's give them a very small sum, TL50, and instead give them a food parcel. As the boy gambles, let's not give them money.'" Thus muhtars' individual moral judgments strongly influence both the decision to grant welfare and the form it takes.

The preponderant role these moral judgments play in muhtars' actions sheds light on practices which do not necessarily seek to "maximize" distribution on instrumental grounds. In turn, the importance of these moral judgments relates back to how muhtars are selected. In other fields where they have much discretion, such as family issues, muhtars often draw on a certain number of personal moral judgments about what is right and good for the family, generally relating to honor and good conduct. When consulted on family issues, many muhtars try to steer people away from divorce, which to their mind would be detrimental to the social order and domestic peace. Bediz said she had been involved in family reconciliation to dissuade couples from separating. She said she pointed out the needs of children, drawing on her personal experience as a woman who had divorced after her husband was unfaithful. She reckoned she had reconciled six or seven couples considering divorce. Despite being less conservative politically, Duran claimed to have brought together households who had got to the stage of divorce, probably feeling that he had a mission to safeguard domestic peace: "It makes me very happy, as a stable home is essential. As far as possible, it is my role to reconcile households." Several works show that other officials (judges or policemen) tended to follow their own ideas about what was right and good, especially in family issues, but that many were told not to do so in training (Babül 2017; Akarsu 2020, 34). Yet muhtars receive no training, are embedded locally, depend on the constituents they administer, and operate largely without oversight. It may be held that "in the absence of professional socialization and explicitly stated norms, social judgements play a greater part" (Siblot 2006, 191). In many ways, therefore, muhtars may implement their own notions of justice and order, even if they are not state-sanctioned. The fact that muhtars are supposed to intervene in such sensitive issues as public order and welfare distribution, and are left to act as social mediators in such sensitive fields as family matters, suggests that we need to reconsider the widespread idea that the Turkish state is heteronomous from society, implementing top-down reforms.

EXCHANGES AS PART OF A BROADER POLITICAL RELATIONSHIP

Let us return to muhtars' distribution activities. While some seek to win recognition for the important role they play in distribution, others seek to downplay it. In the absence of consultable archives, it is difficult to obtain a clear, objective overview of such practices. Things are not made any easier by muhtars' continual performance concerning this matter. Given the impossibility of "measuring" the distribution action of muhtars, the next section analyzes how they position themselves in this domain, on the basis of interviews and observed practices.

Bediz, a "Welfare" Muhtar

Bediz is a good example of a muhtar who endeavors to increase her resources and her capacity to distribute them. When I asked the main reason why people came to see her, she immediately replied "assistance," for 80 to 90 percent of them. That is partly because neighborhood B is home to many needy people, and there are many requests for assistance. Bediz provides residents with as many services and resources as possible. She does not just wait to receive requests, and instead uses all her influence to obtain new resources to distribute. In spring 2014, two buildings in her neighborhood burned down. Although it was the weekend, she set about accompanying those affected to the district municipal building, where she requested financial support to enable the families to move. She also saw to it that they obtained money to buy new furniture. Even though it is hard to know precisely how much her intervention influenced the course of events, she positioned herself as an intermediary, followed matters closely, and was duly thanked by the residents, showing that they credited her for the assistance received. Bediz praised the municipality for its swift action, thus putting herself forward as an effective intermediary.

Far from simply placing herself at the center of public distribution circuits, Bediz helps set up distribution activities that drew on private sources. This

may be linked to the context in the neighborhood, which is undergoing gentrification, and where rich and poor live side by side, in immediate proximity
to a better-off zone. Thus, Bediz pooled gifts of clothes, which she stored on
premises behind her office and then handed out to residents. Additionally, she
tried to elicit gifts to increase the goods distributed, and also to influence the
form of distribution. A private school in this wealthy neighborhood had recently
contacted her to set up a project to distribute the profit from its annual fete to
the needy. "The first year, they handed out TL300 or TL500 to families," she said.
"This year I suggested that we instead give TL200 or TL300, but to more families.
That instead of there being five families, there be ten or twenty. They accepted,
and asked me for a list. But instead of putting down ten families, I put thirty
families on my list." She thus endeavored to force people's hands. Resources were
limited, because the overall amount available to distribute remained fixed. It
thus became a question of arbitration. Bediz tried to drive up the number of
recipients by showing the scale of need, by benefiting more households, and
by trying to raise more money: "Two weeks ago, we were able to give to thirteen
families with the money we had collected, but as there were other families on
the list, the pupils were very sad for the families to whom we hadn't been able to
give anything. They said to me, 'My muhtar, we're going to collect money again,
for we want to give to the families to whom we weren't able to give anything.'"
By emphasizing the scale of need, and especially by distributing assistance in
person, accompanied by pupils faced with the poverty just outside the gates
of their luxurious school, she encouraged the pupils to collect more money.
She assumed a proactive role in distributing assistance by trying to elicit gifts
and by positioning herself as an indispensable intermediary in collection and
distribution.

Is this welfare tendency attributable solely to electoral concern? Cesare
Mattina notes about local elected officials in Marseille, "Like many other activities performed by elected officials, that which consists of satisfying private
and personal demands is wholly inseparable from their concern with being
reelected. However, the interests they defend in rendering a service [. . .] are
equally inseparable from their effective and symbolic interests in satisfying
demands presented to them" (2004a, 136). Bediz's distributive activism should
not be imputed solely to electoral concern, as shown by her "geographical"
arbitration. On the one hand, when approached to help with a distribution

scheme outside her neighborhood (her reputation as a "welfare muhtar" being extensively known), she nevertheless tried to benefit her residents, an action that could be attributable to electoral concern. For instance, when the Red Crescent contacted her to help a school in need, she pointed them to a poor public school in a nearby neighborhood, because the only school in her own neighborhood was a private school. The Red Crescent wanted to help fifteen to twenty needy students, and went along with her suggestion to help fifteen pupils from that public school along with five children from her own neighborhood. Thus, Bediz "rechanneled" some of the assistance toward her own neighborhood. Yet her commitment should not be attributed solely to electoral considerations, because on other occasions she did the opposite. Among the thirty families she recommended to the school that wished to distribute the proceeds from its fete, some did not live in her ward. Likewise, when the Red Crescent asked for the names of a hundred pupils to whom it could hand out clothing, she also designated four families in nearby neighborhoods. A distinction needs to be made here between the the term *mahalle,* meaning a neighborhood as an administrative unit, and the term *semt,* meaning a larger environment based around a place where people gather, such as a mosque, but without any administrative existence. Mahalle B is part of a semt, which is the environment Bediz thinks of as her own. The school where she was active was not in her mahalle, but was in her semt. Though she cannot decently distribute assistance solely in adjacent neighborhoods—certain families reproached her for having allocated schooling assistance to families living outside her neighborhood—she did not limit her distribution to her own mahalle.

Another element showing that reelection is not drving force behind all of Bediz's actions is the affective dimension. Bediz thus said, "Being able to meet their needs . . . I don't know . . . it makes me incredibly happy." It seems to be a major gratification for her. She also expressed great pride about having helped an alcoholic tramp go sober and reintegrate into society: "It is, in my opinion, very important. I am very proud of it." She rejected any definition of the muhtarlık as a mere administrative counter handing out certificates. On the contrary, she defined her role in terms of a social assistance mission: "If you can really provide help to those in need [. . .] then you are a real muhtar."

Bediz's social activism was not solely attributable to the number of destitutes in her neighborhood and the demands with which she was confronted. "The attitude of elected representatives to voters' personal and private demands, their differing propensity to respond [... ,] does not depend solely or principally on a utilitarian strategy to win more votes on an electoral market. The propensity toward proximity with voters needs to be viewed as closely linked to the processes of acquiring political know-how within family contexts and territories historically inclined to a culture of mutual support" (Mattina 2004a, 141). Indeed, brief consideration of Bediz's background helps explain this attitude. She was born in 1966 and has two children. She became involved with their school while they were still pupils there. After having been involved with the parents-teacher association for five years, she then headed it for another five years. She thus became active in social welfare—organizing fetes, for example, and eliciting gifts of used clothing from comparatively well-off families and then personally distributing them to orphans. She was proud that for the past twenty-five years she had given the meat her family sacrificed each Ramadan to the needy in her neighborhood. Her successive commitments—at the school, as head of the AKP women's branch in the neighborhood, and finally as muhtar—enabled her to scale up and institutionalize the private collection and distribution practices she had already put in place. Hence, her social activism was part of a greater trajectory, and no doubt was one of the reasons why she was elected.

Justifying Arbitrations

But this type of activism is far from being the rule. Bediz worked in concert with three other muhtars from adjacent neighborhoods with whom she was on very good terms. They discussed and compared their practices. Her colleagues had different practices when it came to distribution. For instance, Cemil tended not to become involved in distribution, but it must be said that his neighborhood had far fewer residents and fewer needy people. The following anecdote, about which Bediz and her colleagues still laughed a few years later, is revealing. Some time after being elected, Bediz received a visit from a man who said he was closing his factory and had stocks of wood to distribute, and proposed to give them to her. He said he did not have any sacks to transport the wood, but knew where he could find some. Bediz gave him money to buy the sacks. But the man never came back. This anecdote shows that Bediz had the reputation of being swift to come to people's aid, but also of being naive, which can encourage this type of abusive behavior. This mishap led her to alter her practice and become more restrictive. Her three fellow muhtars teased her, and advised her not to distribute anything openly.

Bediz's colleagues were also thereby warning her against the tensions, jealousies, and resentments that distribution practices may cause. They anticipated rumors of arbitrary distribution. And indeed, recipients and those who witness distribution play an important role. Bediz recounted how the day after the distribution of the school fete proceeds, her office was full of people, including some from outside her neighborhood who had heard about her handing out money. She tried to avoid sparking demand. She said, for example, that she downplayed her role in designating which families received assistance from the school, explaining to all and sundry that she merely supplied a long list of families, and that the pupils drew lots to select the recipients. Denying her role in this way was a way of shielding herself from pressure. The distribution of divisible goods, in the absence of objective criteria and when publicly known, requires justification and gives rise to suspicions of favoritism, and even to negotiations. Those involved in these controversies argue about fairness and justice, and discuss the principles underlying the exchanges, to which they feel bound (Combes and Vommaro 2015, 107). Bediz said that when she had to make a selection of recipients that would be publicly known and discussed in the neighborhood, she was often obliged to justify her choices, particularly to "jealous" inhabitants. When designating families for the Red Crescent, she was reproached by one resident for having helped people from outside the neighborhood and neglecting the poor who resided in it. Bediz said she had agreed with the resident, while justifying her choice by the priority given not only to those who were poor but also to the handicapped. The criteria she put forward were not measures of poverty, which are always complex and untrustworthy, but health criteria, which are by definition unassailable. Thus, she had to draw on moral values to support her arbitrations. Bediz said the resident accepted the legitimacy of this criterion and apologized. However, Bediz promised she would help the resident next time there was a distribution, thus showing that a bit of insistence or questioning of the choices made could trigger a favor. The services rendered or assistance given are only likely to fuel a positive image if they are morally justified, in terms of solicitude and justice. Otherwise, they may well spark objections and accusations of favoritism, or even of enlightened self-interest. The transformation of distribution practices into prestige or electoral resource is thus a complex process.

Muhtars who Eschew Distribution

Other muhtars are far less active in distribution activity. Bediz's three (male) colleagues from adjacent neighborhoods interpret her social activism as being related to her being a woman, and hence "naturally" more inclined to look after her fellow citizens. But not all women muhtars behave as she does. Other muhtars, both men and women, merely try to respond to demands. Says Ebru, for instance, "When someone comes who needs something, I try to help with what I can." Ebru administered a wealthy neighborhood and said she had few requests of this type: "My population is not in a position to ask all the time [for poverty certificates]. It is very rare for someone to ask for one; and when they do, it is to obtain a metropolitan municipality coupon, or to receive legal aid. It's not much. I can't even say I give one or two per month—one every three or four months, sometimes one every two months; it depends. But in any case, I don't keep records." Ebru's comparative lack of interest is confirmed by the fact that she did not seem particularly well informed about distribution procedures—thinking, for example, that the subgovernor's office did not offer any social assistance. She said she knew nothing about the existence of a welfare fund (SYDV)—at least of one linked to the subgovernor's office. She said, "If they have one, it is part of their own association, but it's not located in their offices. I don't know anything about it. I'm not involved with that." Clearly, she had no idea. SYDV is not an association, so the way she spoke about it showed that she had quite poor knowledge of it. She also did not know that the subgovernor's office distributed coal. Although she was a university graduate and fully abreast of the regulations, she did not seem aware of the part that muhtars play in according the "conscript salary," thinking that the application had to be made at the municipality.

How to account for this lack of interest? In addition to the socially privileged situation of her neighborhood and the fact that she received requests for assistance only infrequently, the district she depended on was fairly well-off overall. The district municipality had been run by the Kemalist CHP for several decades, and had not introduced any particularly active welfare policies.

Ebru summarized the municipal aids she could channel very briefly: "The municipality only hands out parcels for Ramadan. And it can also help financially for schooling, between TL50 and TL150 per month." She did not seem to do anything to expand her distribution activities. She said the Red Crescent had approached her on two occasions over the previous nine years: "They asked me to check and tell them who was in need, and I drew up a list with as many needy people as I could identify. I sent them fifteen names, fifteen parcels arrived, and I handed them out in the muhtarlık." She did not express any gratification or other feelings about this. She did not inquire as to why the activity had ceased, and apparently had not sought to prolong it. When I asked her why, she said she did not know, and seemed uninterested. As for distribution by associations such as the Rotary Club, which is often handled by muhtars, she was unable to say whether it was happening in her neighborhood, only noting that it was not her responsibility: "If they do that sort of thing, they don't approach me. At the end of the day, they're NGOs. Our thing is the state's share. The Red Crescent,[4] on two occasions, and before that the municipality." The sense of justice Ebru highlighted concerning her battle to recover the young street seller's confiscated cart (see chapter 5) is not reflected in any form of social activism.

Ebru did not even respond very swiftly to requests from residents. During the March 2014 elections, an elderly voter reportedly told the presiding officer of a polling station in her neighborhood that he did not want to vote for Ebru, and she recounted the episode thus: "An elderly man, having been unable to fast at Ramadan, wished to give money, and wanted me to designate a beneficiary. He said that I had not looked after the matter and not found someone, but sent him to someone else. And that is why he did not want to vote for me: because I had not taken any interest in his case." Whereas "strategically," to "maximize her interests," Ebru should have taken the request seriously, and satisfied both the elderly man and someone in need, she neglected this request and the possibility of recompense. Far from regretting this or criticizing how he had acted, Ebru fully assumed what she had done: "At the end of the day, you cannot satisfy ten thousand people. You're bound to upset some. [...] You forget something, but they are little matters." She thus presented the affair as a minimal and even inescapable oversight.

It may also be hypothesized that the elderly man's request, which was religious in nature, did not appeal to Ebru and may even have displeased her.

Her appearance (she wore a short leather skirt) and behavior did not indicate any religious orientation. As a university graduate projecting a modern image of herself, Ebru seemed to show a certain lack of interest, and even scorn, for welfare distribution. A young woman wearing a headscarf arrived at her office with her child aged one and a half, and said, "The fact is, I want to open a shop, but I would like to have some information about Ramadan parcels." Ebru did not know her, but used a familiar form of address. She unceremoniously bombarded her with questions: "Where do you live? Have you just arrived? Whose wife are you?" It turned out that Ebru knew her husband. Ebru then explained that it was the municipality that looked after Ramadan parcels, and that she had no information yet about what would happen that year, and was not even sure that anything would be done. Ebru closed the conversation by saying that the woman would have to wait until Ramadan and should get back in touch then. But she did not take the woman's phone number or give out her own. Ebru reacted coldly to the request. This exchange is hard to interpret. Was it because the woman was wearing a headscarf, which Ebru might have interpreted as a sign of religious practice, or of a political leaning different from her own? Was it because Ebru, in an upmarket neighborhood and clearly from a wealthy background, considered the woman's request for assistance as incongruous or contemptible? Or because it was the first time they had met, and Ebru was trying to assert her symbolic or social dominance over this woman of similar age? Whatever the reason, Ebru had not been elected for her distribution activities, and did not seek to expand them. This stance may be imputed to the context of her wealthy neighborhood, where the muhtarlık is not based on distributing assistance.

Even in neighborhoods with many poor residents, however, certain muhtars steer away from social assistance, or at least do not get too visibly involved. For instance, Duran, whose neighborhood of fifty thousand inhabitants is one of the worst-off in Istanbul, is pleased that he has never distributed coal to the poor: "I have a clear conscience. If there are injustices or illegalities, they are caused by those who distribute." He said there was very strong demand for welfare assistance, and reckoned that out of the twenty certificates he issued each day, at least five, six, or even ten were poverty certificates. He said he was relieved when muhtars were sidelined from assistance distribution. "The subgovernor's office said that from then on, they would look after distribution themselves, ridding us of this burden. It was very good. It's a lot better that way. Muhtars are unable to shrug off requests, and commit injustices. [. . .] If you ask people how they are, they say, 'Things are very bad, I can't manage any more.' Lots of things happen." Duran thus implied that he had been subjected to pressure, criticism, and even threats, described as difficult constraints to manage. This stance may be attributed to the context of his very deprived neighborhood, where the volume of requests for assistance far exceeded the resources available to the muhtarlık. Additionally, in his divided neighborhood any arbitration was no doubt rapidly labeled as favoritism, or criticized as being biased. It is perhaps also why Duran provided poverty certificates to anyone who asked for one—due to lack of time (he could not consider each individual case), and also because issuing poverty certificates is a minimal and especially limitless way of supporting demands and displaying his support without overly committing himself. Distributing limited forms of assistance necessitates arbitration, is more complicated, and requires more justification. Furthermore, Duran was on extremely bad terms with the district municipality, and it is most probable that any recommendation from him would be ineffective or even counterproductive. That could foster the image of an ineffective muhtar unable to knock on the right doors. While Bediz's neighborhood is also home to many disadvantaged residents, it is significantly smaller than Duran's neighborhood, with only a tenth as many residents, and significantly better established, with fewer recent migrants and less tension between groups. The fact that Bediz was on good terms with the municipality meant she could more successfully assume a distributive role. Finally, Duran also claimed to have a keen sense of social justice. His stance was more activist, and he gave more vocal support to collective causes.

In his analysis of American political machinery, Merton argues that it is important to "note not only that aid is provided but the manner in which it is provided" (1949, 74). Independently of the differing degrees of proactiveness in the distribution activities muhtars display, it is important to examine how they act. Indeed, muhtars' activity is also partly about producing an image. Bediz built a self-image as a welfare muhtar. Even though she sometimes downplayed her role in arbitration in order to reduce the pressure of demands, she emphasized her role as a benefactor. She openly distributed aid, she personally telephoned those whom she had designated as recipients, and she personally distributed goods, sometimes on her premises. On her Facebook page she posted photos of herself handing out money in the company of school pupils. The things she had to say about her welfare activity, the reproaches she mentioned, and the criteria she put forward were also partly about producing an image, probably as a defense against suspicions of favoritism and accusations of arbitrary decisions. Duran, on the contrary, without wholly denying his distributive role, nevertheless concealed it. When private donors approached him to find needy families, he said he did not look after the distribution of assistance in person: "From time to time, when there are generous donors, my goal is to put them in touch with the right person, someone who is in need; it's my moral obligation. What I have never done is say: 'Give your money; I will distribute it.' I have never proceeded that way. [. . .] From that point of view, I am happy to say I have a clear conscience." By insisting on his "conscience," Duran highlighted the moral dimension of arbitration, as well as the difficulty in satisfactorily respecting it.

It would be reductive to think that muhtars naturally wish to be more active in distribution, or seek to increase their resources and redistribution practices. In other words, it is reductive to think that the political capital of muhtars is based solely on the quantity of goods they redistribute. The distribution of welfare is not a straightforwardly instrumental exchange for votes. It is one component in long-term relations based on obligation and rooted in moral economies. Looking at how muhtars distribute brings out the prevalence of personal judgements and moral values in their action. It also sheds light on the extent to which the embeddedness of muhtars in popular worldviews implies social conformity and, in a way, conservatism. Distribution of welfare is also bound up with constraints relating to self-presentation and justification. This redistributive dimension is difficult to handle and transform into political capital—especially in certain contexts. Muhtars are caught up in multiple and complex social relations which bring opportunities, but also constraints.

By highlighting the many ways in which muhtars implement their role, I hope to have shown how reductive it would be to suggest any simple or straightforward interpretation of the muhtarlık in terms of resistance or compliance. Examining how muhtars engage with their distributive role brings out the complexity of their arbitrations, which relate to various factors such as neighborhood context, working conditions, or individual dispositions. There is a fascinating diversity and fragmentation of practices at this level. In studying how muhtars assume their role, it is wise to follow Becker's advice and think in terms of combinations, not variables—in other words, to be attentive to the complexity of situations, rather than reducing them to simple factors (Becker 1998). In recent years, however, the institutional constraints on muhtars have become restrictive, changing the rules of the game to some extent. That is the topic to which we shall now turn.

Part 4

LOSS OF AUTONOMY AT THE MICROLOCAL LEVEL

Chapter 7

WORKING WITHIN AND MODULATING INSTITUTIONAL CONSTRAINTS

THE WAY MUHTARS PERFORM THEIR ROLE DEPENDS ON THEIR profile, but also on the contexts in which they operate. Thus far, we have mainly analyzed muhtars in the context of their neighborhoods. But another dimension to their activity concerns their institutional environment.

Considering muhtars as "intermediaries" implies the existence of two separate entities: here, "local society" and "the state." But examination of the environment of constraints and the economy of power in which muhtars operate sheds light on more complex configurations which undermine the state/society dichotomy. As we have seen, local societies are not homogenous, and certain groups or individuals may establish privileged access to the muhtarlık and use it in contrasting ways. Likewise, observation shows that muhtars, rather than interacting with a coherent state entity, maintain differing ties with diverse institutions. In Turkey as elsewhere, what is imagined as the state is not monolithic. Rather, public institutions are dynamic fields of power relations (for Turkey, see Gourisse 2015; Aslan 2015; Babül 2017). Additionally, muhtars do not necessarily engage with these institutions qua substantive entities, instead often addressing individuals who work in them.

Institutions supply muhtars with resources, yet may equally exert pressures and constraints. How do these relations influence the way muhtars perform their job? How do the latter accommodate these limitations? How does the muhtars' position in the institutional environment impact on government–that is to say, on the way the muhtarlık may be a cog of institutional domination, or a relay for social demands and interests? To what extent and in what way do partisan political factors influence how they relate to the authorities? Specifically, do such factors foster opposition or compliance in the way the muhtars perform their role?

The first section of this chapter looks at the importance muhtars attach to how they relate to the authorities. The second analyzes how they accommodate the institutional environment, but also build up and modulate relationships therein. The final section examines what bearing partisan political considerations may have on these relations.

CRUCIAL RELATIONS WITH THE AUTHORITIES

Unlike bureaucrats, muhtars do not really have any identified hierarchy or any performance requirements. So are they autonomous from institutions? It would be more accurate to say they are dependent, but that their dependence takes nonhierarchical forms, and in fact runs in both directions.

Differing Relations and Stakes

Analyzing relations between muhtars and the authorities requires us to distinguish between different institutions, since they are not of equal importance. Depending on the institution in question, muhtars relate to them in different ways. Their crucial partner is their district municipality. Interestingly, relations with the subgovernor's office, with which muhtars are statutorily linked, would not appear to be a significant stake for them. They address relatively few requests to it. In their dealings with subgovernor's offices, muhtars act primarily as implementers: they are meant to maintain local order, relay public policies, and respond to requests for information from administrative authorities–for example, to write reports about Syrians residing in their neighborhood (Genç and Özdemirkıran 2015). For such matters, they are meant to cooperate with security forces.

Subgovernor's offices conduct regular meetings with muhtars to discuss routine matters, particularly relating to traffic and security. Ebru, in her non-problematic neighborhood, describes a pleasant atmosphere: "[The idea] is to inform each other. [...] What complaints have you received? What can we do? The atmosphere is one of a friendly chat. [...] We sit down, tea and little cakes are served, we talk, sometimes we joke. For example, what can we do for the school? We opened a literacy class. What is the best way to inform illiterate people? How can we attract people? Et cetera." These meetings act as channels for institutional communication: "We swap points of view, we talk, we see our subgovernor, we see the heads [of departments]. At least we're not cut off. [...] If something needs doing, we suggest ideas." Ebru said she was consulted, and stressed that she could report situations to ask for advice or action: "In problematic situations I want them to show me what approach to take, so I ask on my own behalf. For example, [...] we had incidents with a woman who was a bit mentally unstable and was bothering her entourage—what could we do about her?" These meetings did not seem to be the occasion to voice demands, certainly not criticism. Ebru admitted she did not voice all her problems there, and that she did not complain much.

In the same way, nearly all the muhtars depicted the metropolitan municipality as a distant institution with which they had few relations. Indeed, its responsibilities cover fields in which they play next to no part—for example, managing main thoroughfares—and muhtars address few requests to it. The Istanbul municipality did not conduct regular meetings with the muhtars. In 2005 it set up an office in charge of muhtarlıks as part of its public relations department.[1] Despite that office's claim to visit all muhtars and to hold meetings by zone, the muhtars in my sample had never had any contact with it, and supposed that it was in fact intended for village muhtarlıks falling within the metropolitan municipality area.

For muhtars, the most important relationship with the greatest stakes is indubitably that with their district municipality. It is the district municipality which receives nearly all requests for infrastructure, social assistance, and services. In Ebru's words, "At the end of the day, our complaints are mainly about things the municipality should do."

Asymmetric Interdependency

Muhtars depend to a large extent on the authorities, especially municipalities, for resources. Nevertheless, they also have things to offer their institutional partners. Their relationship can be described as one of asymmetric interdependency. To what extent does this dominated position constrain the way muhtars operate?

Let us examine to what extent and in what ways muhtars depend on their institutional partners. First, the muhtars' role as intermediaries only really exists insofar as it is recognized by the public authorities. What lends muhtars their importance in the eyes of neighborhood residents is the fact that the institutions recognize them as intermediaries. However, they do not have a monopoly over political intermediation, including at the neighborhood level. This is the case for welfare distribution (see chapter 3), but it is also true in many other fields. Thus, the muhtars have to negotiate and work at establishing their position as intermediaries. In neighborhood F, the district municipality was planning to hold an *iftar* meal to mark the breaking of the fast during Ramadan. The day before, a municipal employee called Fikret to ask him for the phone numbers of the imams in his neighborhood so that he could invite them. Although the muhtar has no official religious role, the employee contacted him, rather than the mufti office which oversees imams.

Fikret did not have the numbers of all three imams, and asked the municipal employee to call back later. He phoned an imam he knew and explained the situation: "The municipality is organizing an *iftar* meal for respected individuals and imams. [...] At the last municipality meeting we had talked about this idea of cooperating for services [*hizmet*]." He asked for the imam's cellphone number, and that of another imam in the neighborhood. He then called up someone else he addressed as "director" (*başkan*)–maybe the head of an association–and asked for the number of a third imam "to include them in welfare distribution." The first imam called back with the number of the second, and Fikret carried on with his explanations: "We decided to involve imams as well in hizmet." The first imam invited Fikret to come and share an *iftar* meal with him, which he accepted. On the basis of an official invitation, neighborhood sociability was set in motion and Fikret had to reply to a return invitation.

Another imam, with whom Fikret had not yet spoken, called a bit later. Fikret recommended that he attend: "It's you who'll do the prayer [*dua sizin*]." Having been contacted as an intermediary, Fikret now had to ensure that the imams attended, so as to prove to the municipality that he was the right intermediary. A few minutes later, a municipal department head phoned Fikret. The latter took him to task, blaming him for not having kept him in the loop, and having a go at him: "My dear director, it's been announced there will be an *iftar* in the neighborhood tomorrow evening. Why hadn't you given me the program? Please, I beg you. . . . What had we said for this term, do you remember? Hand in hand, always together. So why do I hear about it via public announcement, from citizens?" Fikret then returned to his request. "Let's act together, let's share. The place isn't yet decided; do keep me informed. Please don't take it wrong."

A bit later, a woman from the municipality called (perhaps the same employee who had called earlier). Fiktet addressed her politely, respectfully calling her "Mrs. Fatma." He said he had transmitted the contact details of the three imams, and suggested holding the *iftar* in the neighborhood hall. At the end of the conversation he answered: "Of course, I won't fail to be there tomorrow." Fikret thus used the request from the municipality to lay claim to a larger role in organizing the event and, generally, to come across as an intermediary between the municipality and the neighborhood–and this in a field where he had no official powers. He did this first by responding to an official request and making sure "it worked"; second, by committing to visit an imam; and third, by informing an institutional interlocutor, with whom he felt in a place to do so, that he wished to be more closely involved in such initiatives. Fikret, who was in his fifth term of office, was very experienced and had long been well established. Hence, the role muhtars play as mediators for institutions needs to be continually negotiated and reasserted.

Not having any specific means themselves, muhtars have to rely on the authorities to obtain resources: information, services, infrastructure, and welfare assistance. To take up a distinction used in analyses of clientelism (Boissevain 1974), a muhtar is closer to the figure of a broker than to that of a patron, insofar as they have few specific resources but provide access to resources held by others, mainly by the public authorities. They mainly find themselves in the uncomfortable position of petitioner, and readily admit their dependency on partner institutions. Stakes are correlated to the scale of the matter: "routine" and minor collective services, such as cleaning or technical matters, are of little concern. But for bigger issues—Ebru gave the example of a pavement that needed complete redoing—the department staff "no longer handle it, so we ask or send a request to the level above, to the head of service or deputy mayor. [. . .] It won't be done the following day. There is a call for tenders first;

[. . .] we obtain it too; [. . .] but it takes time. Because other neighborhoods want the same thing as I do. . . . There is an order." This question of arbitration is central, since the ranking of priorities would not appear to follow precise criteria, and this could cause a certain degree of rivalry between neighborhoods and uncertainty for the muhtars. Ebru explained: "As muhtar, you can put as much pressure as you want. It's a bit problematic, for the institution that is able to act is above you. [. . .] And there, things can be cumbersome, and citizens' wishes are not always granted." Muhtars thus seek to get the district municipality to act in order to satisfy the requests and collective needs of their residents.

The volume of resources to which muhtars can provide access depends to a certain extent on their relations with the authorities. Said one muhtar: "Given that you don't have any specific powers and aren't holding any trump cards, you need to be on good terms with the people concerned" (Arıkboğa 1998, 142). For her social activism, Bediz draws on her access to institutions able to dispense services. She told of how she had managed to obtain public assistance for an alcoholic tramp for whom she had got papers issued, and had used her knowledge of existing schemes and the institutional context: "I went to see the subgovernor about him. [. . .] I went to a lot of effort. I obtained money from the subgovernor's office for him, and I got him admitted to a hospital. He stayed nearly a month for treatment. When he got out, it was early winter, and my municipality turns over gymnasiums to be used as homeless shelters for three months. They are housed and fed. [. . .] I sent him there. [. . .] Another time he came and said: 'My muhtar, I need a cart to collect papers.' He collected and sold litter. I immediately wrote a request and informed social assistance, and a paper cart arrived for that man, and now he does that job. In the meantime I asked the municipality and we saw to it that he got free social security coverage." Similarly, Fikret claimed, "It is because I have good relations with state institutions that I can obtain aid. Both material and moral. Be it from the subgovernor's office, the district municipality, the metropolitan municipality, or the [SYDV] fund."

In putting services in place, muhtars depend on the willingness of their institutional partners. An unreceptive district municipality that pays no attention to requests relayed by the muhtars shears the job of its meaning. Ebru complained about how unreactive the previous municipal team had been (2009–14): "They didn't do much. I would call. Nobody. I would write a request. No response. [. . .]

I admit [. . .] nobody came to complain anymore; in any case, you can't come up with a solution, except for minor problems. At that point you don't derive any pleasure from the work you do. You don't have any power. I don't have the official power; I can't do anything. You say again and again, you write again and again, but it still doesn't produce any result." Ebru says she boycotted celebrations and inaugurations to which she was invited by the municipality. She admitted that she was thereby expressing her reaction. Implementing a policy of serving inhabitants thus depends on good relations with the authorities.

But muhtars are not mere suppliants, for the public authorities rely on their mediation. What can muhtars offer in exchange for urging the authorities to act? First, the authorities expect muhtars to act as auxiliaries, transmitting information about their neighborhood and requests from residents. An aza in neighborhood D stated this clearly, mimicking a dialogue with a mayor: "You're the mayor, you've got two eyes on the front of your face, and we're your two eyes on the back of your head, so you've got four eyes, [. . .] Because we're going to transmit information." The need to be "in touch" with residents' needs and to satisfy them as far as possible motivates the municipal authorities to value muhtars. In dealings with their institutional partners, muhtars constantly lay claim to their "local knowledge," because of their everyday experience and their proximity to the concrete and the actual. Certain municipalities have even set up what amount to "muhtar policies." Thus, the municipal team elected in 2014 in a fairly recent middle-class ward decided to provide muhtars with premises that also housed a municipal "problem resolution office." The employee in charge of the project presented the muhtars as essential relays and the only ones capable of understanding what was happening inside their neighborhoods. In his opinion, they needed to be bound more tightly to the municipality to boost their effectiveness as communication channels.

Second, muhtars may act as channels to promote (or denigrate) local elected representatives. They talk with their inhabitants, particularly about neighborhood problems. They are central figures in the local public sphere, and are generally considered to be opinion leaders about local affairs. This is especially true during election periods. Bediz thus explained that "friends in the neighborhood come to see me before elections and ask me who to vote for. [. . .] There are many women who say, 'You do know.' There are so many people who ask questions naively, with good intentions. It's so common: 'Come on, my muhtar, you know people, you see them. At the end of the day, you're the muhtar. Come on, who should we vote for?'" Bediz explained how she reacted to these requests: "Personally, I don't spell out my party, but I say the following: 'Look, if you want, vote for him, or for her. But if you ask me to tell you about the municipal services, I can tell you about it, and then you can vote for who you want.' But it is specifically my duty to tell them about services provided. [...] And if they do nothing, to tell them about mistakes too." Bediz claimed not to operate along party lines, but to assess municipal services neutrally. She laid claim to expertise, which she transformed into a "duty" to inform citizens about municipal activities. Muhtars thus present themselves as opinion leaders, enhancing their importance in the eyes of municipal teams and the parties' rank and file.

All the muhtars I observed dispensed value judgements to their residents about the municipality. They did not feel bound to conceal their opinions. Certain muhtars write articles for local newspapers praising or denigrating the merits of such-and-such a municipal team.[2] During protests against a decision by the municipality to increase land taxes in Beykoz–a protest movement with broad backing from the muhtars–the latter openly threatened to advise their citizens to no longer vote for the AKP.[3] Muhtars adopt highly varied positions, ranging from praise to acerbic criticism. Bediz was full of praise for her municipality's services–unlike Fikret who, as seen earlier, did not refrain from portraying his district municipality as corrupt and biased. Duran was also very critical of the team in office at his municipality, imputing their 2009 electoral victory to their tolerance of illegal buildings as a response to property pressure and speculation. Muhtars are aware of wrongdoing not only by inhabitants but by the public authorities too–which they may choose to conceal or disclose. In publicly denouncing certain ruses of the municipal team, Duran and Fikret made public the "guilty knowledge" (Hughes 1958, 81 et seq.) of connivance to which they were habitually bound. By being able to denounce publicly some actions of municipal teams, muhtars exert real power to inflict damage.

Drawing on the idea that muhtars can influence votes, even unelected authorities (civil and military administrative bodies) may use muhtars as a channel to influence voting, especially in conflict situations. Shortly before the 1999 general election, police chiefs in southeastern Turkey, where armed forces were at war with the PKK, summoned the local muhtars on several occasions to warn

them that voting for the pro-Kurdish party would severely harm their relations with the administration.[4] Residents of a village in the province of Batman
complained that they had been urged to vote "yes" in the 2017 constitutional
referendum, due to the absence of voting booths and the presence of the police
and a muhtar sporting a pistol. According to them, the muhtar subsequently
beat up a voter who had filed a complaint with an attorney working for the
HDP, the pro-Kurdish legal party (Cupolo 2017). These episodes concerned villages and conflict situations in which the authorities sought to curb votes for
pro-Kurdish parties.

The judgments that muhtars express about the authorities also acquire particular importance when sensitive, potentially unpopular measures are being
implemented. Mayors and governors expect muhtars' support in getting the
population to accept certain official decisions. This was the case during the
school rezoning in neighborhood B, and is the case more generally when urban
renewal projects are being implemented (see the next chapter).

This interdependency between muhtars and the authorities is, however,
asymmetric. The vast majority of muhtars say they are obliged to stay on good
terms with officials and municipal representatives to get access to resources
(Arıkboğa 1998, 141–42). Poor relations between muhtars and municipal teams
can indeed have significant effects. Duran best exemplifies this kind of situation.
In 2009 he sat for the first time on the quadrennial assessment committee that
fixes the nominal value of land per square meter, which is then used to calculate
certain taxes. During this meeting, the municipal team increased the rate very
significantly. Duran objected to this increase on the grounds that poorer people
would be unable to pay, but his arguments did not prevail.[5] In their capacity as
their inhabitants' representative, muhtars can launch legal appeals. That is what
Duran did–clearly a fairly rare occurrence–on the grounds that the increase
was "disproportionate and arbitrary." In 2011 the court ruled in his favor; the
ruling in Duran's favor was upheld, against an appeal, for 173 streets out of 176.

Duran was proud of having successfully defended the residents' interests.
However, he reported how this episode had triggered a deterioration in his
relations with the municipality, claiming that the latter immediately stopped
paying the salary for his employee. Prior to this, the municipal council had
paid for administrative costs and the salaries of muhtarlık employees, but had
suspended all subsidies to muhtarlık D. These subsidies for muhtarlıks are

decided by the municipal council, and are in no way obligatory, being at the council's discretion and hence granted as a favor. They thus reinforce muhtars' dependency on municipalities. Duran's case shows how material assistance may be a major stake in the relationship, and even a way for municipalities to exert pressure on muhtars. Furthermore, Duran complained that his requests to build a school, police station, and health center were turned down. He said he no longer asked the municipality for anything. Residents in his neighborhood may still claim municipal assistance, but without his intermediation. This context helps explain why he provided a poverty certificate to whoever asked, without getting any further involved.

In 2013 the committee decided once again to raise the tax valuations significantly, but in the meantime the constitutional court had annulled muhtars' right of appeal, so that only individual proceedings were now possible. Duran encouraged such initiatives, and on his premises he displayed the court ruling on this matter, which I did not see in any other muhtarlık. He also filed several individual proceedings against the municipality concerning the land-use plan, and also against the municipality transferring ownership of land under overhead power lines, even though there were dwellings there. He thus made the conflict public. Duran portrayed himself as a "downtrodden muhtar" (*ezilen*), a champion of justice defending his citizens against the power of money. In private, he denounced attempts to corrupt him by the municipal attorney. He insinuated that relations between the municipality and muhtars were based on self-interest: several muhtars reputedly enjoyed–sometimes unofficially– certain benefits from the municipality, such as free sites for stalls in municipal covered markets. He concluded that "you benefit from lots of things like that, and then you can't protect the people in your neighborhood, the rights of the neighborhood against the injustices of a few." He reckoned that certain muhtars were quite simply "bought" by the municipality. Duran's case makes clear that it is possible, but very costly, for muhtars to oppose their municipality. The authorities have more power over the muhtars than vice versa. Their dependency, while reciprocal, thus remains asymmetric.

ADEPTLY MANAGING TIES WITH INSTITUTIONS

In this landscape, muhtars participate in what Babül calls the "risky business of governance," the "slippery terrain of bureaucratic arrangements that shift according to changing constellations of power and influence" (1997, 152). Despite the inherent limits to their own power, they respond creatively to the workings of power. They employ various tactics to get their institutional partners to respond favorably to their requests. We shall now look at how they navigate their institutional partners and their relations with them.

Limiting, Hierarchizing, and Chasing Matters Up

Muhtars have few means of pressuring institutional service providers into acceding to their requests. They therefore limit the number of requests, relaying the ones they view as priorities, thereby seeking to preserve their credibility. Bediz thus said, "If I recommend too many people [for municipal welfare], they won't take me seriously anymore." By limiting the number of requests she supported, she spared the municipality, together with her "credit." Depending on the matter at hand and the ties they have with their interlocutor, muhtars felt able to ask for services of varying importance, and to insist to varying degrees. Thus, they are not in a position where they are merely reacting. Instead, they continually arbitrate to facilitate or block the flow of requests for information and services. To that extent, they resemble Argentinian brokers, whom Auyero depicts as "expert manipulators of information and of people, channeling resources" in one direction or another (2000, 83).

In operating as intermediaries, muhtars deploy discursive strategies. One of these is to insist on the urgency or importance of the situation. An argument they often use is to cite discontent among neighborhood residents. "There is a lot of resentment," Bediz noted to the municipal head of roads, when reminding him of the disastrous state of a road she was asking to have repaired, and insisting that he would be morally responsibile if a resident were injured. She took advantage of his presence at a "people's assembly" to chase up three cases she had already submitted, but which were still pending.

Muhtars also have to mind how they behave. Ebru emphasized the importance of being courteous, and certain muhtars are careful to behave in a seemly fashion, even obsequiously. When Ahmet called a manager of the SYDV welfare fund to ask them to continue assisting an old man who was ill, he called her "my dear director," then "my soul" (*canım*). He discreetly said to the old man with a wink: "I do a bit of sucking up, then I'll ask for something" (*Biraz yağ çekeyim sonra bir şey isteyim*). Several muhtars said they employed a mixture

FIGURE 11. Banner: "We thank the mayor of *x* municipality, [name of mayor], for having embellished our power transformer. The muhtar of *x* neighborhood." Istanbul, May 2014. Photograph by the author.

of sweetness and firmness. Bediz reckons that the key to her success with the municipality is her firm yet amiable approach and "sweet talk" (*tatlı dil*). Fikret also insisted on this aspect: "My style is an iron fist in a velvet glove. What matters is getting something without rubbing anyone the wrong way."

Certain muhtars publicly thank their institutional partners who are responsible for supplying services, even collective ones. They do so through the local media, by hanging banners in the street (figure 11), or even on social media. In the absence of criteria for determining priority, whenever the authorities satisfy a request, it is considered a favor. Publicly thanking them frames the relationship as one of gratitude, and hence as a favor rather than routine work. This in turn fuels the image of public goods as dependent on the willingness of decision makers, and even on favors.

Thus Bediz, who was on good terms with the municipality, explained that when the roads in her neighborhood were redone, she had a banner hung thanking the mayor: "in the name of the neighborhood residents, the muhtar of neighborhood B."[6] Frequently it is not an institution which is thanked, but an individual. This public display promotes the action of the relevant authority and places the institution and person thanked under an obligation, while at the same time vaunting the effectiveness of the muhtar.

Choosing an Interlocutor

Insofar as muhtars may intervene for various types of affairs, they have many potential interlocutors, including the mayor, deputy mayors, heads of municipal departments, council members, and municipal staff. To whom are they to turn? One important aspect of how they navigate institutions is their ability to choose the right interlocutor–who is not always the most obvious choice.

Several principles guide this choice. The first predictable one is hierarchy. One of the key factors is the importance of what is at stake. Mindful of the relative autonomy departments enjoy for routine affairs, muhtars tend to turn to department heads or their staff. Ebru explained that if it was in the power of smaller services and departments to do something, then it was better to solve problems with them directly; but if it looked like things were not going to be sorted, then she preferred to address the mayor directly. Muhtars have direct channels of communication with several municipal departments, she said: "I sort things out with the smaller services. For example, for a hole in the road, I right away ask a friend in the roads department, 'Mr. Erhan, can you sort that out?' And he answers, 'Of course, Ebru, I'll see to it,' and two days later it's sorted."

Muhtars tend to build up personal ties with municipal staff. I often heard them get through to staff directly on the telephone, call them by their first name, and use the familiar second-person form of address. Thus, Bediz said she was on good terms with staff in the district population bureau, calling them all by their first names. She claimed they always answered her, so she did not hesitate to call them, even several times a day. She said she was "perfectly at ease about calling, without feeling awkward, as if I were calling my own mother or daughter." Ebru, too, acted likewise with people at the population bureau. Muhtars often define their relationships with the authorities in terms of personal ties. They often talk about their municipal interlocutors in terms suggestive of friendship, affection, and even kinship. In talking about Burhan, a staff member in the municipal roads department, Bediz said, "He's a brother, I like him a lot."

On being interviewed by Erder in the 1990s, the muhtars of Ümraniye insisted on how they needed to know everybody at the municipality, from the mayor and his deputies through the department heads, and down to the road sweepers (Erder 1996). In a very similar way, Fikret claimed to sort out lots of things using his one-to-one relations (*ikili diyaloğumuz*): "We maintain dialogue with each institution. As an individual, to sort out problems, you need to have good one-to-one relations." Everything indicates that the interpersonal dimension is important for most dealings. Fliche has documented how in the 2000s, the muhtar of an Alevi village in Anatolia was able to draw on political, family, and friendship ties with senior bureaucrats to mobilize public resources that were otherwise hard to access (Fliche 2005). The personalization of relations, far from concerning interactions solely between muhtars and inhabitants, is also extensively employed by muhtars in their interactions with the authorities.[7]

Privileging Privileged Ties

Interestingly, this personalization–or principle of proximity–sometimes supersedes the principle of hierarchy. When muhtars cannot achieve their purpose using a routine procedure, or feel insufficiently close to the person in charge to present their request, they often proceed indirectly via someone else. Rather than approaching the competent individual with whom they lack a privileged relationship, muhtars then contact someone else with whom they are on good terms, even if that person has no authority in the matter at hand. A single muhtar may have very different relations with various people in a given institution—as illustrated above by Fikret having a privileged interlocutor in the municipality with whom he can speak casually and use the familiar pronoun—but may have hierarchical ties with another. Therefore, whenever they can, muhtars privilege their privileged ties. Ebru thus declared: "I try to turn to people for whom what I say counts. And I present the thing in the light of what I want from the person I'm dealing with [*Karşı tarafın isteği doğrultusunda atyorum*]. For example, it was very difficult to get this cart [belonging to the meatball seller] back from the municipal police, but when I approached someone who knew my father very well, then things became simpler. [...] That's why I talk about using one's contacts, one's circle; if you're not particularly appreciated [...], the person won't sort out your case or else they'll drag their heels." Ebru said she enjoyed a certain advantage because of her father, and that people who had already worked at the municipality in her father's day were very helpful to her. She claimed they had "attitudes like,

'What you say must be done immediately.'" To her mind, being on good terms with her interlocutor is primordial.

Muhtars contact somebody with whom they are on good terms to act as a "relay" or "lever"—that is, to put pressure on, or at least put them in touch with, the municipality. Certain muhtars have municipal councillors who act as their privileged interlocutors or "levers" at the municipality. Bediz, for example, very often sought help from an AKP councillor, Bedirhan. She said that it was thanks to him that she obtained things from the municipality, such as container bins or getting a power transformer painted: "He has great influence in all the aid I disperse, in everything I do. In other words, I ask him, and he then asks our municipality, and that way I send my business to him." When she is having trouble getting what she wants from the municipality, she gets Bedirhan to step in: "If I'm having a lot of trouble, then I call Bedirhan, [...] and it works in the end." Indeed, I witnessed Bediz asking him to intervene in requesting municipal transport to drive bedridden people to polling stations. Bediz addressed him using the familiar second-person form, the diminutive form of his name, and the fictitious endearment "elder brother." Bedirhan comes from the province of Siirt in eastern Turkey, and people from Siirt are one of the two main groups in Bediz's neighborhood, where he also happens to reside. Bedirhan said he felt particularly concerned about neighborhood B. Lasting cooperation was built up between Bediz and him on that basis.

Even in the absence of any privileged ties, muhtars often pass via municipal councillors to further their purpose, when their target is the municipality. Former municipal councillors also regularly act as azas. Ebru explained why she had chosen her uncle, a former district municipal councillor from 2004 to 2009, as one of her azas: "He got several neighborhood problems placed on the agenda of the municipal council when he was a member. Because, as aza, he has the right, and competence, for me to say to him tomorrow or some day: 'Come on, uncle, can you go to the district municipality and pass on these requests?' For he knows the municipality well, he knows people there. He knows the neighborhood, shopkeepers. People know him...." Ebru claimed that this was why she had chosen him as aza: "to be able to rapidly sort out neighborhood problems. [...] In situations where I can't fight, I resort to my uncle. [...] He has helped me with the municipal council for people I cannot reach, when I am unable to speak or meet with them."

Having relations in municipalities is thus a significant resource. But it is not necessarily a matter of preexisting networks, of relationships established before being elected as muhtar. Those may also be set up at a later stage. Fliche recounts how an Anatolian village muhtar managed to obtain public services by building up a privileged tie in the bureaucracy. To get a road built, he visited the local branch of the party that controlled the Ministry of Public Works–for if an official is reluctant, the party chair may refer matters to his superiors in Ankara. In exchange for the requested service, the muhtar explicitly used his villagers' votes as a bargaining chip (Fliche 2005). To pressure local decision-makers, muhtars may therefore use party ties–or build them up from scratch. In any event, these ties are built up and maintained through action.

Muhtars are thus careful to treat their privileged interlocutors with consideration, and to stay on good terms with them over time. Fikret insisted on the importance of maintaining two-way relations: "I have to think about the future, for it's a long-term thing. Heads [of municipal departments] change. I pay them visits; we visit each other and call each other up." These relations are also sustained by little favors that muhtars do for certain institutional partners. Likewise, İlhan said he had helped some "friends at municipality" get their children enrolled for a school with a very good reputation in his very upmarket neighborhood: "I do it in the name of mutual assistance [yardımlaşma olsun diye]." These favors were probably granted in exchange for other services. Such exchanges of favors, far from being limited to residents, include strategic ties in the institutions.

THE INCREASING ROLE OF PARTIES

The importance of municipal councillors and the involvement of parties in those circuits raises the question of what role partisan political factors may play in ties between muhtars and institutions. This question leads, in turn, to that of the relations which muhtars in office have with political parties. To what extent do parties help or constrain muhtars? Are muhtars autonomous from party politics?

Parties as Intermediaries with the Authorities

To what extent does the partisan political dimension influence how muhtars relate with the authorities? Though mostly denied, this partisan political dimension comes into play most clearly at the municipal level–though only to a relative and variable degree. Muhtars and district municipalities both tend to deny any partisan political dimension to their ties. Bediz denied that there was any partisan political factor at work in her good relations with the district municipality. She raised the eventuality of another party running the municipality: "If I work with them, I have to spend those five years together without any problem. I'll explain my requests, and if they're not done, I'll ask insistently. And the municipality won't classify me on the basis of whether I'm from the CHP or the MHP or the BDP, but on the basis of what I ask for." Likewise, an official at a district municipality firmly denied that political proximity played any role in the relations between the municipality and muhtars: "The mayor's approach is that if a muhtar has been elected then we, as a local body, are obliged to support them." He later admitted, however, that "there are muhtars who share the mayor's political opinions, and others who don't. And we know that." However, this idealized (and legitimate) vision is only part of the picture.

The partisan political dimension seems to play a fairly important role in relations with the district municipality. Muhtars who were politically aligned with the party running their district municipalities (Bediz and Ebru) clearly judged the municipal team's actions more positively than did muhtars with diverging political opinions (Duran and Fikret). There was obviously a partisan political factor in the poor relations between Duran and his AKP-run municipality. AKP deputies reputedly intervened to prevent Duran's being elected to the SYDV board; likewise, he said he was on poor terms with local AKP leaders. During the 2014 election campaign, there were also rumors about attempts by the municipal authorities to intimidate inhabitants and property developers into distancing themselves from Duran, saying that otherwise they would cut off their welfare or refuse building permits–which threats did not suffice, since Duran was reelected. Among various criticisms that muhtars make of municipalities whose political leanings they do not share, one of the most frequent is the accusation of partisan political favoritism. Thus Duran denounced his municipality for following party criteria in distributing assistance: "In matters of welfare, you should look solely at the citizen's situation, not their language, race, or religion. But they ask what party you belong to." Fikret, too, said that the district municipality provided more services to people who were close to it politically.

Additionally, partisan political networks may provide muhtars with access to those involved in decision making. What part does the partisan political dimension play in the relations that bind muhtar and councillor together? It seems that links to the party running the municipality are more effective in helping muhtars obtain what they request. Accordingly, municipal councillors from the party that runs the district municipality seem to hold a far more "strategic" position, from the muhtars' point of view. Cemil said he only knew municipal councillors from the ruling AKP, not those from opposition parties, even though the CHP had won the most votes in his own neighborhood. Likewise, Ebru said she did not know the district leaders of parties other than the CHP, which ran the municipality in which her neighborhood lay. Finally, Bedirhan was actually a member of the ruling party. However, and irrespective of all this, Ebru and Bediz both belonged to the same political families as those running their district municipalities. To ascertain whether what predominates among muhtars are links with councillors of the party in office or links with councillors who share their political orientation, it is more telling to look at muhtars whose political leanings diverge from those of their district municipalities, such as Duran and Fikret. A CHP municipal councillor (hence from the party running the district municipality) who oversaw neighborhood matters regularly visited Fikret, who belonged to a political family different from his own. So do muhtars seek to preserve and foster their ties to municipal councillors from the party running the district, irrespective of which party it may be? Not exactly. Duran did not receive municipal councillors from the ruling party (the AKP)—only those from the opposition, who no doubt had less power. It is also possible that his relations with the municipality and the AKP had become so poor that he did not even try to obtain anything from the municipality. So while there is indeed an instrumental dimension to the links muhtars maintain with municipal councillors–meaning that those who rule the municipality are, in general, approached more frequently–muhtars' party preferences may also affect their access to them.

The partisan political dimension would also appear to play a part in relations with the metropolitan municipality, which in Istanbul was run by the AKP until June 2019. Muhtars close to the AKP were the only ones to mention drawing on its assistance: Bediz who, with Bedirhan, directed citizens toward the metropolitan municipality assistance services and supplied them with recommendations; and Fikret, in a district run by the CHP. The latter was close to the AKP, but prided himself on being on good terms with the metropolitan municipality. He claimed to be in touch with those who ran the metropolitan municipality assistance fund, and that it was the families he put forward who benefited from it. In the matter of the park in the upper part of his neighborhood, Fikret did not wish to become involved in the movement to defend the park, which had been rehabilitated by the CHP-run district municipality, and which the AKP-run metropolitan municipality was threatening to destroy. It may be considered that his political leanings and ties with the metropolitan municipality were a factor here.

This partisan political dimension comes out even more clearly when, in the absence of any official procedure, it is a matter of passing on exceptional requests to the authorities. Fikret said he dealt with the metropolitan municipality only for major projects, and that he handled them through political channels (*siyaset üzerine*). He gave bus routes as an example. When a subway station was opened, the bus routes changed, meaning that the upper part of the neighborhood was no longer served. Fikret took the opportunity afforded by the official opening of the subway station attended by the Istanbul metropolitan mayor to approach him and request a meeting. He explained the situation to the mayor, and managed to get the routes changed so that the upper part of his neighborhood was served. Fikret's close ties with the AKP may have helped him get this meeting and obtain an answer to his request. He said he used political channels for a certain number of matters: "In the event of problems, I call on the local head of the ruling party. I invite him to do his duty and solve the problem." He said he "used politics for the subgovernorship offices, for ownership deeds. But mainly at the district level." He said he "obviously" knew the AKP local district leaders, as well as those higher up, at the Istanbul level: "But I don't have many dealings with them. [...] Only for major projects." Fikret also mentioned problems with plots of land. But he additionally emphasized the interpersonal dimension, as he did for the bus route changes: "It's not the party; it's one-to-one relations [*ikili*]. The mayor, his deputy, and department heads. [...] If the problem seems insoluble and I think that political power could help solve it, then I give it a go." Fikret thus presented his recourse to politics as a means for resolving problems that otherwise would have gone unanswered, but linking it to personal relations and thus rendering the partisan political aspect invisible.

Party links may also be used to help get a matter passed on to a decision-maker who, though not in charge of the matter, is highly placed. Fikret said that the matter of land status in his neighborhood had been presented to Turkey's prime minister, Tayyip Erdoğan. Apparently a procedure had been put in place to transfer property to residents in two cooperatives, but the residents were not satisfied with it. The prime minister came to the district for an inauguration, and after the ceremony Fikret and others managed to hand him the case file and obtain a meeting, thanks to the intercession of the AKP district head, and also thanks to Fikret having known Erdoğan in the days when the latter was Istanbul's metropolitan mayor (1994–98). Thus, at the metropolitan and higher levels it is primarily party links that may be used to obtain services, and to break out of official channels to get matters settled by highly placed decision makers. Muhtars are thus among those actors who, "in going about their activities, are led to work with political actors, solicit them, advise them, or have some kind of dealings with them–but who also thereby put them back in place when they 'ask too much,' when they risk compromising themselves as social partners and undermining the grounds of their own legitimacy," as Lagroye has observed (2005, 364).

Placing muhtars in the context of institutional constraints sheds new light on certain aspects of their behavior. Bediz enjoyed very good access to municipal and subgovernorate resources, claiming that she could play a role in how they were channeled. Things were more difficult for Duran, who had no contact with the municipality and fairly limited access to subgovernorate assistance. He did not present himself as mediating social assistance, a role he could probably not have played successfully, and instead concentrated on more collective and activist causes. Though he was in open opposition to the municipality and critical of the AKP, Duran did not systematically oppose the authorities. He tried to maintain order in his neighborhood—for example, by seeking to neutralize local repercussions of the Gezi Park protests in the summer of 2013—and this despite his main concerns (participatory democracy, opposition to urban transformation and government authoritarianism, et cetera) being attuned to the key demands of that protest movement. Duran said he had dispersed protesters and prevented Gezi-linked demonstrations in his own neighborhood, advising the demonstrators to take their protest to Taksim Square, the center of the movement, and avoid any local confrontation.

Fikret's position, despite his very different political preferences, was very similar in terms of maintaining order. The neighborhood he administered, though slightly less difficult than Duran's, was just as politically tense. He was pro-AKP and clearly appreciated those in power in both the national government and the Istanbul metropolitan municipality, even though he opposed urban transformation. During the Gezi Park events, he adopted the same attitude as Duran: "They came down from up there banging their saucepans and frying pans.[8] So I told them to stay up there, and bang on their saucepans and frying pans at home. They did not come down again. [...] If a group wants to oppose the government, then they can just go to Taksim." Fikret here acted to attenuate opposition protests, and sought to maintain order and peaceful cohabitation in his neighborhood. Though from a political family different from that of the district municipality, he was considerate of all his interlocutors. An activist from a group in favor of an alternative, participatory form of urbanism, though habitually reserved about political matters, praised Fikret's political nous: "He speaks with everyone." It becomes clear, then, that partisan political orientations do indeed influence relationships between muhtars and authorities—most importantly, municipalities—but only to a certain extent. Only muhtars from even more oppositional backgrounds than Duran, like Kadir with his radical left background, went so far as to fuel Gezi protests in their own neighborhoods–though Kadir avoided doing so openly, so as not to alienate the subgovernors' office.

Targeting Political Parties

Let us mention a final way that links to political parties may impact on how muhtars operate. This concerns muhtars who harbor ambitions of going into politics, and who may regard the muhtarlık as a springboard to a political career. Muhtars try to make the transition to party politics relatively often, in most cases by running for a municipal council seat. The available sources, which are in no way representative, seem to suggest that few muhtars who wish to run are selected by parties, which do not seem to place much store by such a background. Fikret's attempt in 2014 to be selected as an AKP candidate for the municipal council failed. Nevertheless, some muhtars do succeed. For instance, the muhtar of Kayabaşı from 1995 to 1999 went on to become CHP municipal councillor for the district of Başakşehir in 2009. The head of the Istanbul muhtar federation—who is very active politically, including at the national level—was nominated by the MHP as a parliamentary candidate in 2007, and then as candidate for mayor of his district municipality in 2009. In both elections, he was defeated.

Such projects clearly influence how muhtars perform their role. Fikret changed the way he presented himself on his Facebook page once his attempt to win his party's nomination failed. This impact is also clear in muhtars' involvement in optional, "secondary" activities. Although Ebru said there was nothing political about her job as muhtar, but that "some also see it as a way into politics," she admitted that she would envisage the possibility of a political career if the circumstances were right. However, she denied any precise intent or strategy to attain that end: "Personally I'm not like that. That is, I don't say, 'I absolutely have to go into politics.' [. . .] Time will tell. If it's meant to happen, it will happen. If a door opens and a step is taken in that direction, then fine. But I don't do anything for that. It's not my goal." Still, a certain number of initiatives she implemented suggest that she was seeking to expand her field of action. Thus, she decided to engage more actively with the municipal council, unlike other muhtars who had been turning away from it: "In fact, my concern is to learn a bit about politics, to enter politics from the shallow end [uçundan], and see what councillors do, what they discuss." At the same time, Ebru was elected to the board of the city council, on the same party list as the mayor, despite never having attended its meetings. In 2014 she became head of the district muhtar federation. The expansion of her activities and her acquisition of a more central position are linked to her close ties with the municipality. And it is quite possible that this centrality might help her on her path toward politics. Given that muhtars do not on the whole engage with those institutions, it may be considered that muhtars who plan for moving into politics show a proportionally greater tendency to do so.

As stated at the beginning of this book, muhtars are dominated within the administrative and political structure. They depend on their institutional partners to access many resources which are crucial for their work—such as services, assistance, and information—and for which there are no clear criteria. To access these scarce resources, they often use or build up privileged personal ties, which in many cases deviate from the hierarchy. They therefore play a part in the personalization of decision-making, and in fueling the idea that even public services are rendered as favors.

Political parties are one of the main channels for building up such strategic ties. In that respect, the cases of Bediz and Duran are in sharp contrast to each other. Bediz, who had been involved with the party in government, had very good access to her district municipality, the metropolitan municipality (until 2019), and the subgovernor's office. She acted as a generous provider of services and resources to her neighborhood. Duran, on the contrary, was opposed to the party running the national government, the metropolitan municipality (until 2019), and his district municipality. He had scarce access to public resources, and could provide hardly any services or divisible goods. Rather, he increasingly engaged in oppositional stances and activities. He was, however, reelected, thus proving that muhtarlıks still had a fair degree of autonomy from party politics, perhaps acting as counter-spaces in a landscape otherwise dominated by a hegemonic party. But relations between the muhtarlıks and the partisan political and institutional fields have been reconfigured in recent years.

Chapter 8

THE MUHTARLIK'S WANING AUTONOMY

THE PAST FEW YEARS HAVE SEEN A DECLINE IN THE MUHTARLIK'S autonomy, in several ways. First, since the mid-2000s, municipalities have become more heavily involved at the microlocal level, thereby limiting the muhtarlık's relative autonomy. Second, the advent of more assertive urban development policies has often obliged muhtars to adopt a stance on conflictual issues. Finally, the central authorities have become increasingly involved in how the muhtarlıks are run, particularly since Tayyip Erdoğan became president of Turkey in 2014. This threefold evolution has reinforced the muhtarlıks' dependency on other institutions, and has fostered their alignment with partisan political dynamics.

MUNICIPALITIES ENGAGING AT THE NEIGHBORHOOD LEVEL

Since the mid-2000s, municipalities have become more vigorously involved in the neighborhood sphere, particularly in the wake of the 2005 Law on Municipalities (see chapter 1). More generally, they–especially AKP-run municipalities–have advocated more ambitious municipal policies for services to the population at the local level. In the 2000s, AKP municipalities–rapidly emulated by others–set up new amenities at the local level (Joppien 2019). To a certain extent, these new municipal policies and services have competed with the muhtars. But rather than short-circuiting the muhtars, they have sought to integrate them, while at the same time sidelining them and confining them to a subordinate position.

Since the 1990s, parties in the Milli Görüş (National Vision) Islamist movement, from which the AKP stems, have built up a carefully coordinated and effective grassroots organization, keeping a close watch on neighborhoods to identify the needy, and to flag problematic situations. On coming to power in 1994 in many municipalities, such as Istanbul and Ankara, the Islamist Refah Partisi (Prosperity Party) introduced municipal policies that continued the practices the movement had set up while in opposition, of closely monitoring social needs and distributing assistance. The AKP distanced itself from the ideology of the Milli Görüş tradition while nevertheless broadly assuming its mantle, particularly in the many municipalities these parties had continued to run since the 1990s.

Hence in the 2000s, several district municipalities run by the AKP (such as Beyoğlu and Fatih) introduced neighborhood centers at the semt level (*semt konakları*).[1] Certain CHP municipalities, such as Beşiktaş and Sarıyer, followed suit a few years later, calling them neighborhood houses (*semtevleri*). Official discourse refers to hizmet (service), promoting these local amenities as a way of being in closer contact with inhabitants, and better adapting to their needs. These centers provide various public services under a single roof, though their exact nature varies with the local setup: free health clinics and, in certain cases, psychological support centers; educational courses and seminars (in IT, English, literacy, preparation for the university entrance exam, and craftwork for women); and cultural activities such as talks and concerts. They also dispense social services, with social assistance offices and in some cases services for the destitute such as soup kitchens, laundromats, and showers. There was also an administrative aspect, with offices to pay bills and taxes in certain establishments. AKP and CHP neighborhood centers are fairly similar in purpose and functioning, differing primarily in programs and architecture. AKP centers tend to offer lessons in calligraphy and the Quran, whereas CHP centers run seminars on consumer "awareness" and public health. In terms of style, AKP "palaces" tend to be largely neo-Ottoman, and CHP "houses" more modernist. These centers, which are often next to parks, sports facilities, or cafés, are at the heart of neighborhood social life, especially as they sometimes also have banquet rooms for celebrating weddings and engagements. They also house muhtarlık premises, despite there being no hierarchical or organizational link. Muhtars in such places have thus been shorn of some of their mediation and multipurpose functions, and reduced to a minimal role of issuing documents. They are also under the direct scrutiny of municipal staff working in these establishments.

Most recently, several municipalities have set up "muhtar offices," seeking to associate the latter more closely to what they do. Likewise, a district municipality taken over by the CHP in 2014 set up a "neighborhood solution house" (*mahalle çözüm evi*) in each neighborhood, housing the muhtarlık together with a municipal complaints office. For municipal administrators, this was a matter of improving the working conditions of muhtarlıks by providing premises, but also of "better coordinating municipality and muhtarlık." An advisor in this municipality explained it to me:

> When they are paired, this has major advantages. [. . .] For citizens, bureaucracy and the municipality can be problematic. . . . Citizens only come [to the district municipality] as a last resort. [. . .] Muhtars are on very direct and warm terms with inhabitants. [. . .] We, with the muhtars, are able to connect with citizens. In the same way as a citizen goes to the muhtar to talk about a problem [. . .], he will be able to talk about it to the municipal solution center. [. . .] When you enter citizens' daily life, you can connect with realities and produce solutions. [. . .] We need to connect with the field. [. . .] We need to be closer, and muhtarlıks are the most appropriate place and entity for that.

Clearly, the municipal staff endeavored to establish themselves at the level of the muhtarlık and to appropriate the type of relationship built up there with the population.

Another device introduced by several AKP municipalities, "people's assemblies" (*halk meclisi*), incorporates muhtars while sidelining them. On winning municipal power in the 1990s, the Refah party introduced various schemes to receive inhabitants complaints—such as the "people's day" (*halk günü*) and "white table" (*beyaz masa*).[2] Since 2014, no doubt in the wake of the Gezi Park protests, which were critical of top-down urban developments that neglected inhabitants' concerns, several municipalities have switched the level at which such schemes operate, from the district level to that of the semt.[3] Despite their name, they are not assemblies but sessions during which inhabitants come to present requests directly to municipal leaders (councillors and staff). Each semt is placed under the responsibility of one municipal councillor, the most important person at those meetings. The person in charge of the semt containing neighborhood B is none other than Bedirhan. The muhtars from the semt are supposed to attend. However, their role is limited to presenting the cases under consideration for processing by the municipal councillor, and at times suggesting solutions; they no longer oversee the interaction with residents. They address the councillor with deference, and are in a subordinate position–as was already the case in the past, though unseen by citizens. When inhabitants come to the muhtarlık with a request that does not quite fit the habitual framework, the muhtars often advise them to present it at the next people's assembly. Such was the case of the widow discussed in chapter 5.

Certain muhtars regularly attend these assemblies, while others drag their heels. These contrasting attitudes would appear to stem from two main factors. First is the social situation of the neighborhood. Neighborhood B is home to many needy people, and Bediz makes a point of attending, being heavily involved in social affairs and very close to Bedirhan, who is her main support at the municipality. But other muhtars are far less keen. For instance, Cemil, whose neighborhood is smaller than Bediz's, and home to fewer needy people, says that he does not really see the point of the assemblies, since few residents attend.

The second factor is party alignment. Although the "people's assemblies" are a municipal initiative and are advertised as such, they in fact include a significant partisan political aspect. In practice, all the municipal councillors in charge of a semt come from the ruling AKP party; opposition councillors are excluded from the scheme. The form listing the residents heard during the sessions is explicitly marked "AKP."[4] While residents are apparently not always aware of this partisan political dimension, the muhtars are. On June 9, 2015, two days after the general election that was widely viewed as a defeat for the AKP, Bediz, who was preparing to go to the "people's assembly," bumped into a colleague from an adjacent neighborhood. The latter, who was significantly less close to the AKP, said jokingly to her: "Haven't you caught on yet? Playtime is over, stop [going there]!"

Municipalities include muhtars in new microlocal facilities and involve them in new schemes. They thereby diminish muhtars' relative autonomy, and seek to confine them to being mere auxiliaries, in a subordinate position–thereby diminishing their discretionary power.

POLITICIZATION THROUGH URBAN TRANSFORMATION

This is only one dimension to a broader process of politicization. At the same time, the AKP has implemented more interventionist urban policies. These, especially urban transformation policies (*kentsel dönüşüm*), have made local issues more conflictual. Until recently, urbanization in Turkey occurred largely spontaneously, with migrants settling illegally on public land. For a long while the public authorities tolerated this state of affairs before accommodating and then legalizing it. For decades, the public authorities made next to no effort to control urban dynamics. But the AKP put an end to several decades of turning a blind eye, in order to "take back control." In 2004, for the first time, the penal code made it an offense to build a *gecekondu*. The public authorities declared war on informal dwelling zones, which they depicted as backward, unhealthy, and sources of social problems.[5] In 2012 the Law on Catastrophe Risks generalized urban transformation. The purpose of these projects is to raze and rebuild dwellings and rehouse their inhabitants (often only legal owners, who can prove they own the land or buildings) in new accommodations, often some distance away.

The authorities tend not to involve muhtars in drawing up these urban transformation projects.[6] However, muhtars are compelled to adopt a stance on what is a crucial issue for neighborhood residents. The positions they adopt differ from one neighborhood to another. Some have supported them, as in Şahintepe, at times to their own benefit. Others have been opposed, such as Duran, Gaffar, and Kadir.[7] In many neighborhoods these projects have altered the stakes involved in local government, making it more conflictual. They have transformed muhtarlık issues, reinforcing their links to party politics.

The Emergence of, and Limits to, Activist Rationales

One of the best illustrations of how an urban transformation project can make the muhtarlık more conflictual and align it with partisan political divides is the Başıbüyük neighborhood. Petit studied in depth the conflicts and mobilizations around the implementation of this urban transformation project (2009). Başıbüyük is a *gecekondu* neighborhood built in the 1960s, and is home to about twenty-three thousand people. Although hooked up to electricity and water supply networks, the neighborhood is nevertheless deprived, with high levels of unemployment and many households dependent on social assistance. In 2006, the Maltepe district municipality (AKP) and the Istanbul metropolitan municipality adopted a protocol. It entailed demolishing many houses built on public land without rightful ownership or building permits, and set out plans to build 1,700 collective housing units. This protocol was introduced without consulting residents, who were unaware of its existence. When an employee at the district municipality learned about the transformation plan and informed the residents, the project sparked extensive conflict in the neighborhood.

Certain residents protested against the project, setting up a neighborhood defense association, founding a committee to inform residents, and drawing up a joint strategy that they presented to the Maltepe municipality.[8] They viewed the municipality as the main actor behind the operation, protesting several times against the mayor and his party, for instance.[9] But the muhtar also stood accused. When the existence of the project was made public, the residents' first reaction was to hold the muhtar accountable. The protesting inhabitants and city planners who supported them suspected the muhtar of having come to an agreement with the municipality.[10] Slogans chanted at various protests denounced the mayor of Maltepe and the muhtar as traitors, calling on them to resign.[11] In early 2007, residents whose dwellings were threatened with de-molition vandalized the muhtarlık; the muhtar was defended by the police, then evacuated in an armed vehicle to the boos of demonstrators.[12] The next day, teams from the municipality who had come to conduct a field study for implementing the project were chased off by residents, who bombarded the muhtarlık with stones.[13] In March 2008, a crowd of about two thousand demon-strators headed for the muhtarlık, which was protected by a cordon of police, to cries of: "Muhtar, resign!" and "Muhtar, sold out!"[14]

The 2009 local elections showed an alignment between urban policy issues and partisan political divides. The protesters went over to the main opposition party, the CHP. The head of the Başıbüyük neighborhood association driving the protests since 2006, Adem Kaya, was a CHP candidate for the Maltepe district municipal council. This alignment dynamic also extended to the muhtarlık. Although candidates for muhtar are supposed to run independently of any political party, Adem Kaya publicly supported one of the four candidates run-ning against the incumbent muhtar, who was seeking his fourth term.

In the Maltepe district, the CHP took up the urban transformation as a campaign theme in its own right. Its campaign brochure advocated a participa-tory model of urban management, the "Maltepe social participation project," with a platform including all the muhtars. Additionally, it stated that "all studies for urban planning and developments shall take into account the opinion of neighborhood representatives, muhtars, and the [professional] bodies concerned." The CHP's alternative project for local administration and urban planning echoed the one formulated by the İMDP (İstanbul Mahalle Dernekleri Platformu, or Platform for Istanbul Neighborhood Associations), a grouping of several associations representing neighborhoods threatened by such projects, with Adem Kaya emerging as one of its leaders. The İMDP declaration on January 5, 2008, recommended, for instance, that project planning and implementation be improved by municipalities working in cooperation with all those concerned (muhtars, neighborhood associations, experts, academics, and professional bodies).[15] Petit convincingly argues that this similarity suggests that the neighborhood representatives, heads of neighborhood associations, and muhtars involved with this platform played a leading role in drawing up the CHP local manifesto. For her, this also explains why the CHP advocated a local organization based on the muhtars, "committees of elders," and "street representatives," acting to inform the municipal council of residents' demands.

The 2009 local elections showed the extensive polarization affecting Başıbüyük. Residents unaffected by the urban transformation project mainly remained loyal to the incumbent muhtar and the AKP candidates they had elected in 2004. The decision by leaders of the neighborhood defense association to back a candidate running against the incumbent muhtar, to present a CHP candidate for the district municipal council, and to support the CHP candidate for the position of district mayor against the incumbent AKP mayor crystallized a divide among Başıbüyük residents around the issue of urban transformation. Petit convincingly shows how the urban transformation project politicized the muhtarlık in new ways, and aligned the election for muhtar with partisan political dynamics.

New Muhtar Profiles

In the 2009 election, the CHP won the district municipality, and the outgoing muhtar was beaten by the candidate backed by Adem Kaya and the association to safeguard Başıbüyük. Interestingly, the issue of the transformation project also altered the profiles of those running for the muhtarlık. Instead of the habitual "shopkeepers and traders" (see chapter 2), such a situation encourages candidates who come from resident protest movements or have their backing, often with a background in activism. In neighborhoods where urban transformation projects are in the pipeline, this attracts muhtarlık candidates with a background in real estate or construction. Indeed, such projects create openings for private developers and bring opportunities for property investment.

This was obvious in neighborhood h, home to about fourteen thousand people, mainly from the fairly well educated middle classes. A private cooperative of 1,150 housing units, built in the early 1980s, had a prominent place there. In the early 2010s, more than a hundred people from this housing complex requested that risk tests be conducted to assess its seismic resistance. The muhtar passed this proposition on to the authorities, triggering the anger of most of the residents, whom he had not consulted. Following this procedure, part of the neighborhood was decreed a risk zone in 2013, and slated for a transformation project. Many residents were opposed to the demolition of this estate, which was prized for its green surroundings. Two associations were then set up there, one to defend the transformation project and the other to prevent it, with the latter successfully taking legal action to this end. New divides opened up, and the team of the outgoing muhtar fractured along those lines. Most of the azas, who lived on this estate, did not share the position of the muhtar, who had acted without consulting them beforehand. The issue shattered the coalition they had formed to win the muhtarlık.

The matter also became politicized. The association in favor of demolishing the estate aligned with the AKP, which ran the district municipality, whereas CHP supporters founded their own association opposed to its demolition, and put forward their candidate for the post of muhtar. This was the decisive issue in the 2014 elections. There was a sharp increase in the number of candidates, with many of those running working in construction or real estate, probably anticipating potential profits from the development operation. The incumbent muhtar did not run, but his first aza did. He encountered much opposition to the planned demolition, and was not elected. Instead, a former muhtar returned to office.

Since the advent of urban transformation projects, many neighborhood defense associations have put forward or given their backing to candidates running for muhtar. Grassroot collectives and associations promoting participatory urbanism, such as Dayanışmacı Atölye (Solidarity Workshop)[16] or İmece

(Urbanism Movement of Society),[17] have advised, supported, and linked up movements opposing urban transformation. Initially, some of these initiatives did not trust muhtars, viewing them as bound to the central administration, or in hock to municipal authorities. They therefore did not always seek to cooperate with them. More notably since the Gezi Park movements, however, some of the initiatives have focused on the issue of muhtars, promoting their own idea of muhtars sensitive to resident participation. Thus, Dayanışmacı Atölye published a special report in its bulletin just ahead of the 2014 local elections, on the theme of "What type of muhtar do we want?"[18] Some of these associations have generated or backed candidates. In some cases, the incumbent muhtar has been replaced by a more activist figure issuing from neighborhood defense organizations—such as in Derbent, in the district of Sarıyer, in 2014. Openly left-wing activist organizations such as the *halkevleri* ("peoples' houses") have also become more involved in electoral competition for the post of muhtar, presenting candidates in the neighborhoods where they are active–even though the latter are only rarely elected.

Subdued Participatory Involvement

Other than for such projects, activist participatory dynamics rarely manage to take hold at the muhtarlık level. Some of those involved in the Gezi Park protests set up an association called Istanbul Hepimizin (Istanbul Belongs to All of Us), championing the idea of a "locally driven" (*yerelden*), participatory, transparent city. In the 2014 election they asked certain candidates running for the municipal council or muhtarlık to sign up to an "Istanbul charter" promoting participatory democracy. The association activists started working at the neighborhood level, so as to allow citizens to make themselves heard once again and resume responsibilities. One activist explained the initiative to Gaffar: "Locally, people are the best placed to know problems and to produce the best solutions. They need strengthening. [. . .] We want the people [*halk*] to take part in decisions." He had come to see Gaffar as part of the "get to know your muhtar" project (*muhtarınla tanış*), consisting of a series of encounters with muhtars to encourage citizens to find out about problems and take part in solving them–though in fact only a few activists attended these meetings, despite the invitation being widely circulated. This initiative drew up proposals, such as boosting consultation processes and increasing the role of muhtars in municipal decision making. The activist gave the example of the Kadıköy district municipality, run by the CHP, which set up "neighborhood assemblies" composed of one representative per street, working in association with the muhtars. In particular, he gave the example of the Sahrayicedit muhtar who, drawing on these assemblies, had introduced participatory initiatives. Apparently this muhtar proposed solutions to problems such as traffic and parking, which were presented to the municipality and applied by it (İstanbul Hepimizin 2015). But this type of initiative remains an exception. It is not fortuitous that it occurred in a central neighborhood that was home to a socially and economically privileged population.

During the two "get to know your muhtar" visits I observed, the activists and muhtars were not at all attuned to each other. The latter complained mainly about the conditions in which they carried out their duties and their powerlessness to solve certain neighborhood problems, and were not responsive to the pro-participation arguments of the activists. An activist asked İlhan if there was a neighborhood committee (*mahalle heyeti*), and what they discussed there. İlhan answered that he had azas, and that his first aza was his daughter. When asked if they met all the time, he hesitated before replying, "It depends." When the activists talked about the city council, supposedly attended by a sizeable number of muhtars, İlhan said he had never been invited. An activist asked if he had requested an invitation, to which İlhan answered no, adding, "I don't go where I'm not invited." Somewhat annoyed, the activist retorted, "It's not a matter of being invited. It's a citizen's right." The encounter was a series of misunderstandings, and it made clear how different the parties' worldviews were.

In 2014 the muhtar of this old bourgeois neighborhood of twenty-one thousand inhabitants, who had held the post for the previous thirty-five years, trounced a candidate from the Gezi Park movement, despite the movement being fairly strong in that neighborhood. The movement candidate had been advocating transparent participatory management, and had signed up to the Istanbul charter. With few exceptions, candidates who, in the wake of the Gezi Park events, ran on a "citizen" platform of giving inhabitants a voice in a proximity-based approach and reasserting local control over issues–but, significantly, without much neighborhood anchoring–were unsuccessful. In each case they tended to win only a few hundred votes, including in neighborhoods one could have reasonably expected to be receptive to such arguments. This shows the limits to appropriating participatory dynamics at the muhtarlık level.

Using the Muhtarlık as a Channel for Protest

In contrast to this, urban transformation projects with vital implications for inhabitants often spark protests from muhtars. Duran, for instance, directly opposed the municipality about concerns including an urban transformation project. Neighborhood D, like other neighborhoods adjacent to it, is in a state of legal uncertainty. In the absence of any urban plan, dwellings are tolerated, though nearly all of them are illegal. Some cannot be hooked up to the water and electricity networks for this reason. A plan was finally put in place in the 2000s, but was soon suspended when the zone was decreed a "reserve construction zone" for rehousing people from earthquake zones. All building projects were immediately halted. In 2013, Duran held a press conference with the backing of twenty or so local associations. He criticized the district municipality and the Ministry for the Environment and Urbanism for not having settled the question of land ownership before publishing the urban plan, thereby delaying the building of a school, despite its being budgeted, and the scheduled installation of power transformers. He threatened that if nothing were done, he would place a wreath of black flowers in front of the district municipal building–which he did a few weeks later.

Duran thus used his position to operate in activist ways. Given that he had virtually no institutional allies anyway, he mobilized opinion through the local media, particularly pro-opposition media. He openly conducted a legal "crusade" against the municipality. He also filmed a report for the website of the *Istanbul Times*, a local newspaper, in which, standing in a street that had become a pool of mud, he denounced the fact that a road leading to the school was not asphalted. He used these local media as an echo chamber to help him solve a problematic situation. The *Istanbul Times* proclaimed him "muhtar of the year" in 2011 for having "defended the just interests and rights of the people."

Duran did not have a background in activism and had never been a member of any party. In this he differed from more recently elected muhtars who specifically opposed urban renewal projects and had been renowned for their activist engagement prior to being elected. This is the case in neighborhood k, a very poor *gecekondu* neighborhood that leans strongly leftward, and where left-wing activist networks are influential. It was one of the first neighborhoods to have been targeted in 2004 by an urban transformation project. The muhtar elected in 2014, Kadir, is none other than the former head of the neighborhood association that opposed the transformation. Kadir has a background in 1970s radical left activism, and was then active in the SHP party during the early 2000s.[19] His election in 2014 is revealing because the incumbent muhtar he defeated, who had held the position since 2004, was also opposed to the urban transformation project, which he had not approved or been informed about. From then on, the muhtar and the neighborhood association fought the project together. In 2014 the election of the former association head, Kadir, with the more activist background, over the incumbent muhtar amounted to a form of politicization of the position.

Kadir used his position in an activist manner, and was involved in organizing protests against urban transformation. For him, a muhtar "awakens and guides the masses." He considered his support a way of transcending divides, of drawing previously separate groups to the opposition movement. To guarantee the consensual nature of his role and avoid alienating anybody, Kadir operated discreetly. Though he helped organize support for the Gezi Park protests, he did not attend gatherings. "I guide the masses, but I may remain invisible," he said. "If there is a press conference, for example, I may not attend. [. . .] We conduct activities together but [. . .] it is the association that is in charge. At that stage, I cannot put my name to it. Or when an anti-Erdoğan demonstration is being organized. But I can do propaganda for it. I can mobilize people." Still, Kadir tries to pass on the positions and requests of mobilized inhabitants and get them across to the authorities, thus acting as their "ambassador."

These critical and activist ways of enacting the role differ from those of Fikret. The broader context was also quite different. Fikret's CHP-run district municipality did not promote transformation projects. Like many muhtars in relatively long-established *gecekondu* neighborhoods, Fikret supported his residents' landownership interests, and advocated legalizing their tenure. The issue of property rights enjoyed consensus among the residents—a rare phenomenon in this socially and politically divided neighborhood. Fikret played an active role in the neighborhood defense association, and was involved in organizing residents into cooperatives to defend their land interests and prepare the sale of plots of land. His son claimed that they organized people and obtained legal information that they passed on to people. Fikret supported two petitions on this matter, in concert with cooperatives and neighborhood associations. These petitions attracted about a thousand signatures and were sent to the metropolitan municipality, district municipality, and political parties. According to Fikret, they did not achieve their goal but "we got our voices heard, and showed we were united." Fikret said the petitions were signed by people of different political persuasions, though a higher proportion of left-wing residents put their names to them. In a neighborhood not threatened by urban transformation, Fikret's long-term commitment to defending it and legalizing its status, together with his ties with associations in favor of alternative urbanism, enabled him to "straddle divides." Despite being known to have his own political preferences, he was viewed by various circles as a true defender of the neighborhood residents.

RENEWED ENGAGEMENT BY THE CENTRAL AUTHORITIES

The muhtarlıks have been of renewed interest to local authorities since the 2000s. But more recently, Turkey's central government has also turned its sights on them. The national executive has conducted several initiatives to bind muhtars more firmly to it: first, by improving their material circumstances, second, by improving the conditions in which they carry out their functions, and third, by reinforcing their links with devolved administrations and, increasingly, the central authorities.

Improved Working Conditions for Muhtars

First of all, the muhtars' material circumstances have improved. In particular, their compensation has increased to an unprecedented extent. Their pay has been increased, over and above the inflation index, using two different mechanisms on four successive occasions since the AKP came to power. The first type of increase was determined by the executive. The national cabinet may double the pay scale figure used to calculate their remuneration, which it did on two occasions: in 2005 from 3,000 to 6,000 on the pay index, and then again in January 2014, two months before local elections. In tandem, there has been a second form of increase. In July 2013, just after the Gezi Park protests, the national parliament passed a law fixing their remuneration at 5,700 on the pay index (potentially doubleable)—the first time such a law was passed. In 2014 it was indeed doubled, reaching 11,400. In 2016, the parliament raised the figure again, this time to 14,750. Since the 2010s, the muhtars' remuneration has, for the first time, exceeded the national minimum salary. This historic increase has resulted from decisions taken by the government and by the parliament, both dominated by the AKP.

Additionally, until recently, muhtars, whose status did not provide any social insurance coverage, had to pay an insurance premium amounting to almost half their monthly remuneration (TL490.59 in early 2017). Under a legal decree of May 1, 2017, this insurance premium is now paid by the state—a significant financial boost to muhtars' compensation, which for the first time is now enough to live on.[20] As the proportion of the muhtars' income stemming from their compensation increases, the proportion that comes from issuing documents decreases. The muhtars are financially anchored to the state to a greater extent, and their financial dependence on neighborhood residents drops. Hence, their working conditions increasingly resemble those of bureaucrats. This trend has been confirmed by a circular of November 8, 2017, introducing a professional ID card for muhtars, making it possible for people to easily and uniformly identify them.

Over the same period, the national executive has taken a second series of measures to improve muhtars' working conditions. Not all municipalities supply material support for muhtarlıks, but since 2015, Erdoğan has urged municipalities and ministries to provide the "necessary" support.[21] He has also asked the offices of governors and subgovernors to build premises for muhtarlıks who lack such facilities,[22] on land allocated by the national treasury if necessary.[23]

The muhtarlık is clearly being bound more firmly to the national executive. This has also resulted in new forms for muhtars to fill in, intended to inform the Ministry of the Interior of the needs in each neighborhood and village.[24] The central authorities thus present themselves as the recipients of requests hitherto addressed to local authorities. This new development is illustrative of a final series of measures intended to formalize muhtars' activities while linking them more directly to state institutions. A circular dated February 20, 2015, introduced an IT system with a portal to centralize any findings, complaints, or requests sent by muhtars to subgovernor's and governor's offices and to municipalities. The Directorate of Local Administrations is meant to pass this information on to the relevant state agencies, which have two weeks to respond. Procedures already followed by many administrations were thus extended to the muhtars. The circular further affected training and maintenance personnel for this system in the local authorities concerned. The system makes it possible for state institutions to monitor requests, and for quarterly reports to be generated on the number of requests received and the responses given. In 2017 another website was set up, on which it is possible to consult these reports.

These reforms were introduced at a time when muhtars were becoming better organized within a national federation, which managed to take on a consultative role to parliamentary committees. Representation of muhtars' interests thus became more organized. Still, the steps described above were not a straightforward reflection of what muhtars were calling for. Indeed, the reforms seem to indicate an attempt by the central authorities to bind muhtarlıks more closely and formally to central institutions and subject them to greater scrutiny. This is consistent with broader developments in terms of authoritarianization.

Increased Symbolic Value

One may speak of a coherent "muhtar policy" insofar as these changes have been accompanied by an unprecedented increase in the symbolic value attached to the position of muhtar since Tayyip Erdoğan became president of Turkey. Thus, in 2015 the prime minister's office issued a circular introducing a Muhtar Day, to be celebrated on October 19 each year. A travel program was also introduced for muhtars in 2018, under the patronage of the president, to "expose them to different cultures and various countries." The destinations were not chosen by chance, all having connections with Islam: Andalusia, Jerusalem, and holy Islamic places in Saudi Arabia. Plans were for one to two thousand muhtars to travel on this scheme in 2018.[25]

The most obvious manifestations of this enhanced symbolic value are, of course, the "muhtar meetings," described in the introduction to this book. The plan was to receive each of Turkey's fifty thousand village and neighborhood muhtars at least once every five years, though this objective was not fully met. "Only" about twenty thousand–that is, a little under half–had been invited when the meetings ceased in late 2018. However, this visible and extensive initiative was enough to suddenly thrust the muhtars into the spotlight.

These encounters reveal the unprecedented value the newly elected president placed on muhtars in Turkish public life at this time. This transpired in his praise of muhtars in his speeches. Erdoğan opportunely reminded his audience of everything his governments had done for them, pledging to continue bolstering their status and prerogatives and improve their working conditions. He claimed to personally identify with the muhtars, reminding them of an episode in his past. In 1998, when he was mayor of Istanbul, he was sentenced to ten months in prison for having recited a poem deemed tendentious because of its allusions to Islam. The day after the ruling, the biggest-selling newspaper in Turkey ran a front-page article about the probable demise of his political career, headlined "He Won't Even Be Able to Be Muhtar."[26] Particularly in his early speeches, Erdoğan criticized this headline as insulting to muhtars, and as typifying the lack of consideration and scorn political elites and bureaucrats reputedly felt for them–and, he claimed, for elected representatives in general.[27] He countered this, glorifying the sacred nature of the "popular will" whence muhtars emanated, bestowing superiority on elected representatives over nominated officials.[28] He asserted that election, irrespective of the number of votes received, should incite respect. On this basis, and describing himself as the "muhtar of Turkey,"[29] Erdoğan established an unbroken democratic line running from the muhtars to himself, the first Turkish president to be elected by direct universal suffrage: "The chain of election by popular preference, starting at the level of the muhtarlık, now reaches up to the presidency."[30] Erdoğan emphasized the value of muhtars as the first degree and core of democracy. This was all the more true, he argued, given that democracy, as a bottom-up process, emanated from the local level, from the family and village (Denli 2017). He declared that the president was a "başmuhtar"—a muhtar-in-chief of the country.[31] On the basis of this identification, Erdoğan called for a strengthening of the ties between the base and apex of this pyramid of elected representatives: "The stronger and healthier the ties between the president of the Republic, right at the top of the government organization [*yönetim*], and our muhtars, constituting the base of this structure, the better it will be for Turkey."[32]

From this perspective, Erdoğan emphasized the muhtars' importance to the government. He told them he urged their institutional partners to take them seriously: "I hereby warn all those who don't lend an ear or pay attention to requests [by muhtars] or who cause them difficulties. Anyone alienating the muhtar also alienates the neighborhood, that is to say the people [*millet*]. [. . .] A sensible administrator will listen attentively to all requests our muhtars make for their neighborhood, for the people in their neighborhood, and take the necessary steps."[33] Erdoğan thus stated that he wanted muhtarlıks to cease being places for getting certificates stamped, and to instead become effective functional units of government.[34] He argued for their importance on the grounds that "if a government really wants to perform successfully, it has to conduct dialogue with the muhtars at a very good level. [...] For who will act as its hand, its foot, its watchful eye, its listening ear in each neighborhood, in each village? It will be the muhtar."[35] It was because of the "very important position they hold," he said,[36] that muhtars ought to enjoy good working conditions. Erdoğan emphasized that Turkey needed them to be involved in all matters, from economic growth to foreign policy, and including security and the thwarting of threats to the country: "It is both highly important and extremely precious that each of you takes the initiative to solve Turkey's problems, to be pioneers guiding our people."[37] He thus called on the muhtars to back his projects for the country: "Our muhtars will be the most precious helpers in building the new Turkey. [...] That is why I beg you, in particular, to know how important you are, and to be aware of your weighty duty."[38]

On the grounds of promoting the role of muhtars in running the country, Erdoğan devoted most of his speeches to general policy, both national and international. Depending on the political agenda, he justified the process for resolving the Kurdish issue, praised his own achievements in infrastructure and housing policy, vigorously defended himself against accusations of corruption, promoted his Syrian policy, and talked about his visits abroad. At the end of most of these speeches, Erdoğan enjoined the muhtars to transmit his messages about current issues–to send his greetings–to every local community. He closed his address of March 10, 2015, with his plans for a new Turkey, for a new constitution, and for strengthening the presidential system with the following words: "I expect your support [...] on this matter. I want you to explain these realities to the people of the neighborhoods and villages in your wards. I want you to explain to our fellow citizens that we need to seize the historic opportunity of the general election on June 7." He thereby cast the muhtars as his envoys, bearing his message across the country.

These addresses reveal how the president thought of the role of the muhtars, and the missions he assigned to them. What transpired first was an enjoinder to activism. After highlighting how he assumed his role as president, by actively seeking to introduce new services, he specified: "It is in this manner that I expect you to conduct yourselves. You have to mobilize institutions, the governor's and subgovernor's office, municipalities for the needs of your neighborhood, [...] of your village and its inhabitants."[39] But this commitment was not to be limited to institutional partners: "Does a muhtar who does not strive to produce services in cooperation with NGOs, with local shopkeepers and neighborhood notables, deserve his post?"[40] He urged muhtars to become involved in helping the needy: "It is essential that you identify the weak of mind, the poor and needy in your neighborhood, that you look after them, or that you see to it that they are looked after."[41] Erdoğan encouraged muhtars to become personally involved in solving problems, not confining themselves to their official functions but reasserting their social role, "Do people listen to a muhtar who does not apply himself to reconciling those who are offended or in dispute? No."[42]

A central aspect of the expectations voiced by Erdoğan is that muhtars should definitely have intimate knowledge of their neighborhood: "I believe you go from house to house in your village or neighborhood; you are practically a friend of the family. You drink their tea, and you bring food to those who need it."[43] He claimed to expect very precise knowledge: "I say clearly that the muhtar who does not master his neighborhood as well as the back of his hand, who does not know which chimney works well and which does not, cannot, to my mind, fulfil his mission appropriately."[44] He said, "If a muhtar does not know who is who, and know who goes around his neighborhood or village, that means he is not really able to carry out his mission."[45] He thereby asserted that the specific nature of the muhtarlık resides in the intimate knowledge and trust binding muhtars to inhabitants, and he encouraged them to infiltrate people's everyday lives, including private spaces.

Moreover, the way he exhorted them to use the intimate knowledge he supposed them to have of their residents took a highly specific form: that of surveilling for institutions, and even denouncing residents to the public authorities. This took place in the summer of 2015, admittedly in a very specific and troubled context. In the southeast of the country, violence was flaring up once again between pro-Kurdish insurgents and security forces during the months before the rerun of the June legislative election in which Erdoğan's party had lost its absolute majority. This instruction to surveil was confirmed in a December 2016 circular enjoining governors and subgovernors to hold monthly security meetings with muhtars–admittedly once again in a very tense period, after the failed coup, and in the wake of a broader trend toward authoritarianism.

What reactions did these steps trigger? These encounters were widely criticized. First, the explicit desire to turn muhtars into informers attracted extensive media criticism.[46] Several muhtars opposed this role prescription. Indeed, the practice of informing usually had a negative valence, connoting a betrayal of one's community and an abuse of personal trust (Akarsu 2020, 36). Therefore, depicting muhtars as state informers could be expected to weaken the residents' trust in them, especially in settings where the muhtars had a tense relationship with state authorities. The pro-Kurdish opposition party, the HDP, criticized what it considered an attempt to use the muhtars as "law-enforcement forces of the state."[47] A group of muhtars from Suruç–a town on the Syrian border where there was a bloody attack attributed to Daesh, also known as the Islamic State–told the press they would act not as palace "informers," but as "servants of the people" (halkın hizmetkarız).[48] In opposition to this role definition as agents of state surveillance, they put forward an alternative vision of serving citizens. These muhtars stated this openly, but many others–not only from the HDP–admitted in private that they too were upset about this instruction to surveil, and did not intend to comply.

A second, more general criticism came from the opposition media. They portrayed these meetings as a highly political initiative to win over the muhtars, and hence as a step to rallying public opinion. In fact, these encounters, like the measures concerning muhtars, were closely linked to the political and electoral calendar. Thus, the measures to improve the status of muhtars were taken or announced just before elections. The muhtars' pay was increased in January 2014, two months before key local elections, the first to be held after the Gezi Park movement. Likewise, the announcement that the state would pay the muhtars' insurance premiums was made on April 5, 2017, two weeks before the constitutional referendum. Two thousand muhtars were invited to attend the meeting when this announcement was made, as opposed to the usual four hundred or so. A second measure was announced at this meeting, in response to a request by the muhtar confederation, with former muhtars being exempted from paying for weapons permits, a privilege previously reserved to acting muhtars.[49] This electoral dimension also transpired in the content of Erdoğan's speeches. This was apparent during the two meetings following the June 2015 general elections (including the one in which Erdoğan called the muhtars to act as state informers),[50] in which the HDP Kurdish nationalist party won numerous seats in the national parliament, thus preventing the AKP from obtaining an absolute majority. Most of the muhtars invited to these particular meetings came from the southeast of the country, a key election battleground as the prospect of early elections came into focus. On this occasion, Erdoğan reminded his listeners of all his governments had done for the region—investments, the setting up of a Kurdish-language public TV channel, the lifting of the state of emergency—and inveighed against terrorism. His purpose was clearly to win electoral backing for the upcoming November elections. Ülgül (2018) has argued that these meetings were one of the ways Erdoğan prepared public opinion for the presidentialization of the regime. More generally, these encounters were not intended solely for an audience of muhtars—nor even, through their intermediaries, for their constituents. Rather, the meetings received extensive coverage, were broadcast live on the main TV channels, and commented on in the media.[51] To some observers, one objective of these meetings was to make Erdoğan's opinions on contemporary issues known to the Turkish public and to foreign actors (Ülgül 2018, 72). Erdoğan explicitly addressed the muhtars as representatives of the people, admitting that they enabled him to be attuned with the people, given that he could not directly address 79 million inhabitants.[52] In thereby addressing broader audiences, Erdoğan presented himself as a president who was in touch with the lowest tier of elective representatives and the people, an image which chimed with his anti-elitist populist discourse.

Third, certain muhtars said they felt unable to voice their concerns, and complained of having to meekly submit to speeches which were largely irrelevant to them—in short, of being instrumentalized. An Istanbul MP from the main opposition party, the CHP, criticized Erdoğan for using muhtars as onlookers, arguing that the president was playing politics with them.[53] The president, on the contrary, described these "muhtar encounters" as constructive dialogue: "I learn many things from muhtars' expressions, from how they hold their heads or move their hands, from their objections, revolts, silences, and gestures of approval. Most of the time, the message I receive from this communication is far more informative, far more appropriate, far more important than the information I get from speaking privately with dozens or hundreds of people."[54] Nevertheless, these encounters were a limited form of dialogue.

The president did all the speaking from behind his lectern, taking no questions afterward, and any objections were rare. One notable exception occurred when Erdoğan stated that since the 2005 law, municipalities supported the muhtarlıks. This triggered murmurs of protest, and one muhtar stood up to affirm the contrary.[55] Clearly taken aback, Erdoğan retorted that a list of municipalities that did not support the muhtarlıks would be made public, a statement which was welcomed with sustained applause. It was actually in the wake of this episode that he undertook that all central resources would, if required, be mobilized to help improve muhtars' working conditions.

One final criticism related to the partisan political nature of the initiative. The selection of muhtars to be invited to the meetings gave rise to suspicions of party preference. The first two in my sample to be invited were the two closest to the AKP, Bediz and Fikret. Bediz even admitted that some string-pulling had been done in her favor. She said she was delighted by the trip, and described the presidential palace and catering service in proud and emotional terms.[56] But in 2016 a young muhtar from Trabzon was the first to turn down such an invitation, declaring to the press that his obligation of neutrality meant he could not respond to an invitation from a president who did not respect his own duty of neutrality, despite its being laid down in the former constitution. He criticized Erdoğan for addressing the muhtars as a political party leader rather than behaving as an impartial president. Erdoğan was often accused of having acted during the 2015 legislative campaign not as a president above political parties, but as a party leader, and hence of having misused his presidential position. This young muhtar also openly criticized Erdoğan's policies concerning Syrian refugees, Russia, unemployment, and the preferential provision of public jobs and contracts to AKP supporters.[57] He was charged with insulting the president. Interestingly, the main opposition party began gathering and mobilizing muhtars in some situations. Ahead of the April 2017 constitutional referendum, the leader of the main opposition party, the CHP, held a meeting with the muhtars to criticize the constitutional reform, asserting that it would endanger the very survival of the muhtarlık.[58] A prosecutor subsequently launched investigations against more than half of the muhtars who had attended this meeting. In any case, the muhtars have become addressees of political discourse and of efforts at mobilization.

Bediz showed me with great pride the photo she had had taken in the company of Erdoğan. When I asked whether she intended to display it in her muhtarlık, she initially said yes, then hesitated and declared, "In fact, I'm not sure if it's a good idea at the moment." It was in June 2015, just before a legislative election in which Erdoğan was clearly involved. Would he be viewed as the president of all citizens, or as a party leader? This partisan dimension, which could generate divisions, was problematic even for Erdoğan's supporters. In 2017, Bediz was actively involved in campaigning for "yes" votes in the constitutional referendum. She was organizing home visits to distribute AKP goodies, assisted by women she had helped and also accompanied by Bedirhan. The upcoming ballot had an ambivalent status, since the constitutional reform was strongly backed by the executive and the AKP, and the entire state apparatus controlled by the AKP was campaigning in its favor. Did Bediz's position signify that she was in favor of moving toward a regime embodied by the president, or was it a political stance? Behind her back, Cemil criticized Bediz's stance as "political" and incompatible with the role of muhtar.

These presidential addresses have redefined the muhtars at the national level as a channel for mobilizing public opinion and for spreading ideas. The "muhtar policy" has been fairly comprehensive. It has endowed the figure of the muhtar with renewed value, while also providing them with better material conditions. However, it has not reinforced muhtars' prerogatives in any way.[59] Rather, official expectations, guidelines, and limits to their action have been set out more clearly. Interestingly, the policy has not sought to bureaucratize them, in that their role continues to be defined by the specificity of the position: proximity, and intimate and experiential knowledge of a population. But it has added an explicit injunction to use this knowledge and proximity for the executive.

It is enlightening to consider the executive's greater reliance on muhtars in the broader framework of recent reconfigurations of law enforcement at the local level, and especially to relate it the revitalization of another Ottoman figure, the "neighborhood and market watchman" (*mahalle ve çarşı bekçisi*). Watchmen were reinstated in the wake of the failed coup of 2016, and were the first to patrol southeastern Kurdish-majority areas under curfew following military operations to eradicate militants linked to the outlawed PKK. They then returned to the streets of cities all over Turkey, starting with Istanbul in 2017. Watchmen share several similarities with muhtars. The position has a lengthy past—stretching back at least to the seventeenth century, according to the famous traveler Evliya Çelebi—and was neighborhood-based. Watchmen oversaw security, protected people and goods, and policed correct behavior in their neighborhoods. They had strong links to neighborhood residents, who chose them and paid them tips, as they received no salary from the state. Like muhtars, watchmen are popularly viewed as benevolent figures from Istanbul's past (Lévy 2010, 292). Turkish popular culture portrays them with nostalgia (Akarsu 2020, 33). Like the figure of the muhtar, that of the watchman represents a historically rooted quality, a supposedly authentic local "spirit" (Akarsu 2020, 34). In the literature on Ottoman cities and in the social imaginary, the watchman is portrayed as a figure of order, but of a familiar order immanent to the neighborhood, as opposed to one imposed from above by the authorities. Another striking similarity between watchmen and muhtars is that watchmen, as intermediaries between the neighborhood and the authorities, have increasingly been integrated into the state apparatus. In 1896, during the reign of Sultan Abdul Hamid II, known for his attempts at surveillance, the watchmen were attributed the role of informers. For institutions, the watchmen's intimate neighborhood knowledge and the trust residents placed in them provided major reasons for expanding their role (Lévy 2010, 292). This surveillance with a political dimension, based on intimate knowledge of residents, shows striking similarities to the enhanced role the authorities attributed to muhtars just when they were reinstating watchmen.

However, the revitalization of watchmen holds a meaning different from that of the authorities' greater reliance on muhtars. First, watchmen's links to neighborhood residents are far more tenuous: as of the late nineteenth century, watchmen were chosen by the police authorities, not neighborhood residents. The 1914 regulation on watchmen officialized their presence, positioning them within the official law-and-order system, paying them a wage and placing them under close police oversight. This reform thus did away with what had hitherto grounded their specificity, namely their integration within the neighborhood and intimate knowledge of it, precisely because this was felt to present a risk of indulgence towards residents (Lévy 2010, 296). Watchmen continued to be progressively integrated into the state policing structures, until they were finally transformed into regular police officers in 2008.

When the watchmen were reinstated in 2016, the Istanbul governor explicitly referred to this collective imaginary of proximity and noted, "What was most important to us is that they know the neighborhood. That they know the daily life and perceptions of the neighborhood, that they identify the needs and can transmit them to the other authorities they are linked to."[60] However, such an image sits ill with watchmen's selection procedures. They are hired not at the neighborhood level, but by the security directorate at the department level; they do not necessarily work in the neighborhood where they live or hail from; and consequently their work is not grounded in experiential knowledge. So in the end, they have little in common with the watchmen of Evliya Çelebi—or even Abdul Hamid II—except their name and the imaginary associated with it.

It was only in 2020, as the corps continued to expand, that a law clarified the duties of these "new watchmen."[61] Among the powers granted to them are the authority to patrol streets, intervene in incidents, conduct identity checks, carry out searches, carry guns, and take preventative measures until the police arrive, in the event of demonstrations, marches, or disturbances that trouble public order. The law enables them to stop, on "reasonable grounds," any person or vehicle to prevent a crime. Criticism by the opposition has thus mainly targeted the vast powers granted to such poorly trained and poorly educated people: the only educational requirement is for candidates to have completed high school, and the law stipulates a minimum of three months' training, as against one year for police officers. The opposition has also raised concerns about possible misuse or even abuse arising from the vagueness of the law defining this low-cost form of ancillary policing. It has also voiced concerns about the potential for politicized usages, given that the watchmens' powers include that of preventing demonstrations.[62] The re-creation of watchmen is no doubt part of a broader attempt to reassert control over policing in the wake of massive police purges launched in 2016. It shows that institutions seek not only to reinforce but also to renew forms of policing, combining closeness to the population with a desire to exert central control over law and order—a major issue with an increasingly political dimension.

This concern with new forms of policing also transpires very clearly in the creation of another structure in 2006, TDP (*toplum destekli polislik*, or socially supported policing), which appears closer to the muhtarlık—especially in terms of its local but also familiar dimension. Unlike the police–a centrally adminis-tered organization in which officers are required to serve in different parts of the country, excluding their hometowns–a significant objective of introducing socially supported policing relates to the principle of localization. In her analy-sis of TDP in terms of community policing, Akarsu convincingly argues that this localization aims to close the social distance between police and citizens: "TDP officers are expected to build strong relationships with the communities they police" (Akarsu 2020, 29). For example, they would, like muhtars, hand out cards with their name and cellphone numbers so that people can know their police officers by name and contact them directly. Personalization is meant to "generate some familiarity between police officers and citizens" (Akarsu 2020, 32). Akarsu points out that TDP units "had tea in local coffeehouses, visited local residents, played backgammon with shop owners [...] to 'win the hearts of the citizens'" (2020, 30). She convincingly argues that this closeness aims to generate trust: "This is supposed to show that the police not only know the communities they are serving, but also are on the citizens' side" (2020, 29). The similarities with muhtars are striking. The authorities' growing engagement with muhtars makes sense in this broader context of reconfigurations of policing based on the principle of proximity. This broader framework also highlights the muhtars' specificity: they are the only ones among these various figures to be local and elected, therefore depending primarily on their residents. This explains why they are increasingly monitored at various levels.

Forms of municipalization are at work which both integrate and sideline the muhtars. At the same time, more proactive urban planning has increased the stakes, making the muhtarlık more politicized and conflictual. Likewise, central authorities have asserted growing control over muhtars. These three shifts have curtailed the muhtars' autonomy from institutions, which was long the specific characteristic of their position. These trends have often been accompanied by the discreet yet growing importance of partisan political rationales—which therefore now extend to this micro level. In late 2018, the government dismissed 259 muhtars (among whom were 156 urban neighborhood muhtars) in south-eastern parts of the country, for links with terrorist organizations or activities deemed incompatible with their office—and did so without any judicial decision. The muhtars dismissed were in settings and settlements where people had voted overwhelmingly for the HDP.[63] This was part of a major crackdown, with many HDP mayors also being removed for the same reasons. Prior to this, the only instances I have found in which muhtars were collectively dismissed occurred after the 1960 and 1980 military coups.

CONCLUSION

IN 2007 ŞERIF MARDIN, AN ILLUSTRIOUS FIGURE IN TURKISH political science and sociology, launched a debate about *"mahalle baskısı,"* literally "neighborhood pressure," which was amplified by the media to an unexpected degree.[1] In the context of the crisis surrounding the spring 2007 presidential elections, with Kemalist circles raising the specter of the Islamization of the country, the media debate focused mainly on the present day, and on the prospect of bottom-up, repressive, and reactionary Islamization.

Independently of their topicality, Mardin's observations are to be considered within the framework of his ongoing examination of the processes of modernization in the late Ottoman Empire and republican Turkey (Mardin 1974). In an interview, he said, "In Turkey, there is what is called 'neighborhood pressure.' It was one of the things the Young Turks feared the most" (Çakır 2007). This reference to the Young Turks places his comments in a historical perspective which has been largely missing from subsequent debate. The arrival in power of the Young Turks after 1908, symbolizing for Mardin the political modernization of the Ottoman Empire, marked the culmination of a policy of centralizing and strengthening state control over the population. From this perspective, what the neighborhood imperils is the very project of top-down modernization of society.

As Lévy rightly shows, Mardin is careful not to assimilate neighborhood resistance to modernization to some form of immobilism or inertia, instead thinking of it as a neighborhood capacity to impose alternative norms to the modernizing ones promoted by political power (2010, 272 et seq.). According to Mardin, the "lived space" of the neighborhood is a place of pressure. He elliptically defines it as the watchful other. For him, neighborhood pressure is a form of social, religious, and moral control inherently linked to society.

Mardin conceptualizes neighborhood pressure in relation to local configurations which vary in time and space: "Rather than a concept, neighborhood pressure is a form of organization and a reality which changes over time. [...] Neighborhood pressure needs to be examined as part of a historical process." From this perspective, Mardin depicts the neighborhood as a complex entity defined by its influences and interactions between various protagonists: "In this sphere, there is not just the neighborhood, there is the neighborhood mosque, the mosque's imam, the books read by the imam, the *tekke* [dervish lodge], the brotherhood. And then there are the *külliyes* [building complexes next to the mosque], the *esnafs* [craftsmen and tradesmen], et cetera. That is the neighborhood, all of these things which begin to function, which function as a whole." Despite his call to place it in a historical perspective, the description Mardin offers of the Ottoman neighborhood seems to correspond to the classical period, before the Tanzimat reforms. Mardin then conjures up a second representation of the neighborhood, corresponding to the early days of the republic, in which domination by the imam is said to have come into competition with the arrival of a new figure, namely the schoolteacher: "Let us take the structure and now turn to the republic. [...] This structure underwent a change: a rival arrived. [...] A rival such that against this structure, a construct appeared with the teacher of the republic, associating the teacher, the school, the pupil, and the pupil's book, and this construct was in fact a rival construct to the neighborhood structure. In the long run, we may observe that one of these constructs lost. [...] The teacher lost."

From being a configuration with multiple and particularly religious protagonists, outside state control, the neighborhood is said to have become a field to be conquered by the modernizing republican state. As Lévy again convincingly argues, Mardin presents the historical process here in highly schematic form, at the risk of simplifying relations between the state and the neighborhood and reproducing the image of a conservative religious Ottoman neighborhood, insensitive to state influence, alongside that of a radical modernizing state seeking to break traditional social structures. The fact that these observations were made during an interview and the political context of the subsequent debate no doubt partly explain the elliptical nature of the reasoning. Nevertheless, it is surprising that Mardin, despite his unsurpassed knowledge of the nineteenth century, does not mention the figure of the muhtar. This omission may also be because mentioning the muhtar, as a figure of adaptation and mediation between the official order and the social order, would entail nuancing this dichotomous interpretation and the oppositions it sets in play. Muhtars are invested with institutional power by the state, yet are grounded in the social structures of the neighborhood, particularly the social control exerted there. This social control constitutes a resource for them, as indeed it does for other protagonists such as the religious leaders mentioned by Mardin.

VARIATIONS ON STATE HETERONOMY

The longevity of the muhtarlık shows how important a place brokerage and intermediation play in the institutional functioning of the Turkish state. Among the various intermediaries whose key role in Ottoman government has been brought to light by historians, the muhtarlık is the longest-lasting. Far from disappearing with the republic, muhtars have survived for a remarkably long while. While certain reforms did suppress the muhtarlık in the most radical periods— perhaps during the time of the Young Turks from 1913, and more certainly in the early republic from 1933 to 1944—those attempts were soon abandoned, and these periods may be viewed as parenthetical. This being so, the muhtarlık no doubt amounts to more than some accidental historical leftover. As Auyero notes about Argentina: "Resolving problems through personalized political mediation should be taken seriously, and not simply dismissed as vestiges evoking ancient structures" (Auyero 2000, 212). While this observation has become standard for certain states, particularly African ones, it is more surprising for a state reputed to be "strong" and modern, for which the social sciences have customarily deemed anything smacking of intermediation or deviating from an idealized vision of "modernity" to be a throwback destined to disappear.

This longevity is evidence of continuity. During the Ottoman period of reforms, and in the subsequent republican period, intermediaries have been institutionalized in parallel to and at the same time as an administration. We may thus assert that there have been institutional dynamics producing notables and nonbureaucratic modes of government. Studying muhtars thus acts as a reminder of the need to historicize the notion of administration which especially Ottoman and then Turkish reformists, along with most observers, have tended to view as a universal. Descimon, Schaub, and Vincent define administration "as the general imposition on a subject of a measure concerning him, without him having any possibility of defending his point of view, his particular case" (1997, 15–16). They correctly point out the "radical historicity [of this] mode of governing society."

The challenge taken up here has been to cease viewing these intermediaries as "the opposite" of the state, as parasitical figures, or even as signs of some "crisis" of state. The classical literature on corruption examines informal political relations, particularly clientelist ones, as being opposed to the official order, viewing them in terms of circumventing or hijacking the state. Equally, Africa is one of the areas for which base-level intermediaries and administrative brokers have been the most extensively studied. But they have sometimes been analyzed as being symptomatic of situations of state dereliction. Thus Blundo (2001) associates the existence of administrative brokers with a putative critical situation in the administration, and a state crisis. These interpretations are based on an idealized representation, a "grand narrative" of a rational administrative state. I have sought, on the contrary, to apprehend these intermediary figures and their semiformal practices as revealing genuine forms of government and state formation, as certain scholars have done, particularly for Africa. Thus, the notion of a rhizome state, while shedding light on the complex "subterranean" ramifications of state power in society, also offers a way of thinking about a state which both nourishes and is nourished by clientelist networks and informal activities (Bayart 1989).

The specificity of the institution of the muhtarlık is that it does not seek to place officeholders under the entire sway of some state rationale. On the contrary, it grants extensive scope to social rationales, something it largely accepts and accommodates. This "hold" exerted by social rationales is not simply a matter of adapting the ways regulations are applied in the light of circumstances, or of having to make do for want of anything better. On the contrary, it is planned for and integrated into the way the institution functions. It is thus an institution which is linked to, integrates, and to a certain extent institutionalizes social rationales. This simple observation runs counter to interpretations that validate the widespread image of the state as exterior to society. This idea of a state heteronomous from society, reforming it from the top down in an authoritarian manner, has deeply and lastingly marked historiography about Turkey, abetted by the radical nature of the Kemalist "revolution." To that extent, this book breaks with dominant visions of Ottoman and Turkish history in terms of modernization, rationalization, and bureaucratization.

The muhtarlık is an institution with a lax framework, and is highly malleable for the uses made of it, which may well diverge from official definitions. While granting extensive room to social dynamics, it provides a way of exerting institutional pressure. This seems to support Blundo's idea of "institutionalizing informality"—which he uses to describe the generalization of intermediation practices, both spontaneously and at the initiative of the administration. He shows that brokers partake in a process of negotiating and redirecting actions by administrative services, into which they import new rules of functioning and circumvention (Blundo 2001, 89). He puts forward the hypothesis of a de facto privatization of administrative action, which is not the sole preserve of state agents but is, he argues, generated by interactions between bureaucrats, intermediaries, and public service users. He views this as being grounded in ad hoc arrangements made possible by the shared mobilization of practical norms, behaviors, and rationales foreign to the principles meant to govern the public sphere, and reminiscent of ways of functioning in the so-called informal sector (with a predilection for negotiation, bargaining, amicable agreements, and orality).

This conceptualization is relevant to the case of muhtars. However, I wish to make one distinction. Blundo states that, while procedures subject to informal appropriation remain a state prerogative, this is true more in appearance than in substance (2001, 87). He thus adheres to the interpretation of the state in terms of "substance" that I have criticized in the introduction to this book. I believe, on the contrary, that this type of arrangement practice takes part in state formation—or, more precisely, in a nonbureaucratic (or only partly bureaucratic) mode of state formation. This resembles the idea of state involution, developed by Duara for early twentieth-century China. He defines this as "a variation of the state-making process wherein the formal structures of the state grow simultaneously with informal structures—such as tax farmers and mercenary soldiers. While the formal state is dependent upon informal structures to carry out many of its functions, it is unable to extend its control over the latter. As the state grows in the involutionary mode, the informal groups become an uncontrolled power in local society, replacing a host of traditional arrangements of local governance" (Duara 1987, 132–33). This interpretation has the merit of thinking conjointly about the expansion of the state and the proliferation of non–rational-legal forms of government.

If we accept that intermediaries and an administration are institutionalized simultaneously, and that the two processes are intermingled, then we need to examine the forms of government thus produced. Relatively covert practices, which are nevertheless part of daily government functioning—observable at the level of muhtars, though not limited to that level—reveal commonplace forms of interaction between citizens and institutions that tend to be shrouded from view and considered as illegitimate. This is a blind spot in our way of thinking about republican institutions, with their rationalist and "modernizing" pretensions (Aymes 2008). The muhtarlık displays a form of "vernacular government," to adopt Salzmann's apt expression (2004). This observation brings into question the idea that using personal ties and relationships runs counter to state regulation. The muhtarlık, as the institution in most direct contact with the daily life of inhabitants, and vice versa, partakes in everyday state making. The pervasive influence of the informal in institutional functioning does not necessarily indicate some "failure" by the state, but points, rather, to a form of privatization of its functions, which is not necessarily antithetical to state bureaucratic rationale (Cutolo and Banégas 2018). Muhtars hold a place in a form of indirect government with its own rationality (Hibou 1999).

Muhtars hence have effects on governing that are not negligible. By showing their availability, readily acting as administrative brokers, framing their actions in terms of doing favors (even when withholding them), and behaving like local elected representatives while claiming to act on behalf of the state, they help to sustain the idea of a state accessible solely through intercession. Hence there exists a grand narrative of the state as bureaucratic, external, and inaccessible, in tandem with practices that clearly run counter to this grand narrative while nevertheless contributing to its reproduction. Yet these two orders of reality need to be thought of conjointly. How are they linked? The image of an inaccessible state above society continues to inform practice and discourse, something from which muhtars are not exempt. It may even be stated that it is this representation which produces and infuses the muhtarlık's added value as a relay and an accessible, mobilizable means of accessing the state.

If we accept that the Turkish state has never enjoyed the heteronomy from society it has persistently claimed and that, on the contrary, it has been and continues to be a lastingly "socialized" state—how are we then to interpret the recent prominence attached to muhtars? Should we conclude that nothing has really changed, that this is mere staging, a matter of no real consequence? No, for it seems on the contrary to reveal several shifts.

First, the value placed on muhtars makes sense in the context of other concomitant developments, such as the reintroduction of night watchmen. This may be seen as arising from a desire to promote "indigenous" figures from the neo-Ottoman imaginary, made up of nostalgia, and from an assertion that the country is following its own specific path. This initiative signals a break: over the past century and more, the vast majority of institutional reforms have been inspired by foreign models, considered as "universals" with which Turkey has aligned itself, such as nineteenth-century European bureaucracies, the European Union, neoliberal forms of government, and so on.

These recent institutional reforms thus invoke a different imaginary, one that is not modernist. Institutions and the state were long considered the place of universal modern rationality, and society the place of localized traditions. This is the dichotomy to which Mardin refers. The Young Turks, followed by the Kemalists, deemed the muhtarlk destined to disappear, and rightly so. Although the institution lasted, it was the obverse of the modernity to which they laid claim. It was accordingly viewed with scorn by the elite, and in many ways rendered invisible. Recent reforms take a new approach. By summoning a native tradition, they assert a continuity with the Ottoman past and with society. In a sense, giving prominence to muhtars is an attempt to narrow the gap between state and society and to legitimize institutions that seek to appear closer and more familiar.

But it is not solely a matter of an imaginary. When Mardin coined the term "mahalle baskısı," he was referring to social control, and to moral values that affect everyday behavior—social control and moral values that modernists viewed as outdated and wished to combat. What has changed, then, is probably that institutions, abandoning the struggle against moral and social control, now claim to endorse it. By doing so, they engage in localized relational webs and draw on experiential knowledge—without necessarily controlling them.

These forms of state "socialization" acquire new meaning in the broader context of the securitization of the Turkish society. Over recent years, muhtarlıks have been involved in new areas of activity, such as managing migration (especially that of Syrian migrants) and monitoring the COVID crisis in their localities—plus, of course, the call from the authorities to surveil and denounce "terrorists." What these activities have in common is that all are linked to securitization—as are watchmen. So what is at stake, over and above the endorsement of dominant social values, is an attempt to incorporate social control into official channels, or even—and this is not the same thing—to instrumentalize them for state rationales. What we see, then, is that securitization is not necessarily solely a matter of rationalized government devices, or linked to the autonomization of the state from society. I hope this book has sketched out some of the limits and tensions inherent to this project—especially the multiple, complex, and contradicting rationales of muhtars, and the ambivalent political effects of institutions like muhtarlıks.

To return to the more general discussion, state-in-society scholars have convincingly demonstrated the social embeddedness of the Turkish state. What the muhtarlık shows, however, is, first, that the extent of this embeddedness in Turkey, including its biggest city, has been strikingly underestimated—and second, that the degrees, forms, and patterns it takes change over time in nonlinear ways, with evolving consequences.

FRAGMENTING MODES OF GOVERNMENT

The muhtarlık is one component in a largely and ever more bureaucratized landscape. In other words, citizens are at various times in contact with the state through the muhtar, the imam, the police officer, the watchman, or the military, and more systematically through the teacher, as well as through numerous specialized administrations. In many fields, the muhtar is now dispensable. But the disappearance of the muhtarlık, though often foretold, has not yet materialized. On the contrary, the strengthening of the figure of the muhtar which has accompanied recent administrative reforms shows that computerization and rationalization, far from obliging the most embodied figures of government to retreat, have instead compelled them to reconfigure their role into complementary forms. This leads to the coexistence of different government arrangements: on the one hand, the increasingly rationalized administration, based mainly on computer technology, with a debatable handle on social phenomena; on the other hand, lived experience, often accompanied by intercession. And what happens in one arrangement does not necessarily spill through to the other.

Instead of being viewed as arising from the incomplete rationalization of the state, this situation can be interpreted as giving greater, though involuntary, leeway to citizens. To carry out any given request—for example, to obtain a certificate or apply for social assistance—several procedures can be envisaged involving different official interlocutors. As Starr (1978) has documented in another context, in the 1970s, to settle their disputes, farmers in the region of Bodrum sometimes used official channels and sometimes unofficial ones, at times combining both. Rather than systematically avoiding the law, bureaucracy, and the courts, they did not hesitate to use legal channels when they thought it would better serve their interests. But they also knew how to circumvent them if necessary. This plurality tends to expand the range of ways in which citizens may access the state or use institutions for their own goals. In the case studied here, depending on the situations and resources to hand—be they social, partisan-political, or whatever—certain individuals prefer to turn to the muhtar, others not. In general, groups and individuals who are ill at ease with writing and the administration tend to address the muhtar. However, there is also a partisan political dimension to this. In neighborhood D, it may be the case that social welfare applicants close to the AKP turn to the district municipality or party, while those who lack access to the party but can draw on privileged ties to Duran approach him instead. In neighborhood F, the opposite may be observed. The fragmenting of partial spheres of regulation is thus not solely a social and geographical phenomenon (Camau and Massardier 2009), but also—and perhaps increasingly—a political or even partisan one.

Study of the muhtarlık indicates that the standardization of politics in Turkey is incomplete, for the "micro level" follows partly autonomous rationales and has fairly loose links to party politics and institutional dynamics. The muhtarlık, being plugged into local dynamics, produces territorially contrasting forms of power and sources of fragmentation within institutions. In southeastern Turkey, the Kurdish nationalist movement tends to view muhtars as being the state's lackeys (Çelik 2019). In Istanbul, however, the muhtarlık may be used in many different ways: here as a means of opposition (in neighborhood D, where Duran openly criticized the district municipality, AKP, and government), there as a method of monitoring and surveillance (in neighborhood A, where Ahmet kept his personal expanded database and let police officers access it). Here it may work along partisan political lines (in neighborhood B, where Bediz accessed many public resources through Bedirhan and her AKP connections), there it may not (in neighborhood C, where Cemil did not follow partisan political lines). Here it may be dominated by one particular group (in neighborhood D, where Duran was one of the few recourses in the official sphere for many Alevis), there by another (in neighborhood F, where Fikret clearly had closer relationships to the Sunnis than to the Alevis). Yet this autonomy is currently on the wane due to several trends: the ongoing statization of society, the increasing politicization of local issues, and the growing sway of partisan political factors on public action. This declining autonomy may be restricting the range of possibilities, as occurred in the 1970s.

BACK TO DOMINATION

How does this fragmentation of modes of government tie in with the question of domination? To bring out the contribution this book makes to our understanding of domination, it is first necessary to specify how it differs from the key works that have looked at these less visible forms of politics—conceptualized, for example, in terms of "infrapolitics" (Scott) or "street politics" (Bayat). Most of these works have focused on the political role of subordinates and have examined forms of acting outside institutions. Thus, Scott studies practices such as desertion, fleeing, and tax avoidance, analyzing zones of autonomy outside the state sphere (1985; 2010). In his wake, Kerkvliet shows how a policy—the Vietnamese collectivization of agriculture—may fail not because of organized resistance, but due to the everyday political behavior of ordinary citizens not complying with the authorities' expectations (2005).

Likewise, Bayat opposes street politics to the regulating authorities. His nicely worded "quiet encroachment of the ordinary" refers to individual spontaneous practices occurring outside institutional arenas, such as squats or illegal hookups to power lines. Even though these do not seek to undermine the authority of the state, taken together they contest certain fundamental aspects of state prerogatives, such as the control of public space and the protection of public and private goods (1997, 58). Bayat thus states: "In a quest for an informal life, the marginals tend to function as much as possible outside the boundaries of the state and modern bureaucratic institutions, basing their relationships on reciprocity, trust, and negotiation" (2009, 49). He thereby posits the exteriority of—or even the opposition between—on the one hand, the state sphere, held to be intrinsically modern and linked to bureaucratic institutions; and on the other, the practices of the marginal and the excluded, associated with such values as reciprocity and trust.

But reifying these categories precludes envisaging forms of hybridization or unplanned uses. Briquet, for instance, has shown how moral economies based on the values of reciprocity have encouraged the appropriation of electoral democracy in Corsica (1997). Analyzing an institution such as the muhtarlık provides a way of going beyond the presumed alterity and heteronomy of social and institutional rationales, to instead consider how they may be interlinked, or even produce each other; and to duly note that state rationales may tolerate, produce, reproduce, and be based on social and informal practices, and even feed into them. By leaving behind the "society-against-state" perspective, it allows us to tackle the question of domination in new ways.

Many of these works set out to study the political role and leeway available to social groups that are defined by their subordination or marginalization. To that end, they isolate these margins and dominated groups, postulating that they have specific political practices and relations to the state. Scott thus analyzes tax avoidance as a means of resistance by the poor, undermining the instruments of state domination. But such practices are not confined to the dominated. In present-day France, it is the best-off who are the most frequent and successful tax evaders (Spire 2012). My approach, on the contrary, takes as its starting point an institution and the ways in which various groups with different social profiles perceive and engage with it. It includes groups and places of varying degrees of wealth and varying social positions. As a result, rather than just positing the existence of social and territorial differentiation, it enables us to actually examine differences in practice. Even though the findings are incomplete, it can be asserted that uses of the muhtarlık are driven by multiple dynamics, all of them socially situated; but also that such circumvention practices are not the preserve of the "dominated."

Finally, certain of the works mentioned above are based on reductive visions opposing domination and resistance. Most of them intrinsically posit the state as a form of domination, more specifically as an apparatus for domination in the service of the dominant. This type of analysis underestimates the extent to which there may be a desire or demand for the state, including from deprived and marginalized groups.[2] The dominant/dominated duality has been extensively brought into question, as has the simplistic and univocal alternative domination/resistance duality, with the ambivalence of power relations instead being brought to the fore (Hibou 2011, 13–14). The political significations of the muhtarlık are ambiguous. Just like the administrative, economical and social mechanisms discussed by Hibou, it is by nature "ambivalent and equivocal, simultaneously allowing control and room for maneuver, domination and resistance" (2006, 159). The muhtarlık does not amount to some hiatus in the apparatus of state domination. Power relations are played out there, but in a specific manner, following rationales that do not consist merely of straightforward state domination or social resistance. They also include domination, circumvention, resistance, accommodation, and arrangements. From this point of view, the muhtarlık acts as yet another reminder that political practices are by definition incomplete (Bayart 1989).

How have recent initiatives to bind the muhtarlık more closely to the local authorities, and increasingly to the central state, played out in terms of domination? Will these measures transpire in a strengthening of the state dimension of the muhtarlık, to the detriment of the sway exerted by multiple localized social rationales? Will the muhtarlık, just like its premises—ever less private and more exposed to institutional rationales, which are in turn increasingly less local and more influenced by political parties and the center—become a locus of the state, where institutional rationales are imposed on local societies?

Any such outcome is far from certain, for such an interpretation overlooks the fact that muhtars are, first and foremost, elected by inhabitants—admittedly on the basis inter alia of services rendered, which in turn depend on the public resources they manage to channel. Money can finance a campaign, but it is harder for it to influence conversations at the café or between neighbors. Above all, such an interpretation overlooks the fact that it is the trust residents have in their muhtar that underpins the muhtar's neighborhood knowledge, and therefore the interest this figure has for the authorities. The muhtar is not granted this knowledge and trust forever, or even for an entire term in office, but must maintain it on a daily basis by bending rules, discreetly leaking information, negotiating arrangements, and at times conducting crusades in the service of certain inhabitants. The executive has spectacularly reengaged with the muhtarlık. Still, it has not turned the muhtars into appointed bureaucrats with training in public accounting. In a context of greater authoritarianism, the executive has not discarded this type of locally and socially anchored intermediary. The repoliticization of local issues and the increased institutional anchoring of the muhtarlık have not—for the moment—led to muhtars being brought into line, or in their uniformly conforming to central state rationales. On the contrary, these trends have in certain cases helped muhtars with more oppositional profiles to win election. One thing is certain: recent developments will not reduce the tensions inherent in the position of muhtar. Understanding the complex transformations in modes of government requires us to go beyond ideas such as "crisis of state" or even "deinstitutionalization," and to inquire in terms of government effects. This remains a crucial challenge–for social scientists, and for citizens as well.

Appendix

The Muhtars Studied

Neighborhood	Neighborhood population (2014)	Muhtar dates in office*	Party controlling district municipality (2014–19)	Neighborhood urban transformation project?	Neighborhood profile
A	Approx. 14,000	1994–2019	AKP	No	Old central; lower-middle-class
B	Approx. 3,000	2009–19	AKP	No	Old central; poor, undergoing gentrification
C	Approx. 1,000	1994–2019	AKP	No	Old central; populated mainly by shopkeepers and tradesmen; undergoing gentrification
D	Approx. 50,000	2009–19	AKP	Envisaged, but not yet underway	Recent; very disadvantaged, with major social divides
E	Approx. 12,000	2005–19	CHP	No	Central, relatively recent (1950s); very well off, with many gated communities
F	Approx. 8,500	1989–94 and 1999-2019	CHP	No, but also not ruled out	Former gecekondu; now stabilized, with major social divides
g	Approx. 150	1994–2019	AKP	Envisaged	Old central; populated by local shopkeepers and tradesmen
h	Approx. 14,000	(Aza) 2009-14	AKP	Yes, but not yet underway	Populated by educated middle class with cooperative estates
i	Approx. 12,000	1980-2019	CHP	No	Very well- off, populated by old bourgeoisie
k	Approx. 15,000	2014-19	CHP	Yes	Former gecekondu; disadvantaged, with outlawed left-wing organizations

Note: To avoid revealing the identities of muhtars and neighborhoods, I have indicated 2019 as the end of office for every muhtar studied. Some of the muhtars were reelected in that year; others not.

Notes

INTRODUCTION

1. Presidential address to muhtars, Ankara, August 19, 2015.

2. "Vali Yerlikaya 'dan muhtarlara COVID-19' la mücadelede destek çağrısı," TRT, September 10, 2020, https://www.trthaber.com/haber/turkiye/vali-yerlikayadan -muhtarlara-covid-19la-mucadelede-destek-cagrisi-515233.html. Accessed on January 7, 2020.

3. For critical discussion of these ideas, see Gourisse 2015.

4. See, for example, Padioleau 1982; Dupuy and Thoenig 1985.

5. The project called "Order and Compromise: Patterns of Administration and Government in Turkey and the Ottoman Empire since the Late 19th Century" was financed by the French Agence nationale de la recherche for the period 2008–12, and coordinated by me. The results of this research program are to be found in Aymes, Gourisse, and Massicard 2015.

6. . While the title of Bourdieu's book has been translated as The Logic of Practice, I prefer here to use "practical sense," which appears closer to the French sens pratique. The term "practical sense" steers clear of any rationalizing interpretation, insisting on the subjective and interiorized dimension of practices: "There is an economy of practices, the reason immanent in practices, whose 'origin' lies neither in the 'decisions' of reason understood as rational calculation nor in the determinations of mechanisms external to and superior to the agents" (Bourdieu, 1990, 50).

7. The term *ihtiyar* is still used to refer to azas and is mostly translated as "elder," despite its first sense meaning "prominent."

8. Kerem Kocalar, "Gaziantep'te muhtarlık seçimi kavgası: 3 ölü, 6 yaralı," Anadolu Ajansı, March 30, 2019, https://www.aa.com.tr/tr/turkiye/gaziantepte-muhtarlik -secimi-kavgasi-3-olu-6-yarali/1438692.

9. The position is not mentioned in any of the following reference works: Varol 1989; Kurtoğlu 2005; Çitçi 1989; Erder and İncioğlu 2008.

10. Interestingly, muhtars still exist in several post-Ottoman states: Cyprus, Lebanon, Bulgaria, and Iraq, to name a few. But they have also hardly been examined.

11. About two-thirds of them are urban neighborhood muhtars. "2020'de Türkiye'sinde muhtar sayısı," *Haber ne diyor?* January 22, 2020, https://www.habernediyor.com/gundem/ 2020-de-turkiye-deki-muhtar-sayisi-h24063.html. Accessed December 20, 2020.

12. A wave of civil unrest and demonstrations from May to July 2013, initially to contest the plan to transform Istanbul's Gezi Park into rebuilt Ottoman barracks containing a shopping center. The protests were sparked by outrage at the violent eviction of a sit-in held at the park to denounce the plan. Subsequent supporting demonstrations took place across Turkey, voicing a wide range of concerns, at the core of which were issues of freedom of expression and of assembly, as well as the government's alleged authoritarianism and growing interventionism on lifestyles. These protests were the largest Turkey has seen in recent decades, with more than three million people estimated to have actively taken part.

13. "Türkiye Muhtarlar Konfederasyonu Genel Başkanı Akdeniz: 'Türkiye genelinde kadın muhtarların sayısı arttı,'" Haberler.com, August 1, 2014, https://www.haberler .com/turkiye-de-kadin-muhtar-sayisi-artti-6328778-haberi/. Accessed January 15, 2021.

CHAPTER 1: AN INCOMPLETELY FORMED INSTITUTION

1. The *Tanzimat* are considered to have started with the Gülhane Imperial Edict (*Gülhane Hatt-ı Hümayunu*) of 1839, which set out a set of legal, administrative, and fiscal reforms to strengthen the Ottoman state.

2. Behar considers the introduction of muhtarlık in the framework of the Tanzimat (2003, 78).

3. Figures broadly similar to that of muhtar existed, or had previously existed, in certain Ottoman lands, some of which were not formally codified by the Ottoman administration. These included the *ra'îs al-fallâhîn* in Palestine, and the *çorbacı* or *kocabaşı*, mainly found in non-Muslim groups, who were replaced by muhtars in the 1880s (Singer 1990; Veinstein 1987).

4. Both Çadırcı (1970) and Ortaylı (2000) rely on the chronicle of Ahmet Lütfi Efendi (1873).

5. A parallel can be established—though only a loose one—with the shift from the priest to the mayor in French parishes and municipalities. Until 1789, priests—often the only literate inhabitants—carried out administrative functions relating to civil status, weddings, and censuses, as well as acting in rural areas as mediators and representatives in dealings with the political authorities.

6. The relationship between muhtars and imams would, however, appear to have been peaceable, since it was the imam who guaranteed the activities of the muhtar and played an active part in decisions about the neighborhood (Çadırcı 1970, 412; Behar 2003, 66).

7. This procedure was modified in 1864, on the grounds that it was too costly and cumbersome given the communication conditions. It was henceforth the governor who confirmed their appointment (Ortaylı 2000, 110).

8. It would appear that they were not very effective in curbing the rural exodus (Ortaylı 2000, 110).

9. The 1881 Regulation on Population Censuses systematized and centralized civil records. Subsequently muhtars were responsible for recording births, deaths, and marriages, as well as migrations, and for reporting this information to the central population registrar (Behar 2003, 79–80, 160).

10. According to Osman Nuri Ergin, they were elected from the beginning (1936, 121). According to Musa Çadırcı (1970, 410), relying on the newspaper *Takvim-i vekayi*, no. 73, 81, they were appointed by Istanbul but selected in Kastamonu from among successful people who enjoyed the esteem of the residents, and whose word they listened to. Rather than free elections, it was probably a process of co-optation by local notables (Behar 2003, 78). Drawing on Ottoman archival documents, Mehmet Güneş also suggests that it was a matter of co-optation between local officials and notables (2014, 30–33).

11. Municipal structures were extended to the capital as a whole in 1867.

12. According to Arıkboğa, the central authorities have always considered the village as a proper administrative unit, but not the urban neighborhood, regarded as a sort of temporary supplement to the municipality (1999, 107–12).

13. Unlike numerous administrative reforms in the Ottoman nineteenth century, the introduction of the muhtarlık did not draw on foreign experience (Eryılmaz 1988, 465). The dominant interpretation of Ottoman administrative reform in terms of Westernization therefore needs to nuanced. See especially Shaw 1968; Findley 1980.

14. This passage suggests rivalry between state institutions and the single party, to which all muhtars belonged.

15. A more detailed discussion of these legal texts and the attendant debates is beyond the scope of this chapter. See Arıkboğa 1998, 117 et seq.

16. For example, the 1972 social security regulations entrust them with drawing up certificates which confirm that a deceased person's beneficiaries have social security cover.

17. I use the terms "district" or "subgovernorship" for the Turkish *ilçe* (the subdivision of a province or city), and the term "subgovernor's offices" for the *kaymakamlık*. I also use the terms "province" for the Turkish *il* (province or city) and "governor's office" for the *vilayet*. I use the term "neighborhood" for the Turkish *mahalle* (the subdivision of a city or town).

18. In the quotations, in order to differentiate my own cuts from speakers' hesitations, I indicate my cuts by ellipses enclosed within brackets, and use ellipses without brackets to indicate that the speaker paused or hesitated.

19. By direct suffrage, even though there are certain exceptions. The muhtar can be elected by the municipal council if the governor deems it necessary.

20. *Cumhuriyet*, December 30, 1930.

21. *Cumhuriyet*, January 8, 1931.

22. "İntihabattan Sonra," *Cumhuriyet*, October 23, 1930.

23. A 1956 law extended the term for muhtars from two years to four (*Hürriyet*, September 2, 1956).

24. "İlimizde Partilerin Önem Verdiği 11 Muhtar Seçiminden 7'sini CHP, 3'ünü de AP Adayı Kazandı," *Yeni Adana*, September 20, 1965, p. 16.

25. *Yeni Erzurum*, January 11, 1952, quoted by Garapon (2017, 225).

26. See, for instance, "Hürriyet Mahallesi Muhtarlığına Mahmut Pekyapar Aday Adayı Oldu," *Yeni Adana*, November 2, 1977.

27. For testimonies, see M. E 1979, quoted by H. Bozarslan (1999).

28. See, among others, Phélippeau 2002.

29. For an example relating to the Maltepe subprovince in Istanbul, see http://www.maltepe.gov.tr/maltepe-protokol-listesi.

30. The *bağ-kur* is a form of social security insurance providing cover for those who are officially self-employed. Muhtars not otherwise covered are obliged to obtain it.

31. One of the main demands of muhtar associations is that neighborhood muhtarlıks be granted legal personality.

32. Muhtars figure among those who, when they are directly affected by decisions of a commission of the municipal council, are entitled to join its meetings—with no right to vote.

33. Law no.5393 on municipalities, 2005, article 9.

34. Law no. 5393 on municipalities, article 76. The other members include representatives of professional chambers, trade unions, lawyers, universities, civil society organizations, political parties, and public bodies and institutions. The application decree finalized in 2006 fixes the number of muhtar members, which must be between 20 and 30 percent of the number of muhtars in the constituency. This cap on the number of muhtars has come in for much criticism from those sitting on the participatory bodies (Yalçın-Riollet 2015, 283).

35. "The municipality provides the necessary help and support, within the limits of its budget, to pay for the needs and solve the problems of the muhtarlık and the neighborhood." Law no. 5393 on municipalities, 2005, article 9.

36. This remuneration was paid out of the budget of the Ministry for the Interior, transferred to the governors' offices. Law no. 2108 on the remuneration and social security of muhtars, August 29, 1977.

37. In 2010 it stood at about TL330 (about US$225) per month, when the net minimum salary was TL576 (about US$400).

38. In 2009, the net minimum wage was TL477.

39. In 2004, a newspaper estimated the average monthly income of a muhtar in a very populous neighborhood to be somewhere between TL4.5 billion and TL13.5 billion (between about US$3,400 and US$10,300). "Muhtarların 'rant' düellosu," *Milliyet*, March 25, 2004.

40. Interview with the former partner of a muhtar who held his position from 2004 to 2009. Istanbul, March 29, 2013.

41. When the "price per official stamp" stood at TL3.

42. There were about ten candidates per position in the 1994 local elections, as against an average of four in 1984.

43. T. Akkayan, "Mahallesiyle muhtarıyla Istanbul," *Cumhuriyet*, March 18, 1989.

44. T. Akkayan, "Mahallesiyle muhtarıyla Istanbul," *Cumhuriyet*, March 18, 1989.

45. T. Akkayan, "Mahallesiyle muhtarıyla Istanbul," *Cumhuriyet*, March 18, 1989.

46. Particularly Çubukçuoğlu 1944. This is a commentary of the 1944 law written by a member of the Istanbul municipal council. For a similar, more recent "handbook" written by a former subgovernor, see Taylan 1999.

CHAPTER 2: HOW THE MUHTARLIK FUELS THE PRODUCTION OF NOTABLES

1. The term *gecekondu* comes from combining *gece* (night) and *konmak* (being placed), and literally means "placed at night." It is used to designate dwellings built by their inhabitants without a permit, and so by extension entire neighborhoods made up of this type of dwelling. After the mass rural exodus, Turkish cities were largely composed of such habitats, though far fewer of them exist now.

2. In Anatolian villages in the 1950s, muhtars did not come from "grand families," who operated on a different level, but from intermediary families (Scott 1968).

3. For discussion of these organizations, see Hersant and Toumarkine 2005.

4. *Zaman*, March 28, 2004.

5. "Adem Göktaş: yüreğinizdeki Maltepe resmini tamamlayacağım," *Katılımcı Maltepe*, October 27, 2013, http://www.katilimcimaltepe.com.tr/m-haber-1159.html?islem=anahaber&altislem=onecikanlar.

6. The Islamist Prosperity Party, shut down in 1998. The Saadet Party presents itself as its heir.

7. Until the 2009 elections, muhtars and azas were elected separately, using two distinct voting slips. On occasion, muhtars were elected with azas from other lists—this happened to Duran—especially since voters could strike out the names of aza candidates and write in other choices they preferred. Since 2014, a single voting slip has been used for the muhtar and aza candidates. In addition, most electoral committees have accepted that it is muhtars who determine the order of their azas. Candidates for the position of muhtar can thus establish with certainty who will be their first aza.

8. For a full list, see Aytaç 2009, 167–68.

9. Observation at the polls, Istanbul, June 7, 2015.

10. It has the same Arabic root as the term *ihtiyar*, meaning "prominent."

11. See also the Nişanyan etymological dictionary.

CHAPTER 3: THE MUHTARS' CHANGING ROLE

1. See, for example, "Muhtarlık tarih oluyor," *Radikal*, April 11, 2012.

2. In particular, the series *Mahallenin muhtarları* (The Neighborhood Muhtars), broadcast from 1992 to 2002.

3. The notion of "experiential" knowledge seeks to emphasize how knowledge is anchored in practice—its concrete, largely tacit, rarely verbalized, nonsystematic, and largely nonrationalized nature—to distinguish it from other forms of knowledge discussed in this chapter. Experiential knowledge is embodied, largely interiorized, and attached to a person.

4. Entries on "mahalla" and "mahalle" (Encyclopédie de l'Islam², 1985).

5. Banks sometimes ask muhtars their opinion on the solvency of loan applicants. The muhtar is also one of the sources to whom people may turn for information about a family in view of a prospective marriage.

6. See, for example, Raymond 1995.

7. See, in particular, Hourani and Stern 1970.

8. It is interesting that collecting information about the population is expressed in terms of "intelligence," *istihbarat* being the term used for state intelligence, in tandem with the idea of familiarity or even intimacy.

9. Muhtars are officially meant to obtain information about the claimant's situation from the tax, land registry, and municipal authorities, but in practice they continue to issue certificates without so doing (Aytaç 2009, 75).

10. This term refers to the head of the civil administration in a district—a status that muhtars do not actually have, but sometimes inaccurately attribute to themselves.

11. This can be explained by the low level of institutional involvement in this sector, and the fact that few public agents are assigned to it.

12. Republic of Turkey, law no. 4541 on the organization of muhtars and councils of elders in cities and towns, *Official Gazette*, April 15, 1944, article 3/15.

13. Republic of Turkey, law no. 3294, "Sosyal Yardımlaşma ve Dayanışmayı Teşvik Kanunu," *Official Gazette*, June 14, 1986.

14. Previously, its sole task had been to collect revenue and distribute it to the SYDVs. It now became an executive institution with extensive autonomy in charge of monitoring poverty, conducting research, and developing aid programs. Republic of Turkey, law no. 5263, "Sosyal Yardımlaşma ve Dayanışma Genel Müdürlüğü Teşkilat ve Görevleri Hakkında Kanun," *Official Gazette*, Dec. 8, 2004.

15. Registers detailing vehicle ownership, land and real estate ownership, social security, etc.

16. For the distribution of "emergency" assistance, the SYDV boards of trustees continue to decide on a case-by-case basis, based primarily on identification of recipients by muhtars.

17. Admittedly, during a period of confrontation between the judiciary and the government. T.C. Cumhurbaşkanlığı Devlet Denetleme Kurulu (2009, 15). See Dodurka 2014, 89, 111, 146.

18. See, for example, F. Demir, "Tunceli'de seçim öncesi beyaz eşya dağıtımı," *Hürriyet*, February 4, 2009.

19. This formalization by the Deniz Feneri association is no doubt a response to a German court ruling against its German subsidiary for misappropriation of assets and illegal transfers to the Turkish Kanal 7 television channel, close to the AKP.

20. To generate a certificate stating that an individual owned no real estate, the agent could enter the applicant's name in a slightly doctored form (such as one omitting Turkish letters).

CHAPTER 4: THE RESIDENTS' CHAMPION

1. In addition to conditions pertaining to nationality, age, and a clean criminal record.

2. A term-for-term comparison is inappropriate for several reasons. First, the studies were conducted at different times in different places. Second, metropolitan municipal councillors can be regarded as the elite among municipal councillors. The purpose of presenting these two sets of figures in parallel is simply to show that muhtars tend to be significantly less educated than municipal councillors.

3. While the authors focus on intimacy as specific to female muhtars, I tend to think that this a characteristic of the institution as a whole, which also applies to male muhtars.

4. Certain urban districts have provided premises outside the neighborhood. Such a location goes some way towards neutralizing their social embeddedness.

5. It is hard to interpret the use of the familiar or formal second-person pronoun (*sen*), for it can denote both the personal dimension of a relationship, and social hierarchies, particularly those associated with age.

6. In Turkish, the second-person singular (*sen*) is generally used either for a person one knows well or for a person with an inferior status. Using the second-person plural (*siz*) is the proper and polite way to address someone a person does not know well in a formal interaction.

7. As part of a study seeking to "develop awareness of involvement with local authorities." (International Republican Institute 1995).

8. It is also used by adepts to refer to the Gülen movement, a conservative Islamic movement stemming from the *nurcu* neobrotherhood, and inspired by the imam Fethullah Gülen.

9. Türkiye Gazetesi Radyo ve Televizyonu (Turkey Newspaper, Radio and Television), a private conservative television channel.

10. Report on incidents of banditry in the zone of Karaköprü, in Diyarbakır province, and measures to be taken in the zones within the jurisdiction of the first inspectorate general. April 15, 1937, BCA, BMGMK 030.10;128.923.19. Quoted in Belge 2013, 21.

11. An indemnity paid by the state whenever a man who hitherto has provided for his family's needs is drafted for military service.

CHAPTER 5: AMBIVALENT INTERFACE WITH THE OFFICIAL ORDER

1. Until the early 2000s, the status of local governments and the budgets they were allocated depended on the number of residents registered during the five-year census, so these bodies vied with each other for residents. Many people chose to register in their villages of origin, to prevent the villages losing their status should they lack sufficient numbers of residents.

2. Law no. 298 on fundamental electoral provisions, April 26, 1961, article 43.

3. When the mail carrier drops notifications off with the muhtar, he is supposed to leave a note on the person's door or in their mailbox.

4. In blocks of flats, mailboxes are often absent or unused. The mail carrier instead leaves letters under or in front of entrance doors, and bills lie around in the hallways. There is no guarantee of confidentiality. Mail sometimes disappears when relations between neighbors are strained.

5. The *Yeni Şafak* (a conservative Islamic progovernment newspaper) and *Türkiye* (a progovernment newspaper), the "I Too Say Yes" campaign page for the 2010 referendum, and the "I Support the Civil Constitution" page, as well as pages of the AKP Federation, the AKP district youth organization, the AKP candidate for the district municipality in the 2014 local elections, and the head of the Istanbul AKP federation.

6. *Barış ve Demokrasi Partisi*, the Peace and Democracy Party, left-wing and pro-Kurdish. At the 2014 municipal elections, the HDP ran parallel to the BDP, with the BDP running in Turkey's Kurdish-dominated southeast while the the HDP competed in the rest of the country. Shortly afterward, the two parties were reorganized in a joint structure, and the BDP was dissolved.

7. Centers providing all kinds of services, at the level of the *semt*, run by district municipalities (see chapter 8).

CHAPTER 6: ENACTING CONTEXT-DEPENDENT ROLES

1. Muhtars found guilty of abuse of office are generally given a fine, as well as a prison sentence that is often conditional.

2. There are also cases, documented since the nineteenth century, of these certificates being issued in exchange for money, providing muhtars with extra revenue and constituting an abuse of office. "Muhtarlı yeşil kart çetesi," *Türkiye*, December 2, 2007. See also Çadırcı (1970, 414, 417–18).

3. Certain municipalities run a scheme of prepaid cards, replenished by the municipality on a regular basis, enabling holders to buy food, clothing, and school material in certain shops.

4. Which has a semipublic status.

CHAPTER 7: WORKING WITHIN AND MODULATING INSTITUTIONAL CONSTRAINTS

1. The Izmir metropolitan municipality has also set up a muhtar office.

2. For an example of a former muhtar lambasting the municipal team and his successor's political leanings, in defense of of his own former team, see "Eski muhtardan bomba açıklamalar" (Bombshell Declarations by Former Muhtar), *Sarıyermanşet*, November 10, 2012.

3. "Beykoz halkı, 2B için ayakta," *Beykoz Güncel*, March 31, 2013, http://www .beykozguncel.com/2269-beykoz-halki-2b-icin-ayakta.html.

4. As communicated personally by Gilles Dorronsoro. Istanbul, November 1, 2002.

5. This process may also take a less conflictual form. For instance, Fikret said he had put pressure on the committee to maintain the modest value for certain plots of land, to enable their occupiers to buy them at some future date. He declared that "by explaining the problem to friends there," he managed to get the committee to accept his arguments.

6. For a letter of thanks to the chair of the city council (a participatory municipal body) published by a village muhtar in a local paper, see Yalçın-Riollet 2015, 377.

7. This chimes with observations by Alexander 2002.

8. One of the widespread forms of protest was to perform daily outdoor concerts using kitchen utensils.

CHAPTER 8: THE MUHTARLIK'S WANING AUTONOMY

1. The term *konak* refers to the residence of a notable (a bit like an Italian *palazzo*), and is used to designate certain "government palaces" (*hükümet konağı*).

2. For analysis of these schemes, see White 2002.

3. "Vatandaş ile iletişim mahallede kuruluyor," Beyoğlu district municipality press release, January 14, 2015.

4. Together with contact details, the reason they have come, and the proposed solution to their problem.

5. The 2005 law empowered district municipalities to implement "transformation projects" in several cases: to regularize and embellish spontaneously built peripheries, to reduce population density and safeguard natural and historic protection zones, to deindustrialize certain zones, and to produce earthquake-resistant building stock in at-risk zones.

6. Only the Gülsuyu urban transformation project launched in 2004 provided for consultation with the muhtar and local associations. This slowed its implementation, but increased its legitimacy.

7. For certain stances adopted by muhtars towards urban transformation projects, see Advisory Group on Forced Evictions 2009.

8. "Kentsel dönüşüm. Başıbüyük direniyor." *Ekspress* 5, April 23–May 15, 2008, pp. 36–42.

9. "Başıbüyükte kefenli protesto." *Evrensel*, March 22, 2008.

10. Interview with an activist city planner who suspected the former muhtar and the municipality of complicity, July 2014.

11. "Başıbüyük halkı AKP'ye karşı birleşiyor." *Evrensel*, March 6, 2008.

12. "Maltepe'de Evlerinin Yıkım Kararı Çıkan Mahalleli Muhtarlık Binasını Bastı." Haberler.com, January 30, 2007.

13. "Başıbüyük mahallesi halkı yıkıma karşı direndi." *Atılım*, January 31, 2007.

14. "Başıbüyük halkı AKP'ye karşı birleşiyor." *Evrensel*, March 6, 2008.

15. Available at http://www.mimdap.org/?p=3152.

16. This apolitical organization resulted from some students and lecturers in the Department of Urban Planning at Mimar Sinan University becoming individually involved in the Gülensu and Gülsuyu resident protest movement. It is composed of individuals wishing to place their knowledge at the service of the populations at risk of losing their homes due to an urban transformation project.

17. This initiative was set up in 2006 by a small group of highly politicized students against urban transformation, on the basis of a long-term social and political project invoking working-class struggle and combating neoliberalism.

18. *Sarıyer Mahalleden*, February 5, 2014. *"Muhtarlık"* special report, pp. 8–11.

19. *Sosyaldemokrat Halk Partisi*, the Social Democratic People's Party (2002–10).

20. This may partly explain the increased number of candidates for muhtar posts (over 150,000 for about 32,000 posts in the 2014 elections). Z. Kılıç, "Sıra dışı muhtar adaylarından sıra dışı seçim kampanyaları." *Zaman Pazar*, March 23, 2014.

21. Presidential address to muhtars, Ankara, February 17, 2015.

22. Presidential address to muhtars, Ankara, January 11, 2018.

23. Presidential address to muhtars, Ankara, February 8, 2018.

24. Presidential address to muhtars, Ankara, June 8, 2016.

25. "Erdoğan talimat verdi . . . Muhtarlar yurtdışı turunda." *Cumhuriyet*, July 29, 2018; "Muhtarların farklı kültürleri tanıyor." *Yeni Şafak*, July 30, 2018.

26. "Muhtar bile olamaz." *Hürriyet*, September 24, 1998.

27. First presidential address to muhtars, Ankara, January 27, 2015.

28. Presidential addresses to the muhtars, Ankara, August 19 and 26, 2015.

29. Presidential address to the muhtars, Ankara, April 8, 2015.

30. Second presidential address to the muhtars, Ankara, February 17, 2015.

31. Presidential address to the muhtars, Ankara, October 26, 2016.

32. Presidential address to the muhtars, Ankara, November 4, 2015.

33. Presidential address to the muhtars, Ankara, February 24, 2015.

34. Presidential addresses to the muhtars, Ankara, November 9, 2017.

35. First presidential address to the muhtars, Ankara, January 27, 2015.

36. Presidential address to the muhtars, Ankara, February 24, 2015.

37. First presidential address to the muhtars, Ankara, January 27, 2015.

38. Presidential address to the muhtars, Ankara, June 1, 2017.

39. Second presidential address to the muhtars, Ankara, February 17, 2015.

40. Presidential address to the muhtars, Ankara, April 8, 2015.

41. Second presidential address to the muhtars, Ankara, February 17, 2015.

42. Presidential address to the muhtars, Ankara, April 8, 2015.

43. Presidential address to the muhtars, Ankara, March 10, 2015.

44. Second presidential address to the muhtars, Ankara, February 17, 2015.

45. Presidential address to muhtars, Ankara, December 14, 2016.

46. "Erdoğan muhtarlardan muhbirlik istedi." *Cumhuriyet*, August 12, 2015.

47. "HDP: Muhtarlar devletin kolluk güçleri değildir," T24, August 13, 2015; https://t24.com.tr/haber/hdp-muhtarlar-devletin-kolluk-gucleri-degildir,306137.

48. İ. Çelik, "Muhtarlardan Erdoğan'a tepki: İşimiz saray'a devlete muhbirlik değil." *Zaman*, August 13, 2015.

49. Legal decree of December 24, 2017.

50. Presidential addresses to muhtars, Ankara, June 24 and August 19, 2015.

51. The addresses are transcribed virtually in their entirety on the Turkish website of the president's office, and then translated into English, but in shorter versions more focused on international affairs.

52. Presidential address to muhtars, Ankara, April 6, 2016.

53. "Oran: Muhtarlar Bahane, Siyaset şahane." April 25, 2015, *Kamugündemi*, https://www.kamugundemi.com/siyaset/oran-muhtarlar-bahane-siyaset-sahane -h52155.html.

54. Presidential address to muhtars, Ankara, October 26, 2016.

55. Second encounter with muhtars, Ankara, February 17, 2015.

56. The reception included an official meal that apparently impressed many participants.

57. "Saray'ı reddeden ilk muhtar." *Cumhuriyet*, July 13, 2016.

58. "Kemal Kılıçdaroğlu: Muhtarların da ömrü kararnameye bağlı." *Evrensel*, March 13, 2017.

59. A 2015 draft law had been planned to give them the right to perform weddings, but this article was removed from the final version.

60. "Vali Şahin'den Bekçi Açıklaması," Haberler.com, February 21, 2017, https:// www.haberler.com/vali-sahin-den-bekci-aciklamasi-9288436-haberi/.

61. In January 2020 there were 21,300 watchmen, to which an additional 8,200 new recruits were added in July. Expectations were that 11,500 would be hired in 2021.

62. "CHP ve HDP'den bekçi kanununa muhalefet şerhi." *Evrensel*, February 3, 2020.

63. "Muhtar operasyonunun görünmeyen yüzü: HDP'li ve Alevi." *Artıgerçek*, October 17, 2018, https://artigercek.com/haberler/muhtar-operasyonunun-gorunmeyen -yuzu-hdp-li-ve-alevi.

CONCLUSION

1. A work edited by the journalist and columnist Ruşen Çakır (2008), the first journalist to interview Şerif Mardin on this topic, reviews the main components of the debate. The quotations in this passage are taken from this work.

2. For a notable exception, see Secor 2007.

References

Abrams, Philip. 1988. "Notes on the Difficulty of Studying the State (1977)." *Journal of Historical Sociology* 1:59–89.

Adelkhah, Fariba. 2017. *Elections et notabilité en Iran: Une analyse du scrutin législatif de 2016 dans quatre circonscriptions.* Paris: Les Etudes du CERI.

Advisory Group on Forced Evictions. 2009. *Mission to Istanbul, Republic of Turkey, June 8th to 11th, 2009: Report to the Executive Director of the Habitat Program.* Istanbul.

Akarsu, Hayal. 2020. "Citizen Forces: The Politics of Community Policing in Turkey." *American Ethnologist* 47, no. 1: 27–42.

Akın, Yiğit. 2007. "Reconsidering State, Party and Society in Early Republican Turkey: Politics of Petitioning." *International Journal of Middle Eastern Studies* 39:435–57.

Aldan, Mehmet. 1956. "Mahalle Muhtarlığı Teşkilatı." *İdare Dergisi* 27, no. 240: 5–19.

Alexander, Catherine. 2002. *Personal States: Making Connections between People and Bureaucracy in Turkey.* New York: Oxford University Press.

Aretxaga, Begoña. 2003. "Maddening States." *Annual Review of Anthropology* 32:393–410.

Arıkboğa, Erbay. 1998. "Yerel yönetimler, katılım ve mahalle muhtarlığı." Master's thesis, Marmara University.

———. 1999. "Yerel yönetim açısından mahalle muhtarlığına bir bakış." *Çağdaş Yerel Yönetimler* 8, no. 3: 103–25.

———. 2002. "Boşluk doldurucu ve aracı kurum: Mahalle muhtarlığı." In *Yerel Yönetimler Sempozyumu Bildirileri*, edited by Birgül Ayman Güler and Ayşegül Sabuktay, 167–76. Ankara: TODAİE Yayınları.

Ark, Ceren. 2015. "Transformation urbaine et réseaux clientélistes: Le quartier de Şahintepe à Istanbul." PhD thesis, Panthéon Sorbonne University.

Asad, Talal. 2004. "Where Are the Margins of the State?" In *Anthropology in the Margins of the State*, edited by Veena Das and Deborah Poole, 279–88. Santa Fe, NM: School of Advanced Research Press.

Aslan, Senem. 2015. *Nation-Building in Turkey and Morocco: Governing Kurdish and Berber Dissent*. New York: Cambridge University Press.

Aslan, Şükrü. 2013 [2004]. *1 Mayıs mahallesi: 1980 öncesi toplumsal mücadeleler ve kent*. Istanbul: İletişim.

Auyero, Javier. 1999. "'From the Client's Point(s) of View': How Poor People Perceive and Evaluate Political Clientelism." *Theory and Society* 28, no. 2: 297–334.

———. 2000. *Poor People's Politics: Peronist Survival Networks and the Legacy of Evita*. Durham, NC: Duke University Press.

Aymes, Marc. 2008. "Dissipation de l'Etat: L'impensé des institutions ottomanes." Paper presented at the workshop "Servir l'État en Turquie: La rationalisation des institutions en question." Paris, École des hautes études en sciences sociales, December 5. http://halshs.archives-ouvertes.fr/halshs-00723285.

Aytaç, Fethi. 2009 [1996]. *Mahalle muhtarlarının el kitabı*. Ankara: Seçkin Yayınevi.

Bayart, Jean-François. 1981. "Le politique par le bas en Afrique Noire: Questions de méthode." *Politique Africaine* 1:53–82.

———. 1985. "L'énonciation du politique." *Revue française de science politique* 35, no. 3: 343–73.

———. 1989. *L'Etat en Afrique: La politique du ventre*. Paris: Fayard.

Bayart, Jean-François, Achille Mbembe, and Comi Toulabor. 2008 [1992]. *Le politique par le bas en Afrique noire*. Paris: Karthala.

Bayat, Asef. 1997. "Un-Civil society: The Politics of the Informal People." *Third World Quarterly* 18, no. 1 (March 1997): 53–72.

———. 2009. *Life as Politics: How Ordinary People Change the Middle East*. Stanford, CA: Stanford University Press.

Bayramoğlu Alada, Adalet. 2008. *Osmanlı-Türk şehrinde mahalle*. Istanbul: Sümer.

Beaud, Olivier. 1994. *La puissance de l'état*. Paris: Presses Universitaires de France.

Becker, Howard. 1993. "How I Learned What a Crock Was." *Journal of Contemporary Ethnography* 22:28–35.

———. 1998. *Tricks of the Trade: How to Think about Your Research while You're Doing It*. Chicago: University of Chicago Press.

Behar, Cem. 2003. *A Neighborhood in Ottoman Istanbul: Fruit Vendors and Civil Servants in the Kasap İlyas Mahalle*. New York: SUNY.

————. 2004. "Neighborhood Nuptials: Islamic Personal Law and Local Customs: Marriage Records in a Mahalle of Traditional Istanbul (1864–1907)." *International Journal of Middle East Studies* 36:537–59.

Bektaş, Arsev. 1988. *Demokratikleşme sürecinde liderler oligarşisi, CHP ve AP (1961–1980)*. Istanbul: Boğaziçi üniversitesi.

Belge, Ceren. 2013. "Seeing the State': Kinship Networks and Kurdish Resistance in Early Republican Turkey." In *The Everyday Life of the State: Developments in the State-in-Society Approach*, edited by Adam J. White, 14–28. Seattle: University of Washington Press.

Belge, Taciser and Orhan Bilgin, eds. 1997. *Yurttaş katılımı: Sivil toplum kuruluşları ve yerel yönetimler arasında ortaklık ve işbirliği*. Istanbul: Helsinki Yurttaşlar Derneği.

Berger, Peter L., and Thomas Luckmann. 1966. *The Social Construction of Reality: A Treatise in the Sociology of Knowledge*. Garden City, NY: Anchor Books.

Bierschenk, Thomas, Jean-Pierre Chauveau, and Jean-Pierre Olivier de Sardan, eds. 2000. *Courtiers en développement: Les villages africains en quête de projets*. Paris and Mainz: Karthala/APAD.

Bierschenk, Thomas, and Jean-Pierre Olivier de Sardan, eds. 2014. *States at Work: The Dynamics of African Bureaucracies*. Leiden, Netherlands: Brill.

Blau, Peter M. 1955. *The Dynamics of Bureaucracy: A Study of Interpersonal Relations in Two Government Agencies*. Chicago and London: University of Chicago Press.

Blondiaux, Loïc, and Jean-Marie Fourniau. 2011. "Un bilan des recherches sur la participation du public en démocratie: Beaucoup de bruit pour rien?" *Participations* 1, no. 1: 8–35.

Blundo, Giorgio. 2001. "Négocier l'Etat au quotidien: Intermédiaires, courtiers et rabatteurs dans les interstices de l'administration sénégalaise." *Autrepart* 20:75–90.

Boissevain, Jeremy. 1974. *Friends of Friends: Networks, Manipulators and Coalitions*. Oxford, UK: Blackwell.

Bourdieu, Pierre. 1990a. "Droit et passe-droit: Le champ des pouvoirs territoriaux et la mise en œuvre des règlements." *Actes de la recherche en sciences sociales* 81–82:86–96.

————. 1990b. *The Logic of Practice*. Stanford, CA: Stanford University Press.

Bozarslan, Hamit. 1999. "Le phénomène milicien: Une composante de la violence politique en Turquie des années 70." *Turcica* 31:185–244.

Briquet, Jean-Louis. 1997. *La tradition en mouvement: Clientélisme et politique en Corse*. Paris: Belin.

———. 2005. "La politique au village: Vote et mobilisation électorale dans la Corse rurale." In *La politisation*, edited by Jacques Lagroye, 31–45. Paris: Belin.

Briquet, Jean-Louis, and Frédéric Sawicki. 1989. "L'analyse localisée du politique: Lieux de recherche ou recherche de lieux?" *Politix* 2, no. 7–8: 6–16.

Buğra, Ayşe. 2013. *Kapitalizm, yoksulluk ve Türkiye'de sosyal politika*. Istanbul: İletişim.

Buğra, Ayşe, and Sinem Adar. 2008. "Social Policy Change in Countries without Mature Welfare States: The Case of Turkey." *New Perspectives on Turkey* 38 (Spring): 83–106.

Buğra, Ayşe, and Ayşen Candaş. 2011. "Change and Continuity under an Eclectic Social Security Regime: The Case of Turkey." *Middle Eastern Studies* 47, no. 3: 515–28.

Buğra, Ayşe, and Çağlar Keyder. 2005. "Poverty and Social Policy in Contemporary Turkey." Social Forum Working Paper, Boğaziçi University.

Çadırcı, Musa. 1970. "Türkiye'de Muhtarlık Teşkilatının Kurulması Üzerine Bir İnceleme." *Belleten* 34, no. 135: 409–20.

———. 1993. "Türkiye'de Muhtarlık Kurumunun Tarihi Gelişimi." *Çağdaş yerel yönetimler* 2, no. 3: 3–11.

Çakır, Ruşen. 2007. "Mahalle havası diye bir şey var ki AKP'yi bile döver." *Vatan*, Books Supplement, May 15.

Çakır, Ruşen, ed. 2008. *Mahalle baskısı, Prof. Dr. Şerif Mardin'in tezlerinden hareketle Türkiye'de İslam, cumhuriyet, laiklik ve demokrasi*. Istanbul: Doğan Kitap.

Camau, Michel, and Gilles Massardier, eds. 2009. *Démocraties et autoritarismes: Fragmentation et hybridation des régimes*. Paris: Karthala.

Çelik, Adnan. 2019. "Le muxtar: Conflit et enjeu dans les conflits intra-kurdes à l'échelle locale." Paper presented at the congress of the Middle East and Muslim Worlds Scientific Interest Group. Paris, July 4.

Çitçi, Oya. 1989. *Yerel yönetimlerde temsil: Belediye örneği*. Ankara: TODAİE.

Clayer, Nathalie. 2015. "An Imposed or Negotiated Laiklik? The Administration of the Teaching of Islam in Single-Party Turkey." In *Order and Compromise: Government Practices in Turkey from the Late Ottoman Empire to the Early 21st Century*, edited by Marc Aymes, Benjamin Gourisse, and Elise Massicard, 97–120. Leiden, Netherlands: Brill.

Combes, Hélène, and Gabriel Vommaro. 2015. *Sociologie du clientélisme*. Paris: La Découverte.

Copeaux, Etienne. 1996. "*Hizmet*: A Keyword in the Turkish Historical Narrative." *New Perspectives on Turkey* 14:97–114.

Crozier, Michel, and Erhard Friedberg. 1977. *L'acteur et le système: Les contraintes de l'action collective*. Paris: Seuil.

Çubukçuoğlu, Zühtü. 1944. *Muhtar ve ihtiyar heyetleri kılavuzu*. İstanbul: Suhulet Matbaası.

Cumhuriyet Halk Partisi. 1968. *CHP: İl Kongresi 1968*. Istanbul: Özaydın.

Cupolo, Diego. 2017. "What Turkey's Election Observers Saw." *Atlantic*, April 21.

Cutolo, Armando, and Richard Banégas. 2018. "Les margouillats et les papiers kamikazes: Intermédiaires de l'identité, citoyenneté et moralité à Abidjan." *Genèses* 112:81–102.

Das, Veena, and Deborah Poole, eds. 2004a. *Anthropology in the Margins of the State*. Santa Fe, NM: School of Advanced Research Press.

———. 2004b. "State and Its Margins: Comparative Ethnographies." In *Anthropology in the Margins of the State*, edited by Veena Das and Deborah Pool, 3–34. Santa Fe, NM: School of Advanced Research Press.

De Certeau, Michel. 1984. *The Practice of Everyday Life*. Berkeley, University of California Press.

Delaney, Carol. 1991. *The Seed and the Soil: Gender and Cosmology in Turkish Village Society*. Berkeley: University of California Press.

Denli, Özlem. 2017. "Hosting the Nation: Populist Themes in Erdoğan's Muhtar Meetings." In *The Transformation of Public Sphere: An Interdisciplinary Debate about the Recent Development of Publicity in Turkey*, edited by Armağan Öztürk and Ayhan Bilgin, 135–148. Baden Baden, Germany: Nomos.

Descimon, Robert, Jean-François Schaub, and Bernard Vincent, eds. 1997. *Les Figures de l'administrateur: Institutions, réseaux, pouvoirs en Espagne, en France et au Portugal 16e–19e siècles*. Paris: Éditions de l'EHESS.

Devlet Planlama Teşkilatı. 2007. "9. Kalkınma Planı (2007–2013): Gelir Dağılımı ve Mücadele Özel İhtisas Komisyonu Raporu." Ankara: T. C. Başbakanlık Devlet Planlama Teşkilatı.

Dodurka, Berra Zeynep. 2014. "Institutionalization of Social Assistance and Means Testing Mechanisms in the Post-2001 Period." Master's thesis, Boğaziçi University.

Duara, Prasenjit. 1987. "State Involution: A Study of Local Finances in North China, 1911–1935." *Comparative Studies in Society and History* 29, no. 1: 132–61.

Dubois, Vincent. 2010. *The Bureaucrat and the Poor: Encounters in French Welfare Offices*. London and New York: Routledge.

Dupuy, François, and Jean-Claude Thoenig. 1985. *L'administration en miettes*. Paris: Fayard.

E. M., 1979. "Kahramanmaraş faşist katliamından bazı çizgiler ya da Güneş ne Zaman Doğacak?" *Yeni Ülke* 8:252–67.

Ekal, Berna. 2015. "Women's Shelters as State Institutions." In *Order and Compromise: Government Practices in Turkey from the Late Ottoman Empire to the Early 21st Century*, edited by Marc Aymes, Benjamin Gourisse, and Elise Massicard, 317–32. Leiden, Netherlands: Brill.

Elias, Norbert, and John L. Scotson. 1965. *The Established and the Outsiders: A Sociological Enquiry into Community Problems*. London: Frank Cass.

Encyclopédie de l'Islam². Tome V. 1985. Leiden, Netherlands: Brill.

Erder, Sema. 1996. *Istanbul'a bir kent kondu: Ümraniye*. Istanbul: İletişim.

———. 1997. *Kentsel gerilim: Enformel ilişki ağları alan araştırması*. Ankara: Um:ag.

———. 1999. "Where Do You Hail From? Localism and Networks in Istanbul." In *Istanbul: Between the Global and the Local*, edited by Çağlar Keyder, 161–72. Lanham, MD: Rowman and Littlefield.

Erder, Sema, and Nihal İncioğlu. 2008. *Türkiye'de yerel siyasetin yükselişi*. Istanbul: Bilgi Üniversitesi.

Ergin, Osman Nuri. 1936. *Türkiye'de şehirciliğin tarihi inkişafi*. Istanbul: Istanbul University.

———. 1939 [1932]. *Beledi bilgiler*. Istanbul: Osmanbey Matbaası.

Eryılmaz, Bilal. 1988. "Türkiye'de köy ve mahalle muhtarlıklarının ortaya çıkışı ve gelişimi." *Türk İdare dergisi* 378:465–75.

Findley, Carter. 1980. *Bureaucratic Reform in the Ottoman Empire: The Sublime Porte, 1789–1922*. Princeton, NJ: Princeton University Press.

Firat, Bilge. 2019. *Diplomacy and Lobbying during Turkey's Europeanisation: The Private Life of Politics*. Manchester, UK: Manchester University Press.

Fliche, Benoît. 2005. "De l'action réticulaire à la recherche du semblable, ou comment faire lien avec l'administration en Turquie." In *La Turquie conteste: Mobilisations sociales et régime sécuritaire en Turquie*, edited by Gilles Dorronsoro, 147–65. Paris: CNRS Editions.

———. 2015. "Officialdom and the Woman Who Was 'Meant to Be Dead.'" In *Order and Compromise: Government Practices in Turkey from the Late Ottoman Empire to the*

Early 21st Century, edited by Marc Aymes, Benjamin Gourisse, and Elise Massicard, 362–75. Leiden, Netherlands: Brill.

Fontaine, Jacques, and Christian Le Bart, eds. 1994. *Le métier d'élu local.* Paris: L'Harmattan.

Foucault, Michel. 1995 [1975]. *Discipline and Punish: The Birth of the Prison.* New York: Vintage.

———. 2007 [2004]. *Security, Territory, Population: Lectures at the Collège de France, 1977–1978.* New York: Palgrave Macmillan.

———. 2008 [2004]. *The Birth of Biopolitics: Lectures at the College de France, 1978–1979.* New York: Palgrave MacMillan.

Garapon, Béatrice. 2017. "Aux origines de la Turquie conservatrice: Une sociologie historique du Parti démocrate (1946–1960)." PhD thesis, Institut d'Etudes Politiques de Bordeaux.

Garraud, Philippe. 1994. "Le métier d'élu local: Les contraintes d'un rôle." In *Le métier d'élu local,* edited by Jacques Fontaine and Christian Le Bart, 29–54. Paris: L'Harmattan.

Genç, Deniz, and Merve Özdemirkıran. 2015. "Local Perceptions on Syrian Migration to Turkey: A Case Study of Istanbul Neighborhoods." In *Turkish Migration Conference 2015 Selected Proceedings,* edited by Güven Şeker, Ali Tilbe, Mustafa Ökmen, Pınar Yazgan Hepgül, Deniz Eroğlu, and İbrahim Sirkeci, 106–17. London: Transnational Press.

Goffman, Erving. 1959. *The Presentation of Self in Everyday Life.* New York: Anchor Books.

Goodman, Neville M. 1964. "Turkey's Experiment in the 'Socialization' of Medicine." *Lancet* 783, no. 7323: 36–38.

Gourisse, Benjamin. 2010. "L'Etat en jeu: Captation des ressources et désobjectivation de l'Etat en Turquie (1975–1980)." PhD thesis, Université Paris I Panthéon Sorbonne.

———. 2013. "Party Penetration of the State: The Nationalist Action Party in the Late 1970s." In *Negotiating Political Power in Turkey: Breaking up the Party,* edited by Elise Massicard and Nicole Watts, 118–39. London and New York: Routledge.

———. 2015. "Order and Compromise: The Concrete Realities of Public Action in Turkey and the Ottoman Empire." In *Order and Compromise: Government Practices in Turkey from the Late Ottoman Empire to the Early 21st Century,* edited by Marc Aymes, Benjamin Gourisse, and Elise Massicard, 1–24. Leiden, Netherlands: Brill.

Grémion, Pierre. 1976. *Le pouvoir périphérique: Bureaucrates et notables dans le système politique français*. Paris: Seuil.

Grignon, Claude, and Jean-Claude Passeron. 1989. *Le Savant et le populaire, misérabilisme et populisme en sociologie et en littérature*. Paris: Gallimard.

Güçlü, Muhammet. 1999. "Antalya'da ve Salihli'de 1930 Belediye Seçimleri." *Toplumsal tarih*, 65.

Günal, Asena. 2008. "Health and Citizenship in Republican Turkey: An Analysis of the Socialization of Health Services in Republican Historical Context." PhD thesis, Bosphorus University.

Güneş, Mehmet. 2014. *Osmanlı döneminde muhtarlık ve ihtiyar meclisi (1829–1871)*. Istanbul: Kitabevi.

Gupta, Akhil. 1995. "Blurred Boundaries: the Discourse of Corruption, the Culture of Politics, and the Imagined State." *American Ethnologist* 22, no. 2: 375–402.

Gürel, Burak. 2004. "Political Mobilization in Turkey in the 1970's: The Case of the Kahramanmaraş Incidents." PhD thesis, Bosphorus University.

Hacımahmutoğlu, Hande. 2009. *Türkiye'deki sosyal yardım sisteminin değerlendirilmesi*. Ankara: Devlet Planlama Teşkilatı.

Hakyemez, Serra. 2018. "Waiting with Hope and Doubt in the Trials of Terror." Paper presented at the symposium "Politics of Emotions in Turkey and Its Connected Geographies," Consortium of European Symposia on Turkey, London School of Economics, January 11, 2018.

Harris, Leila M. 2009. "States at the Limit: Tracing Contemporary State-Society Relations in the Borderlands of Southeastern Turkey." *European Journal of Turkish Studies* 10, https://doi.org/10.4000/ejts.4122.

Heper, Metin. 1985. *The State Tradition in Turkey*. Beverley, UK: Eothen Press.

———. 1992. "The 'Strong State' and Democracy: The Turkish Case in Comparative and Historical Perspective." In *Democracy and Modernity*, edited by Shmuel N. Eisenstadt, 142–64. Leiden, Netherlands: Brill.

Hersant, Jeanne, and Alexandre Toumarkine. 2005. "Hometown Organisations in Turkey: An Overview." *European Journal of Turkish Studies* 2, https://doi.org/10.4000/ejts.397.

Herzfeld, Michael. 1993. *The Social Production of Indifference: Exploring the Symbolic Roots of Western Bureaucracy*. Chicago: University of Chicago Press.

Hibou, Béatrice, ed. 1999. *La privatisation des États*. Paris: Karthala.

————. 2006. *La force de l'obéissance: Economie politique de la répression en Tunisie.* Paris: La Découverte.

————. 2011. *Anatomie politique de la domination.* Paris: La Découverte.

Hoggart, Richard. 1957. *The Uses of Literacy: Aspects of Working-Class Life.* London: Chatto and Windus.

Horasan, A. Hikmet. 1992. "İstanbul mahalle muhtarlarının çağdaş demokrasi anlayışı." Master's thesis, İstanbul Üniversitesi.

Hourani, Albert. 1968. "Ottoman Reforms and the Politics of Notables." In *Beginnings of Modernization in the Middle East: The Nineteenth Century,* edited by William R. Polk and Richard L. Chambers, 41–68. Chicago and London: University of Chicago Press.

Hourani, Albert, and S. M. Stern, eds. 1970. *The Islamic City: A Colloquium.* Oxford and Philadelphia: University of Pennsylvania Press.

Hughes, Everett. 1958. *Men and Their Work.* London: The Free Press.

International Republican Institute. 1995. *Turkey, Survey Results: Attitudes and Priorities of Citizens of Urban Areas.* Washington: International Republican Institute.

Işık, Damla. 2012. "The Specter and Reality of Corruption: Privatizing Poor Relief in Turkey." *Comparative Studies of South Asia, Africa and the Middle East* 32, no. 1: 57–69.

Istanbul Hepimizin. 2015. *"Muhtarınla tanış" projesi ve muhtarlık raporu.* Istanbul.

Jeannot, Gilles. 2011. *Les métiers flous: Travail et action publique.* Toulouse, France: Octares.

Joppien, Charlotte. 2019. *Municipal Politics in Turkey: Local Government and Party Organization.* London and New York: Routledge.

Kandiyoti, Deniz. 2002. "Introduction: Reading the Fragments." In *Fragments of Culture: The Everyday of Modern Turkey,* edited by Deniz Kandiyoti and Ayşe Saktamber, 1–23. New Brunswick, NJ: Rutgers University Press.

Kayaalp, Ebru. 2013. "If these Machines Could Talk . . . : Experts, Cigarettes and Policymaking in Turkey." *Social Anthropology* 21, no. 4: 479–91.

Kerkvliet, Benedict J. Tria. 2005. *The Power of Everyday Politics: How Vietnamese Peasants Transformed National Policy.* Ithaca, NY, and London: Cornell University Press.

Koğacıoğlu, Dicle. 2008. "Conduct, Meaning and Inequality in an İstanbul Courthouse." *New Perspectives on Turkey* 39 (Fall 2008): 97–127.

Kolars, John F. 1963. "Tradition, Season, and Change in a Turkish Village." Department of Geography research paper 82, University of Chicago.

Kurtoğlu, Ayça. 2005. *Hemşehrilik ve şehirde siyaset*. Istanbul: İletişim.

Kuyucu, Tuna. 2014. "Law, Property and Ambiguity: The Uses and Abuses of Legal Ambiguity in Remaking Istanbul's Informal Settlements." *International Journal of Urban and Regional Research* 38, no. 2 (March): 609–27.

Lafi, Nora. 2011. "Petitions and Accommodating Urban Change in the Ottoman Empire." In *Istanbul as Seen from a Distance: Centre and Provinces in the Ottoman Empire*, edited by Elizabeth Özdalga, Sait Özervarlı, and Feryal Tansuğ, 73–82. Istanbul: Swedish Research Institute in Istanbul.

Lagroye, Jacques. 2005. "Les processus de politisation." In *La politisation*, edited by Jacques Lagroye, 359–72. Paris: Belin.

Lagroye, Jacques, and Michel Offerlé. 2010. "Pour une sociologie des institutions." In *Sociologie de l'institution*, edited by Jacques Lagroye and Michel Offerlé, 11–29. Paris: Belin.

Lascoumes, Pierre, and Patrick Le Galès, eds. 2005. *Gouverner par les instruments*. Paris: Presses de sciences Po.

Le Bohec, Jacques. 1994. "Le travail de mobilisation électorale et de dénégation de leur intérêt effectué par les maires." In *Le métier d'élu local*, edited by Joseph Fontaine and Christian Le Bart. Paris: L'Harmattan.

Legall, Lionel, Michel Offerlé, and François Ploux, eds. 2013. *La politique sans en avoir l'air: Aspects de la politique informelle, XIXè–XXIè siècle*, Rennes, France: Presses universitaires de Rennes.

Lévy, Noémi. 2010. "L'ordre public dans la capitale ottomane: Istanbul, 1879–1909." PhD thesis, Ecole des hautes études en sciences sociales.

Lévy-Aksu, Noémi. 2012. *Ordre et désordres dans l'Istanbul ottomane (1879–1909)*. Paris: Kartala.

Lewis, Bernard. 1968 [1961]. *The Emergence of Modern Turkey*. London: Oxford University Press.

Lipsky, Michael. 1980. *Street-Level Bureaucracy: Dilemmas of the Individual in Public Services*. New York: Russell Sage Foundation.

Lüdtke, Alf, ed. 1995. *The History of Everyday Life: Reconstructing Historical Experiences and Ways of Life*. Princeton, NJ: Princeton University Press.

Lund, Christian. 2006. "Twilight Institutions: An Introduction." *Development and Change* 37:673–84.

Magnarella, Paul. 1974. *Tradition and Change in a Turkish Town*. New York: John Wiley and Sons.

Mardin, Şerif. 1974. *Super Westernization in Urban Life in the Ottoman Empire in the Last Quarter of the 19th Century*. Leiden, Netherlands: Brill.

Massicard, Elise. 2004. "Entre l'intermédiaire et 'l'homme d'honneur': Savoirs-faire et dilemmes notabiliaires en Turquie." *Politix* 67:101–27.

———. 2013. "Post-hérité: Un retour du patronyme en Turquie contemporaine?" *Revue d'histoire moderne et contemporaine* 60, no. 2: 87–105.

Mattina, Cesare. 2004a. "Mutations des ressources clientélaires et construction des notabilités politiques à Marseille (1970–1990)." *Politix* 67:129–55.

———. 2004b. "L'intermédiation politique des présidents de comités d'intérêt de quartier: Le territoire de la notabilité." In *Marseille, entre ville et ports*, edited by Pierre Fournier and Sylvie Mazzella, 82–96. Paris: La Découverte.

Meeker, Michael. 2002. *A Nation of Empire: The Ottoman Legacy of Turkish Modernity*, Berkeley. Los Angeles, and London: University of California Press.

Merton, Robert K. 1949. *Social Theory and Social Structure*. Glencoe, IL: The Free Press.

Metinsoy, Murat. 2011. "Fragile Hegemony, Flexible Authoritarianism, and Governing from Below: Politicians' Reports in Early Republican Turkey." *International Journal of Middle East Studies* 43, no. 4: 699–719.

Migdal, Joel S. 1994. "The State in Society: An Approach to Struggles for Domination." In *State Power and Social Forces: Domination and Transformation in the Third World*, edited by Joel S. Migdal, Atul Kohli, and Vivienne Shue, 7–34. Cambridge: Cambridge University Press.

Migdal, Joel S., ed. 2001. *State in Society: Studying How States and Societies Transform and Constitute Each Other*. Cambridge: Cambridge University Press.

Mitchell, Timothy. 1991. "The Limits of the State: Beyond Statist Approaches and Their Critics." *American Political Science Review* 85, no. 1: 77–96.

Navaro-Yashin, Yael. 2002. *Faces of the State: Secularism and Public Life in Turkey*. Princeton, NJ: Princeton University Press.

Offerlé, Michel, ed. 1999. *La profession politique, XIXe–XXe siècles*. Paris: Belin.

Ortaylı, İlter. 2000. *Tanzimat devrinde Osmanlı mahalli idareleri (1840–1880)*. Ankara: TTK Yayınları.

Oy ve Ötesi. 2014. *Bir gönüllü gözetmenlik hikayesi*. May 8, 2014. http://oyveotesi.org/gecmis-secimler/30-mart-2014-secim-raporu/.

Özelçi Eceral, Tanyel, and Aysu Uğurlar. 2017. "Hanehalkı konut hareketliliği etkileyen faktörler: Ankara örneği." *Planlama* 27, no. 3: 347–61.

Palabıyık, Hamit, and Şermin Atak. 2000. "İzmir büyükşehir bütününde mahalle yönetimleri profili." *Dokuz Eylül üniversitesi sosyal bilimler enstitüsü dergisi* 2, no. 3: 150–68.

Payaslıoğlu, Arif. 1964. "Political Leadership and Political Parties in Turkey." In *Political Modernization in Japan and Turkey*, edited by Robert E. Ward and Dankwart A. Rustow, 420–32. Princeton, NJ: Princeton University Press.

Petit, Clémence. 2009. "Transformation urbaine, mobilisations collectives et processus de politisation: Le cas du projet de rénovation urbaine de Başıbüyük (Istanbul)." Master thesis, Institut d'études politiques de Strasbourg.

Petrov, Milen V. 2004. "Everyday Forms of Compliance: Subaltern Commentaries on Ottoman Reform, 1864–1868." *Comparative Studies in Society and History* 46, no. 4: 730–59.

Phélippeau, Éric. 2002. *L'Invention de l'homme politique moderne: Mackau, l'Orne et la République*. Paris: Belin.

Pierce, Joe E. 1964. *Life in a Turkish Village*. New York: Holt, Rinehart and Winston.

Quataert, Donald. 2008. "Doing Subaltern Studies in Ottoman History." *International Journal of Middle Eastern Studies* 40, no. 3: 379–81.

Raymond, André. 1995. "Ville musulmane, ville arabe: Mythes orientalistes et recherches récentes." In *Panoramas urbains, situation de l'histoire des villes*, edited by Jean-Louis Hervé and Jean-Claude Biget, 309–33. Fontenay aux Roses, France: E.N.S. Editions.

Revel, Jacques. 1996. "Micro-analyse et construction du social." In *Jeux d'échelles: La micro-analyse à l'expérience*, edited by Jaques Revel, 15–36. Paris: Gallimard/Le Seuil.

Salzmann, Ariel. 2004. *Tocqueville in the Ottoman Empire: Rival Paths to the Modern State*. Boston: Brill.

Scott, Richard B. 1968. *The Village Headman in Turkey: A Case Study*. Ankara: Institute of Public Administration for Turkey and the Middle East.

Scott, James C. 1976. *The Moral Economy of the Peasant: Rebellion and Subsistence in Southeast Asia*. New Haven, CT: Yale University Press.

———. 1985. *Weapons of the Weak: Everyday Forms of Peasant Resistance*. New Haven, CT, and London: Yale University Press.

———. 1990. *Domination and the Arts of Resistance: Hidden Transcripts*. New Haven, CT: Yale University Press.

———. 1998. *Seeing Like a State: How Certain Schemes to Improve the Human Condition Have Failed*. New Haven, CT, and London: Yale University Press.

————. 2010. *The Art of Not Being Governed: An Anarchist History of Upland Southeast Asia*. New Haven, CT: Yale University Press.

Scott, James C., John Tehranian, and Jeremy Mathias. 2002. "The Production of Legal Identities Proper to States: The Case of the Permanent Family Surname." *Comparative Studies in Society and History* 44, no. 1: 4–44.

Secor, Anna. 2007. "Between Longing and Despair: State, Space, and Subjectivity in Turkey." *Environment and Planning* 25:33–52.

Şevran, Seçil. 2005. "The Place of Neighborhood Administration in the Turkish Administrative system: The Case of Ankara." Master's thesis, Middle East Technical University.

Sharma, Akhil, and Aradhana Gupta, eds. 2006. *The Anthropology of the State: A Reader*. Malden, MA: Blackwell.

Shaw, Stanford J. 1968. "Some Aspects of the Aims and Achievements of the Nineteenth-Century Ottoman Reformers." In *Beginnings of Modernization in the Middle East: The Nineteenth Century*, edited by William R. Polk and Richard L. Chambers, 29–39. Chicago and London: University of Chicago Press.

Siblot, Yasmine. 2002. "Stigmatisation et intégration sociale au guichet d'une institution familière: Le bureau de poste d'un quartier populaire." *Sociétés contemporaines* 47:79–99.

————. 2006. *Faire valoir ses droits au quotidien: Les services publics dans les quartiers populaires*. Paris: Presses de Sciences Po.

Silverstein, Brian. 2018. "Commensuration, Performativity and the Reform of Statistics in Turkey." *American Ethnologist* 45, no. 3: 330–40.

Singer, Amy. 1990. "The Routine Conduct of Rural Administration." In *V. milletlerarası Türkiye sosyal ve iktisat tarihi kongresi; Tebliğler; Marmara üniversitesi, Türkiyat araştırma ve uygulama merkezi, İstanbul 21–25 Auğustos 1989*, 663–70. Ankara: Türk Tarih Kurumu basımevi.

Spire, Alexis. 2012. *Faibles et puissants face à l'impôt*. Paris: Raisons d'agir.

Starr, June. 1978. *Dispute and Settlement in Rural Turkey: An Ethnography of Law*. Leiden, Netherlands: Brill.

Stirling, Paul. 1965. *Turkish Village*. London: Weidenfeld and Nicholson.

Stycos, J. Mayone. 1965. "The Potential Role of Turkish Village Opinion Leaders in a Program of Family Planning." *Public Opinion Quarterly* 24, no. 1: 120–30.

Szurek, Emmanuel. 2015. "The Linguist and the Politician: The *Türk Dili Kurumu* and the Field of Power in the 1930s–40s." In *Order and Compromise: Government*

Practices in Turkey from the Late Ottoman Empire to the Early 21st Century, edited by Marc Aymes, Benjamin Gourisse, and Elise Massicard, 68–95. Leiden, Netherlands: Brill.

Tamdoğan-Abel, Işık. 2004. "Les relations de voisinage d'après les livres de morale ottomans (XVe–XVIIIe siècles)." *Anatolia Moderna* 10:167–77.

Tanlak, Ömer. 1996. *İtiraf: Eski ülkücü MHP'yi anlatıyor.* Istanbul: Kaynak Yayınları.

Taylan, Ertuğrul. 1999. *Mahalle muhtarlığı ve açıklamalı kanunu.* Ankara: Türk Belediyecilik Derneği / Konrad Adenauer Vakfı.

TBMM. 2010. *TBMM albümü (1920–2010): 2. Cilt (1950–1980).* Ankara: TBMM.

T. C. Cumhurbaşkanlığı Devlet Denetleme Kurulu. 2009. *Investigation Report no. 2009/4.* Ankara.

Thompson, Edward Palmer. 1971. "The Moral Economy of the English Crowd in the Eighteenth Century." *Past and Present* 50:76–136.

Topal, Çağatay. 2005. "Global Citizens and Local Powers: Surveillance in Turkey." *Social Text* 23:85–93.

TÜİK. 2020. "Hanehalkı işgücü istatistikleri: Nisan 2020." *Haber bülteni* 33788. https://data.tuik.gov.tr/Bulten/Index?p=Isgucu-Istatistikleri-Nisan-2020-33788.

Turan, Ali Eşref. 2008. *Türkiye'de yerel seçim.* Istanbul: Bilgi Üniversitesi Yayınları.

Türk Belediyecilik Derneği and Konrad Adenauer Vakfı. 1998. *Mahalle muhtarları ve belediye ilişkileri.* Ankara: Türk Belediyecilik Derneği / Konrad Adenauer Vakfı.

Ülgül, Murat. 2018. "Framing a Presidential Foreign Policy in a Parliamentary System: Erdoğan and Mukhtar's Meetings." *Turkish Journal of Middle Eastern Studies* 5, no. 2: 65–92.

Vannetzel, Marie. 2010. "Secret public, réseaux sociaux et morale politique: Les frères musulmans et la société égyptienne." *Politix* 92:77–97.

Varol, Muharrem. 1989. *Yerel siyasetin demokratikleşmesi.* Ankara: Gündoğan Basım.

Veinstein, Gilles. 1987. "Le patrimoine foncier de Panayote Benakis, Kocabaşı de Kalamata." *Journal of Turkish Studies* 11:211–33.

Warin, Philippe. 2002. *Les dépanneurs de justice: Les "petits fonctionnaires" entre qualité et équité.* Paris: LGDJ.

Watts, Nicole F. 2009. "Re-Considering State-Society Dynamics in Turkey's Kurdish Southeast." *European Journal of Turkish Studies* 10. https://doi.org/10.4000/ejts.4196.

Weber, Max. 1978 [1921]. *Economy and Society: An Outline of Interpretive Sociology.* Berkeley: University of California Press.

————. 1986 [1921]. *The City*. Glencoe, IL: The Free Press.

Wedel, Heidi. 1999. *Lokale Politik und Geschlechterrollen: Stadtmigrantinnen in türkischen Metropolen*. Hamburg, Germany: Schriften des Deutschen Orient- Instituts.

White, Adam J. 2013. "Introduction: A State-in-Society Agenda." In *The Everyday Life of the State: A State-in-Society Approach*, edited by Adam J. White, 3–12. Seattle: University of Washington Press.

White, Jenny. 2002. *Islamist Mobilization in Turkey: A Study in Vernacular Politics*. Seattle and London: University of Washington Press.

Yalçın-Riollet, Melike. 2015. "Construire une participation "acceptable": Importation, institutionnalisation et usages de l'agenda 21 local en Turquie." PhD thesis, Ecole des hautes études en sciences sociales.

Yasa, İbrahim. 1957. *Hasanoğlan*. Ankara: TODAİE.

Yazıcı, Berna. 2012. "The Return of the Family: Welfare, State and Politics of the Family in Turkey." *Anthropological Quarterly* 85, no. 1: 103–40.

Yildirim, Senem, Burcu Ucaray-Mangitli, and Hakki Tas. 2017. "Intimate Politics: Strategies and Practices of Female Mukhtars in Turkey." *British Journal of Middle Eastern Studies* 45, no. 5: 661–77.

Yoltar, Çağrı. 2007. "The Green Card Scheme: An Ethnography of 'the State' and Its 'Poor Citizens' in Adıyaman." PhD thesis, Bosphorus University.

Yonucu, Deniz. 2018. "Urban Vigilantism: A Study of Anti-Terror Law, Politics and Policing in Istanbul." *International Journal of Urban and Regional Research* 42, no. 3: 408–22.

Stanford Studies in Middle Eastern and
Islamic Societies and Cultures

Joel Beinin and Laleh Khalili, editors

The authorized representative in the EU for product safety and compliance is:
Mare Nostrum Group
B.V Doelen 72
4831 GR Breda
The Netherlands

www.ingramcontent.com/pod-product-compliance
Lightning Source LLC
Chambersburg PA
CBHW020455270326
41926CB00008B/611